Google Cloud Certified Professional Cloud Architect
Introducing Google Cloud
Second Edition

Responsibly Architected By Soumen Chatterjee
Design, Concept and Story Telling By Soumen Chatterjee
Consulted SME: Sanjeevan Mahajan

First Released on 18th February 2019 – PDF
Kindle on 15th March 2019
Paperback on 15th March 2019

Revised Second Edition on 19th May 2019

Copyright

Google Cloud Certified Professional Cloud Architect
Introducing Google Cloud

Soumen Chatterjee
PDF Version ISBN: 9781999609603
Print Version ISBN: 9781999609672
Kindle Version ISBN: 9781999609665

© 2019, Soumen Chatterjee, BeClickAware Ltd
Self-publishing
soumenc@beclickaware.com
chatterjee.soumen@gmail.com

©Google LLC All rights reserved. Google Cloud and Google Cloud Platform is a trademark of Google LLC
Google and the Google logo are registered trademarks of Google LLC, used with permission

ALL RIGHTS RESERVED. This book contains material protected under Copyright Laws and Treaties. Any unauthorised reprint or use of this material is prohibited. No part of this book may be reproduced or transmitted in any form or by any means, electronic or mechanical, including photocopying, recording, or by any information storage and retrieval system without express written permission from the author/publisher. For permission requests, email directly to the author.

Be Informed — your first step.

This book is a self-publishing content - conceptualised, designed and developed in my spare time. The views, opinions, thoughts, strategies or intentions expressed in rest of the books are solely mine, and they do not represent my past or present employers or any of my present or past client's views. My views do not share sensitive and confidential information that I have access to my present or past service at these organisations or any of my clients or suppliers or vendors. All information I provided on an as-is, a point in time snapshot and manifestation of the various thinking process running around my human brain. My views may change in future as I learn and understand. All images are drawn using personal licensed productivity improvement tools or software. Image sourced from elsewhere are declared appropriately.

The information provided in my book is for general informational and understanding purposes only. While I tried to keep my content and advice up-to-date and correct, there are no representations or warranties, express or implied, about the completeness, accuracy, reliability, suitability or availability concerning the information, products, services, or related graphics contained in this eBook for any purpose. The author has no share investment or any other vested interest in any of the products or organisations discussed or mentioned in the book in any way whatsoever, and do not assume and hereby disclaim any associated liability to any party for any loss, damage, or disruption caused by errors or omissions, whether such errors or omissions result from negligence, accident, or any other cause, so your use of the information contained in or linked from the content of my book is solely at your own decision.

The views, opinions, thoughts, strategies or intentions expressed within this eBook are the author's thoughts and not instructed, controlled or endorsed in any direction by any of the organisations described in the book. They are not intended to be a definitive set of instructions for your project.

Although I am an adviser and consultant by trade, I am not your adviser or consultant. Reading this book does not create a consultant-client relationship between us. This book is not intended as a substitute for the advisory advice, professional service of experts, consultants or advisors. The reader should regularly consult advisory advice, professional service of subject matter experts, consultants or advisors in matters relating to their business requirements and suitability of the products or tools described in the book.

The author is not responsible for the content of any materials or third-party website to which links are provided from this book. Any links or references to websites are provided for your information and further study only. The author does not endorse or control these websites or their views and cannot guarantee that material on those sites is in all respects accurate, complete and current.

Dedication

This book is my first debut on my own. Previously, I co-authored one chapter of a Big Data Spectrum book published by one of my previous employer organisation. It took a long time since the concept I discussed with one of the best friend Sanjeev and realised the same into this stage of a book. Life has taught me a lot, and I learn every day. This book is the beginning of a series of my other titles lined up this year. Before getting into the actual subject, let me take this opportunity to confess something beforehand.

I am an ordinary person like many others with millions of dreams[1] in my eyes that wake me up every day. I live in the Moments of Truth, where stimulus push us to be in Zero Moments of Truth (ZMOT[2]) but I believe in beyond that, moments are the future and we are driving past the future every moment. I dream to drive back to my future and our future. I would like to know what Leonardo Da Vinci wanted to convey in his paintings, what is in Veda that could give us a direction in our future, hidden marvels in Chinese and Indian herbals, Who were in Inka and Mayan civilisations, is Atlantis a reality, how music impacts our neurons and if music has hidden treasure to change human life. It is not as far as we think, but the technology could unravel a lot of these soon. AI and ML would lead the way as a significant number of behaviours natural patterns to spot and many prediction problems to solve. I love the flowers. My favourites of all are Sun Flower. This book I dedicate to my mom who was the first Sun Flower I ever knew exist in my planet to spread her positivity and strength that helped me becoming a crazy dreamer who could write the previous two paragraphs, blooming and turning to face the sun. I am a technology lover by profession and help people making their technology garden a bit tidy and better.

This book is dedicated to the angel from the heaven, who made me believe in "To see a World in a Grain of Sand/And a Heaven in a Wild Flower/Hold Infinity in the palm of your hand/And Eternity in an hour[3]"; I wake up, and no tears left to cry. "If you see the wonder of a fairy tale, You can take the future even if you fail, I believe in angels, Something good in everything I see, I believe in angels[4]". This book and my upcoming series lined up and my rest of the work I dedicate to my angels who changed the way I think even in my dream and all those dreamers who dare to dream, believe in angels! I have a dream using advanced technologies to reach every corner of humans and society and spread the concepts of the Sun Flowers that even once inspired Vincent Van Gogh, with warmth, positivity, power, strength, and happiness underpinning advanced technologies such as Cloud, Machine Learning, and Contextonomy™.

Google is one of the most advanced technology on the planet to satiate our curiosity. Stay curious with Google and keep smiling. Funny enough, this ordinary man proud to share the same birthday as Google. Without Google, I don't start my day. Without Google and all those brains with millions of dreams who built it, I wouldn't dare to cross the stream. My first book couldn't be dedicated to anybody other than Google, as my next on the list. Now I am ready to cross the stream – I have a dream.

---

[1] Source and Copyright: The Greatest Showman, A Million Dreams lyrics, Songwriters: Benj Pasek / Justin Paul, Released: 2017
[2] Winning the Zero Moment of Truth - ZMOT , Vook Inc.
[3] From Auguries of Innocence by William Blake
[4] Source and Copyright: ABBA, Album: Voulez-Vous, Released: 1979. I encountered this song about a decade ago though.

Acknowledgement

Writing a book is not something we do a regular basis and requires many inspirations that I thought and more satisfaction than I could have ever imagined. None of this would have been possible without a few people who believed me and stood by me all the time that life presented me at various moments in my journey.

Sanj, Ketan, Rahul, Soumen, Ashish, Cyrus, Nilesh – I am grateful to have friends like you and for all your help in various points. I learnt so many things from you that allowed me to believe in dreams. I'm forever indebted to the Almighty to make me meet people like you.
I am forever indebted to the almighty God to give me Aratrika, my daughter and made me believe in an angel in life every day.
I'm eternally grateful to God for giving me my dad who taught me the most critical lesson to stay focused on what you believe in and leave it to its cycle.

I am grateful to Jean-Claude Franchitti for his help and believe in me while I was working for him in one of my previous organisation.
I thank you Arvind Pal Singh for your help when I really needed.
I sincerely appreciate Segun and Rashmi, for their help and believe in me, and without their support, I couldn't have made my journey so far.

I want to add that I am open and honest throughout my life and non-believer in specific religious faith, race, colour or age. I am a firm believer of karmic cycle. My definition of growth, happiness and success those I learnt from you, gave me a rebirth – you wouldn't believe but embedded in my life.

Table of Contents

PREFACE 18

PROFESSIONAL CLOUD ARCHITECT 19

WHAT IS NEW IN THIS SECOND EDITION? 20

CERTIFICATION ASSESSMENT AREAS 21

Assessment Sections **22**

GOOGLE CLOUD PLATFORM: WELCOME TO A WHOLE NEW POSSIBILITIES 25

Google Cloud Platform – Its role in the Digital Revolution **30**

A DATA-CENTRIC ORGANIZATION – HOW GCP ENABLING THE CXO VISION 35

THE GOOGLE CLOUD ADOPTION FRAMEWORK 43

GOOGLE CLOUD PLATFORM FOUNDATIONAL BLOCKS 49

GOOGLE CLOUD PLATFORM (GCP) SERVICES 52

GOOGLE CLOUD PLATFORM COMPONENTS 55

Networking — 61
    Google Cloud Virtual Networks and Interconnect — 62
    Cloud Load Balancers — 68
    Virtual Private Cloud (VPC) — 70
    Other Components — 72
    Putting the puzzle together – High-Level Networking Architecture Example — 73
    Cloud Router — 74
    Managed Instance Autoscaling — 75
    Load Balancer Health Check — 76

Compute Engine — 78
    The life cycle of a single VM — 81
    Preemptible instance — 84
    Shielded VM — 85
    Compute Engine and Application Autoscaling — 85
     — 86
    Google App Engine (GAE) — 88
    Microservices and Google App Engine — 91
    Google Kubernetes Engine — 92
    Container-Optimized OS — 96
    Graphics Processing Units (GPU) — 97

Cloud Platform Storage — 99
    Cloud Memorystore — 102
    Persistent Disk — 102
    Cloud Filestore — 102
    Firestore — 102
    Cloud Platform Storage – Architectural Usage Scenario — 103
    Putting the puzzle together – Data Ingest and Data Storage — 104

Data Transfer and Data Migration — 106
    Cloud Storage Transfer Service — 107
    Transfer Appliance — 107

Cloud Databases — 109
    Google BigQuery — 110

BigQuery - Programmatic Interaction	112
Cloud native Data Warehouse using BigQuery	113
Optimising Large-Scale Ingestion of Analytics Events and Logs	113
Cloud Bigtable	116
Google Cloud SQL	122
Google Cloud Spanner	123
What Database and when?	125

Data Analytics — 126

Cloud Pub/Sub	127
Cloud Dataflow	128
Cloud Dataprep	128
Cloud Dataproc - Cloud-native Apache Hadoop & Apache Spark	130
Usage scenario - Cloud Dataproc vs Cloud Dataflow	130
Cloud Datalab	131
Exploring data using BigQuery and Cloud Datalab	132
Google Data Studio	132
Genomics	132
Cloud Composer	134

Putting the puzzle together – Google Cloud Databases and Analytics Architecture — 136

Complex Event Processing (CEP)	136

Identity and Security — 138

Cloud Security Controls and Threat Management	140
Cloud Security Scanner	140
Cloud Identity	140
Cloud Identity and Access Management	140
Security Keys	143
Cloud Resource Manager	143
Encryption at rest	143
Cloud Data Loss Prevention (DLP) API	144
Forseti Security: Open source tools for GCP security	144

Development Tools — 147

Management Tools — 149
   Cloud API — 149
   Google Stackdriver — 149

API Management — 151
   Cloud Endpoints — 151

Google Cloud Internet Of Things (IoT) — 155
   Cloud IoT Core — 156
   Cloud IoT Edge — 157
   Edge TPU — 159

Cloud AI — 161
   Natural conversational interfaces — 164
   Machine learning and data — 167
   Google Cloud ML Engine — 167

AI FIRST: DEMOCRATIZE AI — 171

GROUPING GOOGLE CLOUD PLATFORM RESOURCES — 172

Filtering by Service account vs Network tag — 173

Putting the puzzle together – A high-level Network Tagging Example — 174

GOOGLE CLOUD PLATFORM – BUILT TO SCALE — 175

Disaster Recovery and Business Continuity — 178
   Application Recovery – DR Scenario — 178
   Data Recovery – DR Scenario — 180

SERVERLESS ARCHITECTURE — 183

Function as a service (FAAS) – Cloud Function — 184

STANDARDS, REGULATORY COMPLIANCE & CERTIFICATIONS	187
GOOGLE CLOUD – CLOUD NATIVE OPERATIONS (DEVOPS CI/CD, DATA OPS, AIOPS AND NO OPS)	193
CI/CD Pipeline using GKE and Spinnaker	193
CI/CD pipeline using GKE clusters	194
Set up a continuous delivery pipeline using Jenkins and GKE	195
Automating Canary Analysis on Google Kubernetes Engine with Spinnaker	195
A/B Testing in the Google Cloud Platform	196
Distributed Load Testing Using Kubernetes	196
Kubeflow: Simplifying machine learning on open hybrid clouds	199
Kubeflow: Cloud-native machine learning with Kubernetes	199
GOOGLE CLOUD PRICING AND BILLING	201
Google Cloud Platform Sustained Discount	204
CLOUD NATIVE, CLOUD NEUTRAL AND MULTI-CLOUD STRATEGY	207
Moving to Multi-clouds	212
Cloud Migration Topology	214
CLOUD FIRST VS CLOUD ENABLED	221
GOOGLE NEXT 19 – KEY ANNOUNCEMENTS	222
CERTIFICATION EXAM: SAMPLE CASE STUDIES	225
Mountkirk Games Case Study	**225**
Dress4Win Case Study	**227**
TerramEarth Case Study	**228**

TEST YOUR EXAM READINESS	229
GOOGLE CLOUD PLATFORM DIAGRAMMING & DOCUMENTATION	230
GOOGLE CLOUD PRODUCT AND SERVICES GLOSSARY	236
REFERENCES	242
COPYRIGHT DECLARATIONS AND ACKNOWLEDGEMENTS	243
SPECIAL MENTION	244
MY OTHER FORTHCOMING TITLES THIS YEAR Q2 AND Q3 2019	245
INDEX	246
ABOUT THE AUTHOR	254
STAY CONNECTED	255

List of Figures

Figure 1: Professional Cloud Certification Assessment Areas at a glace	21
Figure 2: Section 1to 2.1 details	22
Figure 3: Section 2.2 to 5.2	23
Figure 4: GCP Network Spans, Durability and Availability	26
Figure 5: Google Cloud Differentiations	27
Figure 6: RESPONSE Framework	28
Figure 7: ClickAware - Click, Learn, Immerse, Collaborate, Kinesis	30
Figure 8: ClickAware - Areas mastered and Reimagined by Digital Leaders and Brands	31
Figure 9: Divide - Bring together the Data Silos and Decision Making	36

Figure 10: CxO primary areas of interest	37
Figure 11: The Google Cloud Adoption Framework	44
Figure 12: The Google Cloud Adoption Framework Epics	45
Figure 13: Google Cloud Platform building blocks	49
Figure 14: Google Cloud Services	52
Figure 15: GCP Product Components	55
Figure 16: Product Availability in Americas Regions	57
Figure 17: Product Availability in Europe	57
Figure 18: Product Availability Globally	58
Figure 19: Product Availability in APAC	58
Figure 20: Cloud ML Engine and Training Availability	59
Figure 21: GCP Networking Tools and Components	62
Figure 22: Using Cloud Router Global Routing	62
Figure 23: Dedicated Interconnect Locations	63
Figure 24: GCP Dedicated Interconnect Locations Across the Globe	63
Figure 25: Interconnect vs VPN	64
Figure 26: Google Cloud Regions	66
Figure 27: Google Cloud Network	67
Figure 28: How to decide appropriate load balancer	70
Figure 29: Google Cloud VPC Network	70
Figure 30: Google Cloud Networking Components	72
Figure 31: Google Cloud Networking Basics	73
Figure 32: Cloud Router global dynamic routing	74
Figure 33: Google Cloud Compute Components	78
Figure 34: Creation of a Boot instance from disk	80
Figure 35: Sharing images between projects	80
Figure 36: Phases of an instance	81
Figure 37: Live Migration Stages - A High Level View	82
Figure 38: Preemtible VM Instance - Build affordable, short-lived compute instances for batch jobs and fault-tolerant workloads	84
Figure 39: Scaling leveraging Preemptible VMs - Burst from on premises	85
Figure 40: Application scaling with best-of-breed compute options: Standard VMs and Preemptible VMs	86
Figure 41: Mobile app built using both Firebase and App Engine	88
Figure 42: Building a simple web app using App Engine	89
Figure 43: Six Key Considerations when to think about Google App Engine	90
Figure 44: Multi-version Application Hierarchy	91
Figure 45: App Engine App running with multiple services	91
Figure 46: GKE with a Shared Virtual Private Cloud (VPC)	92
Figure 47: Highly Available GKE with Regional Clusters	93
Figure 48: Steps to create a VM instance or a managed instance group running a container	96
Figure 49: Cloud Platform Storage	99
Figure 50: Data Ingest and Storage	104

Figure 51: Data Transfer and Data Migration Tools	106
Figure 52: Cloud Database Components	109
Figure 53: BigQuery Components	111
Figure 54: BigQuery Streaming Ingestion	112
Figure 55: Dataflow to ETL data into BigQuery	112
Figure 56: An example ETL architecture for cloud-native data warehousing on GCP	113
Figure 57: Hot and Cold Path Ingestion	114
Figure 58: Simplified view of Bigtable internal architecture. An instance with a single cluster	116
Figure 59: Financial Analysis	118
Figure 60: IoT	119
Figure 61: AdTech	120
Figure 62: Google Cloud Analytics Components	126
Figure 63: Cloud Pb/Sub message syndication	127
Figure 64: Data Transformation with Cloud Dataflow, Cloud Pub/Sub for Stream Analytics	128
Figure 65: Google Cloud Dataproc - under the hood	130
Figure 66: Cloud Dataproc – integrated	130
Figure 67: Where Cloud Dataproc fits into GCP	130
Figure 68: Exploring data using BigQuery and Cloud Datalab	132
Figure 69: Genomics in Google Cloud	133
Figure 70: Cloud Composer Architecture Overview	134
Figure 71: Complex Event Processing using Google Cloud Platform	136
Figure 72: Identity and Access Management Tools	138
Figure 73: Cloud IAM Policy, Member Identity and Roles View	140
Figure 74: Cloud IAM Policy	141
Figure 75: GCP Resource Hierarchy	142
Figure 76: GCP Development Tools	147
Figure 77: Management Tools	149
Figure 78: API Management Tools	151
Figure 79: Cloud Endpoints	152
Figure 80: Apigee API Platform, Source: https://cloud.google.com/apigee-api-management/	153
Figure 81: Google Cloud Platform IoT	155
Figure 82: Cloud IoT Core	157
Figure 83: Cloud IoT Edge	158
Figure 84: Cloud AI Tools	161
Figure 85: Cloud AI building blocks	162
Figure 86: Example usage of Cloud ML and NLP APIs	162
Figure 87: Customer Sentiment Analysis Leveraging Cloud Natural Language API	163
Figure 88: Running a distributed training job on Cloud ML Engine	164
Figure 89: The high-level architecture of a search engine-enhanced Action for Google Assistant	165
Figure 90: A complete serverless example with Dialogflow	166
Figure 91: ML Workflow	167

Figure 92: Model building and tuning leveraging Tensorflow	167
Figure 93: Firewall Rules leveraging Service Accounts	174
Figure 94: Network Tagging	174
Figure 95: Designing DR - Building Blocks	176
Figure 96: Building Scalable and Resilient Web Applications on Google Cloud Platform	177
Figure 97: An HA Deployment of Applications	178
Figure 98: Cold DR - Deployment of Applications	179
Figure 99: HA Data Recovery leveraging Persistent Disks	180
Figure 100: A comprehensive serverless ecosystem	183
Figure 101: Cloud Functions integrates with other Google Cloud Platform Components	184
Figure 102: Cloud Functions and Video Intelligence	185
Figure 103: Serverless ML Example	185
Figure 104: App Delivery pipeline with Google Cloud Components	193
Figure 105: Continuous Delivery Pipelines with Spinnaker and Google Kubernetes Engine	193
Figure 106: Building a continuous delivery pipeline using Ansible, Spinnaker and Google Compute Engine	194
Figure 107: CI/CD pipeline using two separate GKE clusters	194
Figure 108: A continuous delivery pipeline using Jenkins and GKE	195
Figure 109: Canary Testing on Google Kubernetes Engine with Spinnaker	196
Figure 110: GCP Pricing Calculator Tool	201
Figure 111: GCP Resource Hierarchy	201
Figure 112: Google Cloud Billing Dashboards	202
Figure 113: Google Cloud Billing dashboards	203
Figure 114: Scenario A where Cost is The total monthly cost of the combined resources is **$284.3335035**	204
Figure 115: Scenario B – Sustained Discount where total monthly cost is $312.075.	204
Figure 116: What moves to cloud	214
Figure 117: Cloud Migration – One example variety of Mirror Topology	215
Figure 118: Cloud Migration – One example a variety of Mesh Topology	216
Figure 119: Cloud Migration - Gated Egress and Ingress Topology	216
Figure 120: Migrating On-Premises Hadoop Infrastructure to Google Cloud Platform - In a hybrid setup	218
Figure 121: Migrating On-Premises Hadoop Infrastructure to Google Cloud Platform - In a Cloud Native Setup	219
Figure 122: Google Next 19 Announcement Summary	222
Figure 123: Mindmap - Mountkirk Games Case Study	226
Figure 124: Mind map - Dress4Win Case Study	227
Figure 125: Mind map - TerramEarth Case Study	228

List of Tables

Table 1: Types of Load Balancer	69
Table 2: Compute Engine Features	79
Table 3: Compute Engine, Kubernetes, GAE and Cloud Functions	85
Table 4: Application Scaling	92

Table	Title	Page
Table 5:	Storage Classes	99
Table 6:	MapReduce vs Dremel	110
Table 7:	Planet Scale No-Compromise Relational Database Service	123
Table 8:	Cloud Spanner Availability	123
Table 9:	Cloud Spanner Industry Use Cases	123
Table 10:	Selecting the right database/data storage	125
Table 11:	Cloud Pub/Sub as a Global Service	127
Table 12:	Dataproc workload vs Dataflow workload	131
Table 13:	Google Cloud Developer Tools	148
Table 14:	Labels, Tags and Security Marks	172
Table 15:	GCP Built-in components to enable scale and resiliency	175
Table 16:	GCP Disaster Recovery Components Building Blocks	175
Table 17:	DR Data Transfer Mechanisms in GCP	180
Table 18:	Regulatory Compliance in Finance - GCP Adherence	188
Table 19:	Google Cloud Components and Compliance Standards	190
Table 20:	Moving on-premise infrastructure to GCP	214
Table 21:	Moving Cloud Neutral Technologies to GCP	214

Preface

Congratulations! for your commitment and decision to make your cloud journey leveraging Google Cloud Platform or even being curious about the Google Cloud Platform. This journey could have a range of different origin point or arrival point. Well! Let me unwrap this a bit of decrypted form, and yes you got it correct. No matter whether you are a software / dev-ops / data-ops professional with engineering and development at your heart, You may even perhaps coming from an enterprise architect background and stipulating the enterprise-wide cloud architecture. Alternatively, even you might be a CIO or CDO or Startup visionary and wanted to understand a high-level view about Google Cloud Platform, or you are in a System Integration or Service Organisation engaged in Cloud delivery for a range of corporations. This book would benefit all of you who are interested in demonstrating your commitment to your organisation or industry and becoming a Google Certified Professional Cloud Architect. There could be some reasons you would think about certifying yourself but the key is your passion and commitment to be part of a revolution, and game-changing vision Google has built into their Cloud platform. Unlike thousands of others, I am not interested in spending another many pages arguing why Google Cloud and not other providers or dedicate component by component comparison in many tables and ensuring Google Cloud is the right choice. That discussion would alone, could be another good book on its right. I have one chapter dedicated to introducing the beauty of the platform and Google's vision that would lead the way Cloud adoption shaping up. I have elaborated a set of ten traits that would make you prudent in this consumer behaviour is driven marketplace and how Google Cloud Platform would enable you achieving what you need to stay relevant in the competitive advantage.

Intended Organisations who would benefit from my book

1. Advisory and Consulting
2. Technology Service Providers
3. System integrators
4. End-User Organization
5. Start-ups
6. Product and platforms
7. Digital Disruptors
8. Fintech, Insuretech and Regtech

Professional Cloud Architect[5]

A Professional Cloud Architect enables organisations to leverage Google Cloud technologies. With a thorough understanding of cloud architecture and Google Cloud Platform, this individual can design, develop, and manage robust, secure, scalable, highly available, and dynamic solutions to drive business objectives. A Google Certified Professional - Cloud Architect enables organisations to leverage Google Cloud technologies. Through an understanding of cloud architecture and Google technology, this individual designs develops and **manages robust, secure, scalable, highly available, and dynamic solutions** to drive business objectives. The Cloud Architect should be proficient in all aspects of solution development including implementation details, developing prototypes, and architectural best practices. The Cloud Architect should also be experienced in **microservices and multi-tiered distributed** applications which span multi-cloud or hybrid environments. To earn this certification, you must pass the Professional Cloud Architect exam. The format is multiple choice and multiple select and is available in English and Japanese. The exam has no prerequisites. This exam must be taken in-person at one of our testing centre locations.

Length: 2 hours, Exam fee: $200.00, **Language**: English, Japanese, **Exam Terms and Conditions**: https://cloud.google.com/certification/terms

If you don't pass an exam, you can retake it after 14 days. If you don't pass a second time, you must wait 60 days before you can take it a third time. If you don't pass the third time, you must wait a year before making it again. You may attempt the exam in multiple languages, but each attempt regardless of language counts toward the total permissible efforts and the waiting period between attempts still applies. Payment is required each time you take an exam. Circumventing this retake policy by registering under a different name or any other means is a violation of the exam terms and conditions and will result in a denied or revoked certification.

> **The Google Cloud Certified - Professional Cloud Architect exam assesment areas**
>
> - Design and plan a cloud solution architecture
> - Manage and provision the cloud solution infrastructure
> - Design for security and compliance
> - Analyze and optimize technical and business processes
> - Manage implementations of cloud architecture
> - Ensure solution and operations reliability

If Google discovers that you're in breach of the exam terms and conditions which are presented to you during your exam, your certification(s) will be revoked, you'll be permanently barred from retaking the exam and any other Google Cloud exams. Additionally, Google, in its sole discretion, may choose to terminate any relevant business relationship with you and take necessary legal actions.

---

[5] https://cloud.google.com/certification/cloud-architect

What is new in this second edition?

It is my great pleasure to release a second edition of this study guide within the first three months of the release. I am grateful to all your support. This version introduced a reference architecture for your overall Google Cloud Platform which I hope would be a great handy reference for your study and work.

I have added a summary mind-map to highlight all changes and new relese annouced in Google's flagship conference, Google Next 2019, hosted in Sanfransisco between 8-11th April 2019.

Please ensure, you read all the images and notes, all are for a reason. There are hiddel sublimimal messages for your
As many of you recommended to add some practice questions, I am introducing two separte sample papers to help you to be fully prepared for the exam. Please check the QR Code or the link as instructed.

Wish you all the best for your upcoming certification exam.

Certification Assessment Areas

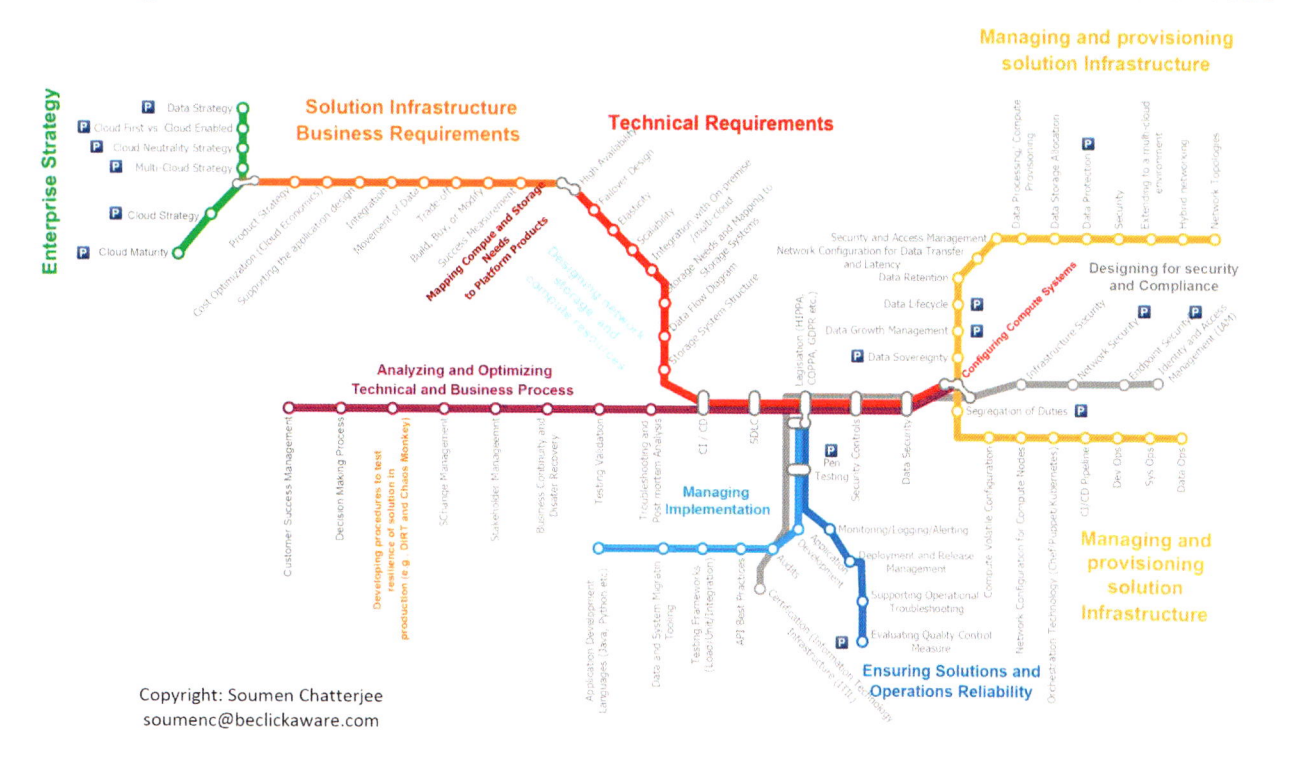

Figure 1: Professional Cloud Certification Assessment Areas at a glace

Google Cloud Certified Professional Cloud Architect, Second Edition

Assessment Sections

Google Cloud Architect Exam Assessment areas

Section 1: Designing and planning a cloud solution architecture

- 1.1 Designing a solution infrastructure that meets business requirements.
  - business use cases and product strategy
  - cost optimization
  - supporting the application design
  - integration
  - movement of data
  - tradeoffs
  - build, buy or modify
  - success measurements (e.g., Key Performance Indicators (KPI), Return on Investment (ROI), metrics)
  - Compliance and observability

- 1.2 Designing a solution infrastructure that meets technical requirements.
  - high availability and failover design
  - elasticity of cloud resources
  - scalability to meet growth requirements

- 1.3 Designing network, storage, and compute resources.
  - integration with on premises/multi-cloud environments
  - Cloud native networking (VPC, peering, firewalls, container networking)
  - identification of data processing pipeline
  - matching data characteristics to storage systems
  - data flow diagrams
  - storage system structure (e.g., Object, File, RDBMS, NoSQL, NewSQL)
  - mapping compute needs to platform products

- 1.4 Creating a migration plan (i.e., documents and architectural diagrams).
  - Integrating solution with existing systems
  - Migrating systems and data to support the solution
  - Licensing mapping
  - Network and management planning
  - Testing and proof-of-concept

- 1.5 Envisioning future solution improvements.
  - cloud and technology improvements
  - business needs evolution
  - evangelism and advocacy

Section 2: Managing and provisioning solution Infrastructure

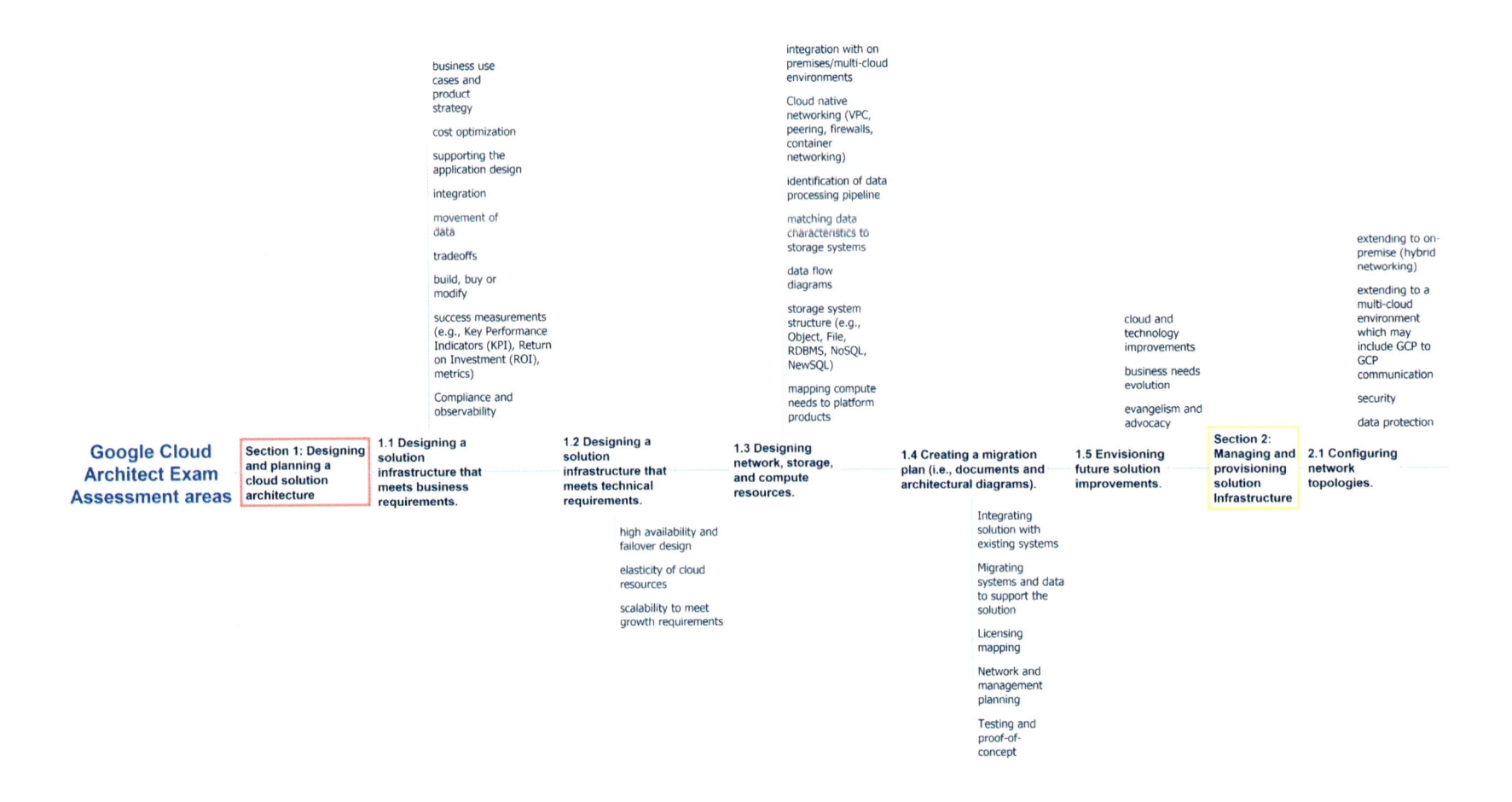

- 2.1 Configuring network topologies.
  - extending to on-premise (hybrid networking)
  - extending to a multi-cloud environment which may include GCP to GCP communication
  - security
  - data protection

Figure 2: Section 1 to 2.1 details

Google Cloud Certified Professional Cloud Architect, Second Edition

Figure 3: Section 2.2 to 5.2

2.2 Configuring individual storage systems.
- data storage allocation
- data processing/compute provisioning
- security and access management
- network configuration for data transfer and latency
- data retention and data lifecycle management
- data growth management

2.3 Configuring compute systems.
- compute system provisioning
- compute volatility configuration (preemptible vs. standard)
- network configuration for compute nodes
- infrastructure provisioning technology configuration (e.g. Chef/Puppet/Ansible/Terraform)
- container orchestration (e.g. Kubernetes)

Section 3: Designing for security and compliance

3.1 Designing for security.
- Identity and Access Management (IAM)
- Resource hierarchy (organizations, folders, projects)
- data security (key management, encryption)
- penetration testing
- Separation of Duties (SoD)
- security controls
- Managing customer-supplied encryption keys with Cloud KMS

3.2 Designing for legal compliance.
- legislation (e.g., Health Insurance Portability and Accountability Act (HIPAA), Children's Online Privacy Protection Act (COPPA), etc.)
- audits (including logs)
- certification (e.g., Information Technology Infrastructure Library (ITIL) framework)

Section 4: Analyzing and optimizing technical and business processes

4.1 Analyzing and defining technical processes.
- Software Development Lifecycle Plan (SDLC)
- continuous integration / continuous deployment
- troubleshooting / post mortem analysis culture
- testing and validation
- IT enterprise process (e.g. ITIL)
- business continuity and disaster recovery

4.2 Analyzing and defining business processes.
- stakeholder management (e.g. Influencing and facilitation)
- change management
- team assessment / skills readiness
- decision making process
- customer success management
- cost optimization / resource optimization (Capex / Opex)

4.3 Developing procedures to test resilience of solution in production (e.g., DiRT and Simian Army)

Section 5: Managing implementation

5.1 Advising development/operation team(s) to ensure successful deployment of the solution.
- application development
- API best practices
- testing frameworks (load/unit/integration)
- data and system migration tooling

5.2 Interacting with Google Cloud using GCP SDK (gcloud, gsutil and bq). Considerations include:
- local installation
- Google Cloud Shell

Figure 3: Section 2.2 to 5.2

"Google is living a few years in the future and sending the rest of us messages."

Doug Cutting, Hadoop's co-creator, Co-Founder Cloudera

Google Cloud Platform: Welcome to a whole new possibilities
Transforming the Neverland into a Magical Wonderland

Cloud war is stirring up the marketplace in an exciting way, and almost all of the cloud providers are edging into the game based on revenue, market share and annual run rates. Being an industry practitioner, I would recommend understanding the rule of the game first before you decide your cloud partner and where necessary keep cloud neutrality in mind while determining your multi-cloud strategy in your enterprise. Revenue of incumbent providers should not create a bias in your decision but one of the feature of the selection criteria, not all. Every organisation has its way to cluster their revenue under a particular category which would include various software products, service, acquisitions revenue and other complex tagging rules. Cloud computing is no longer about how the resources are managed, Google's **mission** is to **organise the world's information** and make it **universally accessible and useful**. To assemble the world's information, Google has been **building the most robust infrastructure on the planet**. Google is heading towards the **Third Wave of Managed Service** where the paradigm is **full elastic storage**, **process** your data **at scale**, make machine learning at a defacto standard and everything you **pay only for what you use**. I can not emphasise enough the importance of **focussing on insights and not the infrastructure**. What Google Cloud indeed offers us: **spend less on ops and administration**, **bring the cloud to us** (in contrary to, we **move to cloud** philosophy) and help to transform our organisation into **a true data-driven enterprise** where we can **put tools into the hands of domain experts**. Pay per use is another misleading term by every vendor where Google differentiates not only per second billings but also guide you by its on-the-fly machine learning based **spend economics**, analysis of your infrastructure use and processing pattern, amount spent, what is the best stack configuration you need to make your investment genuinely pay for what you use. While Google entered a bit late in the game, Google is marching like

> "There was something fundamentally wrong with my conception, in 2008, of what we were doing. It's not realistic to expect people to go de novo, from an original architecture, into App Engine. So we decided that we had to change our strategy...We didn't give the right stepping stone into the cloud."
> **Eric Scmidt, Executive Chairman, Google**

GCP Network Spans, Durability and Availability

Google Cloud Platform has 17 regions, 52 zones, over 100 points of presence across 35 countries, and a well-provisioned global network with 100,000s of miles of fiber optic cable. Google Cloud supports 99.999999999% annual durability, achieved through erasure coding that stores data pieces redundantly across multiple disks located in different power and network failure domains. Such distributed storage means data survives even in the event of the simultaneous loss of two disks.

4 different types of storage: **Coldline storage, nearline, regional storage** (99.99% typical monthly availability, 99.9% availability SLA), and **multi-regional storage (>99.99% typical monthly availability**, 99.95% availability SLA, **Geo-redundant** - which means cloud storage stores your data redundantly in **at least two regions within the multi-regional location** of the bucket ensures you will never lose your data, even in the case of a disaster). It stores data redundantly, with automatic checksums to ensure data integrity.

one of the fastest growing marching like **one of the fastest growing contenders in the game**. What makes Google standing apart, is their vision to be **one of the largest networks in the world**, at the same time no downtime toll to customers.

"This is what makes Google Google: its physical network, its thousands of fiber miles, and those many thousands of servers that, in aggregate, add up to the mother of all clouds." **WIRED Magazine** (https://www.wired.com/2012/10/ff-inside-google-data-center/). The Network is the most substantial foundation of Cloud. Google is the **only provider who allows live migrations of virtual machines**, offers the most secure, flexible, and cost-effective solution. Benefits of live migrations enable the update, patching, repairing, software and hardware, without any machine reboots. Google is committed to **carbon neutrality** with **zero emissions** compute carbon footprint and **100% of renewable energy**. A sustainable cloud is not only good for the environment but good for your business.

In a 2010 interview in the Wall Street Journal, Eric Schmidt, Executive Chairman, Google said that "I actually think most people don't want Google to answer their questions," he explained. "They want Google to tell them what they should be doing next." In March 2017, in a keynote speech at its annual I/O event, Google CEO Sundar Pichai claimed that Google is in a transition path from "**searching and organizing the world's information to AI and machine learning**". He also announced that the company was shifting from a "**mobile-first world to an AI-first world**." Both these statements confirm Google's strategic direction and how it is driving its significant investment in Machine Learning and Artificial Intelligence and keeping that agenda at its forefront of Google Cloud Platform. Has been The announcement more strategic than a fundamental change in vision.

One of the critical objectives, Google is introducing a new Business Model, **democratise AI**. Google Cloud Platform is strengthening its offerings with standard AI building blocks where customers could tailor and optimise models, able to **improve the quality of models much faster with their data**. This is further enhanced by continuous releases of various **automation of technologies** such as transfer learning, training, and model optimisation will be critical. Google Cloud Platform empowers you to lower the barrier of entry and make AI available to the broadest possible community of developers, researchers and businesses. In 2017, Google announced the release of Google **Cloud Machine Learning Engine (MLE)**, the foundation pillar for building machine learning services, to help building ML models that work

Figure 4: GCP Network Spans, Durability and Availability

on any data, of any size. Google ML and AI capabilities could be tapped into via APIs—including Vision, Speech, NLP, Translation and Dialogflow—could be built upon pre-trained models to bring unmatched scale and speed to business applications. It is also worth noting that Kaggle, Google's community of data scientists and ML researchers, has grown to more than one million members where more than 10,000 businesses are leveraging Google Cloud AI services, including leading enterprise like **Box**, **Rolls Royce Marine**, **Kewpie** and **Ocado**.

I use a model, I call **RESPONSE** when I intend to select any technology or vendor, and I would recommend you highly to refer the same. It is pretty self-explanatory – perform your assessment of Google Cloud and compare in all these seven areas and would guide you in the right direction. There are numerous success stories from Google Cloud Customers where organizations were able to reduce costs through sharing information, eliminating delays and innovative example from **Chile's Health Care Sector** where it is helping them overcome the duplication of medical tests. The platform also provides information to apps and websites used by patients, enabling them to see and gradually empower themselves with their health data.

- Google Cloud offers the fastest and most secure way to deliver content globally (offering the fastest SSL) Source: CBInsights research on Cloud Wars
- Blazing fast, private distributed Google's backbone between all the data centers and not over the Internet
- Leaders in providing PAAS and IAAS Service. Source: Gartner and Forrester Reports
- Google Cloud's security model, compliance, transparency & privacy, world-scale infrastructure, unique capability to innovate
- Scale with open, flexible technology
- Solve problems with accessible AI & data analytics

Figure 5: Google Cloud Differentiations

(https://www.blog.google/products/google-cloud/transforming-chiles-health-sector-connectivity/)

Figure 6: RESPONSE Framework

AccuWeather has evolved to offer JSON-formatted, easily cached, and highly efficient APIs that can handle the massive volumes of data required by the mobile world and processing 30B+ API requests per day.
Bazaarvoice provides software that enables e-commerce companies to collect, distribute, and display authentic consumer-generated content about their products online and manages 15B API calls per month without outages.
German fintech startup Billie scales complex infrastructure quickly and efficiently with managed services on Google Cloud Platform, using Google BigQuery to identify the best clients to target.
Evernote moved their more than 200 million users, over 5 billion user notes into Google Cloud Platform in only 70 days and now more securely store billions of records and attachments—the equivalent of roughly ten copies of every modern book ever published. Evernote also chose the Google Cloud Platform for its built-in advanced data analytics and machine learning capabilities. In the future, Evernote plans to add voice recognition and translation features to its service using Google Cloud Machine Learning Engine, giving customers even more power to capture their ideas on the fly. **MainAd** migrated its core infrastructure to Google Cloud Platform to build a high-performance, real-time ad bidding system that can serve up to 50,000 requests per second. It also used Open Bidder, an open source bidding API developed by Google, to craft predictive intelligence algorithms and build custom real-time bidding solutions to meet the unique needs of each customer. Shortly after moving to Google Cloud Platform, MainAd launched Logico, a predictive analytics engine that delivers greater precision in ad retargeting by targeting individuals instead of broadly defined audience groups. MainAd has since expanded the engine into Logico 3C, a comprehensive AI-based retargeting platform with an easy-to-use customer interface. There is a growing list of respected enterprise across the globe who are successfully adopting Google Cloud as part of their strategic move that includes but not limited to **Spotify**, **Apple**, **HSBC**, **Home Depot**, **Target**, **Snapchat**, **HTC**, **Best Buy**, **Philips**, **Coca Cola**, and **Domino's**.

HSBC is among other leading Financial Institutions and Banks, taking their 'Cloud First' journey with Google Cloud Platform. In recent Google Next 2018 in the USA, HSBC CIO Darryl West presented the bank's use cases which are going first on Google Cloud. In an interview with CIO Magazine, recently Darryl West mentioned, "Our strategy is to be multi-cloud, and we will be doing the majority, if not all, of our data warehouse applications and big data applications with Google," he said. "We decided they have the best capability there and have been happy with the way we can work collaboratively with them to solve any problems we have." The liquidity reporting algorithm would give the bank a view of each country in "minutes not hours" therefore leading to a huge productivity boost. The push for more advanced analytics to cut down on money laundering follows the Mexican scandal for which the bank was fined $1.9 billion in 2012. **Source**: https://www.cio.co.uk/it-strategy/hsbc-cio-partners-with-google-cloud-on-machine-learning-drive-3681650/

Google Cloud Machine Learning Engine (MLE), helps data scientists complete Machine Learning model testing and training significantly faster without expensive computational infrastructure constraint. Google Cloud AutoML would empower developers with technology that can automatically create a machine learning model. Google is taking a giant leap forward, next level of Data Economics and Monetisation to Model Monetisation and would soon be offering pre-trained models for companies that do not have the capacity or capability to create custom machine learning models. Google's upcoming API beta could assist with the "dark matter" of the internet, video content analysis leveraging the artificial intelligence to identify and tag content in a video in a timeline. Google's Advanced Solutions Lab would soon assist customers in developing advanced machine learning capabilities. Google is also leading the way supporting a spectrum of cloud open source projects (https://opensource.google.com/projects/list/cloud), a detailed list could be explored here: https://opensource.google.com/projects/explore/featured

There is no wonder that Google Cloud has now proudly secured its leadership position within leading Analysts and Research communities (**Source**: https://cloud.google.com/analyst-reports/). Forrester Research names Google Cloud, a Leader[6] in Public Cloud Platform Native Security Wave[7]. Gartner recently named Google as a Leader in the 2018 Gartner Infrastructure as a Service Magic Quadrant [8] and Google is designated as a leader in the 2018 Gartner Magic Quadrant for Public Cloud Storage Services[9]. Google Cloud has been named as a leader in the Forrester Wave: Insight Platforms-as-a-service, Q3 2017[10], and received the highest score among all the evaluated vendors in both the current offerings and strategy categories.

---

[6] https://cloud.google.com/forrester-public-cloud-platform-native-security-wave/
[7] The Forrester Wave™: Public Cloud Platform Native Security, Q2 2018 report
[8] https://cloud.google.com/gartner-cloud-infrastructure-as-a-service/
[9] https://cloud.google.com/gartner-public-cloud-storage/
[10] https://cloud.google.com/forrester-wave-leader/

Google Cloud Platform – Its role in the Digital Revolution

Digital (Transformation) and Innovation are on almost every corporate agenda these days, and senior leaders overwhelmingly agree as a top strategic priority for sustainable growth that addresses both cost leadership and revenue generation. However, not many organisations can demonstrate their digital leadership. Over the last few years, the industry has noticed the **GAFAM** (Google, Apple, Facebook, Amazon, Microsoft) dominated market determinant with market capitalisation exceeds those of major brands (over $2 trillion). A new economic sensational vibe now originated by **NATU** (Netflix, Airbnb, Tesla, and Uber), the four Chinese internet giants **BATX** (Baidu, Alibaba, Tencent and Xiaomi) challenging every corner of technologies and redefining their boundaries, and now crossed an exceptional financial capital value. Exciting pattern to notice, what is common between GAFAM, NATU and BAFX? All of these organisations are first to develop digital platforms as an innovation strategy since their inception. A lot of today's Cloud and Big Data technologies are their contribution. Their Digital mindset led this technological advancement and not the other way round. There is a list of other digital leaders who have mastered the art of digital – **eBay, GE, 3M, Walmart, Ant Financials, Samsung, IBM, BMW, Daimler, Disney** to name a few, who are consistently generating phenomenal financial growth with unprecedented high market capitalisation valuations. Most seemingly they are all, that I call, ClickAware™. Stay tuned to my www.beclickaware.com for one of my upcoming book due in Q2 2019 that would take you through how a spectrum of exemplifying global 50+ leading organisations are staying relevant and always on a growth trajectory, redefining their success and at the same time making the competition irrelevant. Chris Skinner in his book 'Digital Bank: Strategies to launch or become a digital bank', made a fundamental point. Not only applicable to banks but seamlessly applies to most of the industry that, three key pillars of your organisation - **We are a manufacturer of products** (services), **a processor of transactions** (engage with the customers/consumers) and also at the same time, **a retailer of services**. Real-time enterprise alone is not enough, and we must spend more time on think ahead business, at a speed of thoughts, revisit and de-constitute our digital processes and put our heads together to consider how to reconstitute ourselves. All the digital leaders already mastered the space between order and chaos already or in the process of doing so. They showed us the formula to tame the tide of uncertainty and rewrite the future in every moment as they well understood the **Complex Adaptive Systems (CAS)**. What it transpires into a principle that Human Experience (**HEx**) would always stay on top of Customer and Consumer experience which sits somewhere between a transactional and user experience relationship or engagement spectrum. Human Exchange (**HX**) is the key in Digital. Human is one of the biggest drivers of the behavioural economy of today and coming years, and failing to recognise these shifting demands and subsequently unable to address these behavioural demands would be fatal in many instances, and that might lead

ClickAware™
1. **Connect** – Mechanisms that enterprise (A Complex Adaptive System) as a service provider or consumers interacts with its consumers, social, political, economical systems, Both humans and non-humans devices, processes, algorithms, data, and signals.
2. **Learn** – About the current, and future behaviours of the connected ecosystems including humans and non-humans.
3. **Immerse** – Cognitive and Contextual learning of the connected eco-systems of the enterprise.
4. **Collaborate** – A way of co-creation between internal and extrernal habitant of the enterprise eco-systems
5. **Kinesis** – Stay relevent in behavioural and Contextual Economy and transform into an Adaptive enterprise.

Figure 7: ClickAware - Click, Learn, Immerse, Collaborate, Kinesis

your organisation to a mummification path. In my one of the upcoming title, ClickAware™, you would see another set of 50+ organisations from various sectors who were unable to stay relevant and unable to lead the way they originally planned. Every industry, regardless of the vertical segments, focuses their customer (including B2B, B2E, B2C) - and consumer-centric (end-users) service offerings at a speed of thoughts and some cases even, ahead of the consumer thinking.
What exactly affects enterprises when the market is in continuous flux with significant economic and political events swaying consumer and business confidence, emerging players disrupting the ecosystems with a different class of services, products, platforms or even introducing new inhabitants of sharing economy business models. How soon our organisation respond – Time to Act is the key.
It is

Figure 8: ClickAware - Areas mastered and Reimagined by Digital Leaders and Brands

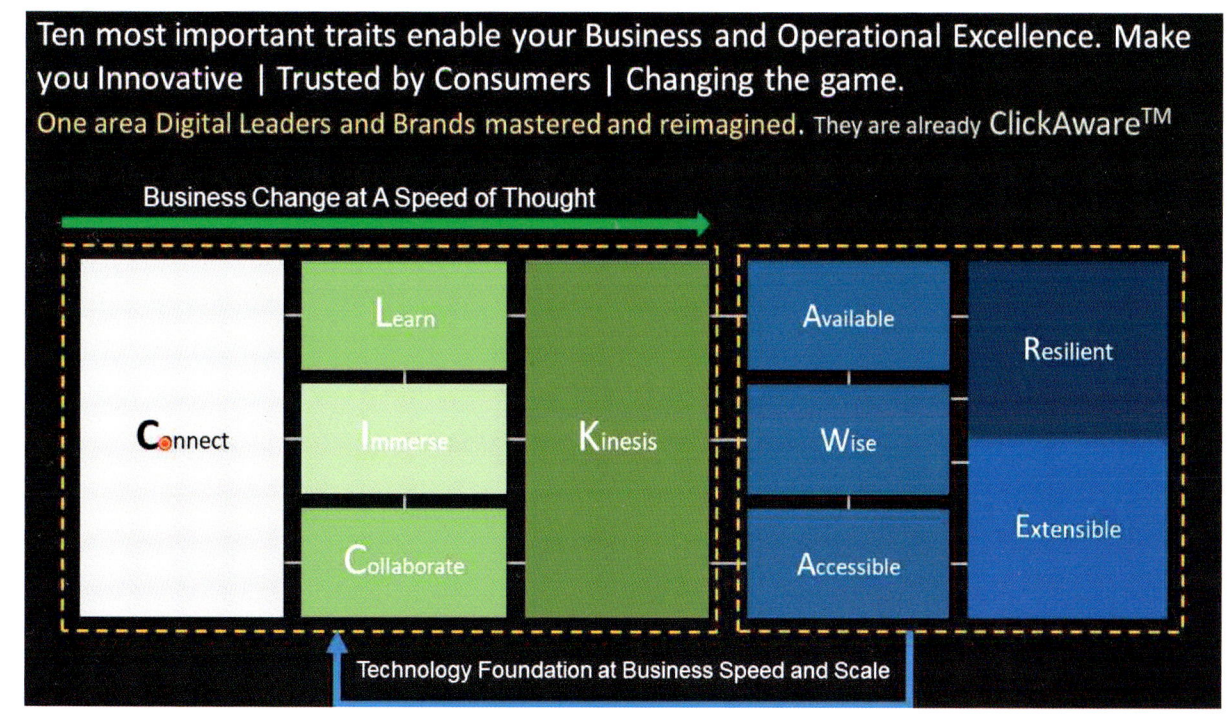

Ten most important traits enable your Business and Operational Excellence. Make you Innovative | Trusted by Consumers | Changing the game.
One area Digital Leaders and Brands mastered and reimagined. They are already ClickAware™

Business Change at A Speed of Thought

Connect | Learn | Kinesis | Available | Resilient
          | Immerse | | Wise | Extensible
          | Collaborate | | Accessible |

Technology Foundation at Business Speed and Scale

ClickAware™
6. **Available** – Always on, lightnight fast, multi-region, earth-scale, eco-friendly data centres.
7. **Wise** – Knows you and your infra economics better than your operations
8. **Accessible** – Every one, every time, every where, every location, every device, and always secure and privacy first
9. **Resilient** – Always-on
10. **Extensible** – Semantically consistent, Flexible, and Interoperable Technology

imperative to put more focus on business thinking and market dynamics where your enterprise can trust on a right shoulder that can help you with a reliable, planet-scale data platform, infrastructure and tools at a Busines Speed and scale.
I have a dedicated title coming later this year illuminating the ClickAware phenomenon. This is already a happening phenomenon with history-making organisations. I thought you would find it useful to know that Google is one of the example organisation which is fully ClickAware to successfully build an emperor with its 'AI First' philosophy and is already leading the front of '**Generation Ci**'. The '**Generation Ci**' is slightly different than the demographic cohorts we are familiar with so far (Baby Boomer, Gen X, Gen Y, Gen Z, iGeneration). Our current generation is the internet, and social technology savvy hugely influenced Gen Z and iGen. However, technologies along with internet and **connected intelligence** with the advent of machine learning and artificial intelligence, would lead the way of wisdom of our upcoming life, the way we would live would be significantly be driven by cognitive intelligence fused with context dimension which would lead us different leadership style, marketplace and introduce the concept of Context Economics (I call it the **Contextonomy**™)– much more real time. The Generation Ci is, very much would experience like a fictional generation who would be a time traveller between generation cohorts to build their contextual intelligence and with the intervention of cognitive technologies, would change the way humankind is advancing at a speed of thought. Your organisation would experience this disruptive force so strong that it could alter the course of your business and the economy.

Google Cloud Certified Professional Cloud Architect, Second Edition

Google Cloud Platform and its foundational Components

COLLABORATE
ACCESSIBLE
EXTENSIBLEE
KINESIS
RESILIENT
CONNECT
AVAILABLE
LEARN
WISE
IMMERSE

© Soumen Chatterjee, soumenc@beclickaware.org

CLICKAWARE™

lead the way to be

Google Cloud Certified Professional Cloud Architect, Second Edition

32

In the last two decades, organisations are rewriting the history, and many are getting on and off the F500 list. A range of disruptive business models avalanche has defined the trajectory of enterprise business systems and therefore the people, process and technology have repelled through the wave. It is now even more significant than ever before to become ClickAware, to stay ahead of the curve. There are many paths to the journey, and the Good News is, the Google Cloud Platform could lead you there. Google Cloud Platform components could enable you to connect with your consumers, marketplaces, supply chain ecosystems and help you to build some game-changing business models. There is a spectrum of components to help you to become the leader, evolving you through the CLICK process. While your business is awakening through the **CLICK**, another range of technologies and components within Google Cloud Platform would keep you **AWARE** of your business and identity-self.

Be ready to be a part of the revolution. A new leader is reborn!

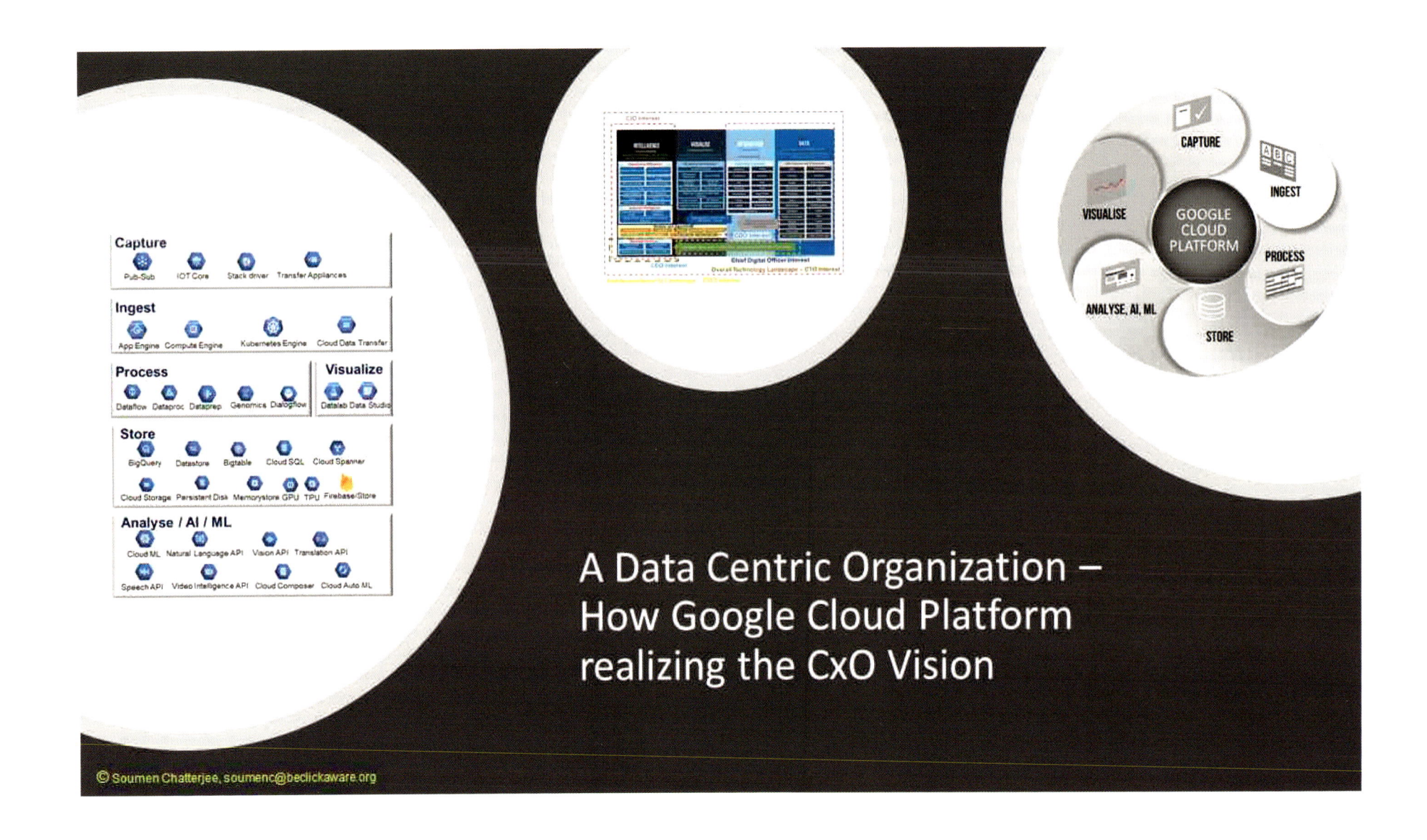

A Data Centric Organization – How Google Cloud Platform realizing the CxO Vision

Google Cloud Certified Professional Cloud Architect, Second Edition

A Data-Centric Organization – How GCP enabling the CxO Vision

The Digital Transformation phenomenon has already reimagined a vast majority of the industry and has charted the leadership and strategy of every sector and its extended ecosystems. Every industry is going through an exciting phase due to a seismic shift in the focus of various business models and subsequent changes in underpinning technology foundational requirements. The Chief Executive role for organisations at its outset has remained mostly unchanged – decision making - to adhere to the vision and mission of the organisation, overall business performance, staying abreast of the curve and maintaining its unique market position and growth trajectory, embracing through its internal and external broader eco-systems. The fun part is the '**decision**' making process and '**actions**'; those have become significantly complex and continually getting elusive. Organisations are in very different phases of maturity in their adoption of data centricity.

As I previously mentioned about the **ClickAware** organisations - one of the key differentiators is their '**Data DNA**' which transformed them into a '**Data Native**' businesses like **GAFAM**, **NATU**, **BATX** and many more. One of the critical characteristics of Data Natives are the data in their DNA. The role of the Chief Data Officer is now mainstream and leading the business transformation that leads those 'Data Immigrant' organisations to become a data-centric, digital organisations. Without a frictionless digital core and a data DNA, '**Right Action**', '**At A Moment in Time**', every time would be immensely obscured under a spectrum of **multi-dimensional contextual information** deluge. Data Native and Data Immigrants are close to consumers to immerse in their behaviours and evolving through the kinesis in response to their market forces including both business and technology disruptions, at a speed of thoughts or well in advance even before thinking happens - is crucial to stay relevant and successful. Data is no longer an IT function. Every decision that business is taking in every moment, it is more informed in 'Data Native' organisations where system yields the right data to either generate reports, deliver a range of analytics or train machine learning models. The vision of the Data Centricity is to design and build a digital business systems where data and information are the lifeblood of every action; an organisation where every business process yields data that helps in business decision-making system. The role of the chief data officer is also constantly evolving and no longer confined into highly regulated industries like banking, finance, insurance, healthcare, telecom and the public sector, and becoming the pillar to cultivate a culture that is building the renewed trust on data among the business leaders and their consumers, encouraging data-sharing, and privacy-first design policy.

Digital Natives and Digital Immigrants, undergoing a digital transformation, require decision-making capabilities embedded within the DNA through an integrated data flow between the parts of the enterprise so that senior leaders are capable of making informed business decisions at any point in time.

One of my upcoming titles has a specific focus on how do we master the formation of a Data Native, Digital Enterprise through a process, I call, DIVIDE:

Google Cloud Certified Professional Cloud Architect, Second Edition

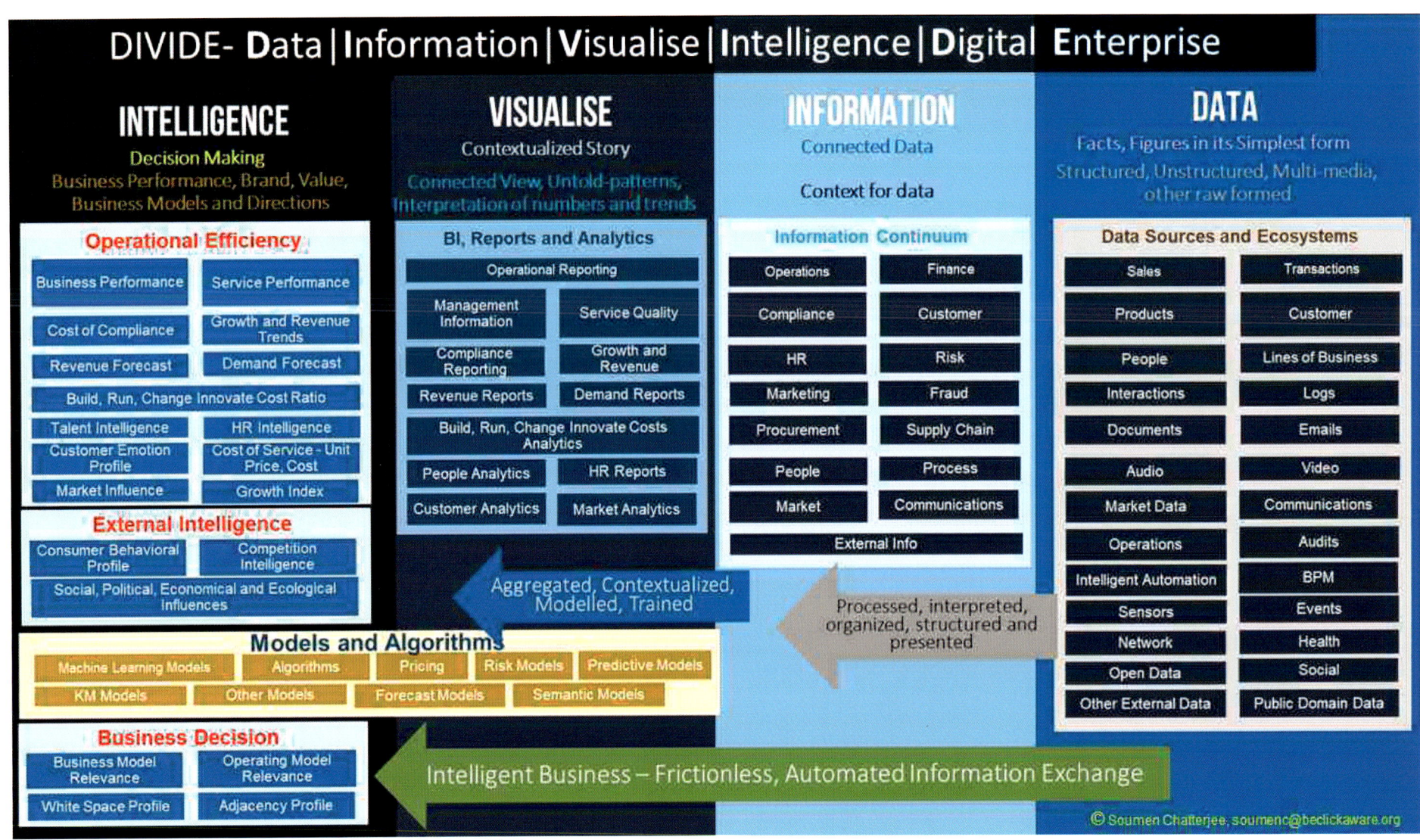

Figure 9: Divide - Bring together the Data Silos and Decision Making

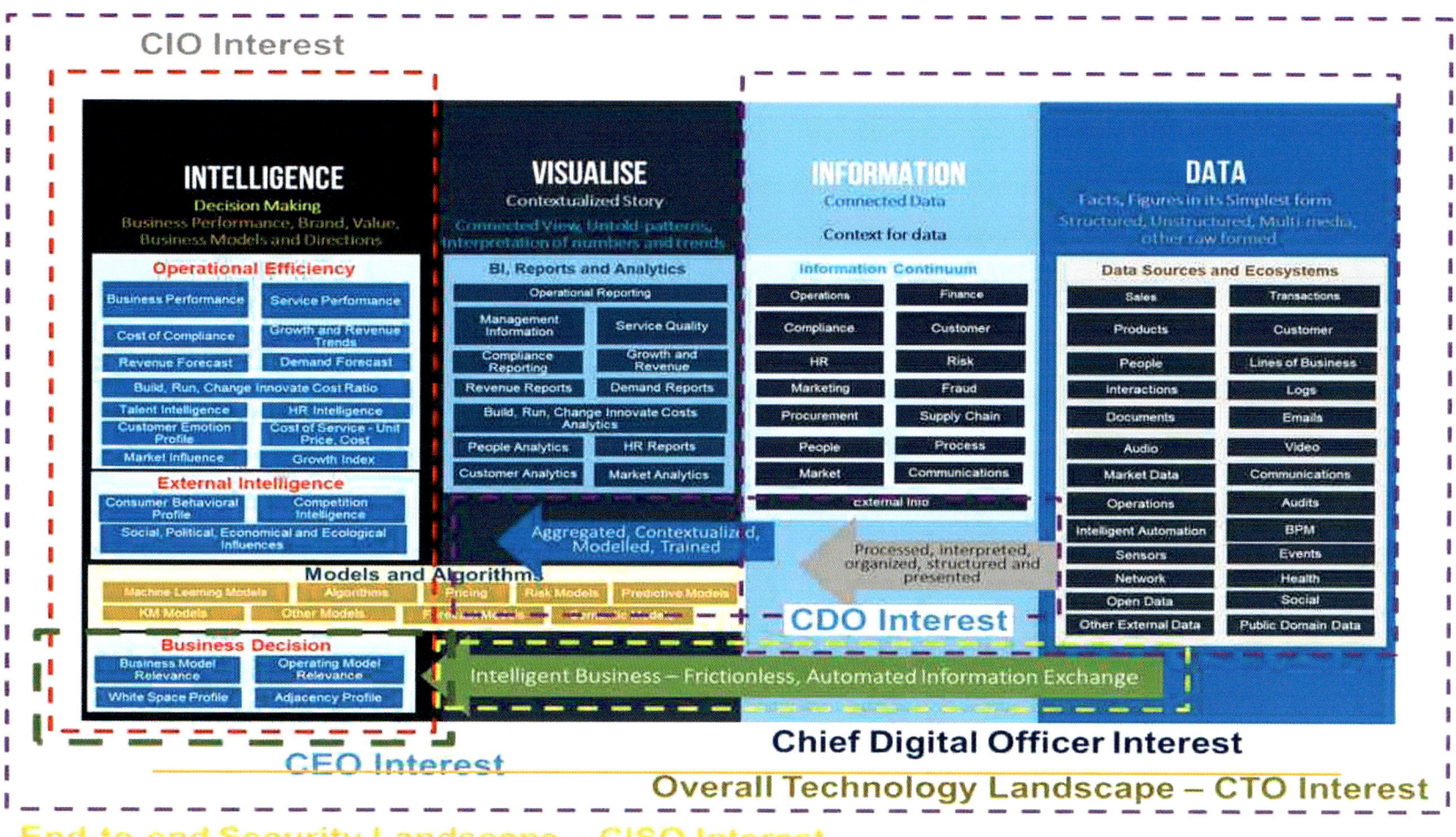

Figure 10: CxO primary areas of interest

It is now imperative to have a seamless function of the CIO, CDO, CTO, Chief Digital Officer and Chief Information Security Officer within your organisation who would work hand-in-hand to become the brain of your business. Building of a Data-Centric Organisation needs a renewed focus beyond a typical data management (data ownership, stewardship, data quality, data lineage, and remediation responsibilities), governance and operating model space – Data Immigrant organisations no longer could ignore the importance of analytics, augmented with an increased adoption of AI and machine learning models embedded into the Digital Native's every decision making processes. CDO organisation now play a pivotal role in their organisation's digital transformation journey, enabling an end-to-end data lifecycle and ensure availability of every information at your fingertips and merely a **CLICK** away. While the CIO and COO organisation is responsible for efficient operations and the CTO would abstract away a best of breed technology foundation at a '**Right Price**', and the CISO organisation becomes the eye and ears to deliver a secure organisation. Together with all these CxO functions, you build an intelligent enterprise that people can trust and be loyal to the products and services – today's enterprises are a reciprocal trust system.

With this shift, it is now essential that the digital transformation agenda delivers a **data production platform** (e.g., business processes and application build) that generates data for revenue growth and a business-friendly **information consumption platform** (MI, reporting, analytics, integration, ML, AI, etc.) that enables adept decision making for senior business leaders. All the Data Centric organisations are consistently maximising the value of data, leveraging through advanced analytics, machine learning, and artificial intelligence, and driving significant revenue growth for organisations.

While technologies are advancing at a remarkable speed, enterprises have embraced cloud computing into their core business strategies and as a significant enabler in the journey to their digital transformations. Cloud providers are every day strengthening their eco-system to unlock, manage and mine massive scale datasets at scale and serving millions and billions of users and handling billions of events real-time from these **data production systems.** Cloud platforms can offer an intelligent **data consumer platform** for your enterprise business leaders as well as other users allowing advanced analytics, machine learning, and artificial intelligence at an affordable price point.

Google Cloud Platform offers you one of the best of its kind compute, storage and networking platform along with a rich set of data and analytics eco-system including BigQuery, a serverless, managed data warehouse, Cloud Dataproc, a managed Spark and Hadoop service, and Cloud Dataflow, which enables you to continuously stream and batch-process your data and allow you to continually tap into its ever-expanding insight generating tools eco-systems.

DIVIDE- Google Cloud Platform Reference Architecture

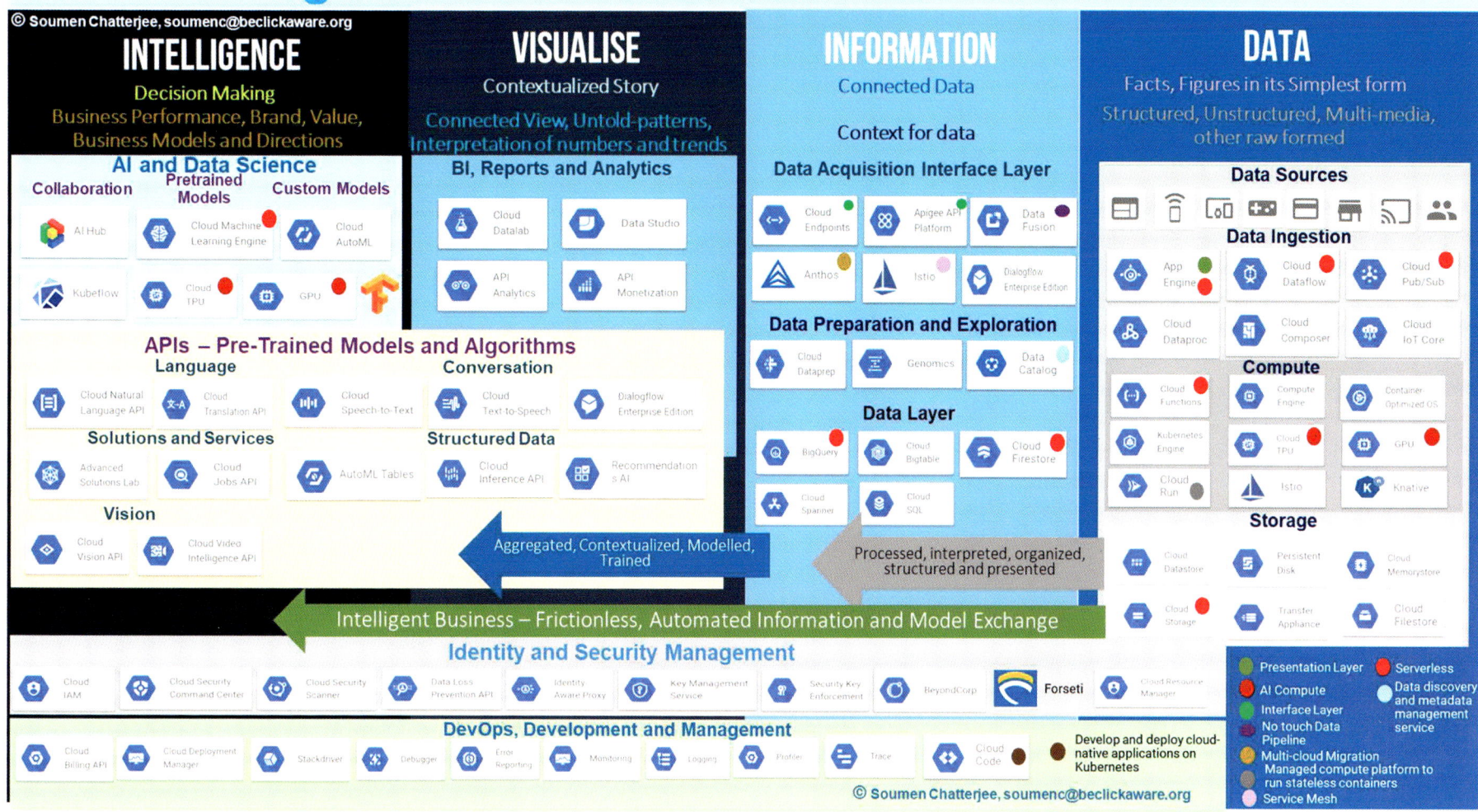

© Soumen Chatterjee, soumenc@beclickaware.org

INTELLIGENCE
Decision Making
Business Performance, Brand, Value, Business Models and Directions

AI and Data Science
Collaboration | **Pretrained Models** | **Custom Models**
- AI Hub
- Cloud Machine Learning Engine
- Cloud AutoML
- Kubeflow
- Cloud TPU
- GPU

APIs – Pre-Trained Models and Algorithms
Language
- Cloud Natural Language API
- Cloud Translation API

Conversation
- Cloud Speech-to-Text
- Cloud Text-to-Speech
- Dialogflow Enterprise Edition

Solutions and Services
- Advanced Solutions Lab
- Cloud Jobs API

Structured Data
- AutoML Tables
- Cloud Inference API
- Recommendations AI

Vision
- Cloud Vision API
- Cloud Video Intelligence API

VISUALISE
Contextualized Story
Connected View, Untold-patterns, Interpretation of numbers and trends

BI, Reports and Analytics
- Cloud Datalab
- Data Studio
- API Analytics
- API Monetization

← Aggregated, Contextualized, Modelled, Trained

← Intelligent Business – Frictionless, Automated Information and Model Exchange

INFORMATION
Connected Data
Context for data

Data Acquisition Interface Layer
- Cloud Endpoints
- Apigee API Platform
- Data Fusion
- Anthos
- Istio
- Dialogflow Enterprise Edition

Data Preparation and Exploration
- Cloud Dataprep
- Genomics
- Data Catalog

Data Layer
- BigQuery
- Cloud Bigtable
- Cloud Firestore
- Cloud Spanner
- Cloud SQL

← Processed, interpreted, organized, structured and presented

DATA
Facts, Figures in its Simplest form
Structured, Unstructured, Multi-media, other raw formed

Data Sources

Data Ingestion
- App Engine
- Cloud Dataflow
- Cloud Pub/Sub
- Cloud Dataproc
- Cloud Composer
- Cloud IoT Core

Compute
- Cloud Functions
- Compute Engine
- Container Optimized OS
- Kubernetes Engine
- Cloud TPU
- GPU
- Cloud Run
- Istio
- Knative

Storage
- Cloud Datastore
- Persistent Disk
- Cloud Memorystore
- Cloud Storage
- Transfer Appliance
- Cloud Filestore

Identity and Security Management
- Cloud IAM
- Cloud Security Command Center
- Cloud Security Scanner
- Data Loss Prevention API
- Identity Aware Proxy
- Key Management Service
- Security Key Enforcement
- BeyondCorp
- Forseti
- Cloud Resource Manager

DevOps, Development and Management
- Cloud Billing API
- Cloud Deployment Manager
- Stackdriver
- Debugger
- Error Reporting
- Monitoring
- Logging
- Profiler
- Trace
- Cloud Code

Legend:
- Presentation Layer
- Serverless
- AI Compute
- Data discovery and metadata management service
- Interface Layer
- No touch Data Pipeline
- Multi-cloud Migration
- Managed compute platform to run stateless containers
- Service Mesh
- Develop and deploy cloud-native applications on Kubernetes

© Soumen Chatterjee, soumenc@beclickaware.org

Google Cloud Certified Professional Cloud Architect, Second Edition

Google Cloud Platform – Data Lifecycle

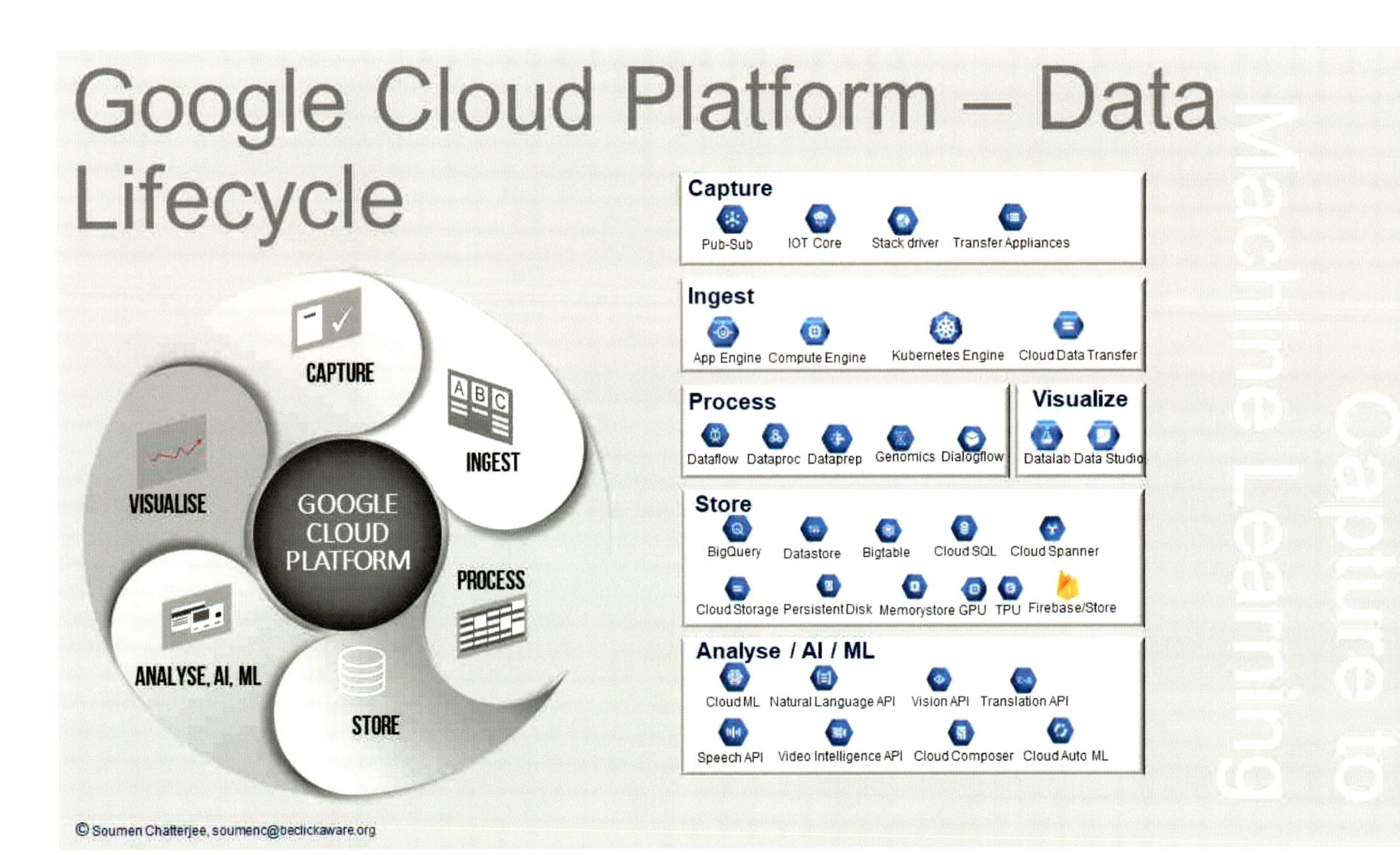

Capture: Pub-Sub, IOT Core, Stack driver, Transfer Appliances

Ingest: App Engine, Compute Engine, Kubernetes Engine, Cloud Data Transfer

Process: Dataflow, Dataproc, Dataprep, Genomics, Dialogflow

Visualize: Datalab, Data Studio

Store: BigQuery, Datastore, Bigtable, Cloud SQL, Cloud Spanner, Cloud Storage, Persistent Disk, Memorystore, GPU, TPU, Firebase/Store

Analyse / AI / ML: Cloud ML, Natural Language API, Vision API, Translation API, Speech API, Video Intelligence API, Cloud Composer, Cloud Auto ML

© Soumen Chatterjee, soumenc@beclickaware.org

Google Cloud Platform allows you to advance your Data Immigrants journey as well as strengthen your Data Native organisation's CxO vision with its planet-scale infrastructure and its strategic Data, Analytics and Machine Learning toolsets. In the rest of the book, we will get into more detailed discussion of various services and components of Google Cloud Platform.

Google Cloud Certified Professional Cloud Architect, Second Edition

Multi-Cloud Enterprise

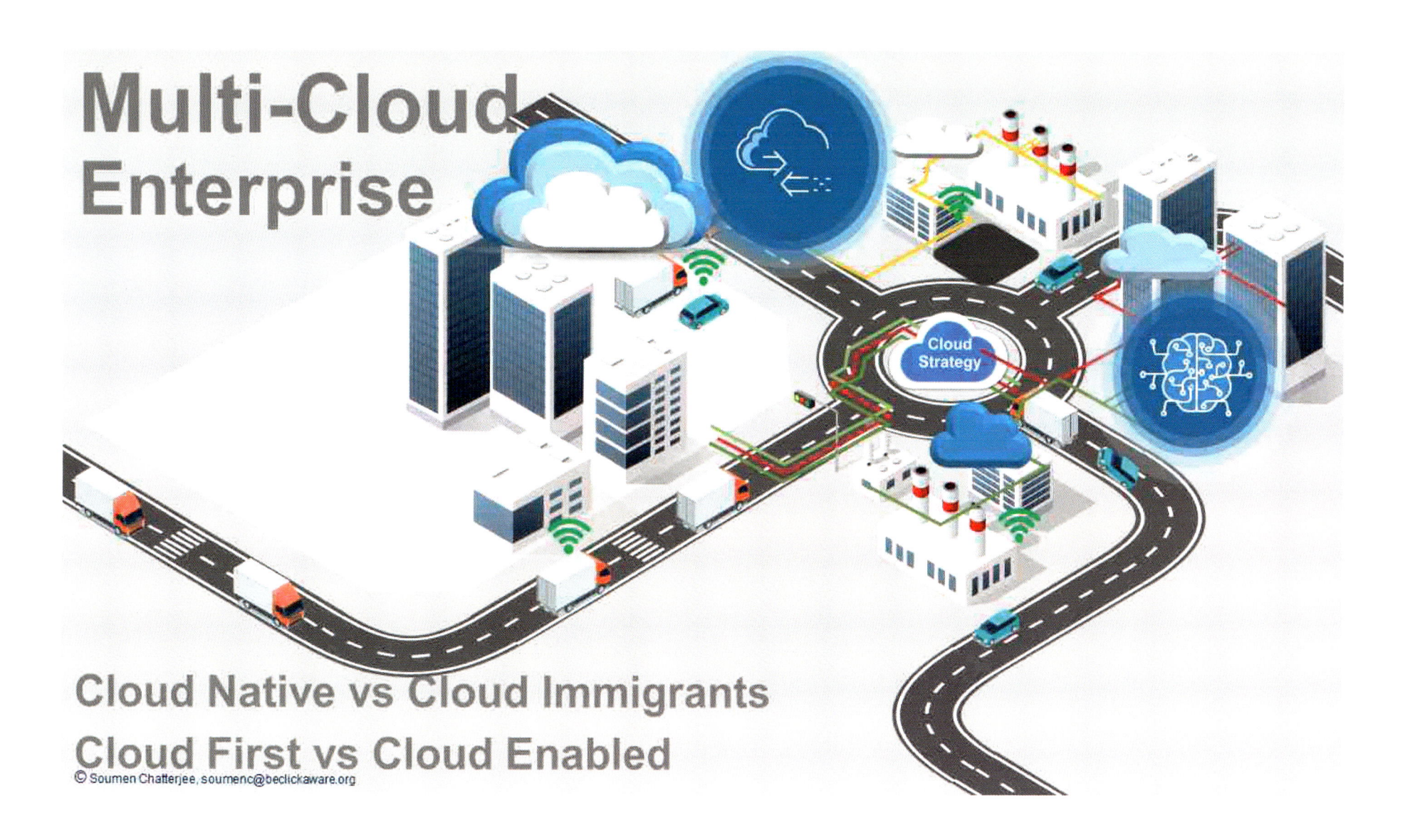

Cloud Native vs Cloud Immigrants

Cloud First vs Cloud Enabled

© Soumen Chatterjee, soumenc@beclickaware.org

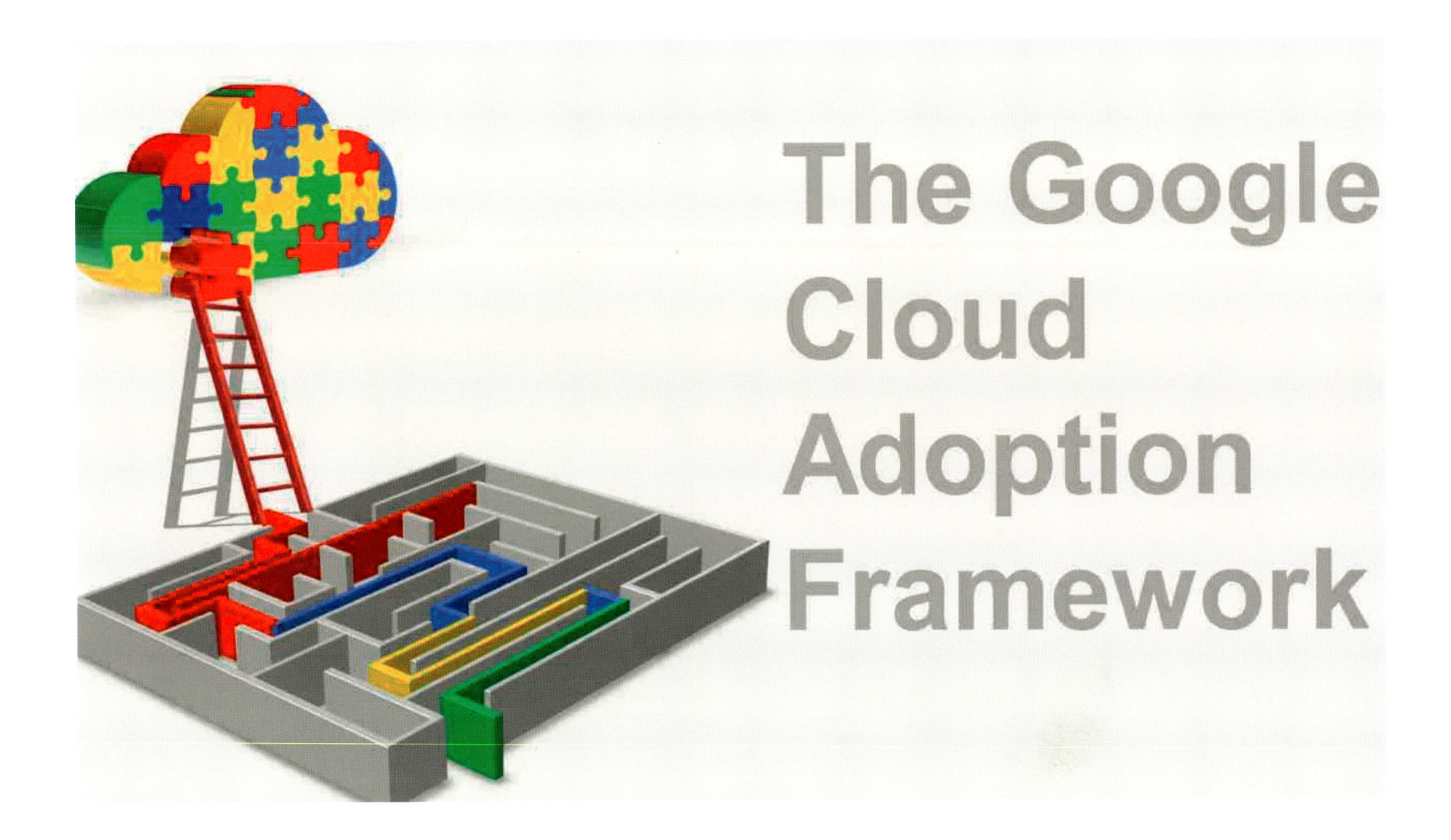

The Google Cloud Adoption Framework

The Google Cloud Adoption Framework

Cloud adoption is no longer an option for your enterprise regardless of whether you are in the process of inducing a new business model, preparing to respond to your competition or revitalising your existing business model. For the first debut and decade of cloud computing, we have gone past the first wave where your kit, someone else's building, yours to mange philosophy. When the second wave of cloud walked into the board room, VM and managed services dominated the market. It was always seen as a cost-cutting initiative—building your "**mess for less**" in the cloud. As we are moving onto the third wave and most interesting phase of the journey, Google is leading the way to their flagship 'no-ops' philosophy to ask ourselves to focus on business performance, game-changing business models and developing connected propositions to our consumers rather than engaging more of our resources and energies into operations. **Google is making the case to rethink and balance between 'Build' vs 'Run' vs 'Change' ratio of tomorrow's successful leading institutions.** With Google cloud, you have an unfair advantage of a platform to focus on **Build** *business models*, **Run** *services but not servers* and **Change** *the business performance.* Google cloud platform enables you to answer visionary questions, often getting boardroom attention quite a lot: "How do I grow X10 vs 10 per cent?", "How do I introduce human experience (HX) and not just customer/consumer/user experience (CX/UX)?", How can I use machine learning to provide better customer service?" "How do I leverage Artificial Intelligence to redefine the way I do my business?", "How do I do predictive inventory planning?" Alternatively, "How do I enable dynamic pricing?". Unlike the other competitors, those have their cloud adoption framework is more of a delivery framework, with the recent introduction of the Google Cloud Adoption Framework, in my opinion, is more of a cloud adoption maturity framework, Google wanted to help you in determining where you are on your cloud journey today, and where you'd like to be. The Google Cloud Adoption Framework is Cloud Neutral and could be tailored to any cloud whereas similar cloud adoption frameworks stress on how do you adopt the cloud of that particular provider along with their tools, components, and platforms.

It is widely observed that many of the cloud-native organisations are already embarking on their journey from a traditional operation to automated cloud-native operation. These organisations are continuously learning, experimenting, and innovating with their fail-fast approach. On the contrary, there is another range of organisations who are often gravitated towards replicating their tried and true governance and operating model in the cloud, spending much time designing process and policies (which are essential), but too little time moving actual workloads into the cloud. Without production workloads, they don't develop the experience needed to manage increasingly complex and business-critical use cases. Moreover, without early successes, they can be reluctant to increase investment and ultimately lose momentum in their cloud strategy.

The Third Wave of Cloud adopters would require a cultural shift and change at the core of the organisation. The ideal is balancing the pace of change across your people, process, and technology. That way, you can **learn** continuously, **lead** effectively, **scale** efficiently, **and secure** your environment comprehensively—the four capabilities we've observed that drive success in the cloud.

The Google Cloud Adoption Framework introduces the four key themes concerning the three phases, as depicted below:

Figure 11: The Google Cloud Adoption Framework

In each of the themes, you can see what happens when you move from adopting new technologies ad hoc to working with them more and more strategically across the organization — which naturally means more in-depth, more comprehensive, and more consistent training for your people, which in turn means streamlined and updated processes, which in its turn drives innovation. The whole organisation gradually transforms. When you are fully invested in the cloud, fully harnessing its capabilities, you are then a **cloud-first** organisation.

Once you've determined where you are in your cloud maturity journey, it's time to move forward. To scope and structure your program of cloud adoption, you will implement many workstreams (which we call epics). The epics are defined so that they do not overlap, they are aligned to manageable groups of stakeholders, and they can be further broken down into individual user stories, making your program planning easier.

Here's a look at those epics within the familiar rubric of people, technology, and process. If you can do only a subset of the epics, focus on the ones in the coloured segments. Those are the epics that align with Learn, Lead, Scale, and Secure; and so those are the epics that will define your journey to successful cloud adoption.

Figure 12: The Google Cloud Adoption Framework Epics

To truly develop a cloud-first organisation, there are four realms (we call them themes) you will need to excel in — whatever your business objectives. These four themes define the foundation of cloud readiness:

Learn: The quality and scale of the learning programs you have in place to upskill your technical teams, and your ability to augment your IT staff with experienced partners. Who is engaged? How public is that engagement? How concerted is the effort? How useful are the results?

Lead: The extent to which IT teams are supported by a mandate from leadership to migrate to the cloud, and the degree to which the units themselves are cross-functional, collaborative, and self-motivated. How are the teams structured? Have they got executive sponsorship? How are cloud projects budgeted, governed, assessed?

Scale: The extent to which you use cloud-native services that reduce operational overhead and automate manual processes and policies. How are cloud-based services provisioned? How is the capacity for workloads allocated? How are application updates managed?

Secure: The capability to protect your services from unauthorised and inappropriate access with a multilayered, identity-centric security model. Dependent also on the advanced maturity of the other three themes. What controls are in place? What technologies used? What strategies govern the whole?

©2018 Google LLC, used with permission. Google and the Google logo are registered trademarks of Google LLC

Your current business practices determine your readiness for success in the cloud in each of these four themes. For each theme, those practices will fall into one of the following phases:

Tactical: Individual workloads are in place, but no coherent plan encompassing all of them with a strategy for building out to the future. The focus is on reducing the cost of discrete systems and on getting to the cloud with minimal disruption. The wins are quick, but there is no provision for scale.

Strategic: A broader vision governs individual workloads, which are designed and developed with an eye to future needs and scale. You have begun to embrace change, and the people and processes portion of the equation is now involved. IT teams are both efficient and effective, increasing the value of harnessing the cloud for your business operations.

Transformational: With cloud operations functioning smoothly, you've turned your attention to integrating the data and insights garnered from working now in the cloud. Existing data is transparently shared. New information is collected and analysed. The predictive and prescriptive analytics of machine learning applied. Your people and processes are being transformed, which further supports technological changes. IT is no longer a cost centre but has become a partner to the business instead.

In the tactical phase, you are reducing costs with a quick return on investment and little disruption to your IT organisation. This is a short-term goal. In the strategic phase, you increase the value delivered by your IT organisation by streamlining operations to be both more efficient and more effective. This is a midterm goal. In the transformational phase, your IT organisation becomes an engine of innovation, making it a partner to the business. This is a long-term goal.

Note: This section was adapted from Cloud Adoption Framework Whitepaper.

Further Reading
- https://cloud.google.com/blog/topics/perspectives/the-google-cloud-adoption-framework-helping-you-move-to-the-cloud-with-confidence
- https://services.google.com/fh/files/misc/adoption_framework_whitepaper_nov12_final.pdf

"The future has arrived — it's just not evenly distributed yet."

- William Gibson

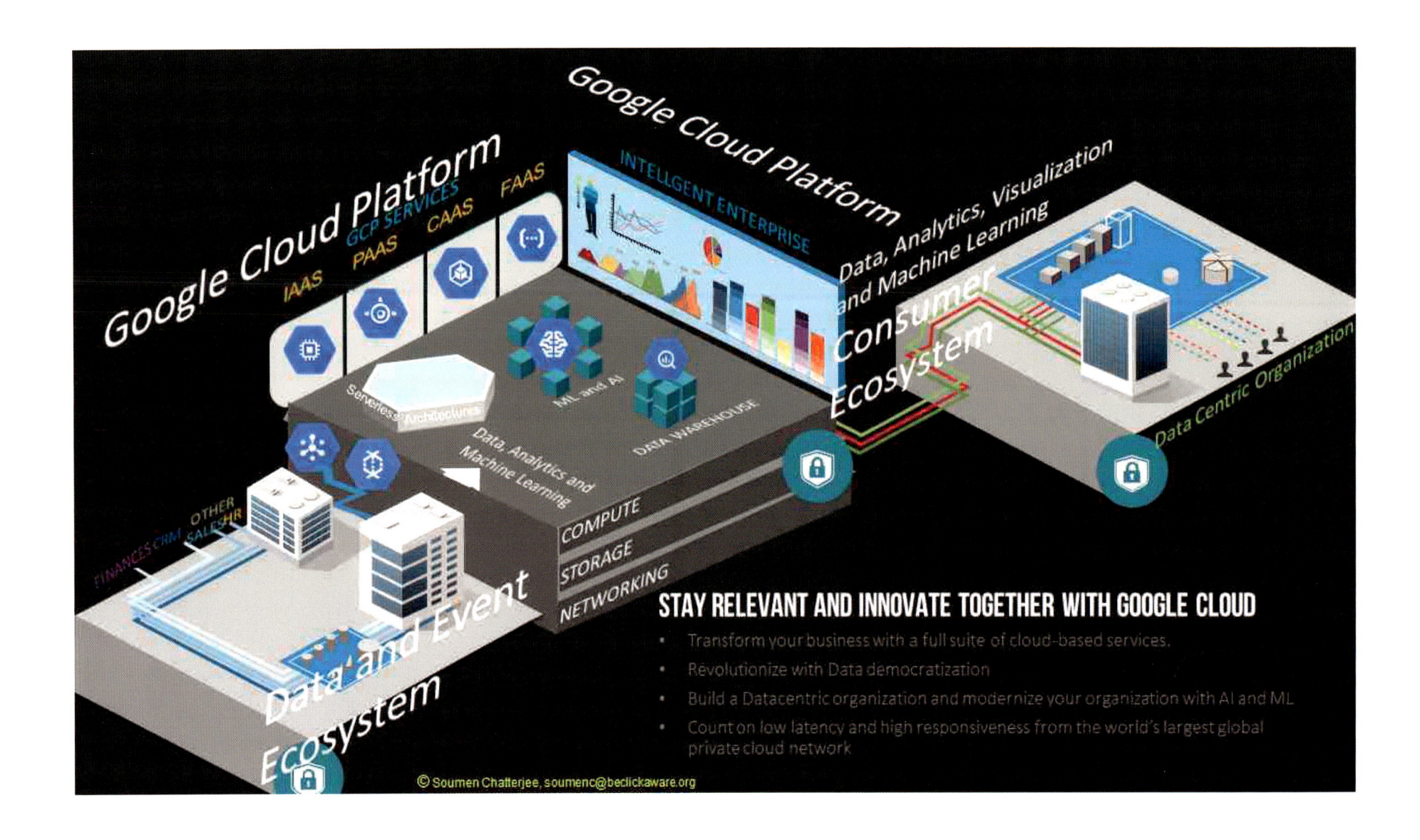

Google Cloud Certified Professional Cloud Architect, Second Edition

Google Cloud Platform Foundational Blocks

Google was the front runner in solving compute and storage problems in various noble ways (including cheaper commodity infrastructure) before the rest of the world, but then others follow. Hadoop and underlying file system (HDFS) was based on the Google File System (GFS). There is no reason to get stuck in Hadoop ecosystems and by nature of it, then locked in by one or the other providers of those technologies/distribution but take advantage of options out there to solve not only your enterprise data problems but also innovate to stay relevant. Google no longer uses GFS. Google Hadoop customers can now run MapReduce jobs directly against data stored in the Google Cloud Storage and leave HDFS out of the big data equation as a result of a new cloud storage Hadoop connector.
Google has moved on from GFS; Colossus is the Successor to the GFS.
Colossus now underpins virtually all of Google's web services, from Gmail, Google Docs, and YouTube to the Google Cloud Storage service the company offers to third-party developers. Whereas GFS was built for batch operations, but Colossus is built explicitly for "real-time" services, where the processing happens almost instantly. With Colossus and its new search infrastructure 'Caffeine' – Google no longer needed to rebuild the index from scratch and able to update the existing index with further information in real time.

Borg is another innovation that enables Google with a highly flexible cluster orchestration service to handle the planet-scale workload without any downtime. At Google-scale, thousands of servers will fail every single day, and Borg protects us from these failures. Someone unplugs a rack in the data centre in the middle of running your query, and you'll never notice the difference.

Google's Jupiter network can deliver 1 Petabit/sec of total bisection bandwidth, allowing us to efficiently and quickly distribute large workloads.
Google BigQuery section would further elaborate how BigQuery is architected by Google leveraging Borg, Colossus, Dremmel and Jupiter.

All these technologies together, with their vision to be **one of the largest networks in the world**, makes Google standing apart
"*This is what makes Google Google: its physical network, its thousands of fiber miles, and those many thousands of servers that, in aggregate, add up to the mother of all clouds.*" WIRED Magazine (https://www.wired.com/2012/10/ff-inside-google-data-center/). The network is the most robust foundation of Cloud. Google is the **only provider who allows live migrations of virtual machines**, offers the most secure, flexible, and cost-effective solution. With Google's planet-scale infrastructure, commitment to innovate together and open cloud philosophy founded – Google Cloud Platform could lead you to the next stage of your enterprise journey.

Borg/Omega are **the father of Kubernetes,** a cluster manager and scheduler for large-scale, distributed data center architecture.

Dataflow Streaming mechanism is underpinned **by MillWheel.**

Dremel
Foundation of Big Query. A column-oriented datastore useful for quick, interactive queries

In GCP data is written using **Reed-Solomon** (1.5x) Client-driven replication, encoding and replication Metadata space has enabled availability analyses.

Colossus
Next-generation cluster-level file system. Nucleus of Google Cloud Infrastructure.

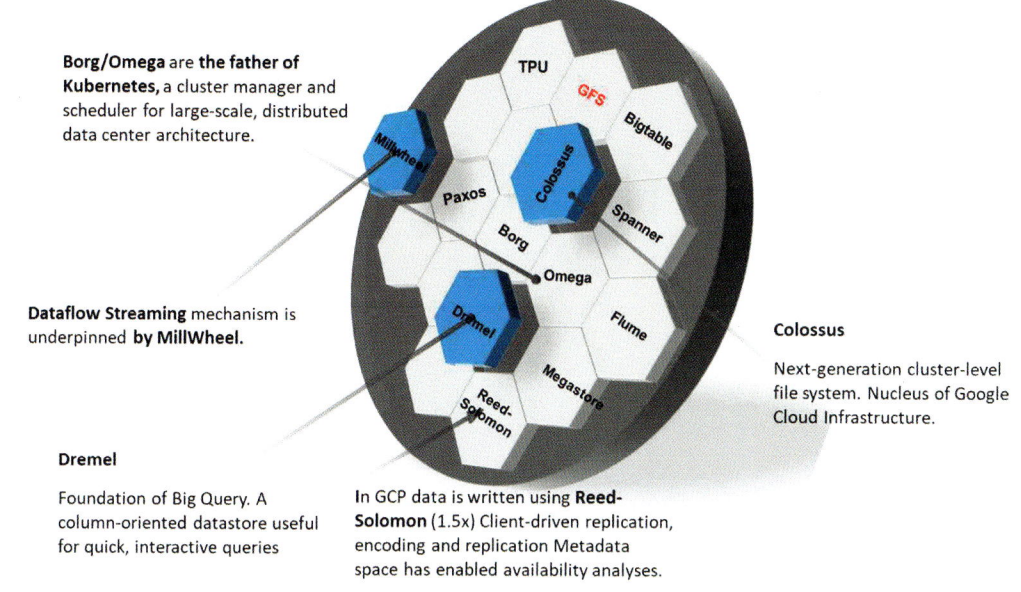

Figure 13: Google Cloud Platform building blocks

https://cloud.google.com/terms/service-terms

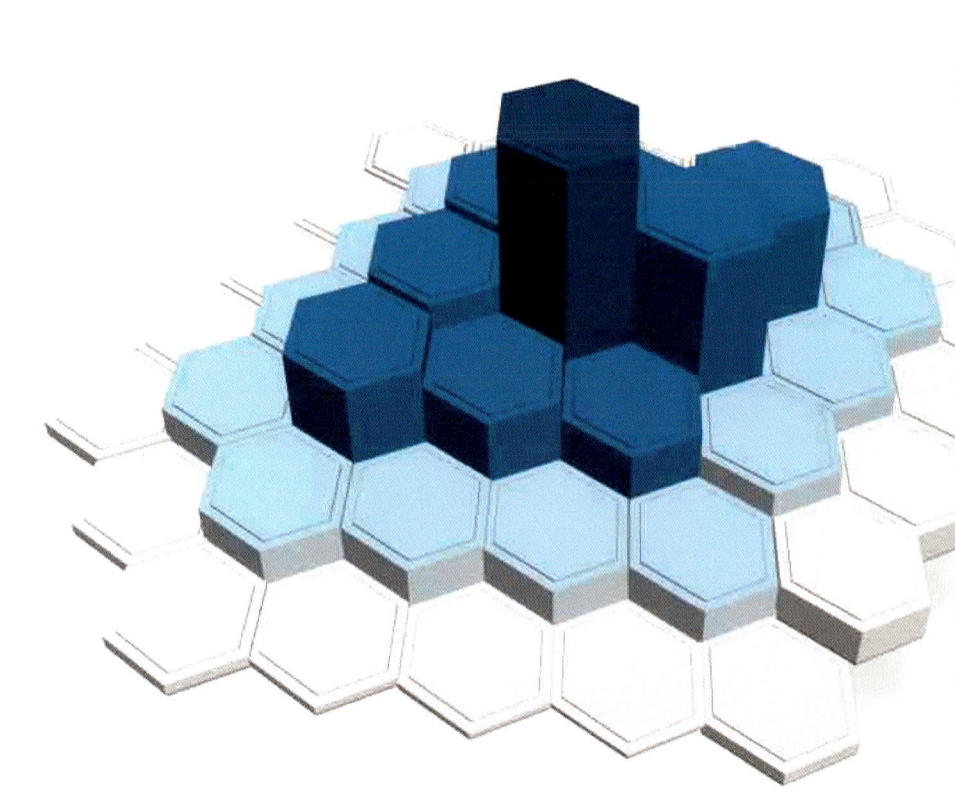

Google Cloud Platform and Services

© Soumen Chatterjee, soumenc@beclickaware.org

Google Cloud Platform Services

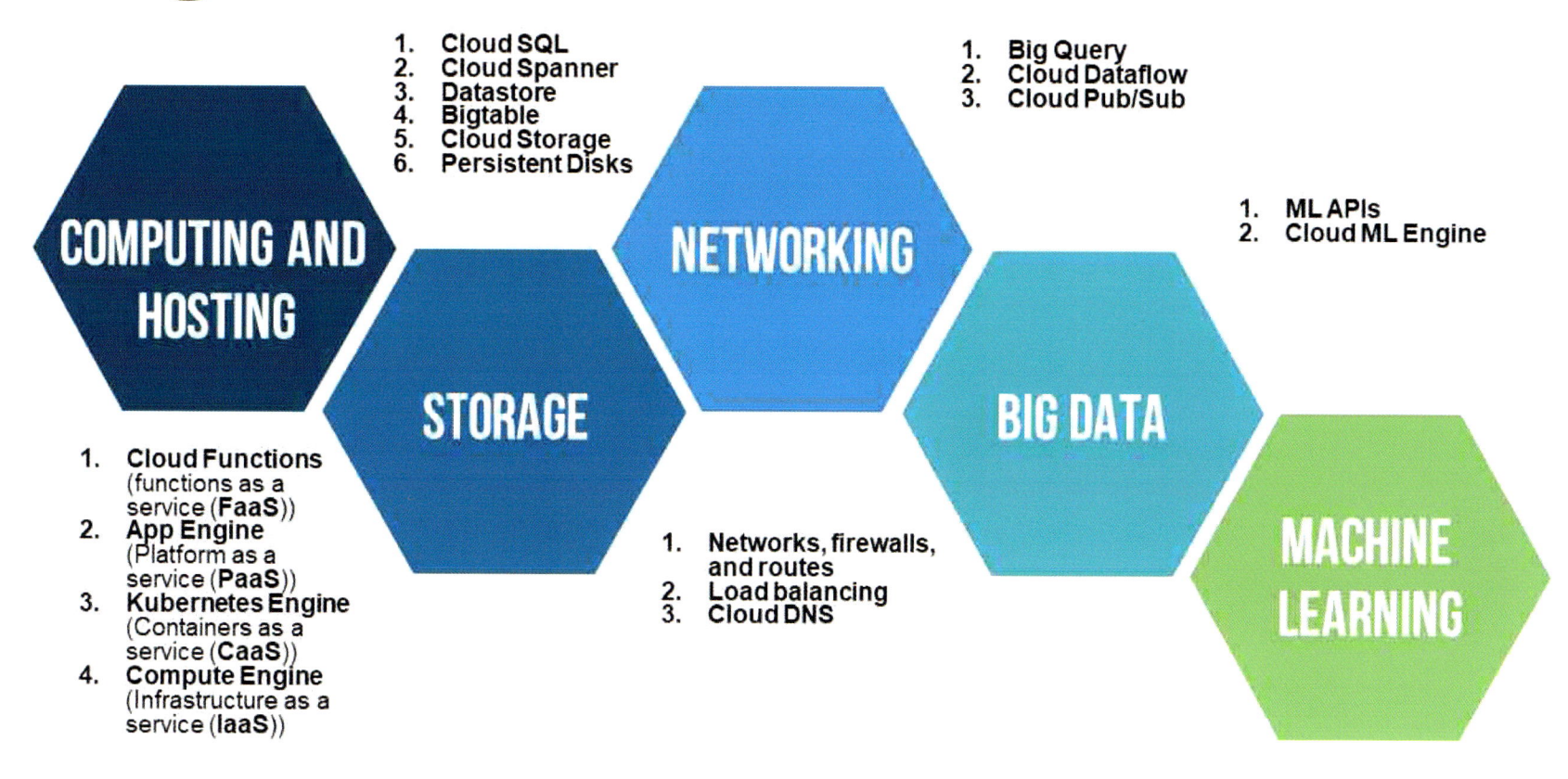

COMPUTING AND HOSTING

1. Cloud Functions (functions as a service (**FaaS**))
2. App Engine (Platform as a service (**PaaS**))
3. Kubernetes Engine (Containers as a service (**CaaS**))
4. Compute Engine (Infrastructure as a service (**IaaS**))

STORAGE

1. Cloud SQL
2. Cloud Spanner
3. Datastore
4. Bigtable
5. Cloud Storage
6. Persistent Disks

NETWORKING

1. Networks, firewalls, and routes
2. Load balancing
3. Cloud DNS

BIG DATA

1. Big Query
2. Cloud Dataflow
3. Cloud Pub/Sub

MACHINE LEARNING

1. ML APIs
2. Cloud ML Engine

Google Cloud Certified Professional Cloud Architect, Second Edition

Google Cloud Platform (GCP) services

Google Cloud Platform represents a full suite of services and spectrum of products/components underneath to help planet-scale computing on one of the world's largest and fastest private networks and bundled together primarily under following five broad types of services:

- Computing and hosting
- Storage
- Networking
- Big data
- Machine learning

Please make a note that Google Cloud Services is different than what Google recently introduced under the name of **Cloud Services Platform** which is a fully managed platform powered by industry-leading open-source technologies from Google. It helps you to transform your IT operations and build applications catering for both today and the future, using containerised infrastructure and microservices-based application architecture. It offers:

- **Service mesh**: Istio 1.0 in open source, Managed Istio, and Apigee API Management for Istio
- **Hybrid computing**: GKE On-Prem with multi-cluster management
- **Ops tooling**: Stackdriver Service Monitoring
- **Serverless computing**: GKE Serverless add-on and Knative, an open source serverless framework
- **Developer tools**: Cloud Build, a fully managed CI/CD platform

©2018 Google LLC, used with permission. Google and the Google logo are registered trademarks of Google LLC

Further Reading
- https://cloudplatform.googleblog.com/2018/07/cloud-services-platform-bringing-the-best-of-the-cloud-to-you.html
- https://cloud.google.com/solutions/cloud-services-platform/

Figure 14: Google Cloud Services

During Google Next 19, Cloud Services Platform has been announced as as a rebrand under Anthos that would allow you build and manage modern hybrid applications across environments. Watch that space as it could be a powerful capabilitiy offering for your multi-cloud startegic direction for your organisation. Please refer here for further details: https://cloud.google.com/anthos/

Your Google Cloud Platform journey starts here...

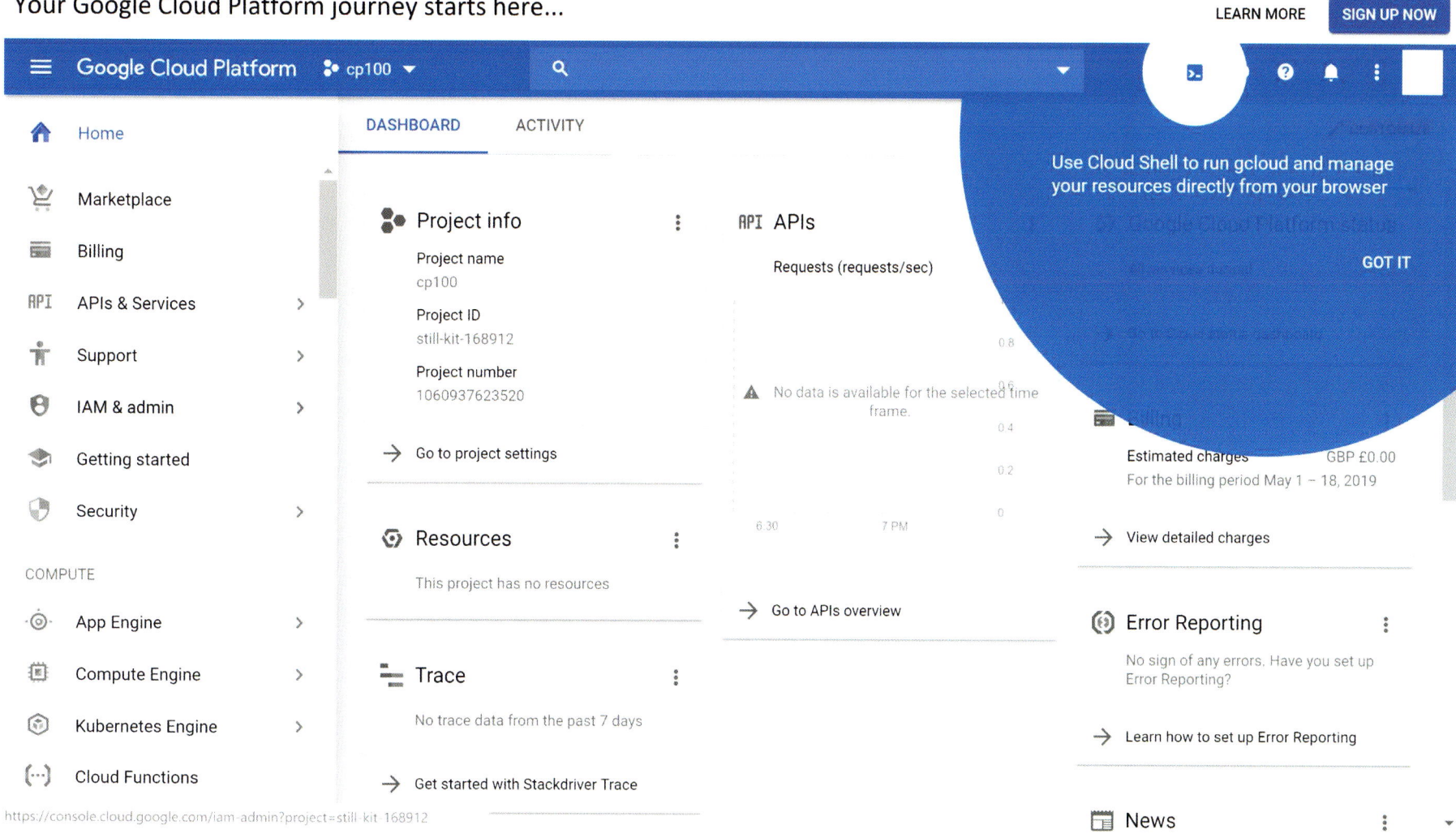

LEARN MORE   SIGN UP NOW

≡ Google Cloud Platform   cp100 ▼

Home

Marketplace

Billing

APIs & Services

Support

IAM & admin

Getting started

Security

COMPUTE

App Engine

Compute Engine

Kubernetes Engine

Cloud Functions

DASHBOARD   ACTIVITY

Project info

Project name
cp100

Project ID
still-kit-168912

Project number
1060937623520

→ Go to project settings

Resources

This project has no resources

Trace

No trace data from the past 7 days

→ Get started with Stackdriver Trace

APIs

Requests (requests/sec)

⚠ No data is available for the selected time frame.

→ Go to APIs overview

Use Cloud Shell to run gcloud and manage your resources directly from your browser

GOT IT

Estimated charges   GBP £0.00
For the billing period May 1 – 18, 2019

→ View detailed charges

Error Reporting

No sign of any errors. Have you set up Error Reporting?

→ Learn how to set up Error Reporting

News

https://console.cloud.google.com/iam-admin?project=still-kit-168912

Google Cloud Certified Professional Cloud Architect, Second Edition

53

https://console.cloud.google.com/home

BIG DATA
- BigQuery
- Pub/Sub
- Dataproc
- Dataflow
- IoT Core
- Composer
- Genomics
- Dataprep

ARTIFICIAL INTELLIGENCE
- ML Engine
- Natural Language
- Talent Solution
- Translation
- Vision

TOOLS
- Cloud Build
- Cloud Scheduler
- Cloud Tasks
- Container Registry
- Source Repositories
- Deployment Manager
- Customer Identity
- Endpoints

- Network Security

STACKDRIVER
- Monitoring
- Debug
- Trace
- Logging
- Error Reporting
- Profiler

Google Cloud Platform — cp100

Home
- Billing
- Support

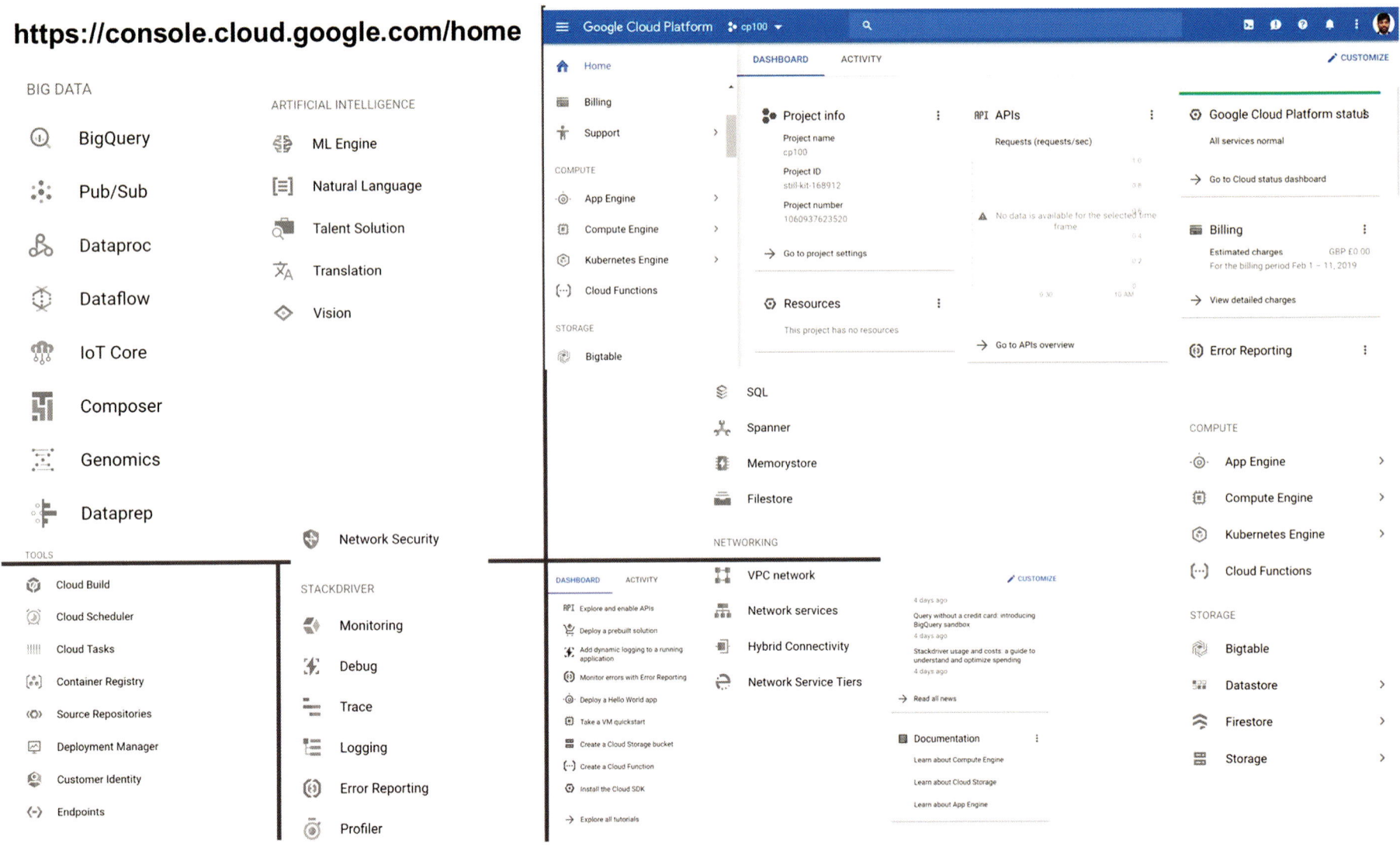

COMPUTE
- App Engine
- Compute Engine
- Kubernetes Engine
- Cloud Functions

STORAGE
- Bigtable
- SQL
- Spanner
- Memorystore
- Filestore

NETWORKING
- VPC network
- Network services
- Hybrid Connectivity
- Network Service Tiers

Dashboard

Project info
- Project name: cp100
- Project ID: still-kit-168912
- Project number: 1060937623520
- Go to project settings

Resources — This project has no resources

APIs — Requests (requests/sec)
- No data is available for the selected time frame
- Go to APIs overview

Explore and enable APIs
Deploy a prebuilt solution
Add dynamic logging to a running application
Monitor errors with Error Reporting
Deploy a Hello World app
Take a VM quickstart
Create a Cloud Storage bucket
Create a Cloud Function
Install the Cloud SDK
Explore all tutorials

Google Cloud Platform status — All services normal
Go to Cloud status dashboard

Billing — Estimated charges GBP £0.00
For the billing period Feb 1 – 11, 2019
View detailed charges

Error Reporting

COMPUTE
- App Engine
- Compute Engine
- Kubernetes Engine
- Cloud Functions

STORAGE
- Bigtable
- Datastore
- Firestore
- Storage

4 days ago — Query without a credit card: introducing BigQuery sandbox
4 days ago — Stackdriver usage and costs: a guide to understand and optimize spending
4 days ago — Read all news

Documentation
- Learn about Compute Engine
- Learn about Cloud Storage
- Learn about App Engine

©2018 Google LLC, used with permission. Google and the Google logo are registered trademarks of Google LLC

Google Cloud Certified Professional Cloud Architect, Second Edition

Google Cloud Platform Components

Google Cloud Platform eco-system transforms your business with a full suite of cloud-based services. Google Cloud Platform offers a rich and comprehensive range of products to create a collaborative, data-driven culture and better customer experiences.

Google Cloud Platform:

- Development Tool
- Data Transfer and Data Migration
- Cloud AI
- Networking
- Management Tools
- Compute
- Databases
- Storage
- Data Analytics
- Identity and Security
- Internet of Things (IoT)
- API Management

GCP consists of a set of physical assets, such as computers and hard disk drives, and virtual resources, such as virtual machines (VMs), that are contained in Google's data centres around the globe. Each data centre location is in a global region. Regions include Central US, Western Europe, and East Asia. Each region is a collection of zones, which are isolated from each other within the region. Each zone is identified by a name that combines a letter identifier with the name of the region. For example, zone an in the East Asia region is named asia-east1-a.

This distribution of resources provides several benefits, including redundancy in case of failure and reduced latency by locating resources closer to clients. This distribution also introduces some rules about how resources can be used together.

GLOBAL
Accessible by any resource in any zone within the same project

REGIONAL
Accessible by any resources within the same region

ZONE
Hosted in a zone. Are unique to that zone and are only usable by other resources in the same zone

Global, Regional, and Zone Resources

Figure 17: Product Availability in Europe

Some resources can be accessed by any other resource, across regions and zones. These global resources include preconfigured disk images, disk snapshots, and networks. Some resources can be accessed only by resources that are located in the same region. These regional resources include static external IP addresses. Other resources can be accessed only by resources that are found in the same zone. These zonal resources include VM instances, their types, and disks.

The scope of an operation varies depending on what kind of resources you're working with. For example, creating a network is a global operation because a network is a global resource while reserving an IP address is a regional operation because the address is a regional resource.

Figure 16: Product Availability in Americas Regions

Google Cloud Certified Professional Cloud Architect, Second Edition

Figure 18: Product Availability Globally

Figure 19: Product Availability in APAC

Cloud ML Engine services for TensorFlow are available in the following regions:

Region	us-west1	us-central1	us-east1	europe-west1	europe-west4	asia-east1	asia-northeast1
Training	✓	✓	✓	✓	✓	✓	✗
Training with GPUs	✓	✓	✓	✓	✓	✓	✗
Online prediction	✗	✓	✓	✓	✗	✗	✓
Batch prediction	✗	✓	✓	✓	✗	✓	✗

Training with Accelerators are available on a region basis:

Region	us-west1	us-central1	us-east1	europe-west1	europe-west4	asia-east1
NVIDIA TESLA K80	✗	✓	✓	✓	✗	✓
NVIDIA TESLA P100	✓	✓	✓	✓	✗	✓
NVIDIA TESLA V100	✓	✓	✗	✗	✓	✓
TPU_V2	✗	✓	✗	✗	✗	✗

Figure 20: Cloud ML Engine and Training Availability

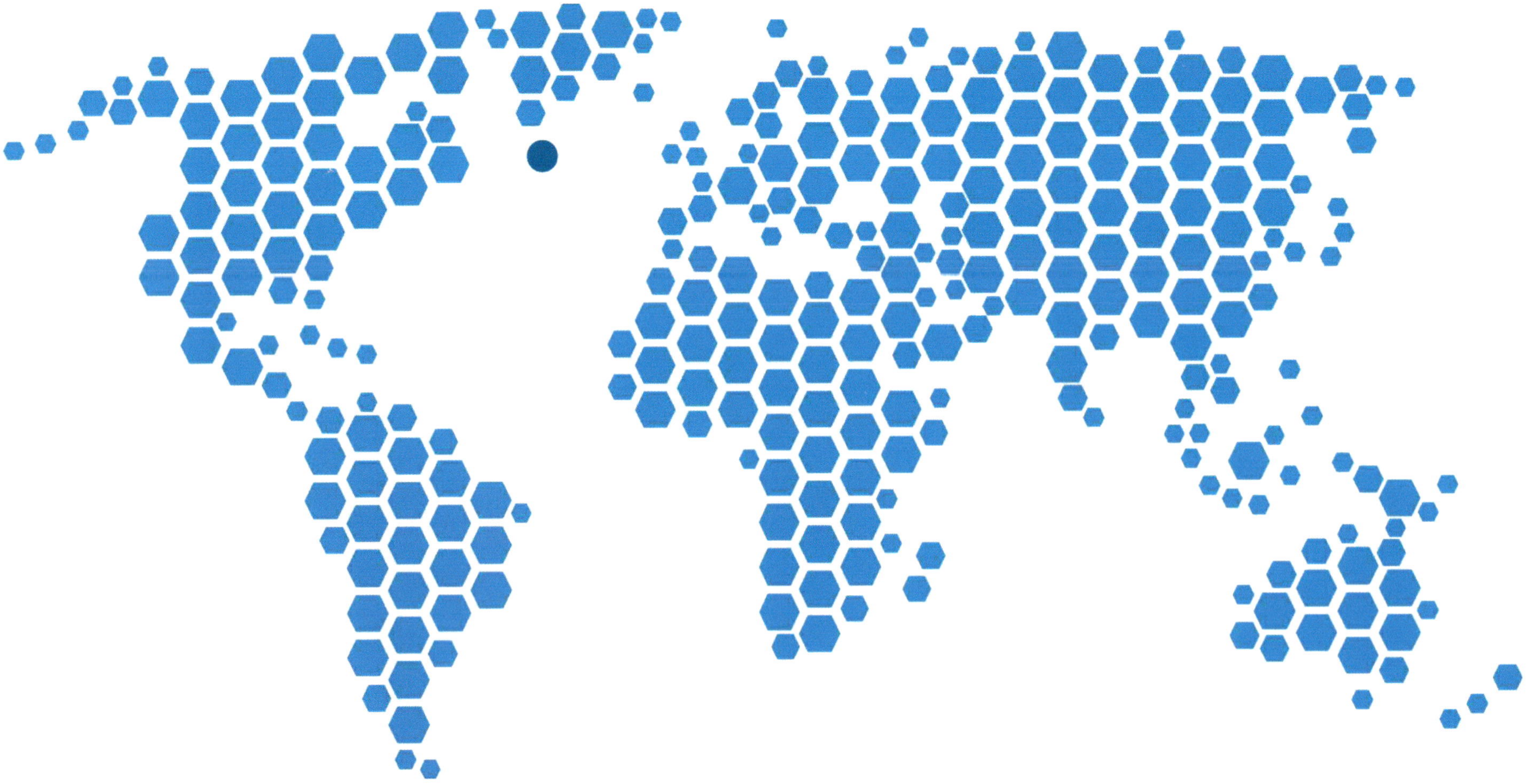

Networking

The Google Cloud Virtual Network is a networking service offering from Google and is one of the foundational blocks of the Google Cloud Platform. The Google Cloud Platform differentiated high-speed services with **one of the best software-defined networking (SDN) solutions** and distributed system technologies to deliver and host services across geographical borders.

Development Tool

Data Transfer and Data Migration

Cloud AI

Network Service Tiers Optimize your network for performance or cost

Virtual Private Cloud (VPC) VPC networking for GCP resources

Cloud DNS Reliable, resilient, low-latency DNS serving

Cloud Load Balancing High performance, scalable load balancing

Networking

Cloud Interconnect Connect directly to GCP's network edge

Cloud Armor BETA Protect your services against denial of service and web attacks

Network Telemetry In-depth network telemetry to keep your services secure

Cloud CDN Content delivery on Google's global network

Management Tools

Google Cloud Platform
- Compute
- Databases
- Storage
- Data Analytics
- Identity and Security
- Internet of Things (IoT)
- API Management

Google Cloud Virtual Networks and Interconnect

The Google's global VPC leverages Google's high-quality private network connects with 18 regions, 52 zones, over 100 points of presence across 225 countries, and a well-provisioned global network with 100,000s of miles of fiber optic cable. The Google Cloud Virtual Networks can contain as many as 7,000 virtual machine instances and can encompass resources or subnets across various regions. The Google Cloud Virtual Networks stands outs from the leading peers such as AWS and Azure, simplifying the complex VPN and peering configurations, and at the same time making it much faster. **Google Cloud Interconnect - Dedicated (Dedicated Interconnect)** provides direct physical connections between your on-premises network and Google's network and enables you to transfer large amounts of data between networks, in a much affordable way than purchasing additional bandwidth over the public Internet. Google Cloud Platform (GCP) now introduced a cutting-edge new **congestion control algorithm, TCP BBR**[11], which achieves higher bandwidths and lower latencies for internet traffic. This is the same BBR[12] that powers TCP traffic from google.com and that improved YouTube network throughput by 4 per cent on average globally — and by more than 14 per cent in some countries. BBR ensures shorter network queues, reducing round-trip time by 33 per cent; enables faster responses and lower delays for latency-sensitive applications like web browsing, chat and gaming.

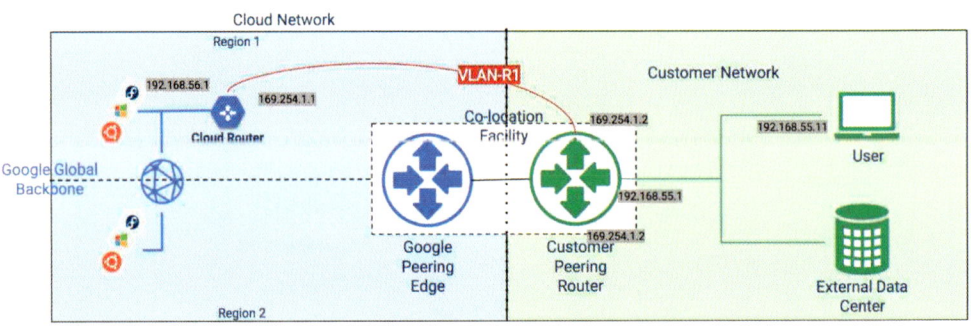

Figure 21: GCP Networking Tools and Components

Figure 22: Using Cloud Router Global Routing

©2018 Google LLC, used with permission. Google and the Google logo are registered trademarks of Google LLC

Source: https://cloud.google.com/blog/products/gcp/google-cloud-dedicated-interconnect-gets-global-routing-more-locations-and-is-ga

Moreover, by not overreacting to packet loss, BBR improves 11 per cent higher mean-time-between-rebuffers allowing substantial improvements for all large user populations around the world, across both desktop and mobile users

---

[11] https://tools.ietf.org/html/draft-cheng-iccrg-delivery-rate-estimation-00

[12] Adapted from source: https://cloud.google.com/blog/products/gcp/tcp-bbr-congestion-control-comes-to-gcp-your-internet-just-got-faster

Dedicated Interconnect - Locations

©2018 Google LLC, used with permission. Google and the Google logo are registered trademarks of Google LLC

Figure 23: Dedicated Interconnect Locations

Figure 24: GCP Dedicated Interconnect Locations Across the Globe

August 2017, Google Cloud Platform launched its premium tier not long ago and the standard tier networks. This makes them the first major public cloud to offer a tiered cloud network. The premium tier delivers traffic over Google's well-provisioned, low latency, highly reliable global network. Redundancy is critical, and that ensures **N+2 redundancy path between any two locations on the Google network, helping ensure that traffic continues to flow between the locations even in the event of a disruption**. Google's network is the largest of any public cloud provider. GCP presents a range of options for us to leverage the cloud in a way that suits

the best for our business scenarios. A High-performance options such as **Dedicated Interconnect** (Direct physical connections between your on-premises network and Google's network with 99.99% availability), **Partner Interconnect** (Flexible bandwidth options (50 Mbps - 10 Gbps) with 99.9% availability), and Cloud IPSec VPN for lower volume and connects your corporate network to the GCP virtual Private Cloud through a unique IPsec Connection.

Please make a note that while some of the core resources in GCP are global, others may be restricted by region or zone. Only Global resources are allowed to share without restriction, but Regional resources can't be used outside the region. Same goes with the zonal resources. Example of resource categories (Reference: https://cloud.google.com/compute/docs/regions-zones/global-regional-zonal-resources)

Global Resources:
- Addresses - Global static external IP addresses
- Images
- Snapshots
- VPC Network
- Firewalls
- Routes
- Global Operations

Regional Resources:
- Addresses – Regional Static external IP addresses
- Subnets
- Regional managed instance groups
- Regional persistent disks
- Regional Operations

Zonal Resources:
- Instances (VMs)
- Persistent Disks
- Machine types
- Zonal managed instance groups
- Per-zone operations

Figure 25: Interconnect vs VPN

Interconnect vs Cloud VPN – When to select What?

1. Dedicated Interconnect provides 10 Gbps for each link to GCP. With up to eight connections per interconnect, you have 80 Gbps at your fingertips.
2. Partner Interconnect provides from 50 Mbps all the way up to 10 Gbps per VLAN.
3. Cloud VPN offers a lower cost option that delivers 1.5–3.0 Gbps over an encrypted public internet connection. Cloud VPN's flexible routing options allow you to use static or dynamic routing to connect to different VPN gateways.

Also refer the useful decision tree here
https://cloud.google.com/hybrid-connectivity/

Google is adding new regions, zones, Network Edge Locations and Countries. Always stay tuned in:
https://cloud.google.com/about/locations/

Google Cloud locations

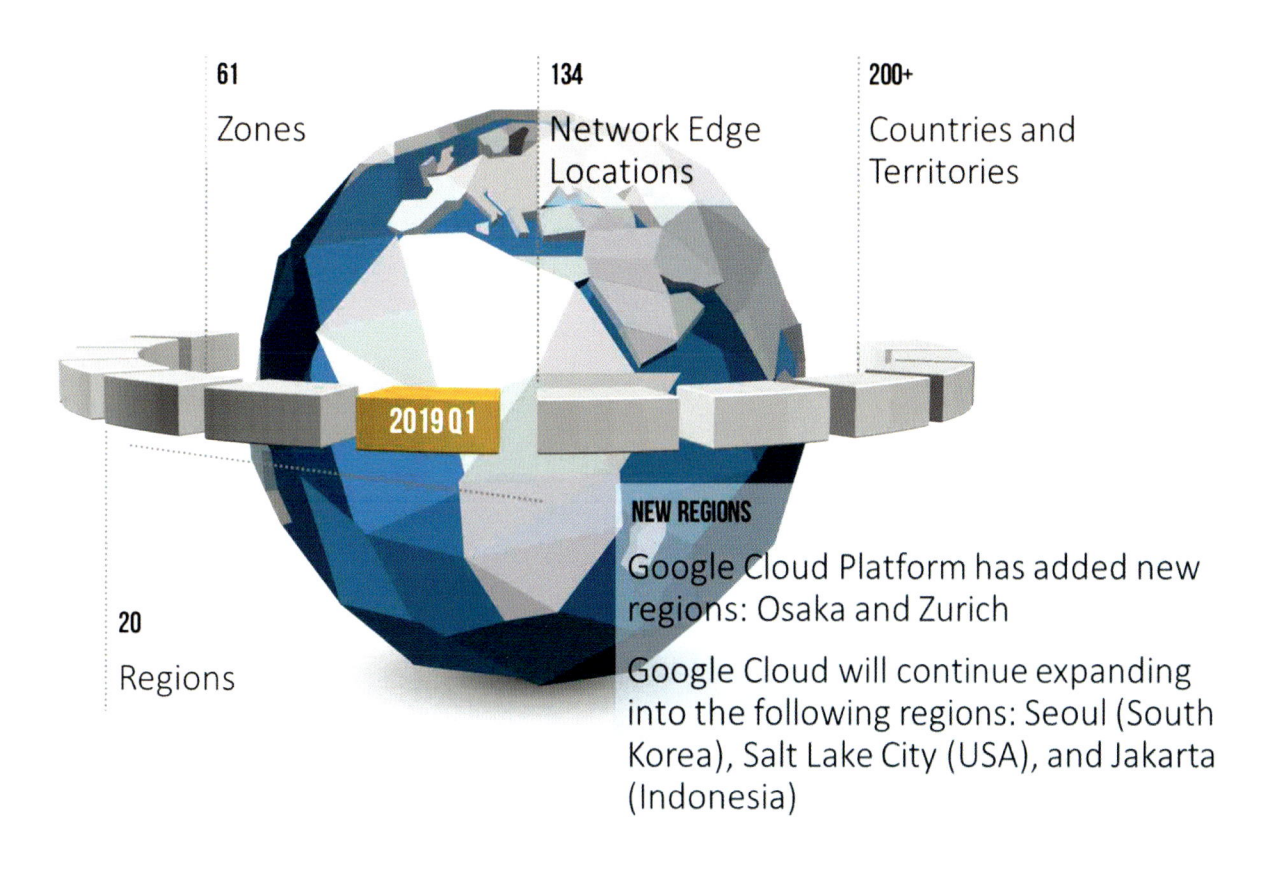

61 Zones

134 Network Edge Locations

200+ Countries and Territories

20 Regions

2019 Q1

NEW REGIONS

Google Cloud Platform has added new regions: Osaka and Zurich

Google Cloud will continue expanding into the following regions: Seoul (South Korea), Salt Lake City (USA), and Jakarta (Indonesia)

Google Cloud Certified Professional Cloud Architect, Second Edition

Figure 26: Google Cloud Regions

©2018 Google LLC, used with permission. Google and the Google logo are registered trademarks of Google LLC

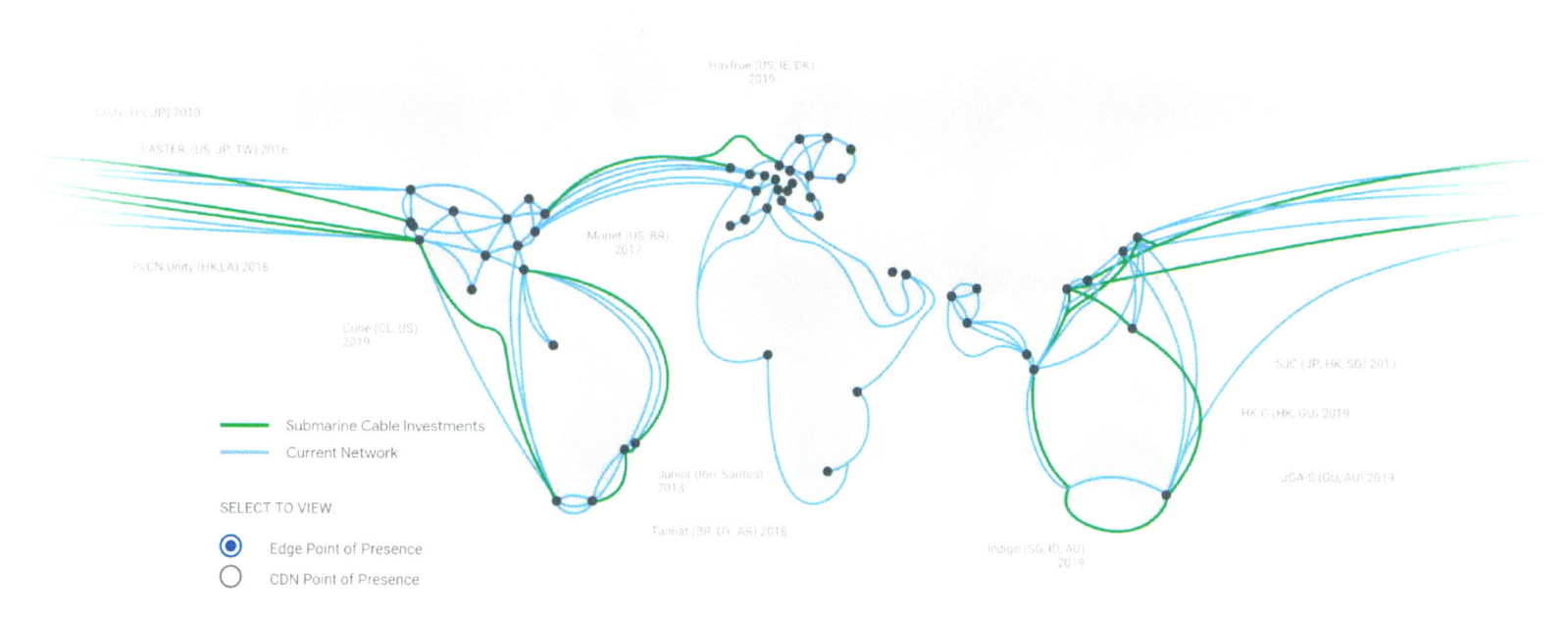

Figure 27: Google Cloud Network

Source: https://cloud.google.com/about/locations/#network-tab

©2018 Google LLC, used with permission. Google and the Google logo are registered trademarks of Google LLC

Cloud Load Balancers
GCP offers **server-side load balancing** distributes incoming traffic across multiple virtual machine instances. Load balancing provides the following benefits:
   a) Application Scaling
   b) Supporting the heavy traffic
   c) Automatically adds or deletes virtual machine instances depending on health checks status. Instances those become healthy, would get added again automatically re-added.
   d) Route traffic to the closest virtual mac.

GCP load balancers uses forwarding rule resources to match specific types of traffic and forward it to a load balancer. **GCP load balancing is a Google managed service**, which comes with redundant and highly available components. When a load balancing component fails, it is restarted or replaced automatically and immediately.

Cloud Load Balancing puts your resources behind **a single anycast IP** IPv4 or IPv6 Virtual IP across multiple regions. It seamlessly expands, overflow or fail-over into other regions and scales your **resources up or down with intelligent Autoscaling**. Cloud Load Balancing is a fully distributed, software-defined, managed service for all your traffic. It is not an instance or device based solution, so you won't be locked into physical load balancing infrastructure or face the HA, scale and management challenges inherent in instance-based LBs. You can apply Cloud Load Balancing to all of your traffic: HTTP(S), TCP/SSL, and UDP. You can also terminate your SSL traffic with HTTPS Load Balancing and SSL proxy.

Cloud Load Balancers serves content as close as possible to your users, on a system that **can respond to over 1 million queries per second**. It is not an instance or device based, so you **do not need to manage a physical load balancing infrastructure.**

GCP provides regional network services in Standard tiers, such as the new regional Cloud Load Balancing service. In this tier, your Load Balancing Virtual IP (VIP) is regional, similar to other public cloud offerings, and adds management complexity compared to Premium Tier Global Load Balancing, if you require multi-region deployment.

The following table summarises types of load balancers available in Google Cloud.
Table 1: Types of Load Balancer

Load Balancer	Traffic type	Global/Regional	External/Internal
HTTP(S)	HTTP or HTTPS	Global	External
SSL Proxy	TCP with SSL offload	Global	External
TCP Proxy	TCP without SSL offload. Does not preserve client IP addresses	Global	External
Network TCP/UDP	TCP/UDP without SSL offload. Preserves client IP addresses.	Regional	External
Internal TCP/UDP	TCP or UDP	Regional	Internal

To decide which Google Cloud load balancer best suits your implementation use cases, it is advisable to think about the following three aspects of Cloud Load Balancing:
- Global versus regional load balancing
- External versus internal load balancing
- Traffic type

The following flow chart helps us to determine which load balancers are available for your client, protocol, and network configuration:
Diagram source: https://cloud.google.com/load-balancing/docs/choosing-load-balancer

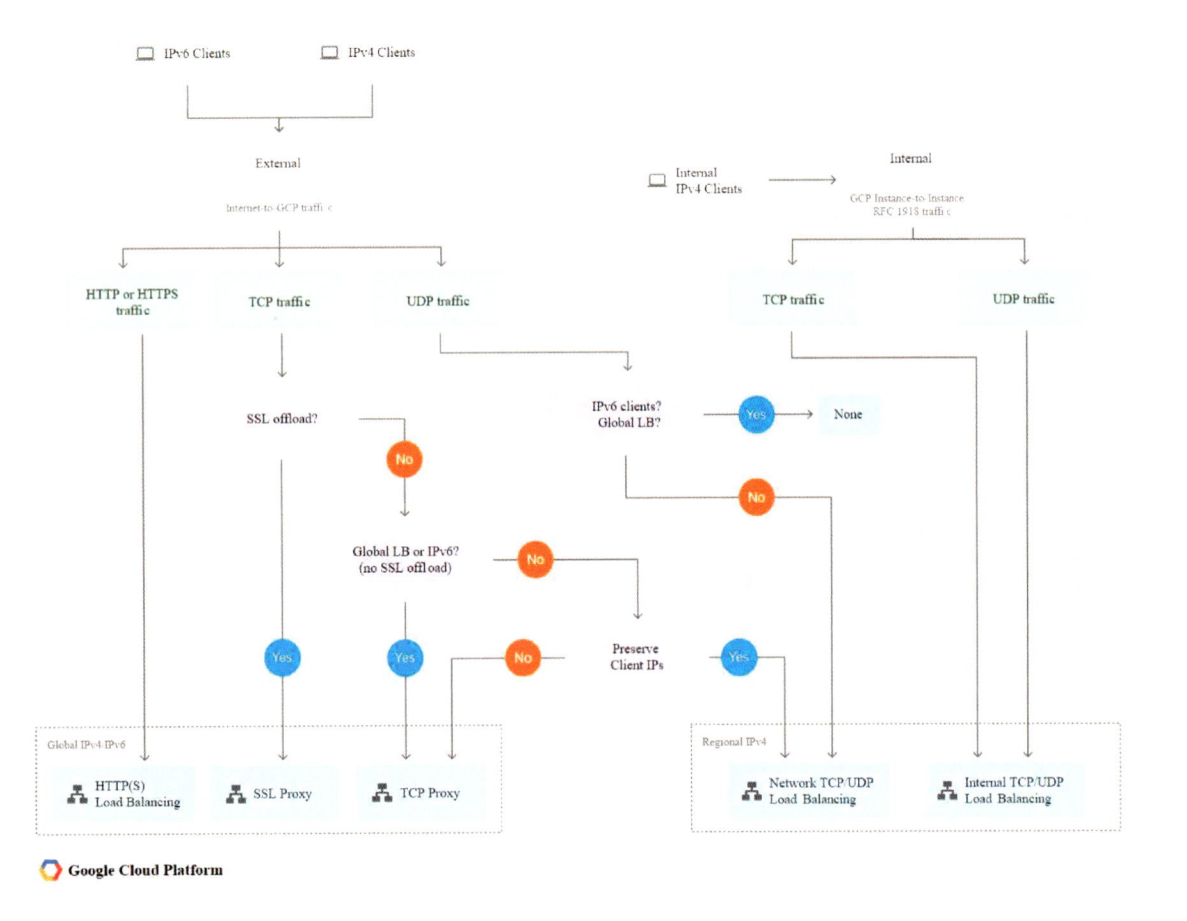

Figure 28: How to decide appropriate load balancer

Google has recently introduced Cloud Armor works with Global HTTP(S) Load Balancer to provide built-in defences against infrastructure DDoS attacks.

Tips: Lot of the cases, you will find HTTP(S) LB is an excellent choice for us. HTTP(S) load balancing can balance HTTP and HTTPS traffic across multiple backend instances, across various regions. Your entire app is available via a single global IP address, resulting in a simplified DNS setup. HTTP(S) load balancing is scalable, fault-tolerant requires no pre-warming, and enables content-based load balancing. For

HTTPS traffic, it provides SSL termination and load balancing.

Virtual Private Cloud (VPC)
Virtual Private Cloud (VPC) provides networking functionality for computing Engine virtual machine (VM) instances, GKE clusters, and App Engine Flex instances. Google Cloud VPC provides global, scalable, flexible networking for your cloud-based resources and services. VPC Network is virtualised. It acts as a global resource which

©2018 Google LLC, used with permission. Google and the Google logo are registered trademarks of Google LLC

Figure 29: Google Cloud VPC Network

consists of a list of regional virtual subnetworks (subnets) in data centres, all connected by a global WAN. VPC networks are logically isolated from each other in GCP.
VPC networks, and their associated routes and firewall rules, are global resources and not limited to any particular region or zone. Whereas, Subnets are regional resources.
An organisation can use Shared VPC to keep a VPC network in a typical host project. Authorised IAM members from other projects in the same organisation can create resources that use subnets of the Shared VPC network.
VPC networks can be connected to other VPC networks in different projects or organisations by using VPC Network Peering. VPC networks can be securely connected in hybrid environments using Cloud VPN or Cloud Interconnect. VPC networks only support IPv4 unicast traffic. They do not support broadcast, multicast, or IPv6 traffic within the network.

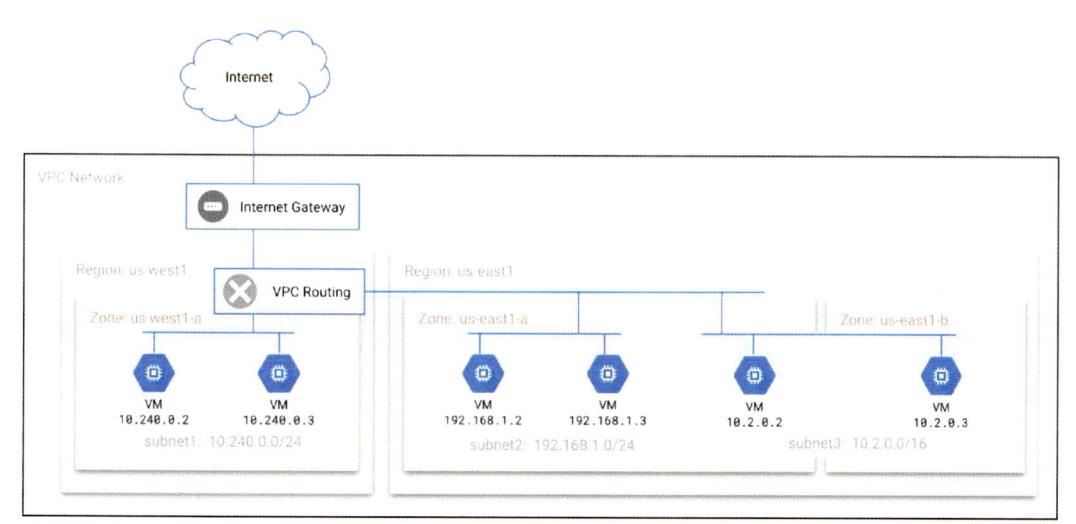

©2018 Google LLC, used with permission. Google and the Google logo are registered trademarks of Google LLC

As networks have no IP address range here, subnetworks don't need to fit into an address hierarchy. Subnetworks can be used to group and manage resources and very useful to represent various departments in an organisation like Finance, HR, Marketing, Sales, IT and so on. Subnetworks can extend across zones in the same region. **Projects can contain multiple VPC networks**. New projects start with a default network that has **one subnet in each region** (an auto mode network). **Subnetworks are not useful for Separation of duties**.
GCP offers two types of VPC networks, determined by their subnet creation mode (Refer: https://cloud.google.com/vpc/docs/vpc):

1. When we build an auto mode network, one subnet from each region is automatically generated. These automatically created subnets use a set of predefined IP ranges which fit within the 10.128.0.0/9 CIDR block. As new GCP regions become available, new subnets in those regions are automatically added to auto mode networks using an IP range from that block. In addition to the automatically created subnets, you can add more subnets manually to auto mode networks, in regions you choose, using IP ranges outside of 10.128.0.0/9.
2. When a custom mode network is created, no subnets are automatically generated. It also gives you complete control over its subnets and IP ranges.
3. Each project starts with a default auto mode network.
4. You can switch a network from auto mode to custom mode. This conversion is one-way; custom mode networks cannot be changed to auto mode networks. Carefully review the considerations for auto mode networks to help you decide which type of network meets your needs

Firewall Rules either allow or deny and is defined to apply either for ingress (incoming) traffic or egress (outgoing) traffic. A single firewall rule can apply to all the VMs connected to a subnet even though they are in different zones.

Google Cloud Certified Professional Cloud Architect, Second Edition

Other Components

Google Cloud CDN is benefitted by Google's **globally distributed edge points of presence (PoP)** resulting in accelerated content delivery for websites and applications served out of Google Compute Engine and Google Cloud Storage. Cloud CDN results in lower network latency, offloading origins, and reduces serving costs. Once you've set up HTTP(S) Load Balancing, enable Cloud CDN with a single checkbox.

Google Cloud DNS provides a **scalable, reliable and managed authoritative Domain Name System (DNS)** service that runs on the same infrastructure as Google. It has low latency, high availability and is a cost-effective way to make your applications and services are available to your users. Cloud DNS translates requests for domain names like www.google.com into IP addresses like 74.125.29.101. **Cloud DNS is programmable.** You can easily publish and manage millions of DNS zones and records using our simple user interface, command-line interface or API.

Further Reading:
1. https://cloud.google.com/network-tiers/
2. https://cloud.google.com/load-balancing/docs/https/setting-up-https
3. https://cloud.google.com/load-balancing/docs/load-balancing-overview
4. An excellent example of how to use LBs for websites: https://cloud.google.com/solutions/web-serving-overview
5. https://codelabs.developers.google.com/codelabs/gcp-infra-vpn-and-cloud-router/index.html?index=..%2F..cloud#0
6. https://cloud.google.com/vpc/docs/overview
7. https://cloud.google.com/interconnect/docs/concepts/dedicated-overview
8. https://cloud.google.com/compute/docs/instances/live-migration
9. https://cloud.google.com/about/locations/
10. https://cloud.withgoogle.com/infrastructure/

Figure 30: Google Cloud Networking Components

Google's cloud Stackdriver logging feature ensures that all of the load balancing requests sent to the load balancer are managed property and could be processed further by Cloud Pub/Sub and analysed in Google BigQuery.

Further Reading: https://cloud.google.com/vpc/docs/using-firewalls

Putting the puzzle together – High-Level Networking Architecture Example

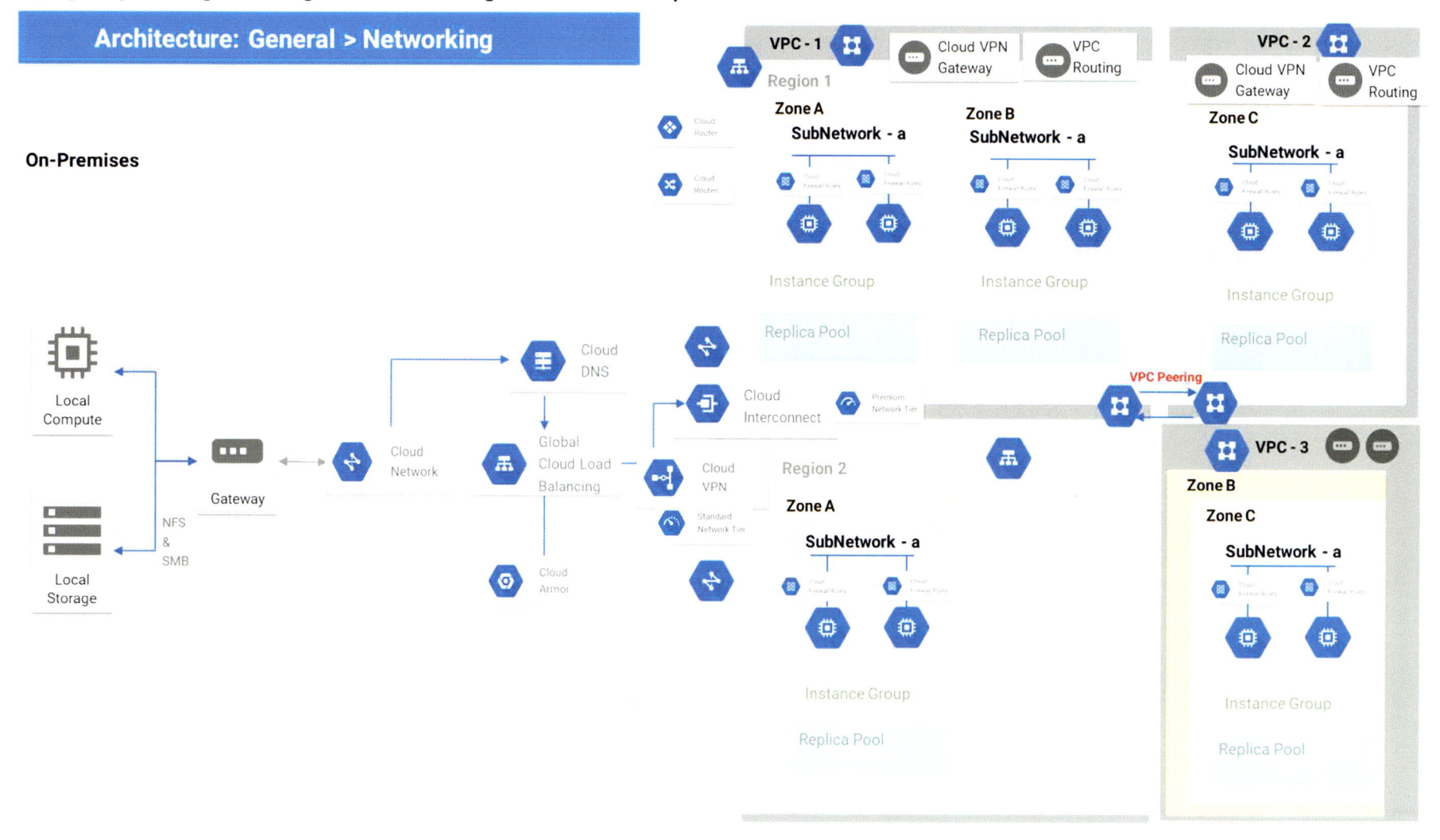

Figure 31: Google Cloud Networking Basics

Cloud Router

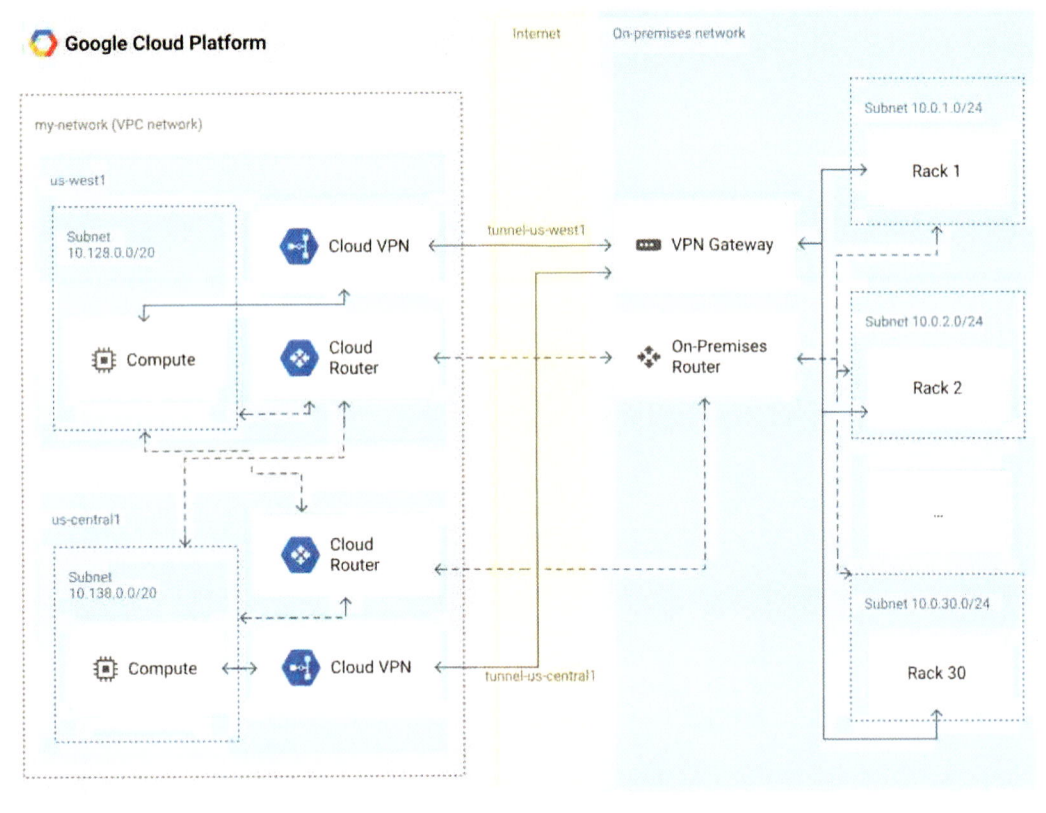

Figure 32: Cloud Router global dynamic routing

Cloud Router is a fully distributed, scalable and managed Google cloud service and not a physical device that might cause a bottleneck.

Cloud Router dynamically exchange routes between your Google Cloud networks and your on-premises network. Cloud Router peers with your on-premises VPN gateway or router. The routers exchange topology information through Border Gateway Protocol (BGP). Topology changes automatically propagate between your VPC network and on-premises network. You don't need to configure static routes.

Further Reading:
https://cloud.google.com/router/docs/concepts/overview

Data path vs Logical Control path: Fast packet forwarding happens through Datapath, but high-level routing decisions happen through a control path.

©2018 Google LLC, used with permission. Google and the Google logo are registered trademarks of Google LLC

Managed Instance Autoscaling

Autoscaling is a feature of managed instance groups. A managed instance group is a pool of homogeneous instances, created from a common instance template. Autoscaling adds or deletes instances from a managed instance group. Although Compute Engine has both managed and unmanaged instance groups, only managed instance groups can be used with autoscaler. A managed instance group uses an instance template to create a group of identical instances. You control a managed instance group as a single entity. Applicable autoscaling policies include **scaling based on CPU utilisation, load balancing capacity, Stackdriver monitoring metrics, or by a queue-based workload like Google Cloud Pub/Sub**.
Managed instance groups maintain high availability of your applications by proactively keeping your instances available, which means in RUNNING state. A managed instance group will automatically recreate an instance that is not RUNNING. However, relying on instance state may not be sufficient. You may want to recreate instances when an application freezes, crashes or runs out of memory. **Application-based auto healing** will improve application availability by relying on a health checking signal that detects application-specific issues such as freezing, crashing, or overloading. If a health check determines that an application has failed on an instance, the group automatically recreates that instance.

Further Reading: https://cloud.google.com/solutions/about-capacity-optimization-with-global-lb

Instance Groups Limitations

- Regional instance groups can have a maximum number 2,000 instances and The number of instances that would produce 9,000 endpoints, calculated in the following way: instances * (number of ports in the named port that contains the most port numbers) <= 9,000
- Zonal instance groups can have a maximum number of 1,000 instances and The number of instances that would produce 3,000 endpoints, calculated in the following way: instances * (number of ports in the named port that contains the most port numbers) <= 3,000
- Network endpoint groups can include up to 10,000 endpoints. Only global backend services with a load balancing scheme EXTERNAL can use NEGs, so the backends are not limited to any particular region.

Further Reading:
https://cloud.google.com/compute/docs/instance-groups/
https://cloud.google.com/compute/docs/instance-groups/distributing-instances-with-regional-instance-groups

Load Balancer Health Check

Google Cloud Platform (GCP) provides health checking mechanisms that determine whether VM instances respond correctly to traffic. GCP organises health checks by category and protocol. There are two health check categories: **health checks** and **legacy health checks**. Each category supports a different set of protocols and a means for specifying the port used for health checking. **Most load balancers perform non-legacy health checks, but Network Load Balancing requires that you use legacy health checks**. A health check runs continuously, and its results help determine which instances should receive new requests.

Unhealthy instances do not receive new requests and continue to be polled. If an unhealthy instance passes a health check, it is deemed healthy and will begin accepting new connections.
The best practice when configuring a health check is to check the health and serve traffic on the same port. However, it is possible to perform health checks on one port while serving traffic on another. **If you use two different ports, ensure that firewall rules and services running on instances are configured appropriately**.
If you run health checks and serve traffic on the same port, but decide to switch ports at some point, be sure to update both the backend service and the health check. Backend services that do not have a valid global forwarding rule referencing it will not be health checked and will have no health status.

Further Reading:

https://cloud.google.com/load-balancing/docs/health-checks
https://cloud.google.com/load-balancing/docs/backend-service

Google Cloud Certified Professional Cloud Architect, Second Edition

Serverless
Apps and Functions

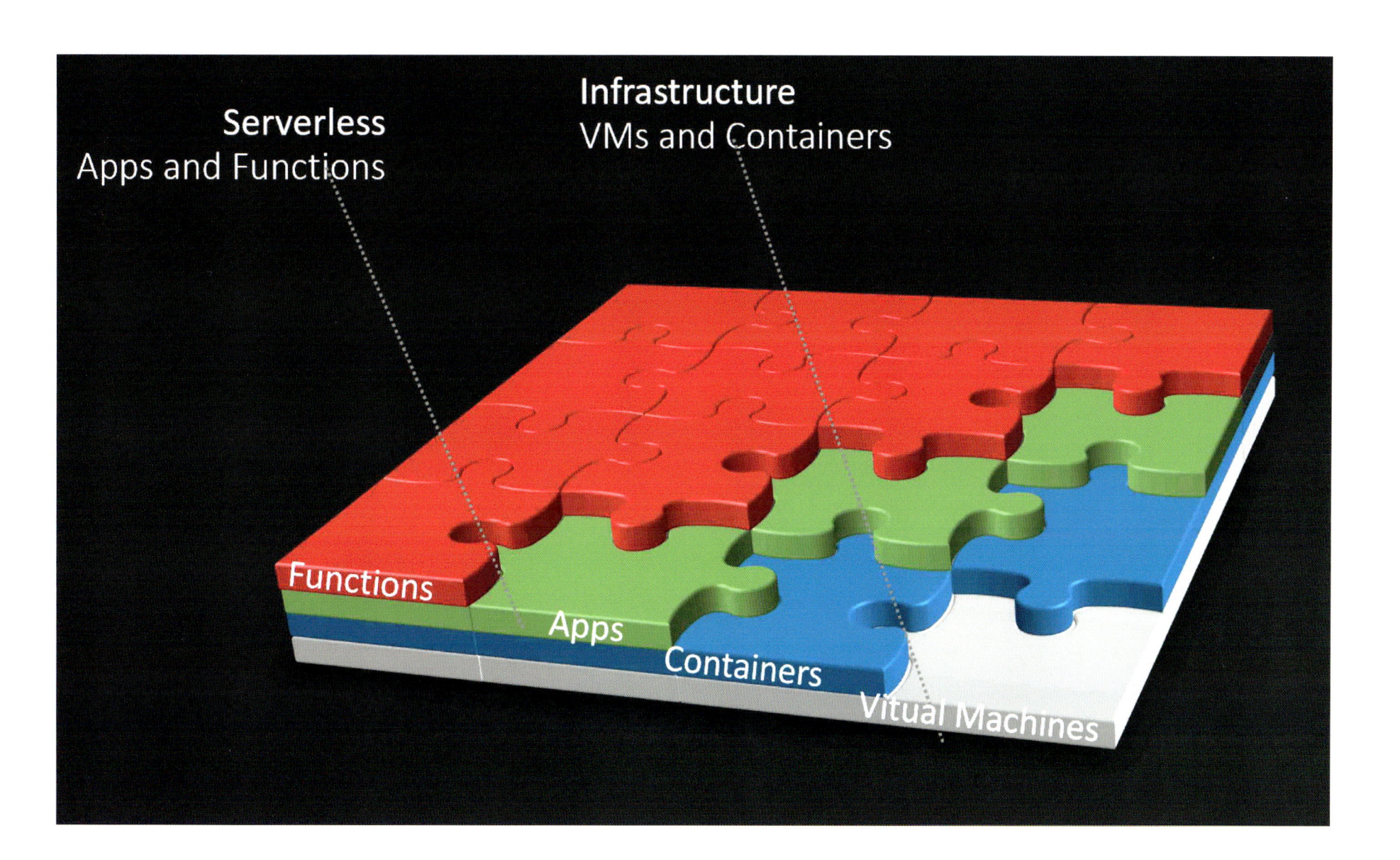

Infrastructure
VMs and Containers

- Functions
- Apps
- Containers
- Vitual Machines

Compute Engine

Google Cloud Platform

- Development Tool
- Data Transfer and Data Migration
- Cloud AI
- Networking
- Management Tools
- Compute
  - **Compute Engines** Scalable, High-Performance Virtual Machines
  - **App Engine** PaaS for apps and backends
  - **Kubernetes Engine** Run containers on GCP
  - **Cloud Functions Serverless** Environment to build and connect Cloud Service
  - **GKE On-Prem** Make apps "Cloud Raady" and move them to the cloud at your own pace
  - **Knative** Components to create modern Kubernetes-native cloud based software
  - **Shielded VMs** BETA Hardened VMs on GCP
- Databases
- Storage
- Data Analytics
- Identity and Security
- Internet of Things (IoT)
- API Management

The Compute Engine is Google's **infrastructure-as-a-service (IaaS)** offering that enables you to run workloads on a large scale on virtual machines on Google's planet-scale infrastructure. Google Compute Engine delivers virtual machines running in Google's innovative data centres and worldwide fibre network - from global, load-balanced, resilient services to flexible single-instance VMs, a scalable range of computing options that could easily be tailored to match your enterprise requirement. Compute Engine's tooling, and workflow support enables scaling from single instances to global, load-balanced cloud computing.

Compute Engine's VMs boot quickly, come with high-performance persistent and local disk options, and deliver consistent performance.

Flexible pricing and automatic sustained use discounts make Compute Engine the leader in price/performance.

Google Compute Engine has completed ISO 27001, SSAE-16, SOC 1, SOC 2, and SOC 3 certifications,

Compute Engine Features	Points to remember
Predefined Machine Types	From micro instances to instances with up to 160 vCPUs and 3.75 TB of memory
Custom Machine Types	VMs with the shape (i.e. vCPU and memory) that is right for your workloads
Persistent Disks	• Network storage, up to 64 TB in size, in HDD or SSD formats • If a VM instance is terminated, its persistent disk retains data and can be attached to another instance and create new persistent disks from that snapshot. • Encrypted on the fly and then transmitted and stored in encrypted form
Local SSD	• Always-encrypted local solid-state drive (SSD) block storage • Physically attached to the server hosting the VMs • Very high input/output operations per second (IOPS) and very low latency compared to persistent disks • Sizes up to a 3 TB with at least one vCPU.

Table 2: Compute Engine Features

An image in Compute Engine is a cloud resource that provides a reference to an immutable disk. That disk representation is then encapsulated using a few data formats.

©2018 Google LLC, used with permission. Google and the Google logo are registered trademarks of Google LLC
Figure 34: Creation of a Boot instance from disk

Figure 35: Sharing images between projects

The life cycle of a single VM

An instance can have the following states:

- **Provisioning** - Resources are being allocated for the instance. The instance is not running yet.
- **Staging** - Resources have been acquired, and the instance is being prepared for first boot.
- **Running** - The instance is booting up or running. You should be able to ssh into the instance soon, but not immediately after it enters this state.
- **Stopping** - The instance is being terminated. This can be because a user has made a request to stop the instance or there was a failure. This is a temporary status, and the instance will move to TERMINATED once the instance has stopped.
- **Terminated** - A user stopped the instance, or the instance encountered a failure. Restart the instance or delete it.

The following diagram describes the transition between each instance state:

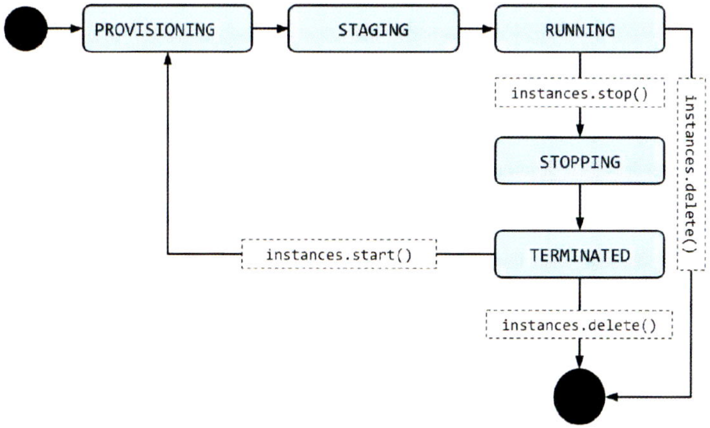

Boot disks could be created from the following image types:

- Public images are provided and maintained by Google, open-source communities, and third-party vendors. By default, all projects have access to these images and can use them to create instances.
- **Custom images** are available only to your project, created from boot disks and other images.

You can use most public images at no additional cost, but some premium images do add additional cost to your instances. Custom images that you import to Compute Engine add no cost to your instances, but do incur an image storage charge while you keep your custom image in your project.

Figure 36: Phases of an instance

©2018 Google LLC, used with permission. Google and the Google logo are registered trademarks of Google LLC

Compute Engine offers live migration to keep your virtual machine instances **running in the same zone** instead even when a host system event occurs, such as a software or hardware update. This allows Google to perform maintenance that is integral to keeping infrastructure protected and reliable without interrupting any of your VMs.

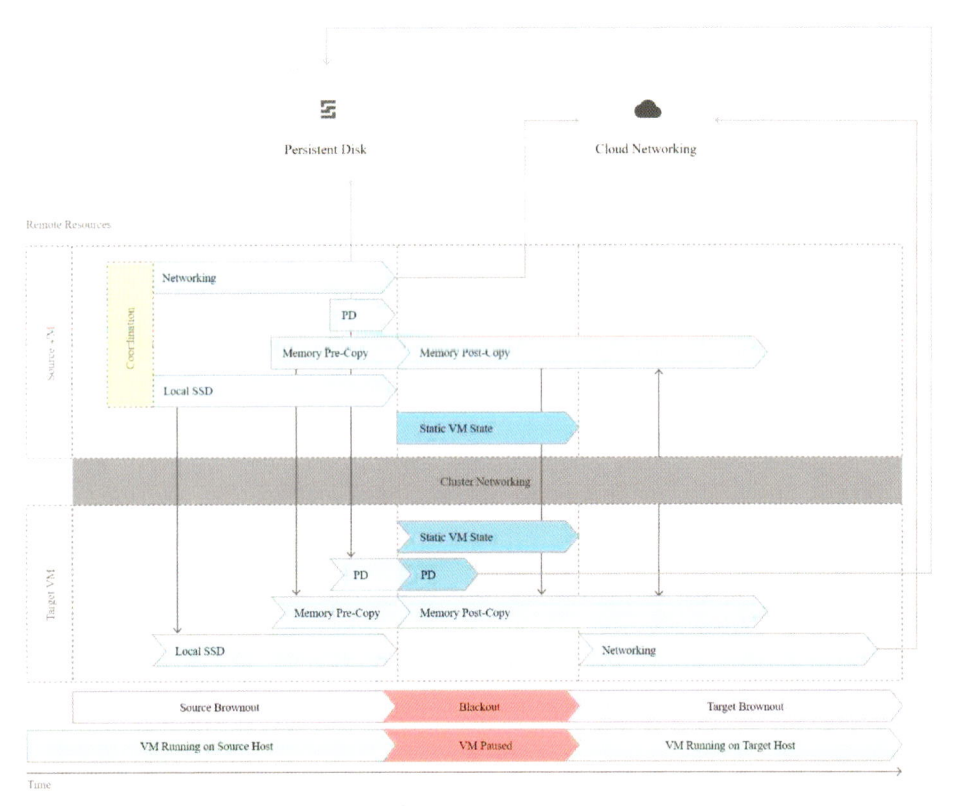

Live migration keeps your instances running during:

- Regular infrastructure maintenance and upgrades.
- Network and power grid maintenance in the data centres.
- Failed hardware such as memory, CPU, network interface cards, disks, power, and so on. This is done on a best-effort basis; if hardware fails completely or otherwise prevents live migration, the VM crashes and restarts automatically, and a hostError is logged.
- Host OS and BIOS upgrades.
- Security-related updates, with the need to respond quickly.
- System configuration changes, including changing the size of the host root partition, for storage of the host image and packages.

All VM properties and attributes would remain unchanged, including internal and external IP addresses, instance metadata, block storage data and volumes, OS and application state, network settings, network connections, and so on.

©2018 Google LLC, used with permission. Google and the Google logo are registered trademarks of Google LLC

Figure 37: Live Migration Stages - A High Level View

High Performance Computing

Powerful, flexible infrastructure to support scalable workloads

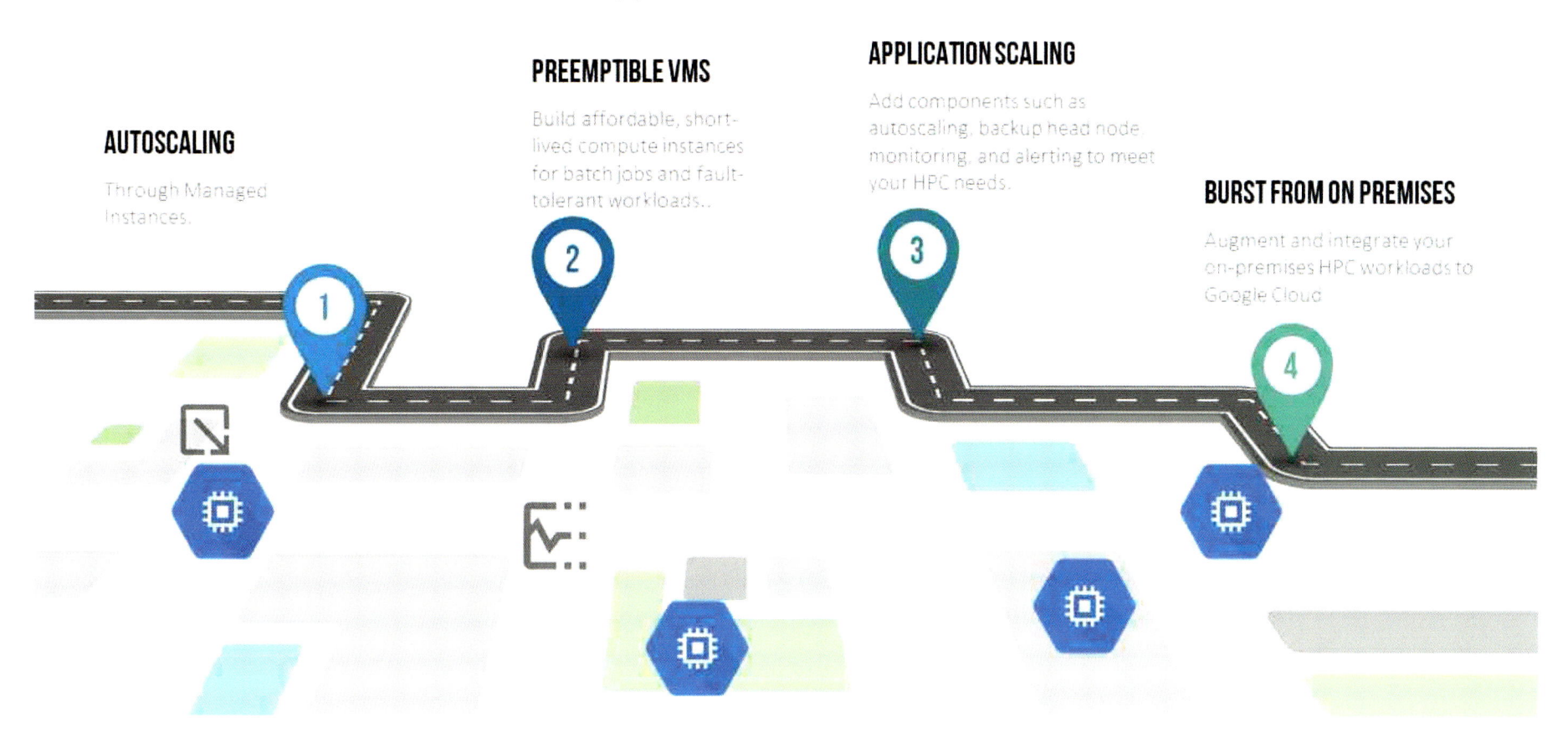

AUTOSCALING

Through Managed Instances.

PREEMPTIBLE VMS

Build affordable, short-lived compute instances for batch jobs and fault-tolerant workloads.

APPLICATION SCALING

Add components such as autoscaling, backup head node, monitoring, and alerting to meet your HPC needs.

BURST FROM ON PREMISES

Augment and integrate your on-premises HPC workloads to Google Cloud.

Preemptible instance
A preemptible VM is an instance that you can create and run at a much lower price than normal instances. Preemptible instances are excess Compute Engine capacity, so their availability varies with usage.

Applications designed to be fault-tolerant and can withstand possible instance preemptions could reduce your Compute Engine costs significantly leveraging preemptible instances. For example, batch processing jobs can run on preemptible instances and get completed without impacting with any additional load to your existing instance and without requiring you to pay full price for additional normal instances.

Preemptible instance limitations
Preemptible instances function like normal instances, but have the following limitations:

- Compute Engine might terminate preemptible instances at any time due to system events. The probability that Compute Engine will terminate a preemptible instance for a system event is generally low but might vary from day to day and from zone to zone depending on current conditions.
- Compute Engine always terminates preemptible instances after they run for 24 hours. Certain actions will reset this 24 hour counter.

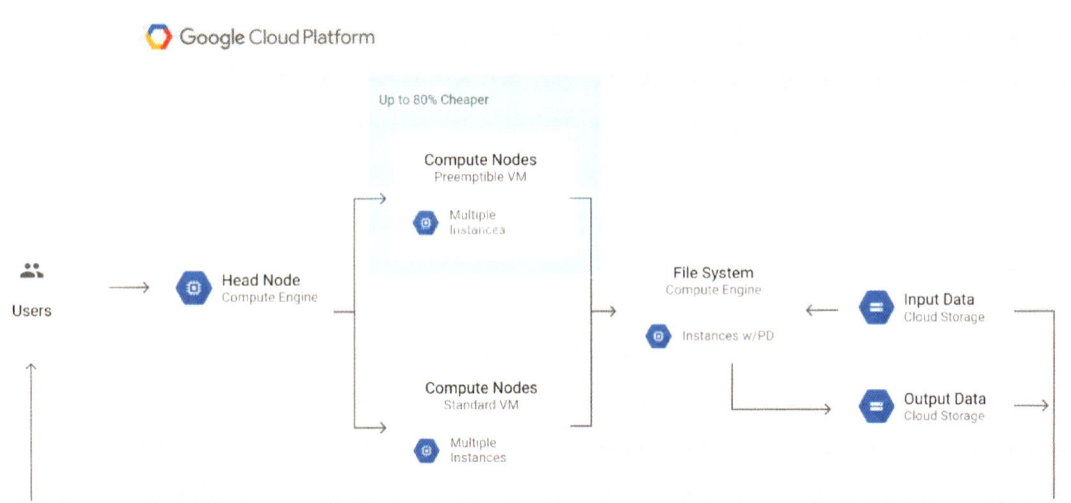

Figure 38: Preemtible VM Instance - Build affordable, short-lived compute instances for batch jobs and fault-tolerant workloads

©2018 Google LLC, used with permission. Google and the Google logo are registered trademarks of Google LLC

- Preemptible instances are finite Compute Engine resources, so they might not always be available.
- **Preemptible instances cannot live migrate to a regular VM instance**, or be set to restart when there is a maintenance event automatically.

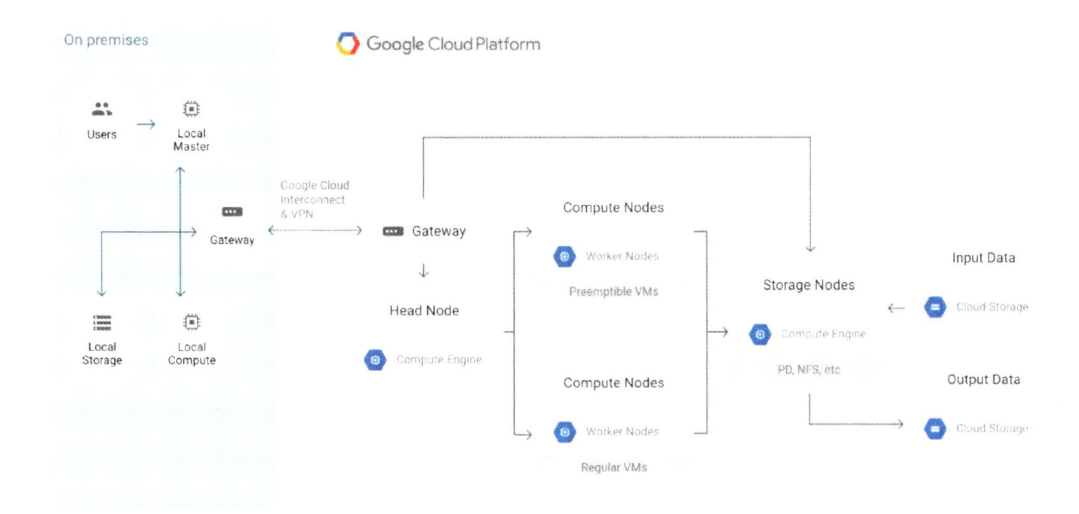

Figure 39: Scaling leveraging Preemptible VMs - Burst from on premises

©2018 Google LLC, used with permission. Google and the Google logo are registered trademarks of Google LLC

Shielded VM
Shielded VM provides an even more secure foundation for all of Google Cloud Platform (GCP) by providing verifiable integrity and offering features, like vTPM shielding or sealing, that help prevent data exfiltration.

Shielded VM offers verifiable integrity of your Compute Engine VM instances, so you can be confident your instances haven't been compromised by boot- or kernel-level malware or rootkits. Shielded VM's verifiable integrity is achieved through the use of Secure Boot, virtual trusted platform module (vTPM)-enabled Measured Boot, and integrity monitoring.

Compute Engine and Application Autoscaling
Google Cloud Compute Engine comes with a scalable range of tailored computing options to meet your needs, from global, load-balanced, resilient services to flexible, single-instance VMs. With preemptible VMs, you can perform batch jobs and fault-tolerant workloads in affordable, 24-hour instances. Google Compute Engine provides highly customizable virtual

- Preemptible instances are **not covered by any Service Level Agreement** (and, for clarity, are excluded from the Google Compute Engine SLA).
- Preemptible instances are not included in the Google Cloud Platform Free Tier.

Preemptible instances help in building affordable; short-lived compute instances for batch jobs and fault-tolerant workloads.

Preemptible instances help managing burst from on-premises, augment and integrate your on-premises HPC workloads to Google Cloud.

Leveraging Preemptible instances, you could achieve application scaling and add components such as autoscaling, backup head node, monitoring, and alerting to meet your HPC needs.

Table 3: Compute Engine, Kubernetes, GAE and Cloud Functions

Compute Engine, Kubernetes, GAE and Cloud Functions

Compute Engine allows you to create your own virtual machines by allocating hardware specific resources whereas Kubernetes Engine is an abstraction above the Compute Engine, and enables you to use Containers to manage your application.
App Engine is a further level abstraction of Kubernetes Engine allowiing us to focus only on your code, whilst all the underlying platform requirements are managed by Google.
Cloud-Functions is the top of the compute pyramid, and enables us to write simple functions that leverages all the underpinning compute infrastructure.

machines with best-of-breed features, friendly pay-for-what-you-use pricing, and the option to deploy your code directly or via containers.

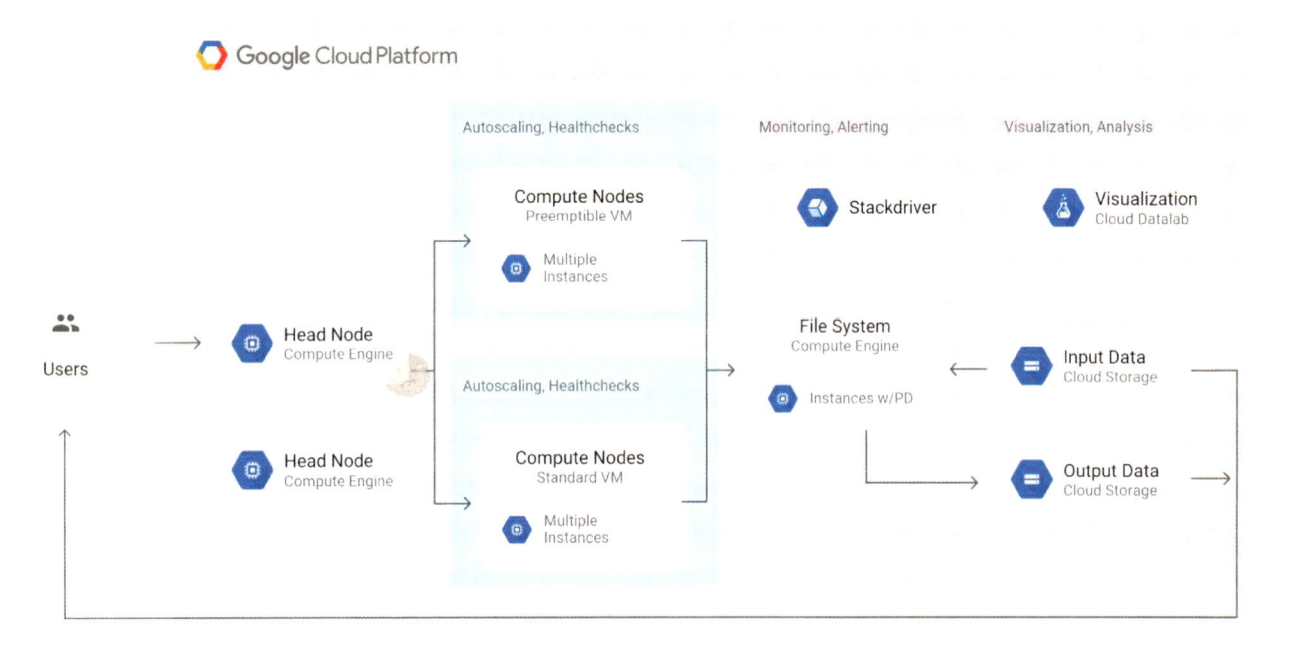

Figure 40: Application scaling with best-of-breed compute options: Standard VMs and Preemptible VMs

©2018 Google LLC, used with permission. Google and the Google logo are registered trademarks of Google LLC

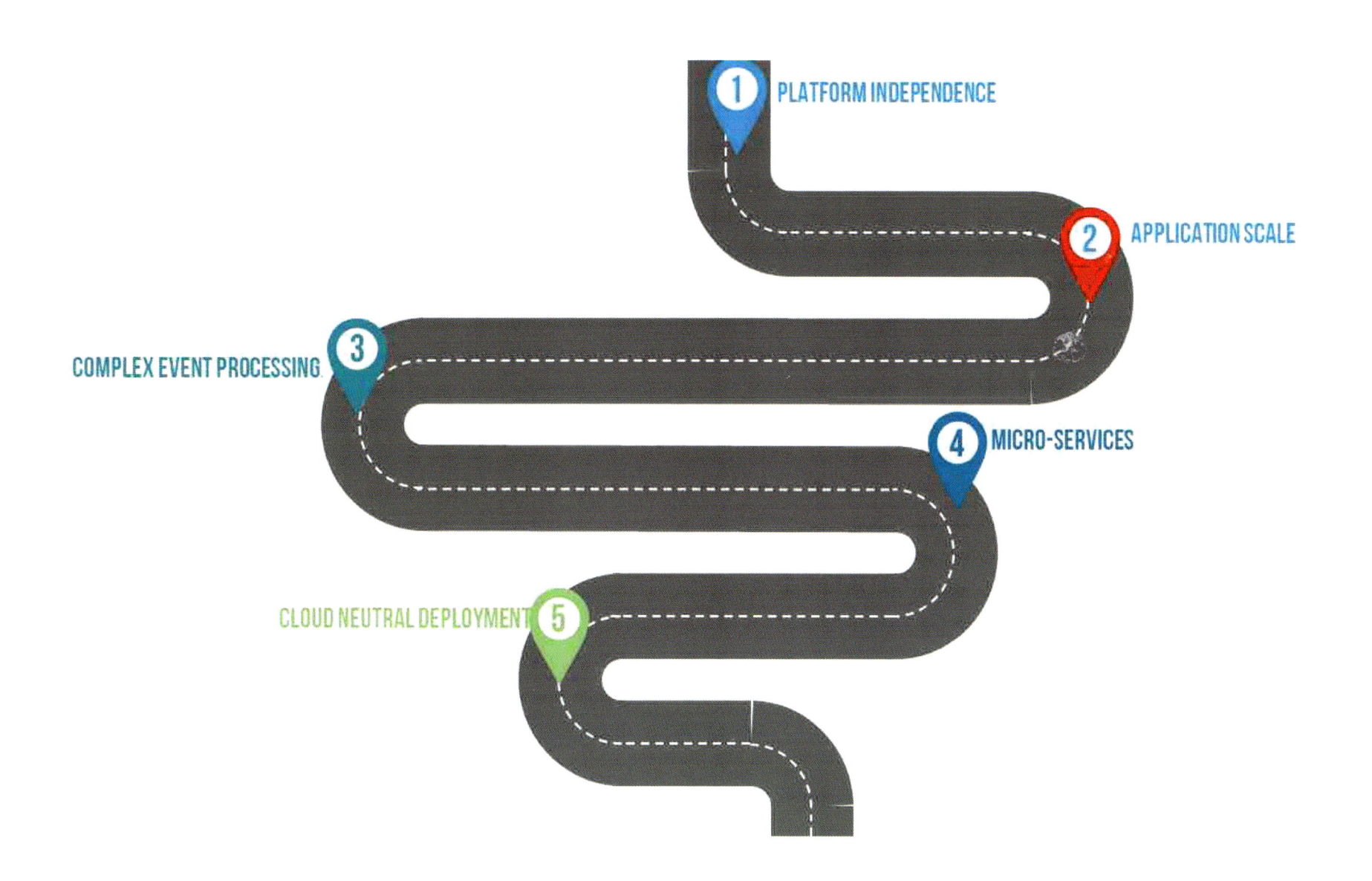

1. PLATFORM INDEPENDENCE
2. APPLICATION SCALE
3. COMPLEX EVENT PROCESSING
4. MICRO-SERVICES
5. CLOUD NEUTRAL DEPLOYMENT

Google App Engine (GAE)

Google App Engine is a **fully managed serverless application platform** for building scalable web applications and mobile and IoT backends. App Engine provides you with built-in services and APIs, such as NoSQL datastores, Memcache, and a user authentication API, common to most applications.

AppEngine enables zero server management and zero-configuration deployments; With AppEngine, developers can focus only on building great applications without the management overhead. App Engine enables developers to stay more productive and agile by supporting popular development languages and a wide range of developer tools.

Following is an excellent example of a reference architecture for a typical mobile app built using both Firebase and App Engine along with other services in Google Cloud Platform.

GAE enables you to build and deploy applications using many of the popular languages like Java, PHP, Node.js, Python, C#,.Net, Ruby and Go or bring your language runtimes and frameworks if you choose. Resources are managed from the command line, debug source code in production and run API backends efficiently using industry-leading tools such as Cloud SDK, Cloud Source Repositories, and other IDEs.

Another excellent example of a reference architecture for building a simple web app using App Engine and Google Cloud Platform:

Figure 41: Mobile app built using both Firebase and App Engine

©2018 Google LLC, used with permission. Google and the Google logo are registered trademarks of Google LLC

Figure 42: Building a simple web app using App Engine

App Engine Limitations

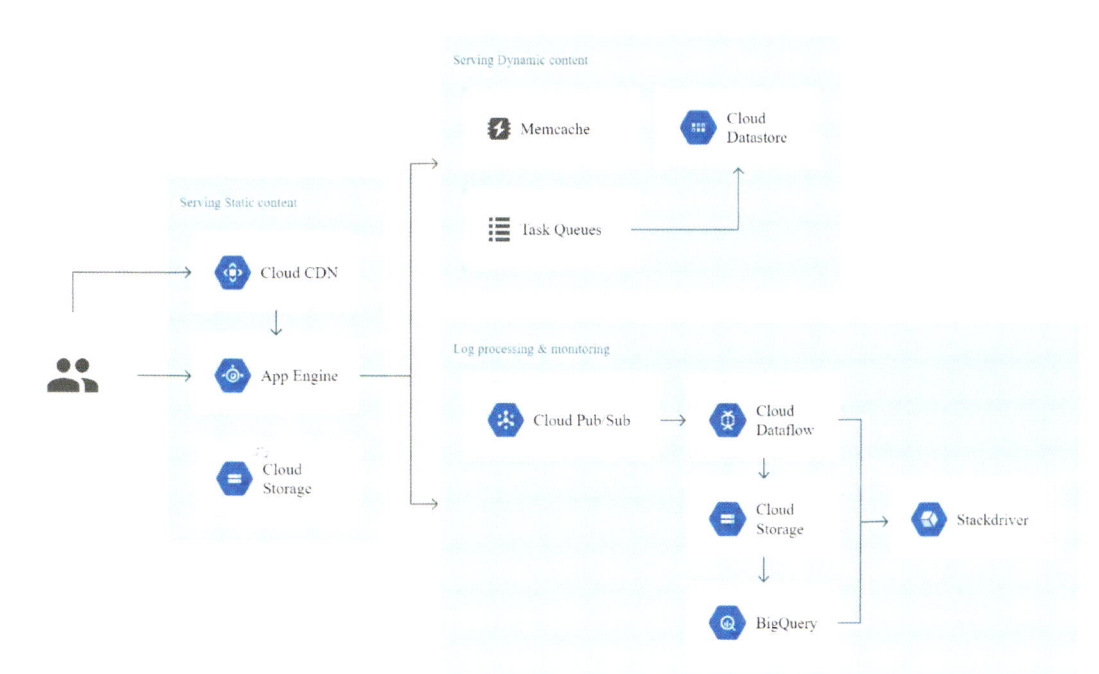

- For apps running in the App Engine standard environment, all database requests must finish within the HTTP request timer, around 60 seconds. For apps running in a flexible environment, all database requests must complete within 60 minutes.
- Offline requests like cron tasks have a time limit of 10 minutes.
- Requests to Cloud SQL have limitations based on the scaling type of the App Engine module and how long an instance can remain in memory (residence).
- Each App Engine instance running in a standard environment cannot have more than 100 concurrent connections to a Cloud SQL instance. For applications written in Java 7, Go 1.6, or PHP 5.5, the limit is 60 concurrent connections.

©2018 Google LLC, used with permission. Google and the Google logo are registered trademarks of Google LLC

App Engine has three kinds of quotas or limits:

- **Free quotas**: Every application gets an amount of each resource for free. Free quotas can only be exceeded by paid applications, up to the application's spending limit or the safety limit, whichever applies first.
- **Spending limits**: If you are the project owner and the billing administrator, you can set the spending limit to manage application costs in the Google Cloud Platform Console in the App Engine Settings. Spending limits might be exceeded slightly as the application is disabled.
- **Safety limits**: Safety limits are set by Google to protect the integrity of the App Engine system. These quotas ensure that no single app can over-consume resources to the detriment of other apps. If you go above these limits, you'll get an error whether you are paid or free.

Daily quotas are replenished daily at midnight Pacific time. Per-minute quotas are refreshed every 60 seconds.

App Engine is a better solution when numerous pieces of functionality are behaving in various inter-related (or even unrelated) ways, while cloud functions are more specifically built and deployed services at the level of a single function that responds to some event and performs some specific action.

For resources that are required to initiate a request, when the resource is depleted, App Engine by default returns an HTTP 403 or 503 error code for the request instead of calling a request handler. The following

resources have this behaviour: Bandwidth, incoming and outgoing, and Instance hours

App Engine could have two types of environments: Flexible and Standard

Open Cloud
Supply your Docker image and bring your software. Deploy it to a container-based system such as Kubernetes on-prem or the public or private cloud

Compute for every workload
Regardless of the amount of data or number of users that your app stores, the app engine can meet your needs by scaling up or down as required

Infrastructure On Demand
Well managed. Integrate easily into your DevOps process, SSH straight into your instances

Move all data to another environment without any difficulty

Route incoming requests to different app versions, A/B test and do incremental feature rollouts

BUILD ONCE, DEPLOY ANY CLOUD — AT SCALE — JUST ADD CODE — PLATFORM INDEPENDENCE — TRAFFIC SPLITTING — VERSIONING

When to choose the flexible environment
- Application instances run within Docker containers on Compute Engine virtual machines (VM).
- Applications that receive consistent traffic, experience regular traffic fluctuations, or meet the parameters for scaling up and down gradually.

When to choose the standard environment
- Application instances run in a sandbox, using the runtime environment of a supported language listed below.
- Applications that need to deal with rapid scaling.

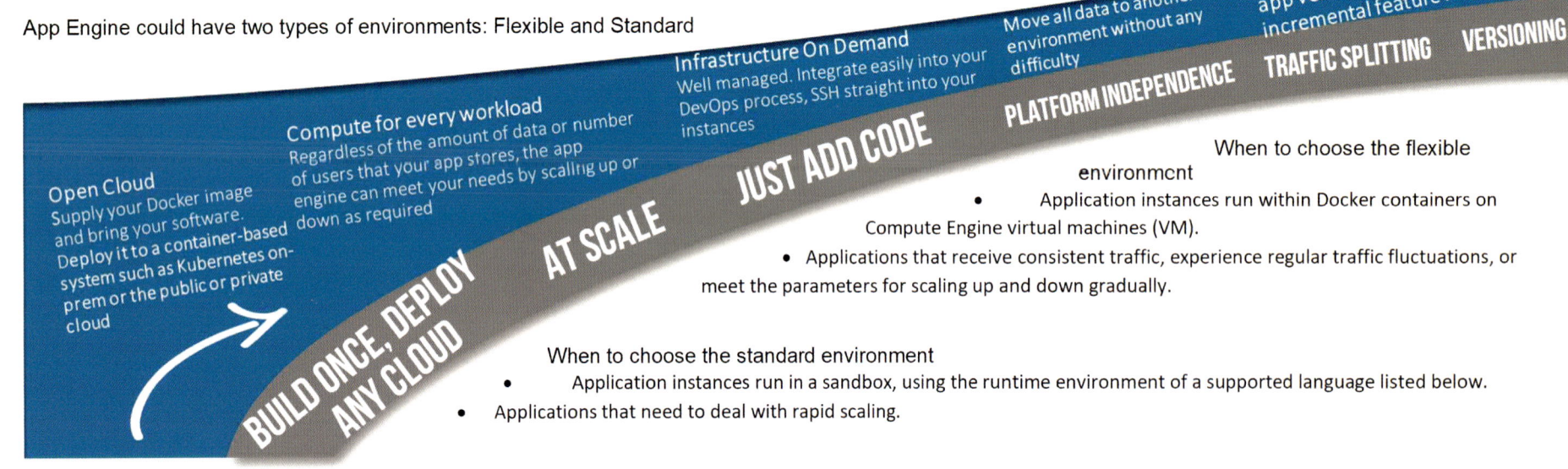

Figure 43: Six Key Considerations when to think about Google App Engine

Microservices and Google App Engine

Microservices refers to an architectural style, inspired by a robust design by contacts philosophy that allows construction of a large application into independent collections of loosely coupled services. Microservices are independently built systems, each running in their process and often communicating with REST API.

An App Engine project can have services and versions. Though mostly isolated, services share some App Engine resources. For example, Cloud Datastore, Memcache, and Task Queues are all shared resources between services in an App Engine project. While this sharing has some advantages, it's essential for a microservices-based application to maintain code- and data-isolation between microservices. There are architecture patterns that help mitigate unwanted sharing.

The following diagram illustrates the hierarchy of an App Engine app running with multiple services. In this diagram, the app has two services that contain multiple versions, and two of those versions are actively running on multiple instances:

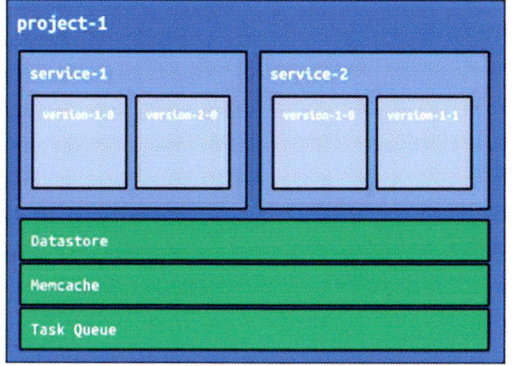

Microservices allows building systems composed of small, independent units of functionality focused on doing one thing well.

Figure 45: App Engine App running with multiple services

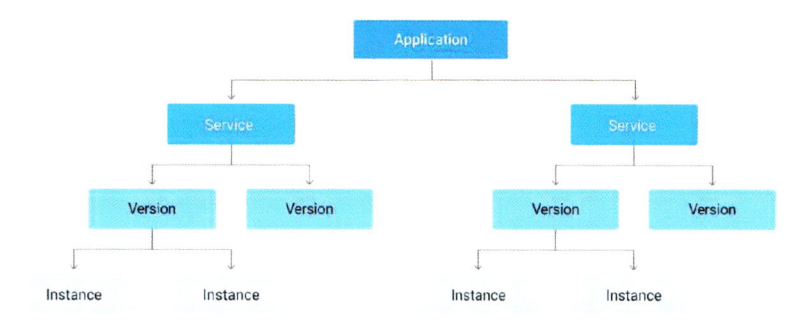

Figure 44: Multi-version Application Hierarchy

A properly implemented microservices-based application can help you to facilitate concurrent, A/B release testing on subsystems and minimise test automation and quality-assurance overhead.

©2018 Google LLC, used with permission. Google and the Google logo are registered trademarks of Google LLC

Google Kubernetes Engine

Kubernetes Engine is a managed, cloud service for deploying containerised applications and enables rapid application development and iteration by making it easy to deploy, update, and manage your applications and services. **Kubernetes Engine could be stateless, but you could also attach persistent storage**, and even run a database in your cluster. GKE allows you to get up and running with Kubernetes in no time, by eliminating the need to install, manage, and operate your Kubernetes clusters. GKE leads in developer productivity, resource efficiency, automated operations, and open source flexibility to accelerate your time to market.

Table 4: Application Scaling

When we configure the compute, memory, and storage resources for our application containers, and GKE provisions and manages the underlying cloud resources automatically. Kubernetes Engine enables us to run Machine Learning, General

Application Scaling
When you deploy an application in GKE, you define how many replicas of the application you'd like to run. When you scale an application, you increase or decrease the number of replicas. Each replica of your application represents a Kubernetes Pod that encapsulates your application's container(s).

Purpose GPU, High-Performance Computing, and other workloads that benefit from specialised hardware accelerators.

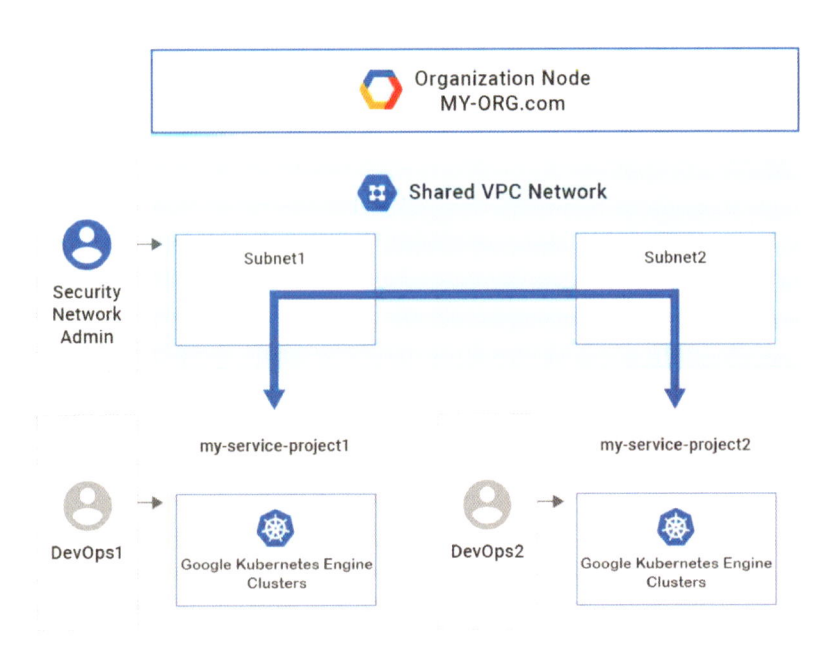

Figure 46: GKE with a Shared Virtual Private Cloud (VPC)

©2018 Google LLC, used with permission. Google and the Google logo are registered trademarks of Google LLC

High availability with Regional Persistent Disks
To make it easier to build highly available solutions, the Kubernetes Engine provides support for the new Regional Persistent Disk (Regional PD).

Reliability GKE improves uptime with Regional Clusters, node auto-repair. Regional clusters also offer a zero-downtime upgrade experience when upgrading Kubernetes Engine masters.

Google Kubernetes Engine Overview | Highly Available with Regional Clusters

Figure 47: Highly Available GKE with Regional Clusters

©2018 Google LLC, used with permission. Google and the Google logo are registered trademarks of Google LLC

Auto-scaling: Horizontal Pod Autoscaling with custom metrics supports three different custom metrics types such as scaling based on Cloud Pub/Sub queue length or scaling based on the average number of open connections per pod and Object such as scaling based on Kafka running in your cluster.

Multi-cloud workload portability

GKE runs Certified Kubernetes ensuring portability across clouds and on-premises.

There's no vendor lock-in: you're free to take your applications out of Kubernetes Engine and run them anywhere Kubernetes is supported, including on your on-premises servers.

Container Registry is a single place for your team to manage Docker images, perform vulnerability analysis, and decide who can access what with fine-grained access control.

GKE Top 5 benefits

1. **Auto Scale** — Automatically scale your application deployment up and down based on resource utilization
2. **Fully Managed** — Kubernetes Engine clusters are fully managed by Google Site Reliability Engineers (SREs), ensuring your cluster is available and up-to-date All phrases can be replaced with your own text.
3. **Auto Upgrade** — Automatically keep your cluster up to date with the latest release version of Kubernetes
4. **Auto Repair** — When auto repair is enabled, if a node fails a health check Kubernetes Engine initiates a repair process for that node
5. **GPU support** — Supports GPU and makes it easy to run ML, GPGPU, HPC, and other workloads

Success with GKE

Kubernetes Engine runs Certified Kubernetes, **enabling workload portability** to other Kubernetes platforms **across clouds and on-premises**.

SECURITY AND COMPLIANCE

PRIVATE CONTAINER REGISTRY

OS Built for Containers
Docker Image Support

Workload Portability, on-premises and cloud

Kubernetes Engine is both **HIPAA and PCI DSS 3.1 compliant**.

Integrating with Google Container Registry makes it easy to store and access your **private Docker images**.

Container-Optimized OS

Container-Optimized OS is an operating system image based on the open source Chromium OS project for your Compute Engine VMs that is optimised for running Docker containers. Container-Optimized OS comes with the Docker container runtime and all Kubernetes components pre-installed for out of the box deployment, management, and orchestration of your containers. **Container-Optimized OS powers many GCP services such as Kubernetes Engine and Cloud SQL**, making it Google's go-to solution for container workloads.
The Container-Optimized OS image pulls the container image from the repository and starts the container when the VM starts, using the docker run command configuration stored in the instance's metadata.

©2018 Google LLC, used with permission. Google and the Google logo are registered trademarks of Google LLC

Figure 48: Steps to create a VM instance or a managed instance group running a container

Use cases for Container-Optimized OS

- You need support for Docker containers or Kubernetes with minimal setup.
- You need an operating system that has a small footprint and is security hardened for containers.
- You need an operating system that is tested and verified for running Kubernetes on your Compute Engine instances.

Container-Optimized OS may not be the right choice for you in the following cases:

- Your application is not containerised, or your containerised application depends on kernel modules, drivers and other additional packages that are not available in Container-Optimized OS.
- You need professional customer support from a Linux provider (Canonical, Core OS, Redhat, SUSE).
- You want your image and OS application to be fully supported outside the Google Cloud Platform.

Limitations
Container-Optimized OS has limited or no support for some of the standard features you may be familiar with on other operating systems:
- Container-Optimized OS does not include a package manager; as such, you'll be unable to install software packages directly on an instance. However, you can use CoreOS toolbox to install and run debugging and admin tools in an isolated container.
- Container-Optimized OS does not support the execution of non-containerized applications.
- The Container-Optimized **OS kernel is locked down**; you'll be unable to install third-party kernel modules or drivers.
- Container-Optimized OS is not supported outside of the Google Cloud Platform environment.
- Container-Optimized OS is the default node OS Image in Kubernetes Engine and other Kubernetes deployments on Google Cloud Platform. Container-Optimized OS could be used to quickly bring up a Docker container on a Compute Engine instance with minimal setup.

Graphics Processing Units (GPU)
You would benefit from GPUs when you require to compute-intensive heavy machine learning, scientific computing, and 3D visualisation. Accelerated Cloud Computing
Scientists, artists, and engineers need access to massively parallel computational power. Google Cloud offers virtual machines with GPUs capable of up to 960 teraflops of performance per instance. Deep learning, physical simulation, and molecular modelling are accelerated with NVIDIA Tesla K80, P4, P100, and V100 GPUs. Regardless of the size of your workload, GCP provides the perfect GPU for your job.

Further Reading

- https://cloud.google.com/appengine/docs/standard/python/microservices-on-app-engine
- https://cloud.google.com/appengine/quotas
- https://cloud.google.com/sql/docs/mysql/quotas
- https://cloud.google.com/appengine/quotas
- https://cloud.google.com/solutions/image-management-best-practices
- https://cloud.google.com/appengine/docs/standard/python/microservices-on-app-engine
- https://cloud.google.com/appengine/
- https://cloud.google.com/kubernetes-engine/docs/concepts/network-overview
- https://cloud.google.com/compute/docs/containers/deploying-containers
- https://cloud.google.com/blog/products/gcp/regional-clusters-in-google-kubernetes-engine-are-now-generally-available

Data is everywhere

Assets are your Data....

Cloud Platform Storage

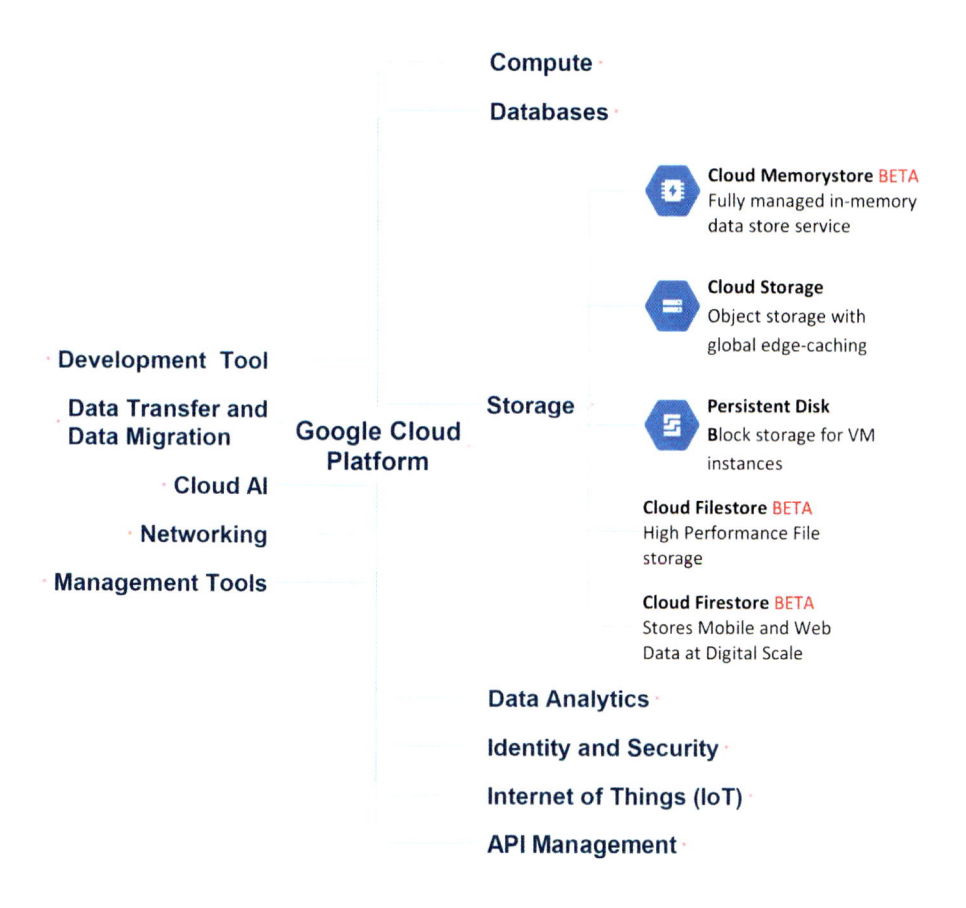

```
                                    Compute
                                    Databases
                                              ┌─ Cloud Memorystore BETA
                                              │  Fully managed in-memory
                                              │  data store service
                                              │
                                              ├─ Cloud Storage
                                              │  Object storage with
                                              │  global edge-caching
  · Development Tool                           │
                                    Storage   ├─ Persistent Disk
  · Data Transfer and   Google Cloud          │  Block storage for VM
    Data Migration      Platform              │  instances
                                              │
  · Cloud AI                                  ├─ Cloud Filestore BETA
                                              │  High Performance File
  · Networking                                │  storage
                                              │
  · Management Tools                          └─ Cloud Firestore BETA
                                                 Stores Mobile and Web
                                                 Data at Digital Scale

                                    Data Analytics
                                    Identity and Security
                                    Internet of Things (IoT)
                                    API Management
```

Figure 49: Cloud Platform Storage

Table 5: Storage Classes

Storage Class	Characteristics	When do you use it?	Deployment / Network	Architectural Considerations / Trade-off
Multi-Regional Storage	• 99.99% typical monthly availability • 99.95% availability SLA* • Geo-redundant	Use when data is frequently accessed ("hot" objects) multi-region, such as serving website content, streaming videos, or gaming and mobile applications.	Multi-Regional Storage can be placed only in multi-regional locations, such as the United States, the European Union, or Asia, not specific regional locations such as us-central1 or asia-east1	• Application Design Time Consideration based on the type of contents. • Geo-redundant stores your data redundantly in at least two geographic places separated by at least 100 miles within the multi-regional location of the bucket
Regional Storage	• 99.99% typical monthly availability • 99.9% availability SLA* • Lower cost per GB stored • Data stored in a narrow geographic region • Redundant across availability zones	Use when data is frequently accessed in the same region for data analytics. Usually considered storing data in the same regional location as Cloud DataProc or Google Compute Engine instances, or Google Kubernetes Engine	Regional Storage can be placed only in regional locations, such as us-central1 or asia-east1	Note the design time considerations. Trade-off: • Better performance for data-intensive computations, as opposed to storing your data in a multi-regional location. • Can reduce network charges.
Nearline Storage	• 99.9% typical monthly availability • 99.0% availability SLA* • Very low cost per GB stored • Data retrieval costs • Higher per-operation costs • 30-day minimum storage duration	Data do not expect to access frequently (i.e., **no more than once per month**).		Ideal for back-up and serving long-tail multimedia content.
Coldline Storage	• 99.9% typical monthly availability • 99.0% availability SLA* • Lowest cost per GB stored • Data retrieval costs • Higher per-operation costs	Data accessed infrequently (i.e., no more than once per year).		• Stored for **legal or regulatory** reasons • Ideally archived data that may be needed near future and **purpose of disaster recovery**. • Remain available for **infrequent viewing by auditors for at least ten years**. Cost optimisation is your top priority

Google Cloud Certified Professional Cloud Architect, Second Edition

- 90-day minimum storage duration

The availability SLA is the monthly uptime percentage backed by the Cloud Storage SLA. If Google fails to meet that uptime, customers are eligible to receive a credit as described in the Cloud Storage SLA.

All storage classes are designed for:
- Creating buckets in locations worldwide.
- It is accessed through the XML API and JSON API, the command-line gsutil tool, the Google Cloud Platform Console, and the client libraries.
- Using the same OAuth and granular access controls to secure your data.
- 99.999999999% annual durability, achieved through erasure coding that stores data pieces redundantly across multiple disks located in different power and network failure domains. Such distributed storage means data survives even in the event of the simultaneous loss of two disks.
- No minimum object size.
- Low latency (time to the first byte is typically tens of milliseconds).
- The same data security through encryption at rest.
- Using with other Cloud Storage features like object versioning, object notification, access logging, lifecycle management, per-object storage classes, and composite objects and parallel uploads.
- Unlimited storage that can be accessed worldwide.

Cloud Storage acts as a distributed storage layer, accessible by apps and services running on App Engine, GKE, or Compute Engine, and through other services such as Logging. Consider the following use cases for storing data.

- Data backup and disaster recovery: Cloud Storage offers highly durable and more secure storage for backing up and archiving your data.
- Content distribution: Cloud Storage enables the storage and delivery of content. For example, storing and delivering media files is scalable.
- Storing ETL data: Cloud Dataflow can access cloud Storage data for transformation and loading into other systems such as Cloud Bigtable or BigQuery.
- Storing data for MapReduce jobs: For Hadoop and Spark jobs, data from Cloud Storage can be natively accessed by using Cloud Dataproc.
- Storing query data: BigQuery can import data from Cloud Storage into datasets and tables, or queries can be federated across existing data without importing. For direct access, BigQuery natively supports importing CSV, JSON, and Avro files from a specified Cloud Storage bucket.
- Seeding machine learning: GCP machine learning APIs, such as the Cloud Vision or the Cloud Natural Language, can access data and files stored directly in Cloud Storage.
- Archiving cold data: Nearline Storage and Coldline Storage offer low latency, lower cost storage for objects that you plan to access less than once per month or less than once per year, respectively.

Points to remember
- In case you have a Standard Storage object in the us multi-regional location, it is treated as a Multi-Regional Storage object and charged accordingly. Please take some extra care when you create these objects.
- Data movement from Standard Storage to other storage classes is entirely possible by **performing a storage transfer** or **using Lifecycle Management**.

- Advised to leverage Regional Storage in place of Durable Reduced Availability (DRA) with an advantage of lower pricing for operations, but otherwise the same price structure.
- Object Lifecycle Management supports setting a Time to Live (TTL) for objects, archiving older versions of objects, or "downgrading" storage classes of objects to help manage costs. An example includes but not limited to downgrade the storage class of objects older than 365 days to Coldline Storage, Delete objects created before any specified date, Keep only the three most recent versions of each object in a bucket with versioning enabled.
- Lifecycle configurations achieved via the Console, gsutil tool, JSON API, or XML API
- Updates to your lifecycle configuration may take up to 24 hours to go into effect. Google doesn't charge for storage after the object expiration time even if the object is not deleted immediately. However, responsibility lies to you for other charges involved (request, network bandwidth).
- It is possible to enable Cloud Pub/Sub Notifications for Cloud Storage for buckets and send notifications to a Cloud Pub/Subtopic of your choice when specified actions occur. However, **this feature does not record who performed the operations**.

Cloud Memorystore
Cloud Memorystore for Redis provides **sub-millisecond data access** with a fully managed in-memory data store service built on scalable, secure, and highly available infrastructure managed by Google.

Persistent Disk
Google Persistent Disk is durable and high-performance **block storage** for the Google Cloud Platform. Persistent Disk provides **SSD and HDD** storage which can be attached to instances running in **either Google Compute Engine or Google Kubernetes Engine**. With **no downtime**, Storage volumes can be transparently resized and backed up. Persistent Disk offers unique multi-reader capability to support simultaneous readers.
SSD offers consistently high performance for both random access workloads and bulk throughput and could be up to 64TB in size.
Persistent Disks are **automatically encrypted** to protect your data.

Cloud Filestore
Cloud Filestore is a managed file storage service for applications that require a filesystem interface and a shared filesystem for data. Filestore gives users a simple, native experience for standing up **managed Network Attached Storage (NAS)** with their **Google Compute Engine** and **Kubernetes Engine** instances. The ability to fine-tune Filestore's performance and capacity independently lead to predictably fast performance for your file-based workloads.

Firestore
Cloud Firestore is a fast, fully managed, serverless, cloud-native NoSQL document database built for automatic scaling, high performance, and ease of application development. It is a best of breed Cloud Datastore and the Firebase Real-time Database. It is the next major version of Cloud Datastore and a rebranding of the product. Cloud Firestore is Firebase's new flagship database for mobile app development.
  a. Cloud Firestore simplifies storing, syncing, and querying data for your mobile, web, and IoT apps **on a global scale**.
  b. It is a strongly consistent storage layer and provides Real-time updates
  c. Cloud Firestore delivers massive improvements for Datastore users — **up to 99.999% availability** SLA, **no more eventual consistency**, no more entity group limits on writes per second, and no more cross-entity group transaction limits.
  d. Could access Cloud Firestore directly from your mobile or web-based applications in a true serverless fashion

Here are a couple of use cases for Cloud Firestore.
- **Chat and social**: To store and retrieve images, audio, video, and other user-generated content.
- **Mobile games**: To track of game progress and statistics across devices and device platforms.

It is highly recommended to read the article in https://cloud.google.com/datastore/docs/firestore-or-datastore
https://firebase.google.com/docs/firestore/rtdb-vs-firestore

Cloud Platform Storage – Architectural Usage Scenario

Cloud Storage has multiple uses in your Google Cloud Platform Architecture. Cloud Storage is one of the critical components, would be part of your architecture, in almost all the architecture. Cloud Storage improves the reliability of your data architecture and minimises data transfer time. You could directly transfer your files in a different Google Cloud Regional Storage bucket location across the geography using Google APIs over HTTP(S) and leverage the data pipeline or ETL process to retrieve the data from each Regional bucket. Cloud Storage best practices are one of the **must read** and could be found here https://cloud.google.com/storage/docs/best-practices.

A few key points are worth highlighting:
- ✓ **Avoid using sequential filenames** such as **timestamp-based filenames** if you are uploading many files in parallel. Because files with sequential names are stored consecutively, they are likely to hit the same backend server, meaning that **throughput will be constrained**. To achieve optimal throughput, you can add the hash of the sequence number as part of the filename to make it non-sequential.
- ✓ Always use TLS (HTTPS) to transport your data to ensures that your credentials, as well as your data, are protected as you transport data over the network.
- ✓ Make it a practice to ensure that authentication credentials are revoked that when applications no longer need access to your data.
- ✓ Make sure that you securely store your credentials.
- ✓ Bucket and object ACLs are independent of each other, which means that the ACLs on a bucket does not affect the ACLs on objects inside that bucket. It is possible for a user without permissions for a bucket to have permissions for an object inside the bucket. For example, you can create a bucket such that only GroupA is granted permission to list the objects in the bucket, but then upload an object into that bucket that allows GroupB READ access to the object. GroupB will be able to read the object, but will not be able to view the contents of the bucket or perform bucket-related tasks.
- ✓ If you need to make content available securely to users who don't have Google accounts we recommend you use signed URLs.

Putting the puzzle together – Data Ingest and Data Storage

Architecture: General > Data Ingest

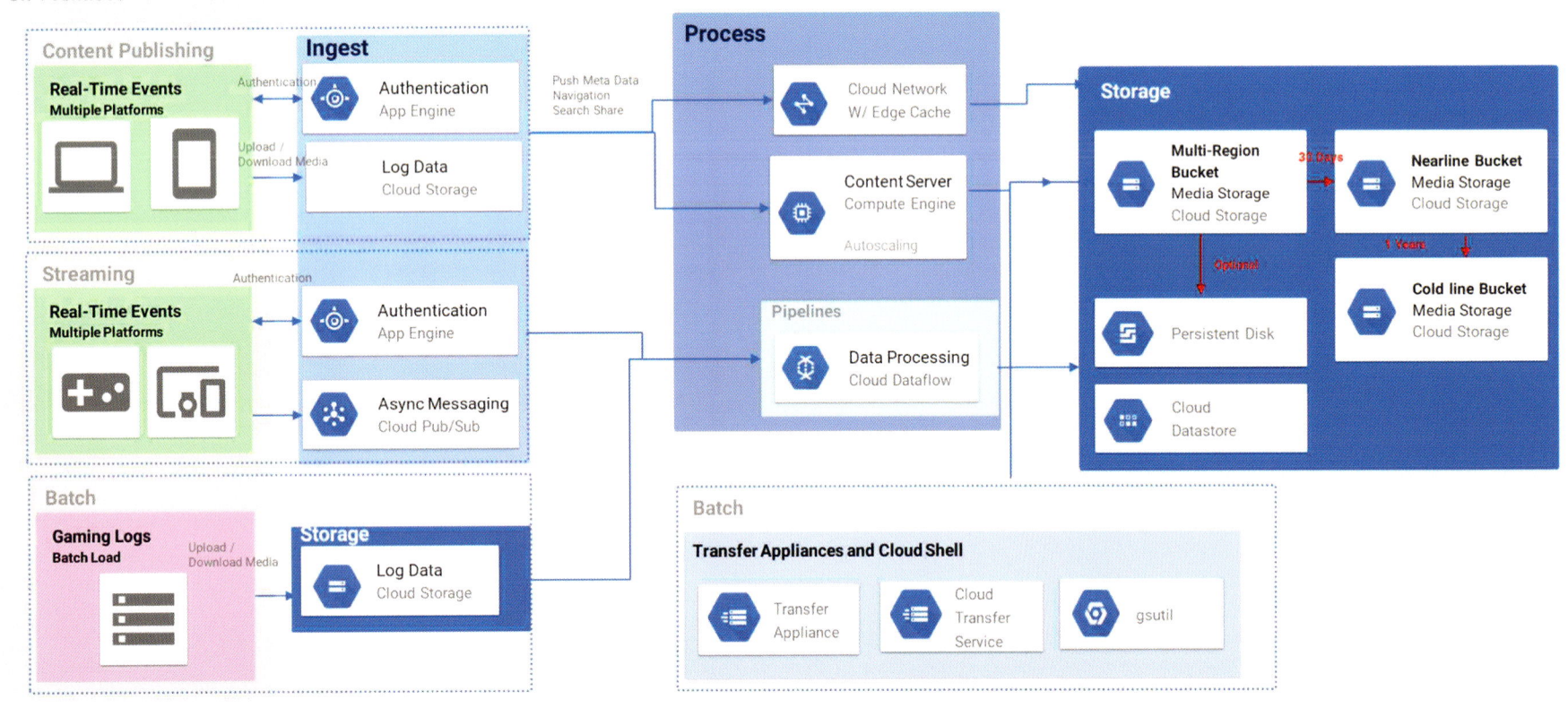

Figure 50: Data Ingest and Storage

An example is showing various components together firming a Data Ingest (both Batch and Stream) and Processing the same to destine to appropriate Cloud Storages.
A great way to build a Data Pipeline and Lambda Architecture within Google Cloud. We will discuss the Service / Consume part separately in our Analytics and other relevant sections.

Google Cloud Storage is widely used for ClickStream Data processing too (https://zulily-tech.com/2015/08/10/leveraging-google-cloud-dataflow-for-clickstream-processing/). Retaining data as a long-term disaster recovery backup is another excellent use case for GCS. Google Cloud Storage best practices are one of the **must read** and could be found here https://cloud.google.com/storage/docs/best-practices. A few key points are worth highlighting:

- ✓ **Avoid using sequential filenames** such as **timestamp-based filenames** if you are uploading many files in parallel. Because files with sequential names are stored consecutively, they are likely to hit the same backend server, meaning that **throughput will be constrained**. To achieve optimal throughput, you can add the hash of the sequence number as part of the filename to make it non-sequential.
- ✓ Always use TLS (HTTPS) to transport your data to ensures that your credentials, as well as your data, are protected as you transport data over the network.
- ✓ Make it a practice to ensure that authentication credentials are revoked that when applications no longer need access to your data.
- ✓ Make sure that you securely store your credentials.
- ✓ Bucket and object ACLs are independent of each other, which means that the ACLs on a bucket does not affect the ACLs on objects inside that bucket. It is possible for a user without permissions for a bucket to have permissions for an object inside the bucket. For example, you can create a bucket such that only GroupA is granted permission to list the objects in the bucket, but then upload an object into that bucket that allows GroupB READ access to the object. GroupB will be able to read the object, but will not be able to view the contents of the bucket or perform bucket-related tasks.
- ✓ If you need to make content available securely to users who don't have Google accounts we recommend you use signed URLs.
- ✓ **Tips:** Please remember, when local read/write is involved, the persistent disk would be fine but global access of data, the variable would require Cloud Storage.
- ✓ **Tips:** When the design would require compliance, your original thinking should be around the keeping track of a lineage of the transaction, an audit in the form of logs, trends and would involve storages and further analysis of the data.

Data Transfer and Data Migration

gsutil

Google BigQuery Data Transfer Service
Fully managed data import service for Google BigQuery

Cloud Storage Transfer Service
Transfer data between cloud storage services such as AWS S3 and Google Cloud Storage

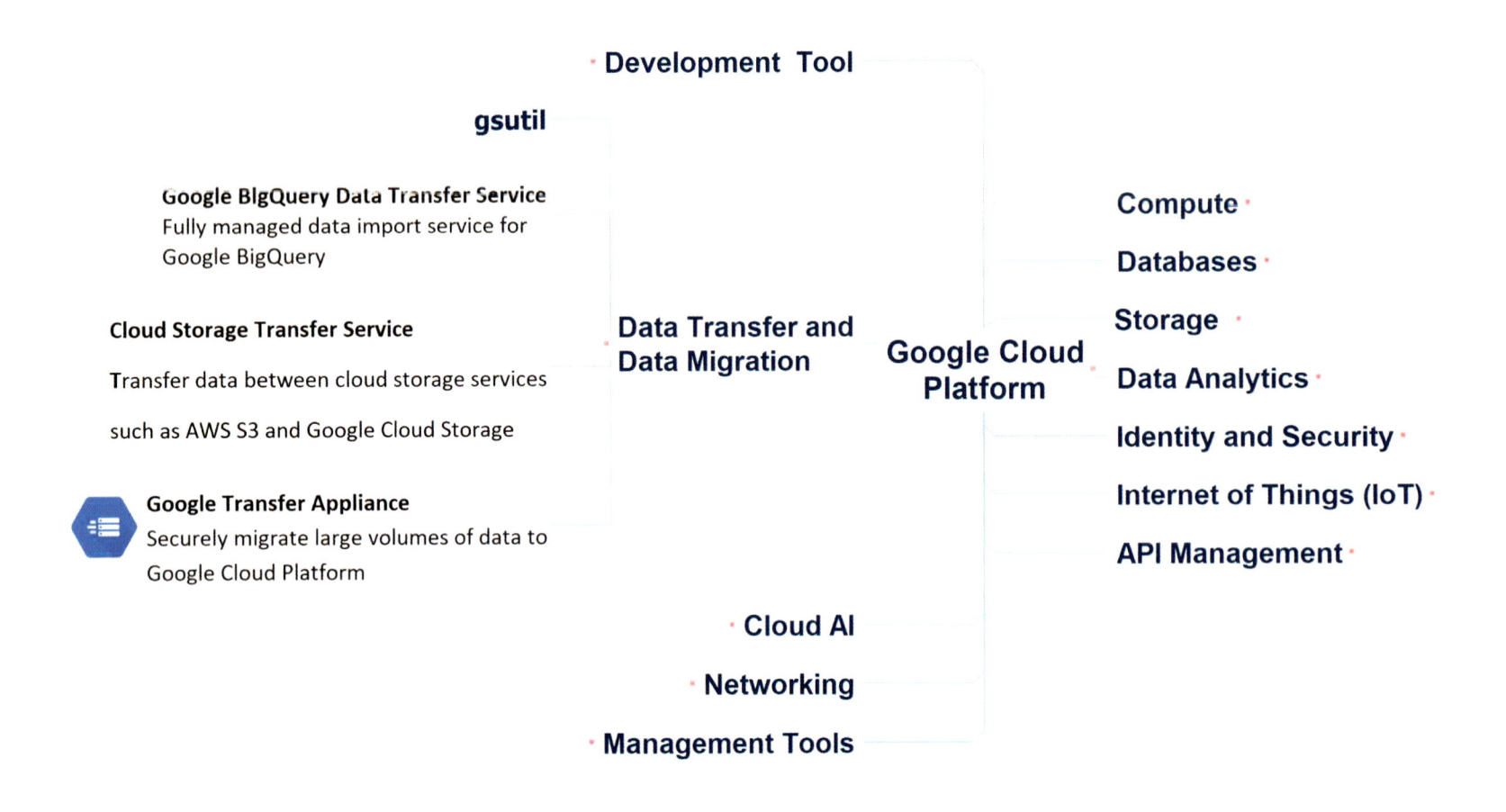

Google Transfer Appliance
Securely migrate large volumes of data to Google Cloud Platform

- Development Tool
- Data Transfer and Data Migration
- Cloud AI
- Networking
- Management Tools

Google Cloud Platform
- Compute
- Databases
- Storage
- Data Analytics
- Identity and Security
- Internet of Things (IoT)
- API Management

Figure 51: Data Transfer and Data Migration Tools

Google Cloud Certified Professional Cloud Architect, Second Edition

Cloud Storage Transfer Service

Storage Transfer Service enables transferring data from an online data source (Amazon Simple Storage Service (Amazon S3) bucket, an HTTP/HTTPS location, or a Cloud Storage bucket) to a data sink (always a Cloud Storage bucket).
Some other good usage of Storage Transfer Service to:
- Back up data to a Cloud Storage bucket from other storage providers.
- Move data from a Multi-Regional Storage bucket to a Nearline Storage bucket to lower your storage costs.
- Schedule one-time transfer operations or recurring transfer operations.
- Schedule periodic synchronisation from a data source to data sink with advanced filters based on file creation dates, file-name filters, and the times of day you prefer to import data.
- Follow these rules of thumb when deciding whether to use gsutil or Storage Transfer Service:
    - ✓ When transferring data from an on-premises location, use gsutil.
    - ✓ When transferring data from another cloud storage provider, use Storage Transfer Service.

Storage Transfer Service supports one-time transfers or recurring transfers. It provides advanced filters based on file creation dates, filename filters, and the times of day you prefer to import data. It also supports the deletion of the source data after it's been copied.

Transfer Appliance
Transfer Appliance is a rackable high capacity storage server that you set up in your datacentre and could be used to ship data (Choose from 100TB or 480TB's of raw capacity per appliance) to an ingest location where the data is uploaded to Google Cloud Storage. Transfer Appliance helps in collecting significant amounts of **geographic, environmental medical or financial data** for analysis. Once **transferred to Google Cloud Storage or BigQuery,** data is accessible via our **Google Cloud Dataflow** processing service and **Cloud Machine Learning Engine**.

To determine when to use Transfer Appliance, calculate the amount of time needed to upload your data by using a network connection. If you discover that it would take a week or more, or if you have more than 60 TB of data (regardless of transfer speed), it might be more reliable and expedient to transfer your data by using the Transfer Appliance.

Transfer Appliance deduplicates, compresses, and encrypts your captured data with strong AES-256 encryption using a password and passphrase that you provide. When you read your data from Cloud Storage, you specify the same password and passphrase. After every use of Transfer Appliance, the appliance is securely wiped and re-imaged to help prevent your data from being available to the next user.

Must Read Reference: https://cloud.google.com/solutions/transferring-big-data-sets-to-gcp

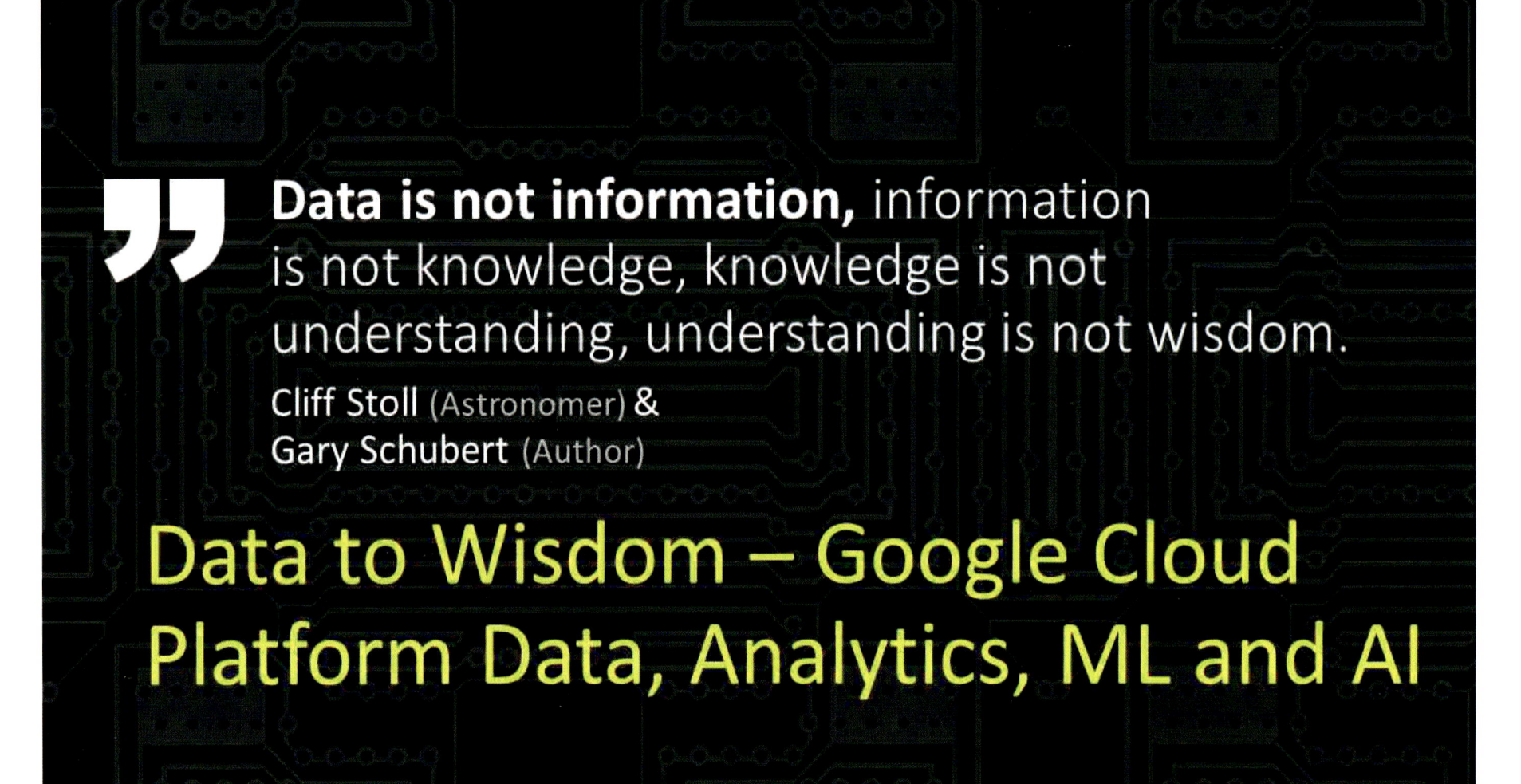

> **Data is not information,** information is not knowledge, knowledge is not understanding, understanding is not wisdom.
>
> Cliff Stoll (Astronomer) &
> Gary Schubert (Author)

Data to Wisdom – Google Cloud Platform Data, Analytics, ML and AI

Cloud Databases

Compute

- **Cloud Memorystore** BETA
  Fully managed in-memory data store service
- **Cloud SQL**
  Fully-managed MySQL and PostgreSQL database service
- **Cloud Bigtable**
  Fully managed NoSQL database service

Databases

- **Cloud Datastore**
  NoSQL database for non-relational data
- **Cloud Spanner**
  Mission-critical, relational database service
- **Cloud Firestore** BETA
  Stores Mobile and Web Data at Digital Scale
- **Firebase Realtime**
  Database Store and Sync Data at Realtime

Development Tool
Data Transfer and Data Migration
Cloud AI
Networking
Management Tools

Google Cloud Platform

Storage
Data Analytics
Identity and Security
Internet of Things (IoT)
API Management

Google Cloud Platform includes object storage for different needs and price points, block storage for your VMs, file storage for applications that need a shared filesystem, as well as managed MySQL and globally scalable NoSQL databases.

We have already discussed Cloud Storage, Cloud MemoryStore, DataStore and Cloud Firestore in section Cloud Platform Storage.

GCP has several target databases suitable for migrating data from external databases.

- **Relational databases**: Data stored in a relational database management system (RDBMS) can be migrated to Cloud SQL and Cloud Spanner.

- **Data warehouses**: Data stored in a data warehouse can be moved to BigQuery.

- **NoSQL databases**: Data stored in a column-oriented NoSQL database, such as HBase or Cassandra, can be migrated to Cloud Bigtable. Data stored in a JSON-oriented NoSQL database, such as Couchbase or MongoDB, can be migrated to Cloud Datastore.

In this section, we would introduce BigQuery, Big Table, Cloud SQL, and Cloud Spanner.

Google Cloud Certified Professional Cloud Architect, Second Edition

Google BigQuery

BigQuery is built on **Dremel** technology and Google's flagship **serverless, highly scalable, enterprise data warehouse** designed to provide your data organisation with unparallel productivity at an unmatched price-performance. Because there is no infrastructure to manage, you can focus on analysing data to find meaningful insights using familiar SQL without the need for a database administrator. BigQuery is **columnar storage**. BigQuery allows organisations to capture and analyse data in real time using its powerful streaming ingestion capability so that your insights are always current, and it's free for up to 1 TB of data analysed each month and 10 GB of data stored. **Build and operationalise machine learning solutions with simple SQL**. BigQuery's managed columnar storage, massively parallel execution, and automatic performance optimisations make it possible for all your users to quickly and simultaneously analyse data regardless of the number of users or the size of the data.

BigQuery supports favourite BI tools like Tableau, MicroStrategy, Looker, and Data Studio out of the box, so anyone can easily create stunning reports and dashboards.

BigQuery eliminates the data operations burden by providing automatic data replication for disaster recovery and high availability of processing for no additional charge. BigQuery offers a 99.9% SLA and adheres to the Privacy Shield Principles. BigQuery makes it easy to maintain strong security with fine-grained identity and access-management control. BigQuery data is always encrypted, at rest and in transit.

BigQuery ML [BETA] enables data scientists and data analysts to build and operationalise ML models on planet-scale structured or semi-structured data, directly inside BigQuery, using simple SQL — in a fraction of the time.

Table 6: MapReduce vs Dremel

Mapreduce vs Dremel
Google has been using MapReduce for Big Data processing and its open source implementation, we all are familiar with – Hadoop. However, Google moved on from MapReduce to Dremel and BigQuery is the Enterprise level Externalization of Dremel. Why Dremel? • Dremel is designed as an interactive data analysis tool for large datasets. It finishes queries with billions of rows in seconds, and can even be used by non-programmers.   • MapReduce is designed as a programming framework to batch process large datasets. Map Reduce is significantly slower that takes at least minutes, and sometimes even hours or days) and requires programmers to be involved.

BigQuery requests are served by the **Dremel query engine**, which orchestrates your query by breaking it up into pieces and reassembling the results. The first thing that Dremel does, it turns your SQL query into an execution tree. The leaves of the tree it calls 'slots', and do the heavy lifting of reading the data from Colossus and doing any computation necessary. The branches of the tree are 'mixers', which perform the aggregation. In between is 'shuffle', which takes advantage of Google's Jupiter network to move data extremely rapidly from one place to another. The mixers and slots are all run by Borg, which doles out hardware resources.

Dremel dynamically apportions slots to queries on an as needed basis, maintaining fairness amongst multiple users who are all querying at once. A single user can get thousands of slots to run their queries. BigQuery relies on Colossus, Google's latest generation distributed file system. Each Google data centre has its Colossus cluster, and each Colossus cluster has enough disks to give every BigQuery user thousands of dedicated disks at a time. Colossus also handles replication, recovery (when disks crash) and distributed management (so there is no single point of failure). Colossus is fast enough to allow BigQuery to provide similar performance to many in-memory databases, but leveraging much cheaper yet highly parallelised, scalable, durable and performant infrastructure that gives you thousands of CPU cores dedicated to processing your task, BigQuery takes advantage of Borg, Google's large-scale cluster management system. Borg clusters run on dozens of thousands of machines and hundreds of thousands of cores, so your query which used 3300 CPUs only used a fraction of the capacity reserved for BigQuery, and BigQuery's capacity is only a fraction of the capacity of a Borg cluster. Borg assigns server resources to jobs; the job, in this case, is the Dremel cluster. Google's Jupiter network can deliver 1 Petabit/sec of total bisection bandwidth, allowing us to efficiently and quickly distribute large workloads. BigQuery architecture separates the concepts of **storage (Colossus)** and **compute (Borg)** and <u>will enable them to scale independently - an essential requirement for an elastic data warehouse</u>. This way, it empowers your analytics queries at a speed and fraction of the cost of other competitors.

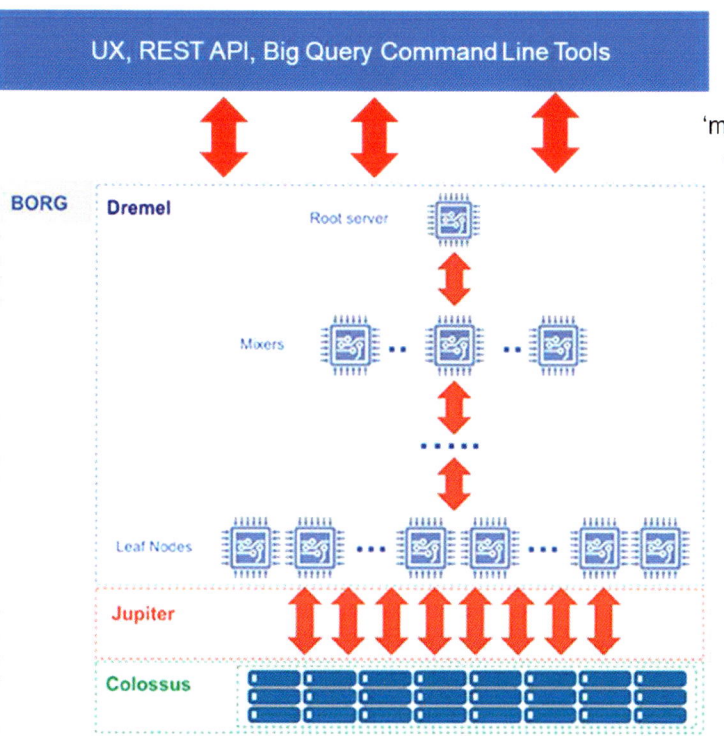

Figure 53: BigQuery Components
©2018 Google LLC, used with permission. Google and the Google logo are registered trademarks of Google LLC

Federated Query and Logical Data Warehousing
BigQuery breaks down data silos so you can analyse all your data assets from one place. Through powerful federated query, BigQuery can process data in object storage (Cloud Storage), transactional databases (Cloud Bigtable), or spreadsheets in Google Drive — all without duplicating data. One tool lets you query all your data sources.

Data Locality
You have the option to store your BigQuery data in the US, Japan, and European locations while continuing to benefit from a fully managed service. BigQuery gives you the opportunity of geographic data control, without the headaches of setting up and managing clusters and other computing resources in-region.

Foundation for AI
BigQuery provides a flexible, robust foundation for machine learning and artificial intelligence. Besides bringing ML to your data with BigQuery ML, integrations with Cloud ML Engine and TensorFlow enable you to train powerful models on structured data. Moreover, BigQuery's ability to transform and analyse data helps you get your data in shape for machine learning.

Google Cloud Certified Professional Cloud Architect, Second Edition

Geospatial Datatypes and Functions
BigQuery GIS BETA brings SQL support for the most commonly used GIS functions right into your data warehouse. With support for arbitrary points, lines, polygons, and multi-polygons in WKT and GeoJSON format, you can simplify your geospatial analyses, see your location-based data in new ways, or unlock entirely new lines of business with the power of BigQuery.

BigQuery - Programmatic Interaction
BigQuery provides a REST API for easy programmatic access and application integration. To enable programmers of all types, BigQuery offers client libraries in Java, Python, Node.js, C#, Go, Ruby, and PHP. Business users can use the Google Apps Script to access BigQuery from Google Sheets.

Streaming data producers send the data for streaming directly into BigQuery or via Dataflow to ETL data into BigQuery in batch or streams. Typically this could be custom code or by Google Cloud services such as Google Cloud Dataflow or Cloud Logging.

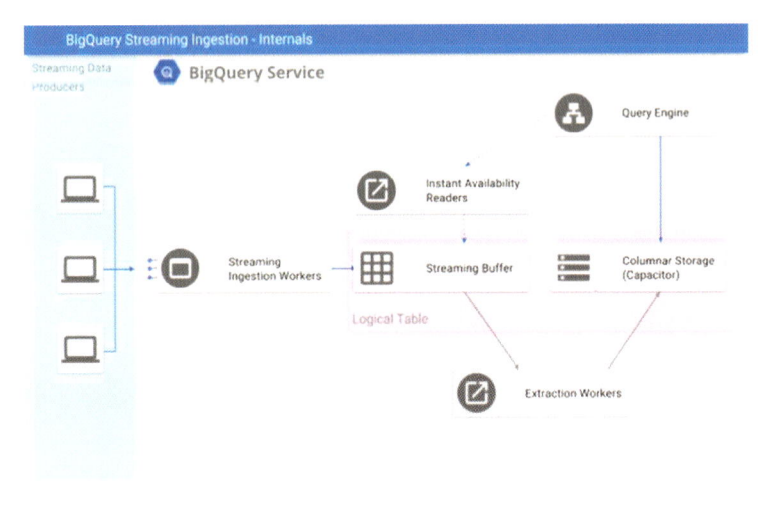

Figure 54: BigQuery Streaming Ingestion

©2018 Google LLC, used with permission. Google and the Google logo are registered trademarks of Google LLC

Figure 55: Dataflow to ETL data into BigQuery

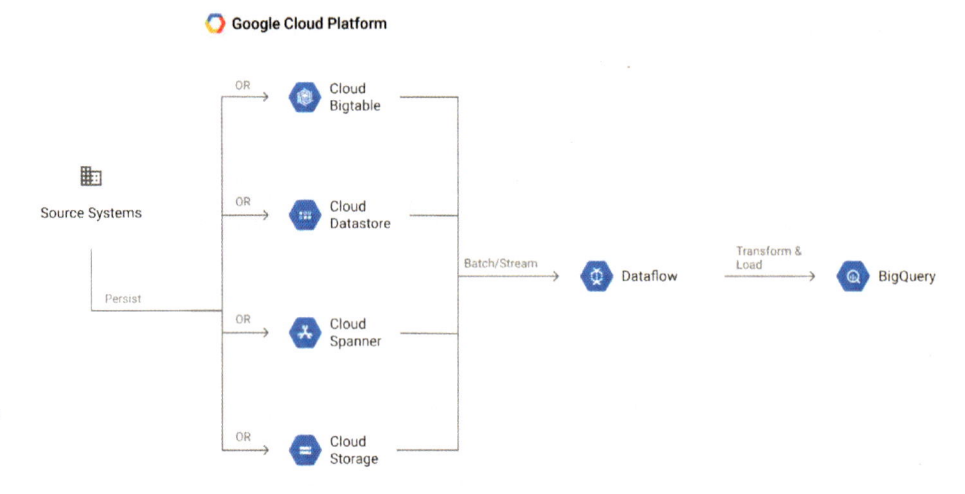

©2018 Google LLC, used with permission. Google and the Google logo are registered trademarks of Google LLC

Cloud native Data Warehouse using BigQuery

Modernising the existing data warehouses and building a cloud-native data warehouse or migrating an on-premises data warehouse to Google Cloud Platform (GCP) is a widespread use case across the industry. This would involve developing an end-to-end data ingestion ETL pipeline solutions that would automate the tasks of extracting data from operational databases, making fundamental transformations to data, loading data records into Google BigQuery staging tables and initiating aggregation calculations. The components of this architecture include:

- A task orchestrator built using Google App Engine Cron Service, Google Cloud Pub/Sub control topic and Google Cloud Dataflow in streaming mode
- Cloud Dataflow for importing bounded (batch) raw data from sources such as relational Google Cloud SQL databases (MySQL or PostgreSQL, via the JDBC connector) and files in Google Cloud Storage
- Cloud Dataflow for importing unbounded (streaming) raw data from a Google Cloud Pub/Sub data ingestion topic
- BigQuery for storing staging and final datasets
- Additional ETL transformations enabled via Cloud Dataflow and embedded SQL statements
- An interactive dashboard implemented via Google Sheets and connected to BigQuery

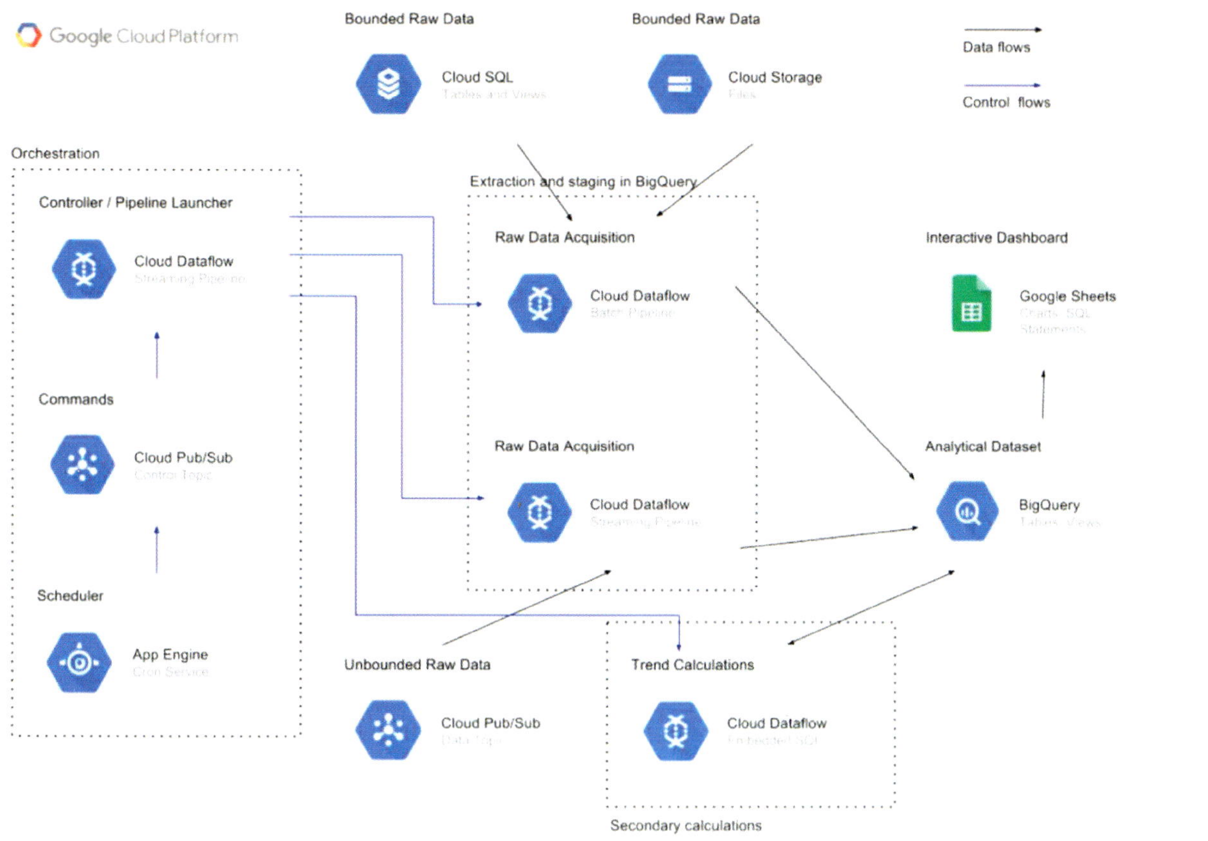

All these components are examples of fully-managed services on GCP; with this architecture, there's no infrastructure for you to deploy, manage, secure or scale and you only pay for what you use.

Optimising Large-Scale Ingestion of Analytics Events and Logs

Any architecture for ingestion of significant quantities of analytics data should take into account which data you need to access in near real-time and which you can handle after a short delay, and split them appropriately. A segmented approach has these benefits:

- Log integrity. You can see complete logs. No logs

Figure 56: An example ETL architecture for cloud-native data warehousing on GCP

©2018 Google LLC, used with permission. Google and the Google logo are registered trademarks of Google LLC

are lost due to streaming quota limits or sampling.

- Cost reduction. Streaming inserts of events and logs are billed at a higher rate than those inserted from Cloud Storage using batch jobs.
- Reserved query resources. Moving lower-priority logs to batch loading keeps them from having an impact on reserved query resources.

The following architecture diagram shows such a system, and introduces the concepts of hot paths and cold paths for ingestion:

Analytics events could get published to a Cloud Pub/Subtopic and Logs could be collected using Stackdriver Logging.
After ingestion from either source, based on the latency requirements of the message, data is put either into the hot path or the cold path. The **hot path uses streaming input**, which can handle a continuous dataflow, while the **cold path is a batch process**, loading the data on a schedule you determine. In this example diagram, red lines indicate a hot path and blue is the cold path.

Figure 57: Hot and Cold Path Ingestion

©2018 Google LLC, used with permission. Google and the Google logo are registered trademarks of Google LLC

In summary, BigQuery could be used in a variety of ways.

- **User analysis**: Ingest large amounts of user-generated activity (adtech, clickstream, game telemetry) and determine user behaviour and characteristics.
- **Device and operational metrics**: Collect streaming information from IT systems, IoT devices, and so on. Moreover, analyse data for trends and variations.
- **Business intelligence**: Store business metrics as a data warehouse, and drive a BI tool or partner offerings, such as Tableau, QlikView, or Looker.

Further Reading

Big Query Under the hood - https://cloud.google.com/blog/products/gcp/bigquery-under-the-hood
12 Components of Google Big Query: https://medium.com/google-cloud/the-12-components-of-google-bigquery-c2b49829a7c7
https://cloud.google.com/storage-options/
https://panoply.io/data-warehouse-guide/bigquery-architecture/
https://cloud.google.com/blog/products/gcp/life-of-a-bigquery-streaming-insert
https://cloud.google.com/solutions/architecture/optimized-large-scale-analytics-ingestion
An Inside Look at Google BigQuery: https://cloud.google.com/files/BigQueryTechnicalWP.pdf
https://cloud.google.com/bigquery/streaming-data-into-bigquery
https://cloud.google.com/solutions/bigquery-data-warehouse
https://cloud.google.com/blog/products/gcp/designing-etl-architecture-for-a-cloud-native-data-warehouse-on-google-cloud-platform
https://cloud.google.com/solutions/architecture/optimized-large-scale-analytics-ingestion
https://cloud.google.com/solutions/architecture/complex-event-processing

Cloud Bigtable

Google Bigtable is a petabyte-scale, Low latency, massively scalable, fully managed NoSQL database service for large analytical and operational workloads. Bigtable is a sparsely populated table that can scale to billions of rows and thousands of columns, enabling you to store terabytes or even petabytes of data. A single value in each row is indexed; this value is known as the row key. Cloud Bigtable is ideal for storing enormous amounts of single-keyed data with very low latency. Cloud Bigtable is perfect for applications that need very high throughput and scalability for non-structured key/value data, where each value is typically no larger than 10 MB. Cloud Bigtable also excels as a storage engine for batch MapReduce operations, stream processing/analytics, and machine-learning applications. Bigtable provides consistent sub-10ms latency. Bigtable is highly available, durable, and resilient in the face of zonal failures.

Cloud Bigtable is useful for storing and querying all of the following types of data:
- **Time-series data**, such as CPU and memory usage over time for multiple servers.
- Marketing data, such as purchase histories and customer preferences.
- Financial data, such as transaction histories, stock prices, and currency exchange rates.
- IoT data, such as usage reports from energy meters and home appliances.
- Graph data, such as information about how users are connected.

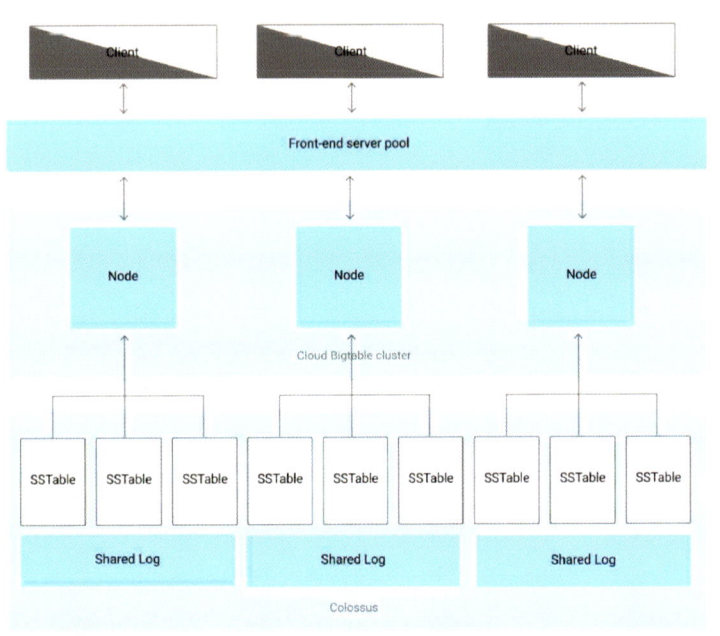

Figure 58: Simplified view of Bigtable internal architecture. An instance with a single cluster

©2018 Google LLC, used with permission. Google and the Google logo are registered trademarks of Google LLC

In Bigtable, all client requests go through a front-end server before they are sent to a Cloud Bigtable node. The nodes are organised into a Cloud Bigtable cluster, which belongs to a Cloud Bigtable instance, a container for the cluster.

Each node in the cluster handles a subset of the requests to the cluster. By adding nodes to a cluster, you can increase the number of simultaneous requests that the cluster can handle, as well as the maximum throughput for the entire cluster. If you enable replication by adding a second cluster, you can also send different types of traffic to different clusters, and you can fail over to one cluster if the other cluster becomes unavailable.

A Cloud Bigtable table is sharded into blocks of contiguous rows, called tablets, to help balance the workload of queries. Tablets are stored on Colossus, Google's file system, in SSTable format. An SSTable provides a persistent, ordered immutable map from keys to values, where both keys and values are arbitrary byte strings. Each tablet is associated with a specific Cloud Bigtable node. In addition to the SSTable files, all writes are stored in Colossus's shared log as soon as they are acknowledged by Cloud Bigtable, providing increased durability.

Please remember, data is never stored in Cloud Bigtable nodes themselves; each node has pointers to a set of tablets that are stored on Colossus.
Cloud Bigtable is not a relational database; it does not support SQL queries or joins, nor does it support multi-row transactions. Also, it is not a good solution for storing less than 1 TB of data.
- If you need full SQL support for an online transaction processing (OLTP) system, consider Cloud Spanner or Cloud SQL.
- If you need interactive querying in online analytical processing (OLAP) system, consider BigQuery.
- If you need to store immutable blobs larger than 10 MB, such as large images or movies, consider Cloud Storage.
- If you need to store highly structured objects in a document database, with support for ACID transactions and SQL-like queries, consider Cloud Datastore.

A Cloud Bigtable instance is mostly just a container for your clusters and nodes, which do all of the real work. Tables belong to instances, not to clusters or nodes. So if you have an instance with 2 clusters, you can't assign tables to individual clusters or create individual garbage-collection policies for each cluster. You also can't make each cluster store a different set of data in the same table. An instance has a few essential properties that you need to know about:
- The instance type (production or development)
- The storage type (SSD or HDD)
- The application profiles, for instances that use replication

When you create a Cloud Bigtable instance, you choose whether its clusters store data on solid-state drives (SSD) or hard disk drives (HDD):
- SSD storage is the most efficient and cost-effective choice for most use cases.
- HDD storage is sometimes appropriate for extensive datasets (>10 TB) that are not latency-sensitive or are infrequently accessed.
- Regardless of which type of storage you choose, your data is stored on a distributed, replicated file system that spans across many physical drives.

Cloud Bigtable is well suited for a variety of large-scale, high-throughput workloads such as advertising technology or IoT data infrastructure.
- **Real-time app data**: Cloud Bigtable can be accessed from apps running in App Engine flexible environment, GKE, and Compute Engine for real-time live-serving workloads.
- **Stream processing**: As Cloud Pub/Sub ingests data, Cloud Dataflow can be used to transform and load the data into Cloud Bigtable.
- **IoT time series data**: Data captured by sensors and streamed into GCP can be stored using time-series schemas in Cloud Bigtable.
- **Adtech workloads**: Cloud Bigtable can be used to store and track ad impressions, as well as a source for follow-on processing and analysis using Cloud Dataproc and Cloud Dataflow.
- **Data ingestion**: Cloud Dataflow or Cloud Dataproc can be used to transform and load data from Cloud Storage into Cloud Bigtable.
- **Analytical workloads**: Cloud Dataflow can be used to perform complex aggregations directly from data stored in Cloud Bigtable, and Cloud Dataproc can be used to execute Hadoop or Spark processing and machine-learning tasks.
- **Apache HBase replacement**: Cloud Bigtable can also be used as a drop-in replacement for systems built using Apache HBase, an open source database based on the original Cloud Bigtable paper authored by Google. Cloud Bigtable is compliant with the HBase 1.x APIs so it can be integrated into many existing big-data systems. Apache Cassandra uses a data model based on the one found in the Cloud Bigtable paper, meaning Cloud Bigtable can also support several workloads that leverage a wide-column-oriented schema and structure.

While Cloud Bigtable is considered an OLTP system, it doesn't support multi-row transactions, SQL queries or joins. For those use cases, recognise either Cloud SQL or Cloud Datastore.

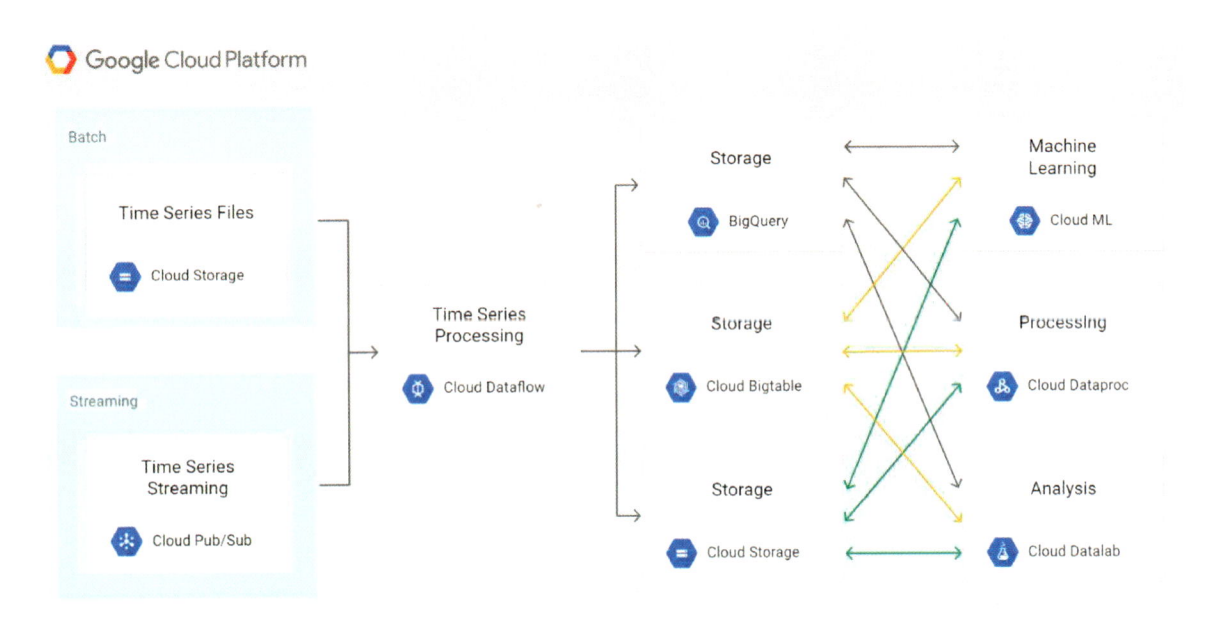

Figure 59: Financial Analysis

©2018 Google LLC, used with permission. Google and the Google logo are registered trademarks of Google LLC

Figure 60: IoT

©2018 Google LLC, used with permission. Google and the Google logo are registered trademarks of Google LLC

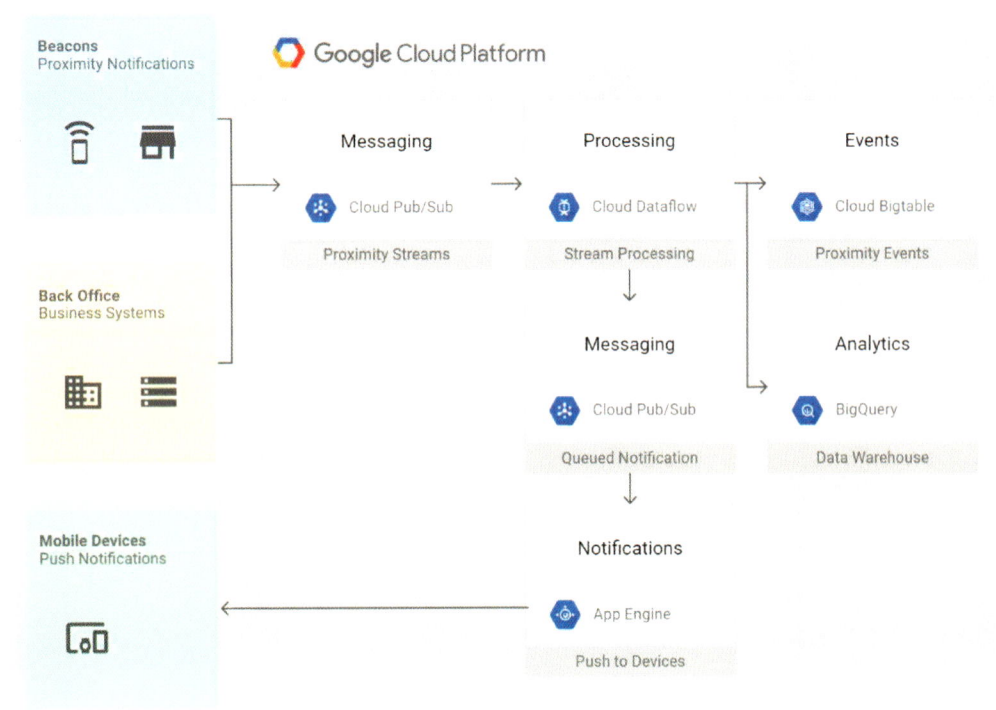

Figure 61: AdTech

©2018 Google LLC, used with permission. Google and the Google logo are registered trademarks of Google LLC

Further Read:

https://static.googleusercontent.com/media/research.google.com/en//archive/bigtable-osdi06.pdf
https://cloud.google.com/bigtable/docs/overview
https://cloud.google.com/bigtable/docs/choosing-ssd-hdd
https://cloud.google.com/bigtable/docs/instances-clusters-nodes

Google Cloud SQL

Cloud SQL is a fully Google managed database service offering a high performance, and scalability. Hosted on Google Cloud Platform, Cloud SQL provides a database infrastructure for applications running anywhere. You can **use Cloud SQL with either MySQL or PostgreSQL.**

Cloud SQL data is encrypted when on Google's internal networks and when stored in database tables, temporary files, and backups. Cloud SQL supports private connectivity with Virtual Private Cloud (VPC), and every Cloud SQL instance includes a network firewall, allowing you to control public network access to your database instance.

Some of the key features of Cloud SQL include:
- Fully managed MySQL Community Edition databases in the cloud.
- Second Generation instances support MySQL 5.6 or 5.7, and provide up to 416 GB of RAM and 10 TB data storage, with the option to automatically increase the storage size as needed.
- First Generation instances support MySQL 5.5 or 5.6 and provide up to 16 GB of RAM and 500 GB data storage.
- Instances available in the **US, EU, or Asia**.
- Customer data encrypted on Google's internal networks and in database tables, temporary files, and backups.
- Support for secure external connections with the Cloud SQL Proxy or with the SSL/TLS protocol.
- **Support for private IP** (private services access).
- Data replication between multiple zones with automatic failover.
- Automated and on-demand backups, and point-in-time recovery.
- Integration with Stackdriver logging and monitoring.
- ISO/IEC 27001 compliant.

Cloud SQL is appropriate for typical online transaction processing (OLTP) workloads.

- **Financial transactions**: Storing financial transactions requires ACID database semantics, and data is often spread across multiple tables, so complex transaction support is required.
- **User credentials**: Storing passwords or other secure data requires complex field support and enforcement along with schema validation.
- **Customer orders**: Orders or invoices typically include highly normalised relational data and multi-table transaction support when capturing inventory changes.

Cloud SQL is not an appropriate storage system for online analytical processing (OLAP) workloads or data that requires dynamic schemas on a per-object basis. If your workload requires dynamic schemas, consider Cloud Datastore. For OLAP workloads, consider BigQuery. If your workload requires wide-column schemas, consider Cloud Bigtable.

Google Cloud Spanner

Google Cloud Spanner is a **globally-distributed, and strongly consistent** database service built for the cloud specifically to combine the benefits of a relational database structure with a non-relational horizontal scale. This combination delivers high-performance transactions and strong consistency across rows, regions, and continents with an industry-leading 99.999% availability SLA, no planned downtime, and enterprise-grade security.

In today's always-on, globally-distributed world, IT and developer efficiency, measured in-app downtime and time to market, is one of an organisation's most critical requirements.

Table 7: Planet Scale No-Compromise Relational Database Service

	Cloud Spanner	Traditional Relational	Traditional Non-Relational
Schema	✓	✓	✗
SQL	✓	✓	✗
Consistency	**Strong**	Strong	Eventual
Availability	**High**	Failover	High
Scalability	**Horizontal**	Vertical	Horizontal
Replication	**Automatic**	Configurable	Configurable

Google Cloud Spanner is Horizontally scalable across rows, regions, and continents, from 1 to hundreds or thousands of nodes.

Covered Service	Monthly Uptime Percentage
Cloud Spanner - Multi-Regional Instance	>= 99.999%
Cloud Spanner - Regional Instance	>= 99.99%

Table 8: Cloud Spanner Availability

Table 9: Cloud Spanner Industry Use Cases

Use Cases	Before Cloud Spanmner	With Cloud Spanner
Financial trading	Inconsistencies lead to potential monetary loss during reconciliation. Global synchronous replication of trades is not feasible.	Cost savings and a consistent, unified, global view.
Insurance	Inconsistencies lead to incomplete views of customers.	Up-to-date customer views provide more accurate, real-time data.
Global call centers	Eventual and out-of-touch.	Real-time and up-to-date.
Supply-chain management and manufacturing	Global supply chain presents an inconsistent global view and/or data must be shipped in batches.	Global, real-time, consistent view enables real-time decision making.
Telecom and billing	Processing capacity limited to finite scale-up compute resources.	Scale-out allows improved processing speed.
Logistics and Transportation	Regional reach with many systems glued together.	Global reach with lower latency and a consistent view.
Gaming	Each server or cluster is its own universe.	Consistent, global view delivers a unified experience.
E-Commerce (High Availability)	Limited availability SLA or no SLA guarantees. In practice, potential missed sales.	Guaranteed max of 5 minutes of downtime (including planned downtime) on paper and in practice.

Cloud Spanner scales horizontally and serves data with low latency while maintaining transactional consistency and industry-leading 99.999% (five 9s) availability - 10x less downtime than four nines (<5 minutes per year). Cloud Spanner helps future-proof your database backend. It can scale to arbitrarily large database sizes to help avoid rewrites and migrations. The use of multiple databases or sharded databases as an alternative solution introduces unnecessary complexity and cost.

Cloud Spanner is ideal for relational, structured, and semi-structured data that requires high availability, strong consistency, and transactional reads and writes.

The following are typical uses cases for Cloud Spanner.

- **Financial services**: Financial services workloads require strong consistency across read/write operations. Cloud Spanner provides this consistency without sacrificing high availability.

Google Cloud Certified Professional Cloud Architect, Second Edition

- **Ad tech**: Latency is a crucial consideration in the ad tech space. Cloud Spanner facilitates low-latency querying without compromising scale or availability.
- **Retail and global supply chain**: The need for a global scale can force supply chain experts to make a trade-off between consistency and maintenance costs. Cloud Spanner offers automatic, global, synchronous replication with low latency, which means that data is always consistent and highly available.

Further Reading:
https://ai.google/research/pubs/pub39966

What Database and when?
The following table would help you to decide what databases to be used and when:

Table 10: Selecting the right database/data storage

What to think?	Type	Load Type	Complex Query	When to think?	Capacity	Unit Size	Key Usage
Cloud Storage	Blobstore	• Objects and blobs • Unstructured data	No	• Storing and streaming multimedia • Storage for custom data analytics pipelines • Archive, backup, and disaster recovery • Images, pictures, and videos	PB+	5 TB/ object	Structured or Unstructured binary or object
Cloud Datastore / Firestore	NO SQL	Document	No	• User profiles • Product catalogues • Game state	TB+	1 MB / entity	Web, AppEngine Semi-structured application data Hierarchical data Durable key-value data
BigQuery	Columnar	OLAP	Yes	• Analytical reporting on large data • Data Science and advanced analysis • Big Data processing using SQL	PB+	10 MB / row	Interactive Query / DW / Offline Analytics
Bigtable	NO SQL Wide Column, non-structured key/value data		No	• IoT, finance, adtech • Personalisation, recommendations • Monitoring • Geospatial datasets • Graphs	PB+	10 MB / cell 100 MB/ row	Heavy Read / Write events, Low Latency, High Throughput
Cloud SQL	Relational	OLTP / Transactional	Yes	• Websites, blogs, and content management systems (CMS) • Business Intelligence (BI) applications • ERP, CRM, and eCommerce applications • Geospatial applications	500 GB	varies	Web Framework and existing applications
Cloud Spanner	Relational	OLTP / Transactional	Yes	• Adtech • Financial services • Global supply chain • Retail	PB+	10, 240MiB / row	Planet-scale, Globally Distributed, Strong Consistency, HA Mission-critical applications High transactions

Google Cloud Certified Professional Cloud Architect, Second Edition

Data Analytics

Figure 62: Google Cloud Analytics Components

Google Cloud Platform comes with a range of tools to help in various stages of Data Analytics lifecycle. These tools include Event or Stream ingestion tool, Real-time Message processing, Data preparation, Data Exploration, Reporting and Data Visualisation tool, and Interactive Data Analytics. Google Cloud's stream analytics solution, with the help of Cloud Pub/Sub, allows us to ingests event streams and delivering the same to Cloud Dataflow for processing and BigQuery for analysis as a data warehousing solution. Google has also introduced Cloud Dataproc, Google-managed clusters to deploy Hadoop on GCP. Cloud Pub/Sub is a simple, reliable, scalable foundation for stream analytics and event-driven computing systems.

Cloud Pub/Sub

Cloud Pub/Sub is a real-time scalable, durable event ingestion and message delivery service that serves as a foundation for modern stream analytics pipelines you to send and receive stream and event messages between apps. Cloud Pub/Sub is founded upon Google's **serverless computing** infrastructure and enables the ingest **event streams from anywhere, at any scale, in real time**. As Cloud Pub/Sub is following serverless architecture, Cloud Pub/Sub automatically manages the details of sharding, replication, load-balancing, and partitioning of the incoming data streams. Fine-grained access controls allow for sophisticated cross-team and organisational data sharing. Moreover, end-to-end encryption adds security to your pipelines. **Cloud Pub/Sub is a global service**: **The clients are unaware of the physical location (or data centre location) of any servers or data and can publish and subscribe from anywhere in the world to anywhere in the world**. Cloud Pub/Sub has global endpoints and leverages Google's global front-end load balancer to support data ingestion across all GCP regions, with minimal latency. Google products including Ads, Search, and Gmail uses this infrastructure to send over 500 million messages per second, totalling over 1TB/s of data. Cloud Pub/Sub doesn't maintain message order but ensures at-least-once delivery at any scale. Cloud Pub/Sub doesn't provide guarantees about the order of message delivery. Strict message ordering can be achieved with buffering, often using Cloud Dataflow. Cloud Pub/Sub distributes data across projects and applications running on other clouds, or between cloud and on-premises apps. Cloud Pub/Sub easily fits in your existing environment via efficient client libraries for multiple languages, open REST/HTTP and gRPC service APIs, and an open source Apache Kafka connector.

Cloud Pub/Sub is a 'Topic' based messaging system. It organises all the received events and messages from various sources and apps as a topic and attaches a unique identifier and timestamp. Later point, apps could receive these events/messages through a topic subscription mechanism which could be pulled or push based. This can be done in either a pull or push model. In a push subscription, the Cloud Pub/Sub server sends a request to the subscriber app at a preconfigured URL endpoint. In the pull model, the subscriber requests messages from the server and acknowledges receipt. Cloud Pub/Sub guarantees message delivery at least once per subscriber. Everyday use of Cloud Pub/Sub is to move streaming data into Cloud Dataflow for real-time processing, per actual event time. When processed, you can move the data into a persistent storage service, such as Cloud Datastore and BigQuery, which support queries ordered by app timestamps.

Figure 63: Cloud Pb/Sub message syndication

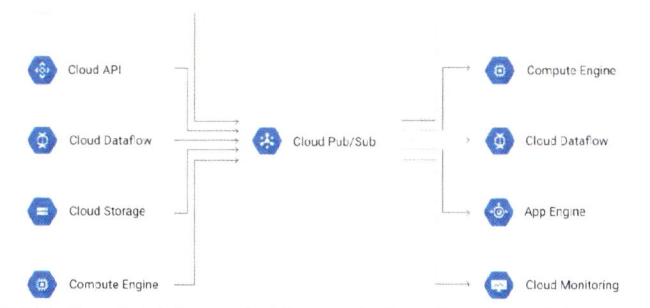

©2018 Google LLC, used with permission. Google and the Google logo are registered trademarks of Google LLC

Table 11: Cloud Pub/Sub as a Global Service

Cloud Pub/Sub – A Global Service

When a service is a Global Service, it wouldn't guarantee the physical location (or data center location) of any of its servers. In case your architecture requires data sovereignty, you may need to relook at the usage of such compoents. It is advisable to consult with Google to make arrangements of these compoents customised for your organization.

Google Cloud Certified Professional Cloud Architect, Second Edition

Cloud Dataflow

Cloud Dataflow is a fully-managed service that transforms and enrich data both in stream (real time) and batch (historical) modes with equal reliability and expressiveness. Cloud Dataflow's serverless approach frees you from operational tasks like capacity planning, resource management, and performance optimisation while you only pay for what has been used. Cloud Dataflow unlocks transformational use cases across industries, including:
- Clickstream, Point-of-Sale, and segmentation analysis in retail
- Fraud detection in financial services
- Personalised user experience in gaming
- IoT analytics in manufacturing, healthcare, and logistics

Cloud Dataflow is a consistently, and that reliably provides built-in support for fault-tolerant execution with 'Exactly-once Processing' regardless of data size, cluster size, processing pattern or pipeline complexity.

Cloud Dataflow seamlessly integrates with GCP services for streaming events ingestion (Cloud Pub/Sub), data warehousing (BigQuery), machine learning (Cloud Machine Learning), and more. Its Beam-based SDK also lets developers build custom extensions and even choose alternative execution engines, such as Apache Spark via Cloud Dataproc or on-premises. For Apache Kafka users, a Cloud Dataflow connector makes integration with GCP easy

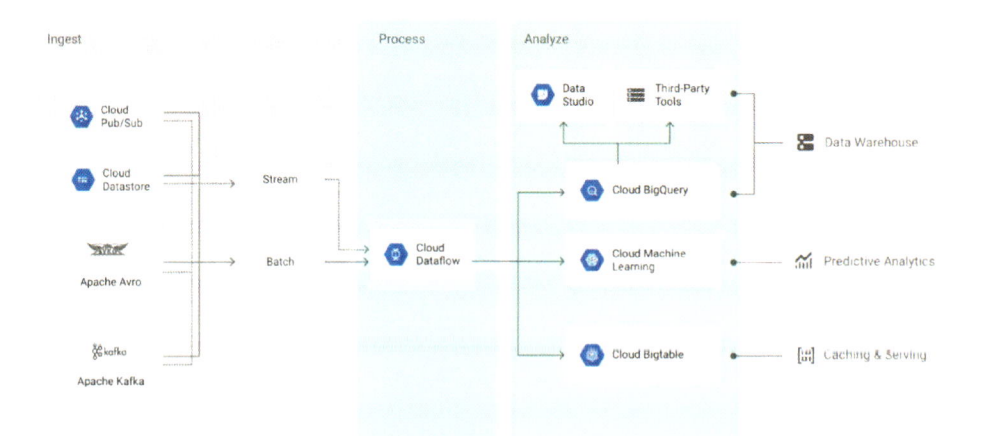

Figure 64: Data Transformation with Cloud Dataflow, Cloud Pub/Sub for Stream Analytics

©2018 Google LLC, used with permission. Google and the Google logo are registered trademarks of Google LLC

Cloud Dataprep

Cloud Dataprep by Trifacta is an intelligent data service for visually exploring, cleaning, and preparing structured and unstructured data for analysis. Because Cloud Dataprep is serverless and works at any scale, there is no infrastructure to deploy or manage. Your next ideal data transformation is suggested and predicted with each UI input, so you don't have to write code. Also, with automatic schema, datatype, possible joins, and anomaly detection, you can skip time-consuming data profiling and focus on data analysis.

Cloud Dataprep automatically identifies data anomalies and helps you to introduce corrective action faster and come up with data transformation suggestions based on your usage pattern. Standardise, structure, and join datasets easily with a guided approach. Cloud Dataprep:
- Processes both structured and unstructured data
- Transforms stored data in CSV, JSON, or relational table formats, and
- Also prepares datasets of any size, megabytes to terabytes, with equal ease.

A great example of a serverless real-time end-2-end ML pipeline shown below built entirely on Google Cloud Platform services - AppEngine, PubSub, Dataflow, BigQuery, Cloud ML Engine, Deployment Manager, Cloud Build and Cloud Composer. One significant advantage introduced by this architecture is staying in full control and ownership of your data and data platform along with pseudonymizing personal and sensitive data.

Data Products

Architecture: E-commerce Data Products

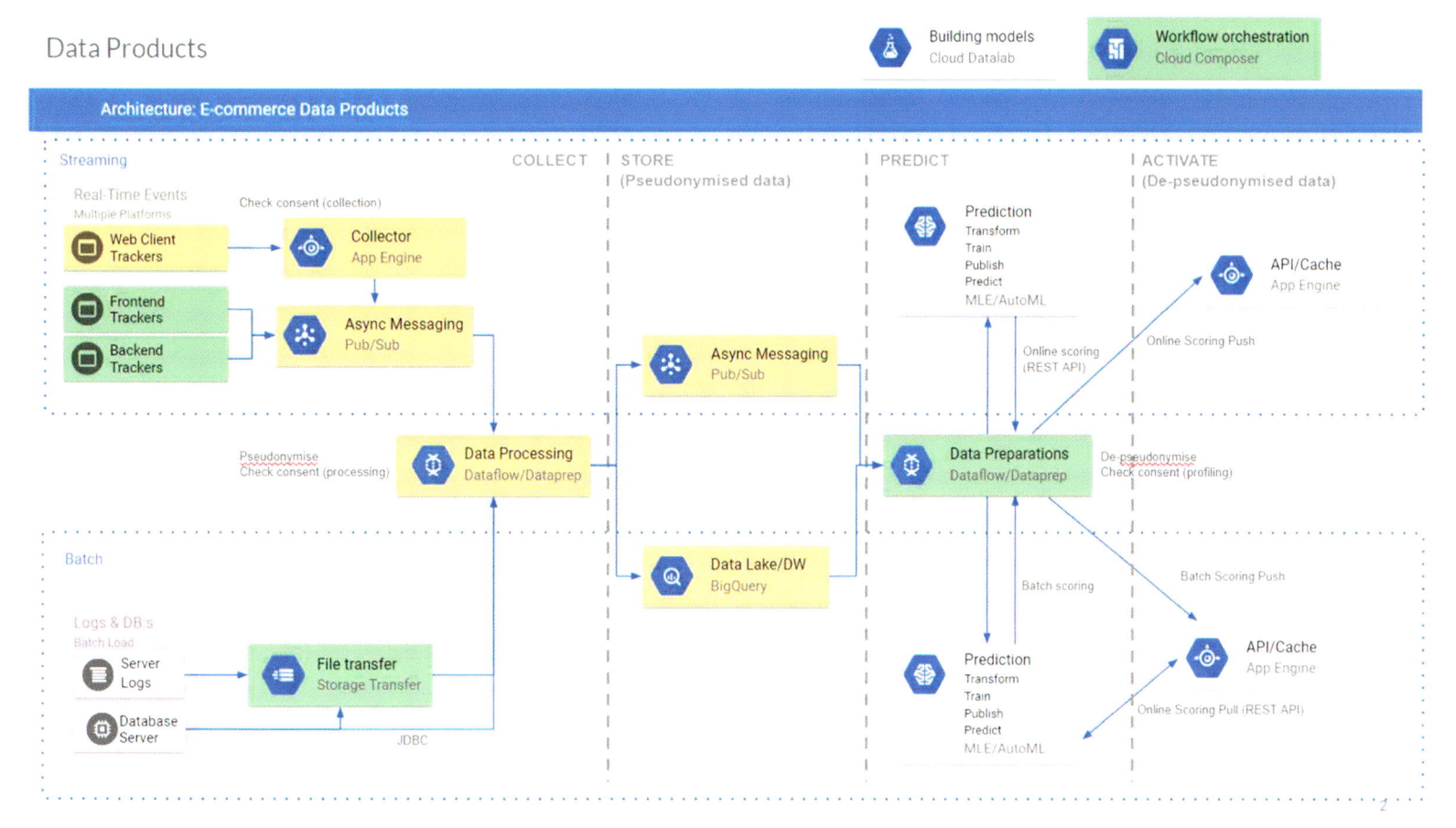

Building models: Cloud Datalab

Workflow orchestration: Cloud Composer

Streaming

COLLECT

- Real-Time Events, Multiple Platforms
  - Web Client Trackers
  - Frontend Trackers
  - Backend Trackers
- Check consent (collection) → Collector (App Engine)
- Async Messaging (Pub/Sub)
- Pseudonymise / Check consent (processing) → Data Processing (Dataflow/Dataprep)

Batch

- Logs & DB:s, Batch Load
  - Server Logs
  - Database Server
- File transfer (Storage Transfer) — JDBC

STORE (Pseudonymised data)
- Async Messaging (Pub/Sub)
- Data Lake/DW (BigQuery)

PREDICT
- Prediction: Transform, Train, Publish, Predict (MLE/AutoML)
- Data Preparations (Dataflow/Dataprep)
- Prediction: Transform, Train, Publish, Predict (MLE/AutoML)
- Online scoring (REST API)
- Batch scoring
- De-pseudonymise / Check consent (profiling)

ACTIVATE (De-pseudonymised data)
- API/Cache (App Engine) — Online Scoring Push
- API/Cache (App Engine) — Batch Scoring Push / Online Scoring Pull (REST API)

Source and Copyright: https://robertsahlin.com/datahem-open-source-serverless-real-time-and-end-2-end-ml-pipeline-on-google-cloud-platform/
Used with kind permission from Robert Sahlin, https://github.com/mhlabs/datahem

Cloud Dataproc - Cloud-native Apache Hadoop & Apache Spark

Cloud Dataproc is Google's fully-managed cloud service offering for running Apache Spark and Apache Hadoop clusters. Cloud Dataproc runs operations in seconds or minutes which otherwise would take hours or days instead. Cloud Dataproc is one of the critical data processing platforms in an offer by Google cloud to enable a cost-efficient migration of Hadoop platform into Google Cloud Platform, integrating with storage, compute, and monitoring services across Google Cloud products and enabling you with a powerful data processing, analytics and machine learning.

Cloud Dataproc is natively integrated with several Google Cloud Platform products as part of an **integrated data platform**.

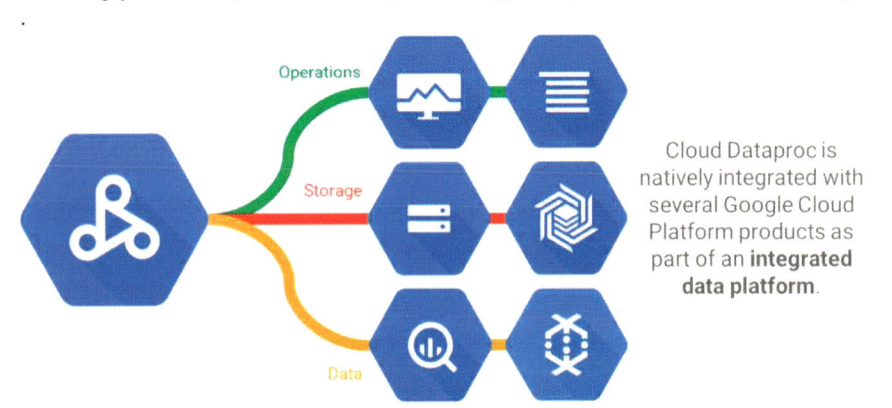

Figure 66: Cloud Dataproc – integrated

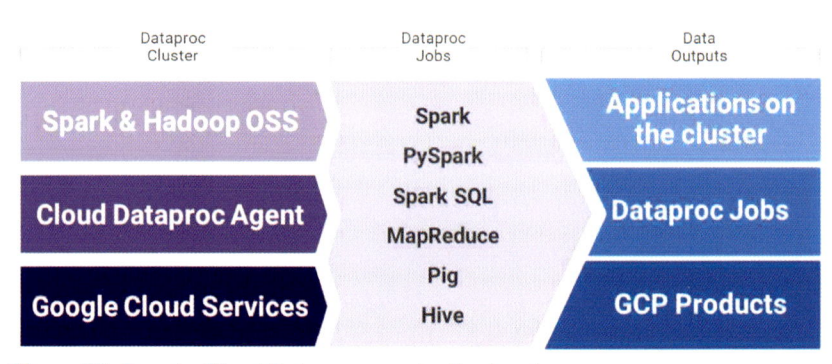

Figure 65: Google Cloud Dataproc - under the hood

©2018 Google LLC, used with permission. Google and the Google logo are registered trademarks of Google LLC

©2018 Google LLC, used with permission. Google and the Google logo are registered trademarks of Google LLC

Typically Dataproc operates both on-premise or in the cloud and fundamentally, a new approach through which **Dataproc lets you think regarding jobs, not clusters**. Dataproc is an excellent option for stateful clusters such as Impala and HBase on HDFS. Fundamentally,

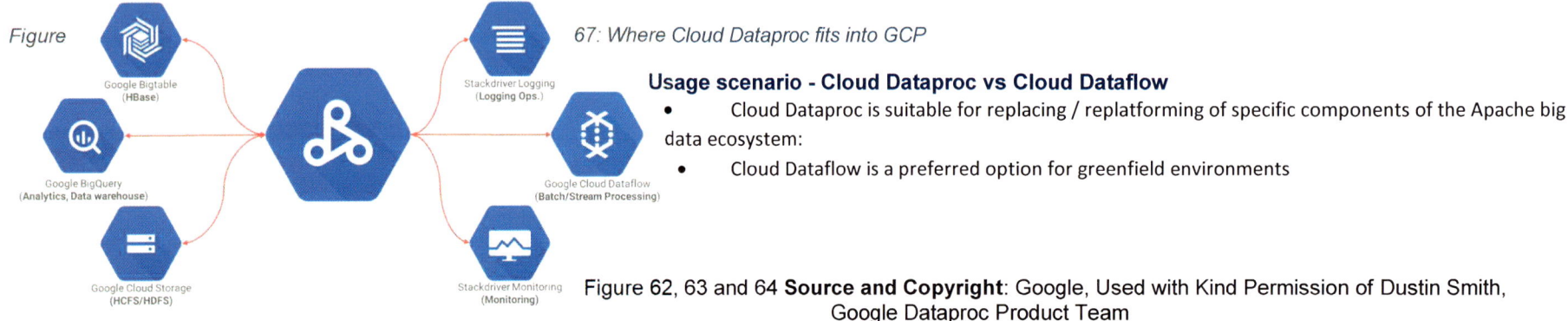

Figure 67: Where Cloud Dataproc fits into GCP

Usage scenario - Cloud Dataproc vs Cloud Dataflow

- Cloud Dataproc is suitable for replacing / replatforming of specific components of the Apache big data ecosystem:
- Cloud Dataflow is a preferred option for greenfield environments

Figure 62, 63 and 64 **Source and Copyright**: Google, Used with Kind Permission of Dustin Smith, Google Dataproc Product Team

©2018 Google LLC, used with permission. Google and the Google logo are registered trademarks of Google LLC

Google Cloud Certified Professional Cloud Architect, Second Edition

Table 12: Dataproc workload vs Dataflow workload

Workloads	Cloud Dataproc	Cloud Dataflow	
Stream processing (ETL)		✓	
Batch processing (ETL)	✓	✓	
Iterative processing and notebooks	✓		
Machine learning with Spark ML	✓		
Preprocessing for machine learning		✓	with Cloud MLE

Cloud Datalab

Cloud Datalab is a powerful **interactive data exploration** tool that allows you to explore, analyse, transform, visualise data, and build ML models on the Google Cloud Platform. Cloud Datalab is **built on Jupyter** (formerly IPython), that boasts a thriving ecosystem of modules and a robust knowledge base. Cloud Datalab enables interactive analysis of your data on Google BigQuery leveraging a combination of toolsets - Cloud Machine Learning Engine, Google Compute Engine, and Google Cloud Storage using Python, SQL, and JavaScript (for BigQuery user-defined functions).

Cloud Datalab combines code, documentation, results, and visualisations in an intuitive notebook format and supports TensorFlow-based deep ML models in addition to scikit-learn.

Exploring data using BigQuery and Cloud Datalab

©2018 Google LLC, used with permission.
Google and the Google logo are registered trademarks of Google LLC

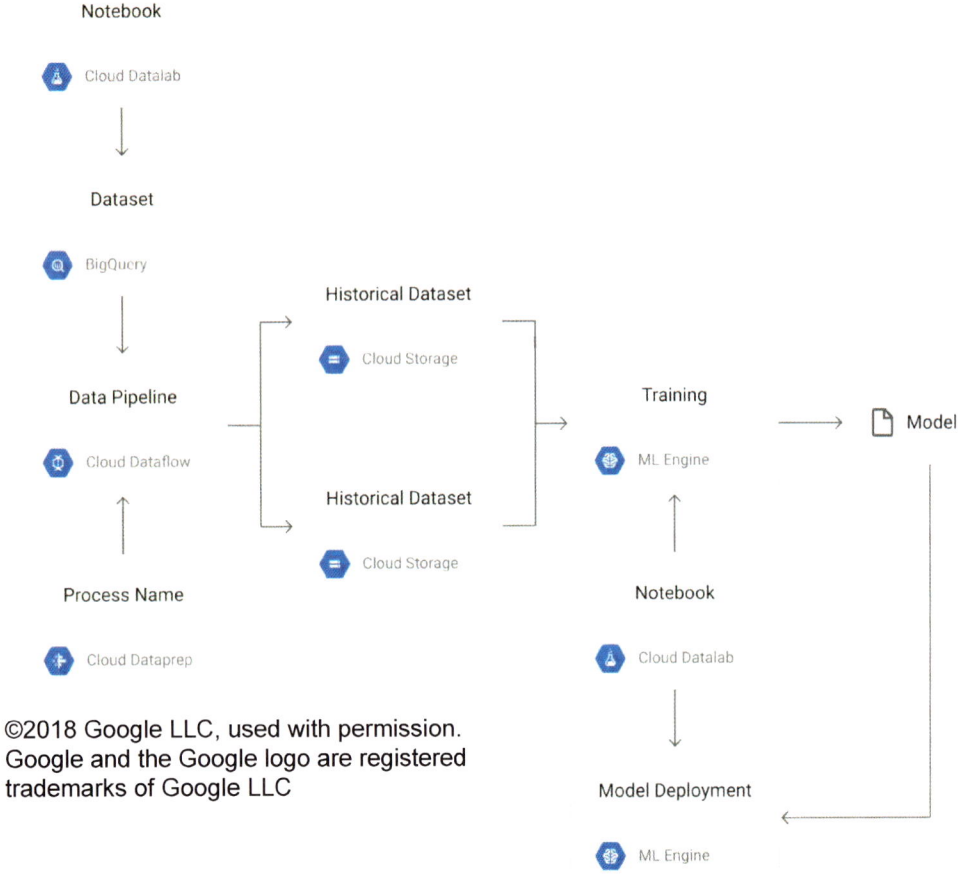

Figure 68: Exploring data using BigQuery and Cloud Datalab

Through Cloud Datalab and BigQuery, you can:

- Explore and visualise TBs of data.
- Filter the inputs that might otherwise not have a substantial impact on the prediction scenario and model.
- Create a sample set of representative data to start creating your model.
- Possibly split data for training, evaluation, and test.
- Preprocessing data using Cloud Dataprep and Cloud Dataflow

Google Data Studio
Google Data Studio allows you to build interactive dashboards, and engaging reports that inspire smarter business decisions. It makes insights easy to read, share, and customise. Integrations between BigQuery, Data Studio, and Sheets and popular BI and ETL tools translate to flexibility for how data is ingested and presented. Data Studio also uses Google Drive's sharing model, enabling teams to collaborate in real time. Moreover, with pre-built report templates, teams can focus on telling compelling stories, not handling data.

Genomics
Google Genomics helps the life science community to organise and access the world's genomic information and make it useful. Big genomic data is here today, with petabytes rapidly growing toward exabytes. Through our extensions to Google Cloud Platform, you can apply the same technologies that power Google Search and Maps to securely store, process, explore, and share large, complex datasets.

Architecture: LifeSciences > Genomics, Secondary Analysis

©2018 Google LLC, used with permission. Google and the Google logo are registered trademarks of Google LLC

Google Genomics supports open industry standards, including those developed by the Global Alliance for Genomics and Health, so you can share your tools and data with your group, collaborators, or the broader community, if and when you choose.

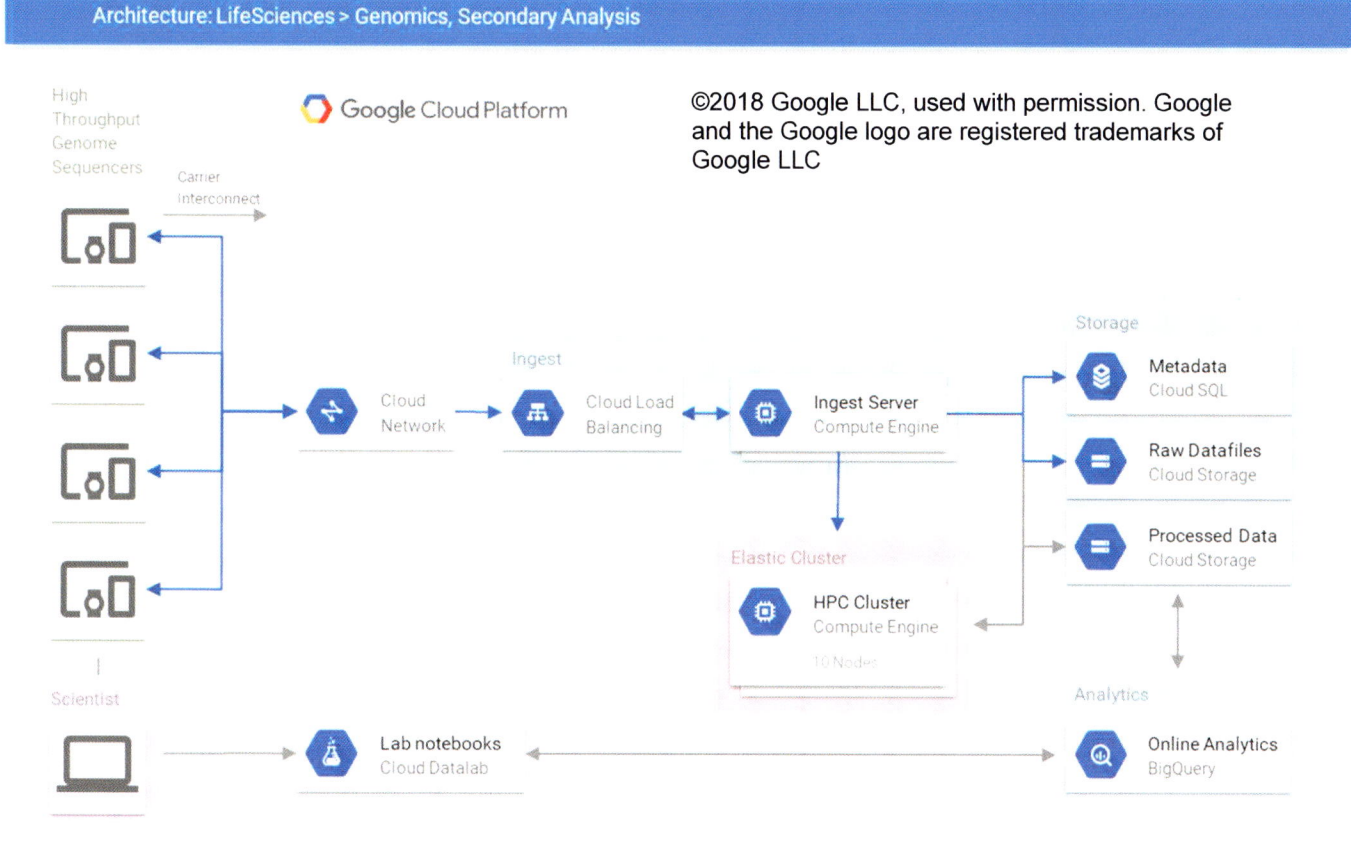

Figure 69: Genomics in Google Cloud

Cloud Composer

Cloud Composer is a fully managed workflow orchestration service empowering you to build a full pipeline weaving all of Google Cloud's big data products - BigQuery, Dataflow, Dataproc, Datastore, Cloud Storage, Pub/Sub, Cloud ML Engine, and giving you the ability to orchestrate end-to-end GCP workloads. Cloud Composer allows you to author, schedule, and monitor pipelines that span across clouds and on-premises data centres. Cloud Composer is built on the popular Apache Airflow open source project and operated using the Python programming language, and Cloud Composer removes vendor-lock-in. Cloud Composer provisions a unified data environment that allows us to connect, process, and provide services across clouds, and thus ease your Multi-cloud journey.

Environments are self-contained Airflow deployments based on Google Kubernetes Engine. These environments work with GCP services through connectors that are built into Airflow.

You create Cloud Composer environments in supported regions, and the environments run within a Compute Engine zone. For simple use cases, you can create one environment in one region. For complex use cases, you can create multiple environments within a single region or across multiple regions. Airflow communicates with other GCP products through the products' public APIs.

Cloud Composer pipelines are configured as **directed acyclic graphs (DAGs) using Python**, making it easy for users of all type of experience level to the author to build and schedule a workflow. Its one-click deployment yields instant access to a rich library of connectors and multiple graphical representations of your workflow in action. Automatic synchronisation of your directed acyclic graphs ensures your jobs stay on schedule.

©2018 Google LLC, used with permission. Google and the Google logo are registered trademarks of Google LLC

Figure 70: Cloud Composer Architecture Overview

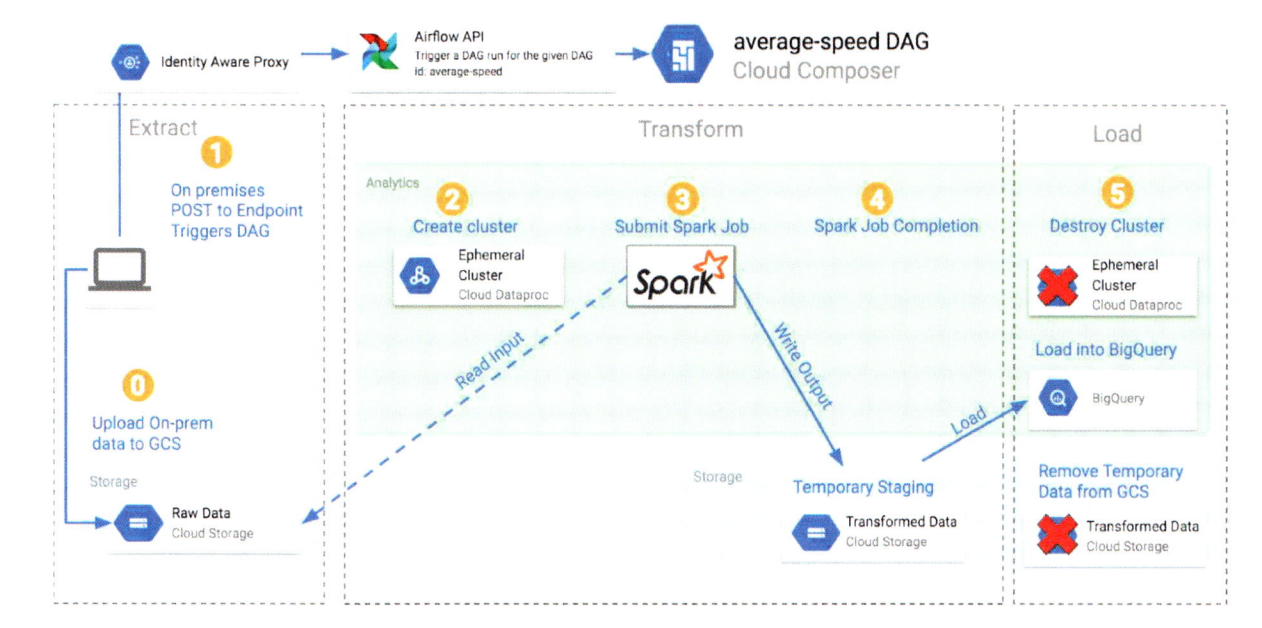

Google Cloud Composer helps to automate the transform and load steps of an ETL data pipeline that will create a Dataproc cluster, perform transformations on extracted data (via a PySpark job), and then upload the results to BigQuery. You'll then trigger this pipeline by authenticating with Google Identity Aware Proxy (IAP) and posting to the Airflow endpoint for your DAG.

An excellent example architecture is demonstrating using HTTP POST to an endpoint to trigger an Airflow DAG that also automates spins up/tear down of a Dataproc cluster to run a Spark job to enhance data and writes the enhanced data to BigQuery.

Source: https://medium.com/google-cloud/using-airflow-experimental-rest-api-on-google-cloud-platform-cloud-composer-and-iap-9bd0260f095a
Copyright: Used with kind permission from Jacob Ferriero

Putting the puzzle together – Google Cloud Databases and Analytics Architecture

Complex Event Processing (CEP)

Google Cloud Platform enables you to build the elastic and scalable infrastructure needed to import vast amounts of data from multiple, heterogeneous sources, process events, apply complex business rules and execute business rules to drive outbound actions. The following architecture diagram depicts a high-level solution and the components involved.

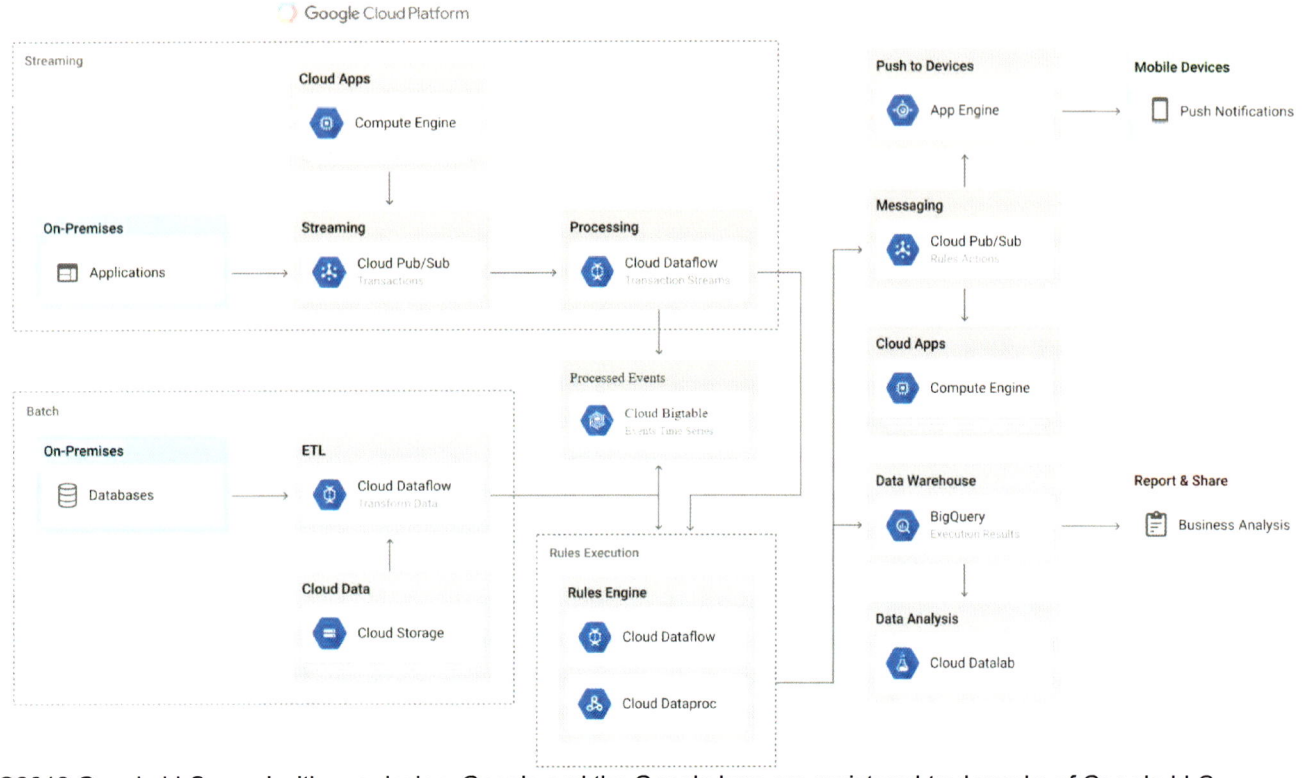

©2018 Google LLC, used with permission. Google and the Google logo are registered trademarks of Google LLC

Figure 71: Complex Event Processing using Google Cloud Platform

User-generated events (UGEs) often originate from interactions within applications that are hosted on-premises or in the cloud (Google App Engine, Kubernetes Engine or Google Compute Engine) and can be in the form of clickstreams, user actions such as adding items to a shopping cart or wish list, or financial transactions. Google Cloud Pub/Sub, is used as a globally durable message-transport service between applications and downstream processing. Cloud Dataflow transforms, enriches, aggregates, or apply general-purpose computations across the data, and executes these pipelines by using a simple pipeline-based programming model on a managed service that elastically scales, as needed.

In CEP workloads, Cloud Dataflow plays a vital role in normalising data from heterogeneous sources and format it into a single, consistent representation. At the heart of CEP systems rule that must be executed across incoming events. Regardless of the rules engine's complexity, it can be deployed in a distributed fashion using either Cloud Dataflow or Google Cloud Dataproc, a managed service for running Hadoop or Spark clusters. Please refer Usage scenario - Cloud Dataproc vs Cloud Dataflow.

After the rules execution mechanism has processed inbound events, results can be turned into a series of outbound actions. These actions can include push notifications for mobile devices, notifications for other applications, or sending email to users. To deliver these actions, you can send messages through Cloud Pub/Sub to applications hosted on-premises or on Google Cloud Platform, whether running on App Engine, Kubernetes Engine, or Compute Engine.
These results even could be stored in Google BigQuery to perform exploration and analysis for business intelligence or reporting purposes. For data-science-oriented analysis, Google Cloud Datalab offers powerful data exploration capabilities based on Jupyter notebooks. For reporting or dashboard use cases, Google Data Studio 360 supports creating customizable and shareable reports, backed by BigQuery's query and storage capabilities.

Further Reading

https://cloud.google.com/solutions/architecture/optimized-large-scale-analytics-ingestion
https://cloud.google.com/solutions/architecture/complex-event-processing
https://cloud.google.com/composer/
https://cloud.google.com/composer/docs/concepts/overview
https://cloud.google.com/pubsub/architecture
https://cloud.google.com/pubsub/docs/faq
https://cloud.google.com/pubsub/
https://cloud.google.com/dataprep/
https://cloud.google.com/dataflow/
https://cloud.google.com/solutions/migration/hadoop/hadoop-gcp-migration-overview
https://hackernoon.com/why-dataproc-googles-managed-hadoop-and-spark-offering-is-a-game-changer-9f0ed183fda3
https://cloud.google.com/blog/products/gcp/visualizing-the-mechanics-of-on-demand-pricing-in-big-data-technologies
https://cloud.google.com/blog/products/gcp/understanding-bigquerys-rapid-scaling-and-simple-pricing
https://www.slideshare.net/huguk/google-cloud-dataproc-easier-faster-more-costeffective-spark-and-hadoop-65909195

Identity and Security

This section covers high-level GCP Security and IAM area keeping in mind for your certification assessment areas. IAM is a significant area and deserves a good book on its own.

Figure 72: Identity and Access Management Tools

The Google Cloud Platform offers comprehensive security products and capabilities. These products include:

- Infrastructure Security
- Network Security
  - Virtual Private Cloud
  - Cloud Load Balancing
  - Encryption in transit
  - Application Layer Transport Security
- Endpoint Security
- Data Security
  - Encryption at rest
  - Cloud KMS
- Identity and Access Management
- Cloud Identity
  - Cloud IAM
  - Cloud Identity-Aware Proxy
  - Security Keys
  - Cloud Resource Manager
- Application Security
  - Cloud Security Scanner
- Security monitoring & operations
  - Stackdriver Logging
  - Forseti Audit

GCP Infrastructure Security Layers

OPERATIONAL

Intrusion Detection
(sophisticated data processing pipelines to integrate host-based signals on individual devices, network-based signals from various monitoring points in the infrastructure, and signals from infrastructure services. Rules and machine intelligence built on top of these pipelines give operational security engineers warnings of possible incidents

Reducing Insider Risk
(Active Monitoring)

Safe Employee Devices & Credentials
(U2F-compatible Security Keys)

Safe Software Development
(libraries and frameworks to eliminate XSS vulnerabilities. Automated tools for automatically detecting security bugs including fuzzers, static analysis tools, and web security scanners).

INTERNET COMMUNICATION

Google Front End
(The Google Front End (GFE) ensures that all TLS connections are terminated using correct certificates and following best practices such as supporting perfect forward secrecy. The GFE additionally applies protections against Denial of Service attacks (which we will discuss in more detail later). The GFE then forwards requests for the service using the RPC security protocol discussed previously)

DoS Protection
(Multi-tier, multi-layered DDoS)

STORAGE SERVICES

Encryption at rest
(Use keys from the central key management service to encrypt data before it is written to physical storage. This key management service supports automatic key rotation, provides extensive audit logs, and integrates with the previously mentioned end user permission tickets to link keys to particular end users)

Detection of Data
(most often starts with marking specific data as "scheduled for deletion" rather than actually removing the data entirely.
After having been marked as "scheduled for deletion," the data is deleted in accordance with service-specific policies.
The services can then schedule data associated with the deleted end user account for deletion.)

SERVICE DEPLOYMENT

Access Management of End User Data
(Service identity, automatic mutual authentication, encrypted inter-service communication and enforcement of access policies defined by the service owner, Multi-factor authentication)

Encryption of Inter-Service Communication
(Cryptographic privacy and integrity)

Inter-Service Access Management
(Global namespace, rich identity management workflow, fine-grained access control)

Service Identity, Integrity, Isolation
(cryptographic authentication and authorization at the application layer, ingress and egress filtering at various points, Linux user separation, language and kernel-based sandboxes, and hardware virtualization, enable very sensitive services, such as the cluster orchestration service and some key management services, to run exclusively on dedicated machines)

HARDWARE INFRASTRUCTURE

Secure Boot Stack and Machine Identity
(a lockable firmware chip, a microcontroller, Cryptographic Signature)

Hardware Design and Provenance
(Intelligent chips to detect securely identify and authenticate legitimate Google devices)

Security of Physical Premises
(biometric identification, metal detection, cameras, vehicle barriers, and laser-based intrusion detection systems)

USER IDENTITY

Authentication
(Beyond asking for a simple username and password, uses the Universal 2nd Factor (U2F) open standard user authentication)

Login Abuse Protection
(Intelligently challenges users for additional information based on risk factors such as whether they have logged in from the same device or a similar location in the past. After authenticating the user, the identity service issues credentials such as cookies and OAuth tokens that can be used for subsequent calls)

Adapted and Consolidated from Google Cloud Security White Paper. ©2018 Google LLC, used with permission. Google and the Google logo are registered trademarks of Google LLC

Google Cloud Certified Professional Cloud Architect, Second Edition

Cloud Security Controls and Threat Management

Cloud Security Scanner
Cloud Security Scanner is an automated Vulnerability Scanning for common vulnerabilities including cross-site-scripting (XSS), Flash injection, mixed content (HTTP in HTTPS), and outdated/insecure libraries in App Engine, Compute Engine, and Google Kubernetes Engine applications. It enables early identification and delivers very low false positive rates.

Cloud Identity
Cloud Identity is an Identity as a Service (IDaaS) and enterprise mobility management (EMM) product to manage your users, apps, and devices from a central location—the Google Admin console.

Cloud Identity and Access Management

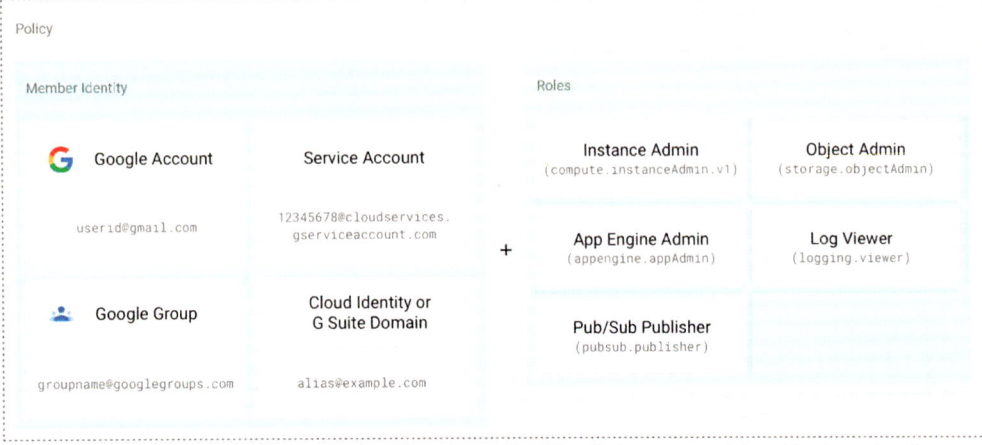

> **CLOUD SECURITY CONTROLS AND THREAT MANAGEMENTS**
>
> It is highly recommended to do some pre-read about security threats and matrix to make yourself familiar with the subject. The Cloud Security is a vastly complex area. Please read: https://cloudsecurityalliance.org/artifacts/security-guidance-v4/
> Allso, make yourself embedded into The Cloud Security Alliance (CSA) Cloud Controls Matrix (CCM) in case you are involved in any Google Cloud Security and architectural role.

Cloud Identity & Access Management (Cloud IAM) is Google's Enterprise-grade access control capability **by defining who (identity) has what access (role) for which resource**, enabling specific resources full control and visibility to manage cloud resources centrally. Cloud IAM is a **context-aware**, offering a **fine-grained** resource level of authorisation granularity, rather than just project level and provides a **unified view into security policy** across your entire organisation, with built-in auditing to ease compliance processes.

Figure 73: Cloud IAM Policy, Member Identity and Roles View

In Cloud IAM, you grant access to members which can be of the following types:
- Google account
- Service account
- Google group
- G Suite domain
- Cloud Identity domain

©2018 Google LLC, used with permission. Google and the Google logo are registered trademarks of Google LLC

Cloud IAM can grant roles to users by creating a Cloud IAM policy, which is a collection of statements that define who has what type of access. A policy is attached to a resource and is used to enforce access control whenever that resource is accessed.

Figure 74: Cloud IAM Policy

In the GCP resource hierarchy, where the organisation is the root node, the projects are immediate next level children of the organisation, and the other resources are the descendants of projects. The following diagram is an excellent example of a GCP resource hierarchy

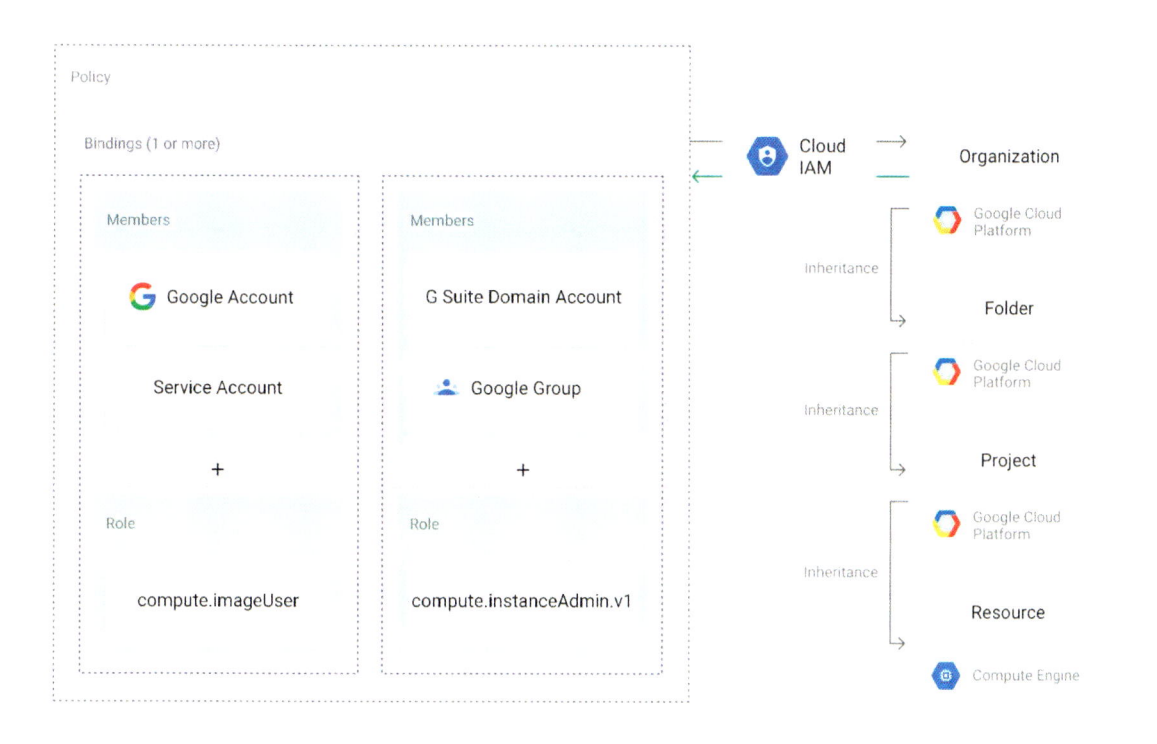

©2018 Google LLC, used with permission. Google and the Google logo are registered trademarks of Google LLC

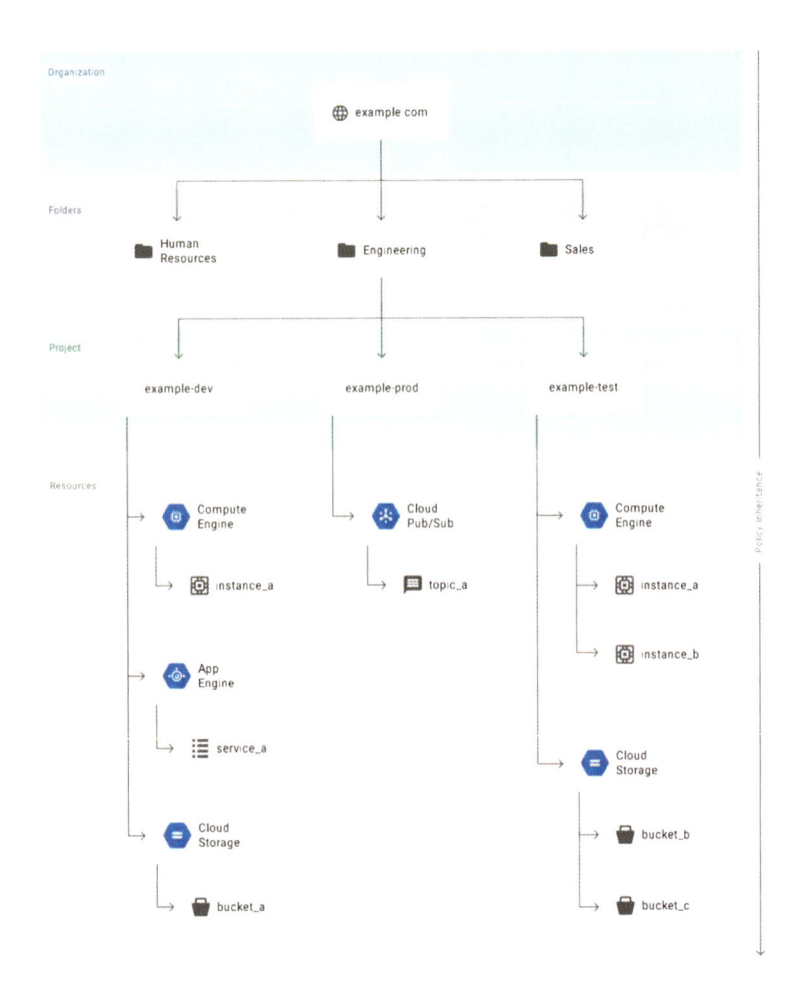

Figure 75: GCP Resource Hierarchy

Google Cloud Certified Professional Cloud Architect, Second Edition

The following products offer Cloud IAM predefined roles:

- Google Cloud Platform project
- GCP Organization
- Compute Engine
- Cloud Source Repositories
- App Engine
- Cloud Storage
- BigQuery
- Cloud Bigtable
- IAM for Cloud SQL

- Stackdriver Debugger
- Cloud Deployment Manager
- Cloud Genomics
- Cloud Key Management Service
- Cloud Pub/Sub
- Cloud Machine Learning Engine
- Cloud Spanner
- Stackdriver Logging
- Cloud IAM for Stackdriver Monitoring

- Cloud Dataflow
- Cloud IAM for Cloud Datastore
- Cloud IAM for Cloud Dataproc
- Cloud IAM for Google Kubernetes Engine
- Cloud IAM for Cloud DNS
- Cloud IAM for Stackdriver Trace
- Cloud IAM for Cloud Billing API
- Cloud IAM for Service Management

There is another level of data access control we could put to restrict access to a dataset, called **an authorised view in BigQuery**. An authorised view allows you to share query results with particular users and groups without giving them access to the underlying tables. You can also use the view's SQL query to restrict the columns (fields) the users can query.

Security Keys
Google Titan Security Keys are phishing-resistant two-factor authentication (2FA) devices that help protect high-value users such as IT admins. Titan Security Keys work with popular browsers and a growing ecosystem of services that support FIDO standards. They are built with a hardware chip that includes firmware engineered by Google to verify the integrity of the key.

Cloud Resource Manager
Google Cloud Resource Manager centrally manages resource containers such as Organizations, Folders, and Projects, that allow you to the group and hierarchically organise other Cloud Platform resources.

Encryption at rest
Data in Google Cloud Platform is broken into smaller units of chunks for storage, and each chunk is encrypted at the storage level with an individual encryption key, called a data encryption key (DEK). These keys are stored near the data that they encrypt to satisfy the low latency and high availability requirements and encrypted with (or "wrapped" by) a key encryption key (KEK). Customers can choose which key management solution they prefer (Customer-managed encryption keys (CMEK) using Cloud KMS and Customer-supplied encryption keys (CSEK)) for managing the KEKs that protect the DEKs that protect their data.
CMEK is supported with BigQuery, Cloud Build, Cloud Dataproc, Cloud Storage and Compute Engin, whereas the Compute Engine and Cloud Storage support Customer-supplied encryption keys (CSEK).

Cloud Data Loss Prevention (DLP) API
The Cloud DLP API automatically discover and redact sensitive data within GCP. It comes with a rich set of 90+ pre-defined detectors with a focus on quality, speed, scale.

Forseti Security: Open source tools for GCP security
Forseti Security helps you secure your Google Cloud Platform organisation. Forseti gives you tools to understand all the resources you have in Google Cloud Platform (GCP). The core Forseti modules work together to provide complete information so you can take action to secure resources and minimize security risks.
- Inventory regularly collects data from your GCP resources and makes it available to other modules.
- Scanner periodically compares your rules about GCP resource policies against the policies collected by Inventory and saves the output for your review.
- Explain helps you understand, test, and develop Cloud Identity and Access Management (Cloud IAM) policies.
- Enforcer uses Google Cloud APIs to change resource policy state to match the state you define.
- Notifier keeps you up to date about Forseti findings and actions.

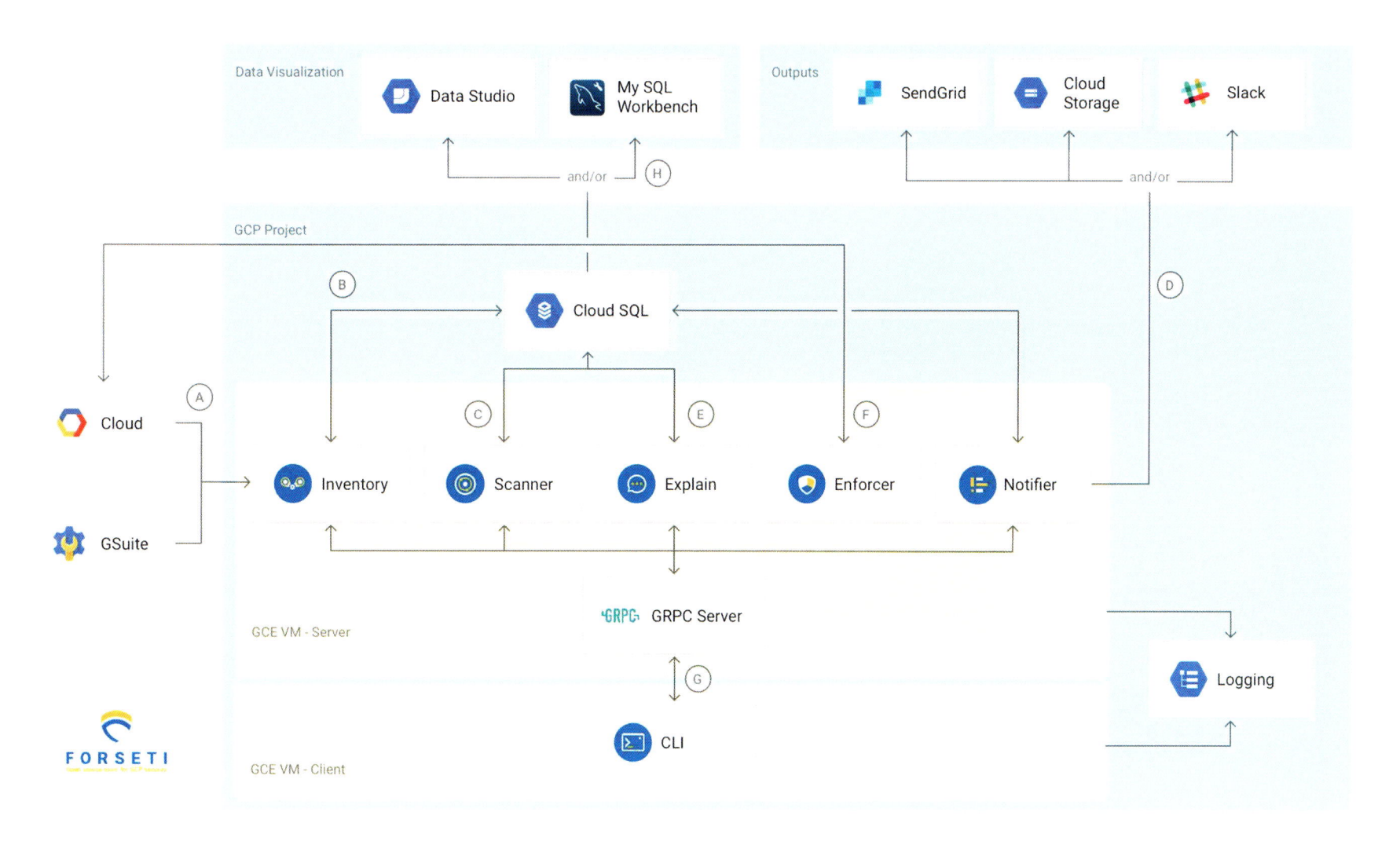

© 2019 The Forseti Security. A Google Open Source Project https://opensource.google.com/projects/forseti-security

Further Reading

- https://cloud.google.com/security/products/
- https://cloud.google.com/iam/docs/overview
- https://services.google.com/fh/files/misc/security_whitepapers_march2018.pdf
- https://cloud.google.com/resource-manager/docs/cloud-platform-resource-hierarchy
- https://cloud.google.com/security/encryption-at-rest/
- https://cloud.google.com/security/encryption-in-transit/
- https://cloud.google.com/kms/
- https://cloud.google.com/dlp/
- https://cloud.google.com/storage/docs/best-practices
- https://cloud.google.com/storage/docs/gsutil/addlhelp/SecurityandPrivacyConsiderations
- https://cloud.google.com/storage/docs/gsutil/addlhelp/SecurityandPrivacyConsiderations
- https://opensource.google.com/projects/forseti-security
- https://forsetisecurity.org/docs/v1.1/howto/deploy/gcp-deployment.html
- https://forsetisecurity.org/

Development Tools

Cloud SDK
CLI for GCP products and services

Container Registry
Fast, private image storage

Container Builder
Fast, consistent, reliable builds

Cloud Source Repositories
Private Git repositories hosted on GCP

Cloud Test Lab
On-demand app testing in a cloud service

Development Tool

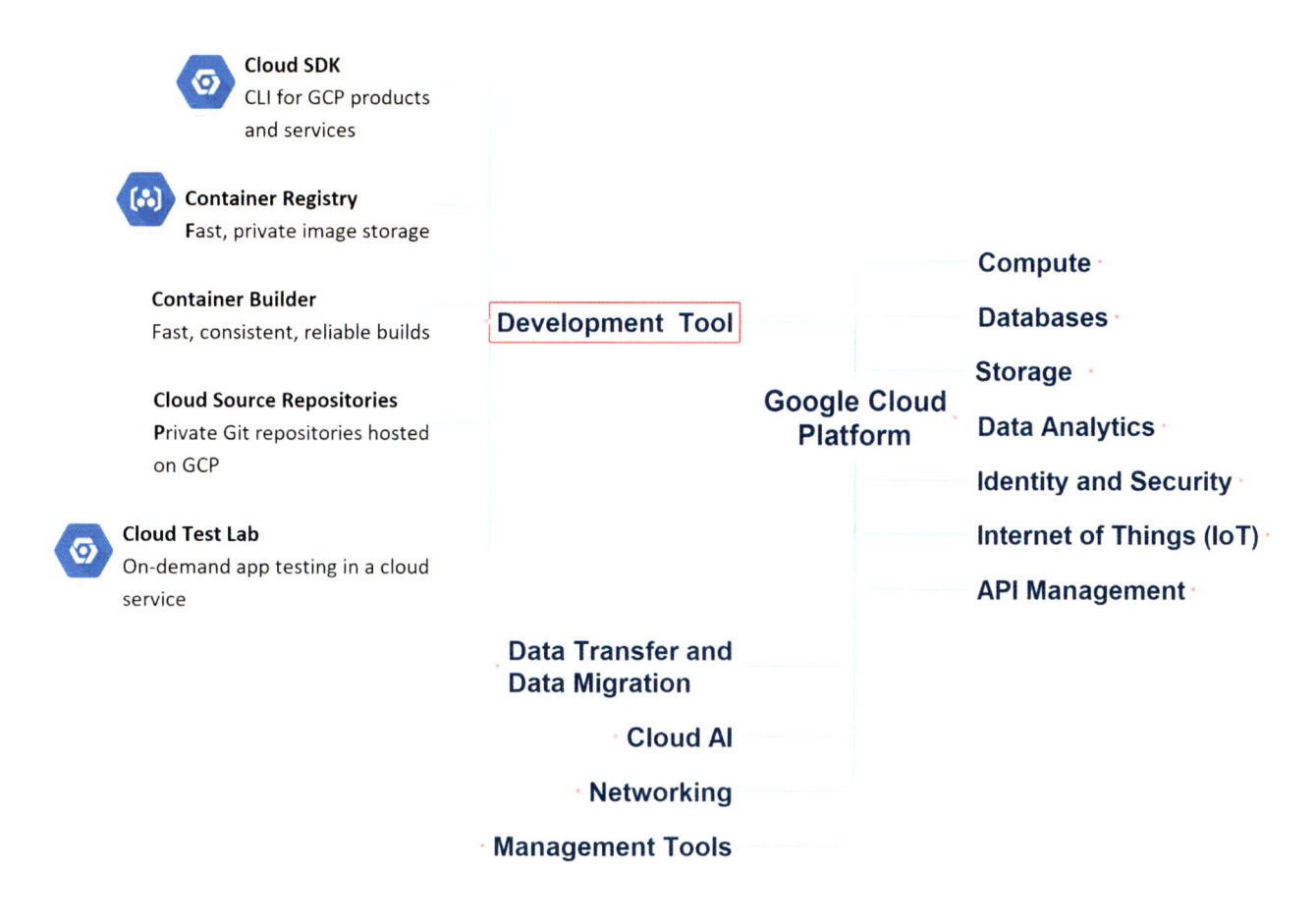

Google Cloud Platform
- Compute
- Databases
- Storage
- Data Analytics
- Identity and Security
- Internet of Things (IoT)
- API Management
- Data Transfer and Data Migration
- Cloud AI
- Networking
- Management Tools

Figure 76: GCP Development Tools

Google Cloud Platform provides a rich collection of tools and libraries to help the developer and software engineer community developing and managing every phase of the SDLC (Software Development Lifecycle). These tools include command line manipulations, Software Development Kit, Deployment tools and Integrated Development Environments. Some of the excellent tools include Cloud SDK, Cloud Shell, Cloud Build, Container Registry, Cloud Source Repositories and Cloud Deployment Manager. The table below briefly describes some of these tools:

Table 13: Google Cloud Developer Tools

TOOL	DESCRIPTION	BENEFITS
Cloud SDK	Command-line interface for Google Cloud Platform products and services	Manage all of your Google Cloud Platform projects from the command line including compute, networking, storage and development products.
Cloud Shell	Manage your infrastructure and applications from the command-line in any browser	Your own Linux VM accessible from your browser allows you to manage your GCP resources with all of the necessary tools pre-installed and up-to-date.
Cloud Build	Build, test, and deploy software on Google Cloud.	Help you to define custom workflows for building, testing, and deploying across multiple environments such as VMs, serverless, Kubernetes, or Firebase.
Container Registry	Securely store and manage Docker images in the Cloud.	Container Registry is a single place for your team to store and manage Docker images, perform vulnerability analysis, and decide who can access what with fine-grained access control.
Cloud Source Repositories	Private Git repositories hosted on Google Cloud Platform	Enable collaborative development with hosted Git repositories and improve developer productivity with automatic integration with Stackdriver Debugger and other Google Cloud Platform diagnostic tools.
Cloud Deployment Manager	Create and manage cloud resources with simple templates	Google Cloud Deployment Manager allows you to specify all the resources needed for your application in a declarative format using yaml.

Further Reads:
https://cloud.google.com/tools/docs/

Management Tools

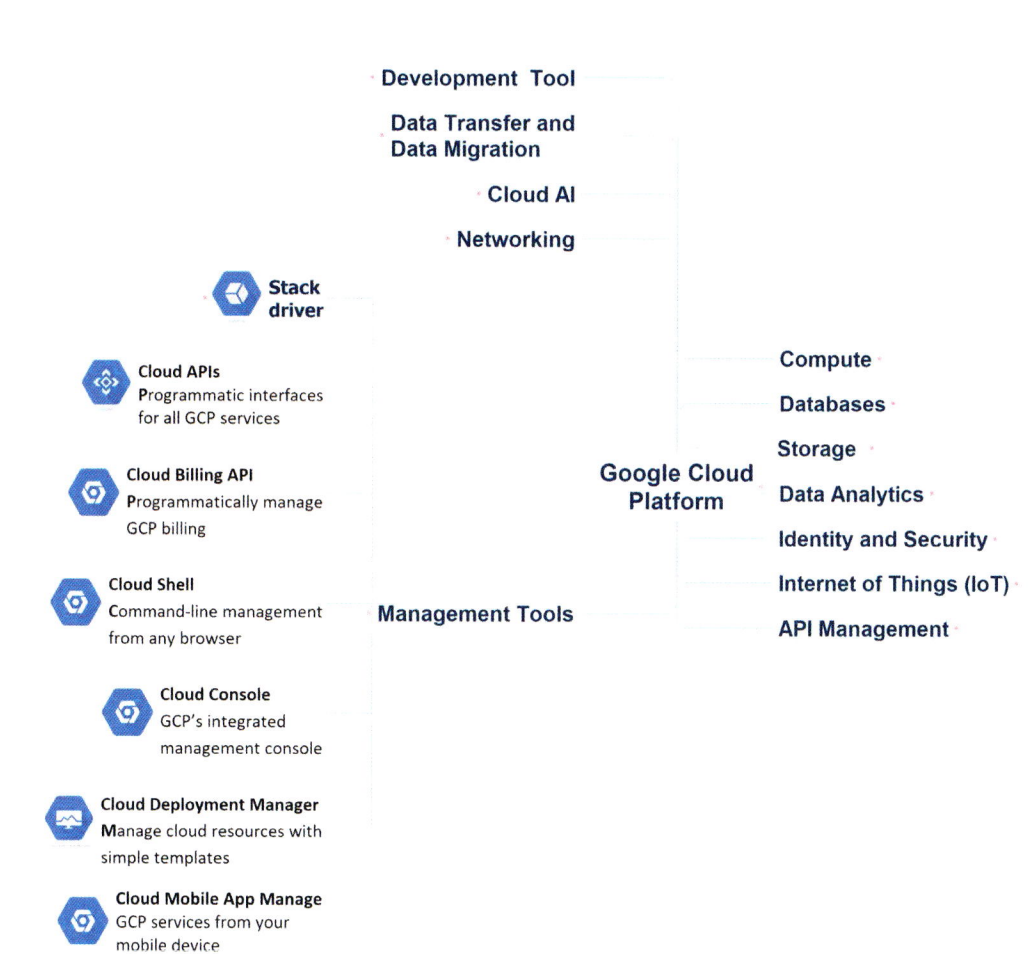

Figure 77: Management Tools

Google Cloud Management Tools help you to develop, deploy and manage your cloud applications.

Cloud API
Cloud APIs are programmatic interfaces allowing you to place REST calls or access client libraries in favourite programming languages and enable you to access Google Cloud Platform products from your code. Cloud APIs provide similar functionality to Cloud SDK and Cloud Console and allow you to automate your workflows leveraging your favourite language.
A detailed API listing is found here:
https://cloud.google.com/apis/

Google Stackdriver
Google Stackdriver allows you to monitor and manage all of the Google Cloud services, containers, applications, and infrastructure. Stackdriver aggregates metrics, logs, and events from infrastructure, giving developers and operators a rich set of observable signals that speed root-cause analysis and reduce mean time to resolution (MTTR). Stackdriver doesn't require extensive integration or multiple "panes of glass," and it **works with multiple clouds and on-premises infrastructure**.
Stackdriver Debugger connects your application's production data to your source code by inspecting the state of your application at any code location in production without stopping or slowing down your requests.
Stackdriver Error Reporting analyses and aggregates the errors in your cloud applications. Notifies you when new errors are detected.
Stackdriver Monitoring provides endpoint checks to web applications and other internet-accessible services running on your cloud environment. You can **configure uptime checks associated with URLs, groups, or resources, such as instances and load balancers**.
Stackdriver Trace provides latency sampling and reporting for Google App Engine, including per-URL statistics and latency distributions.

Google Cloud Certified Professional Cloud Architect, Second Edition

Stackdriver Logging provides you with the ability to filter, search, and view logs from your cloud and open source application services. Allows you to define metrics based on log contents that are incorporated into dashboards and alerts. Enables you to export logs to BigQuery, Google Cloud Storage, and Pub/Sub.

Stackdriver Profiler provides continuous profiling of resource consumption in your production applications, helping you identify and eliminate potential performance issues.

Further Reading

https://cloud.google.com/stackdriver/

API Management

Figure 78: API Management Tools

Cloud Endpoints

Cloud Endpoints is a distributed API management system comprising services, runtimes, and tools and provides API console for management, monitoring, and authentication of APIs on any Google Cloud backend. It enables user authentication through JSON Web Token validation and streamlined developer experience for Firebase Auth, Google Auth and Auth0. It also generates API keys in the Google Cloud Platform Console and validate on every API call and share your API with other developers to allow them to generate their keys.

Cloud Endpoints comprises of:

- Extensible Service Proxy (ESP) - for injecting Endpoints functionality and provide low latency and high performance for serving even the most demanding APIs. ESP runs in its own Docker container with better isolation and scalability and is distributed in the Container Registry. ESP can be used with App Engine flexible, Google Kubernetes Engine (GKE), Compute Engine or Kubernetes.
- Service Control - for applying API management rules.
- Service Management - for configuring API management rules.
- Cloud SDK - for deploying and management.
- Google Cloud Platform Console - for logging, monitoring and sharing.

Google Cloud Platform

- Compute
- Databases
- Storage
- Data Analytics
- Identity and Security
- Internet of Things (IoT)
- Development Tool
- Data Transfer and Data Migration
- Cloud AI
- Networking
- Management Tools
- API Management

API Management tools:

- **Cloud Endpoints** — Develop, deploy and manage APIs on GCP
- **Apigee Sense** — Intelligent behavior detection to protect APIs from attacks
- **API Analytics** — Insight into operational and business metrics for APIs
- **Apigee Open Banking APIx** — Accelerate Open Banking and PSD2 compliance
- **Cloud Heathcare API** — Secure APIs powering actionable healthcare insights
- **Apigee Healthcare APIx** — Accelerate building new FHIR API based digital services
- **API Monetization** — Flexible, easy-to-use solution to realize value from APIs
- **Apigee API Platform** — Develop, secure, deploy, and monitor your APIs everywhere
- **Google Maps Platform** — Discover new insights with targeted location data

Figure 79: Cloud Endpoints

To use Endpoints for OpenAPI, you start with configuring Endpoints and then deploy the Endpoints configuration through the Cloud SDK to a supported GCP backend, such as Compute Engine. ESP coordinates with Endpoints backend services to secure and monitor your API at runtime.

Similarly, you can develop a gRPC API with Endpoints.

Cloud Endpoints are also a great way to maintain two different versions of APIs and continue using the same till you disable one of the version. When you intend to make a backwards-compatible change, such as adding a new method, increment the minor version number (1.2, 1.3, etc.) in the **info.version** field and redeploy.

Cloud Endpoints is API management gateway whereas Apigee is a comprehensive API management platform built for Enterprises, with deployment options on cloud, on-premises or hybrid.

Apigee is a full lifecycle API management platform as depicted below that enables API providers to design, secure, deploy, monitor, and scale APIs.

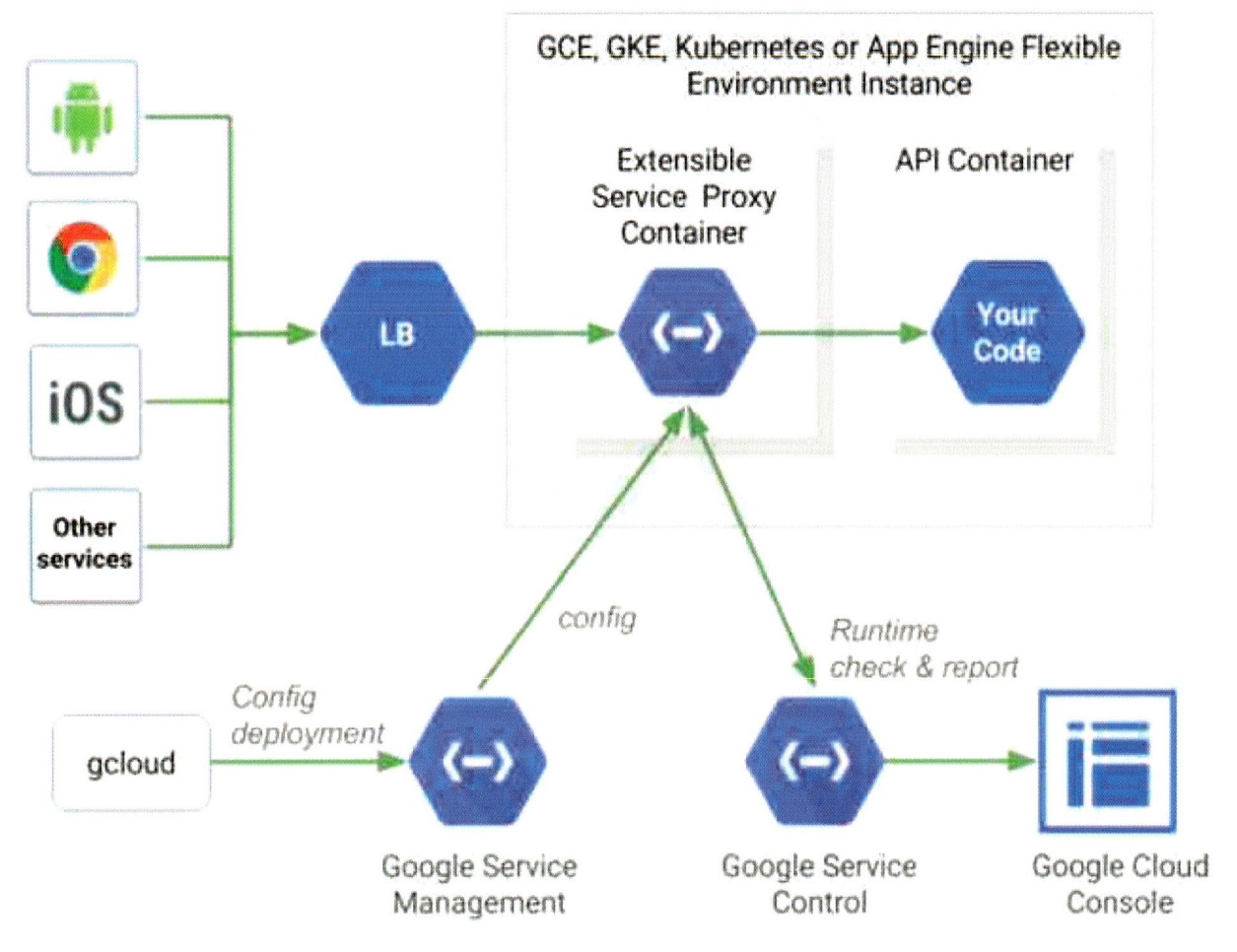

©2018 Google LLC, used with permission. Google and the Google logo are registered trademarks of Google LLC

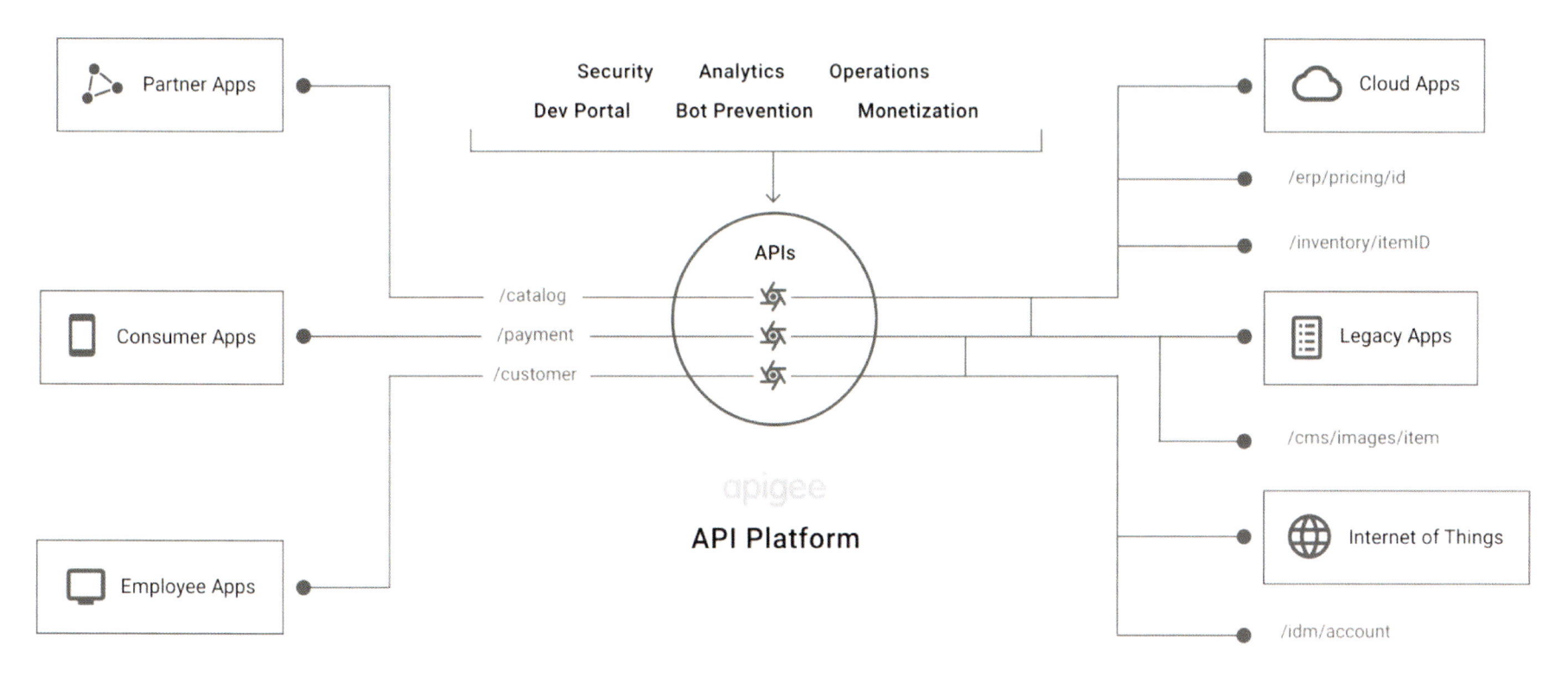

Figure 80: Apigee API Platform, Source: https://cloud.google.com/apigee-api-management/

©2018 Google LLC, used with permission. Google and the Google logo are registered trademarks of Google LLC

Further Reading:
- https://cloud.google.com/endpoints/
- https://cloud.google.com/blog/products/gcp/google-cloud-endpoints-now-ga-a-fast-scalable-api-gateway
- https://cloud.google.com/endpoints/docs/openapi/architecture-overview
- https://cloud.google.com/endpoints/docs/openapi/about-cloud-endpoints
- https://cloud.google.com/endpoints/docs/openapi/lifecycle-management
- https://cloud.google.com/monitoring/api/v3/metrics
- https://cloud.google.com/apigee-api-management/

Google Cloud Internet Of Things (IoT)

- Development Tool
- Data Transfer and Data Migration
- Cloud AI
- Networking
- Management Tools

Google Cloud Platform

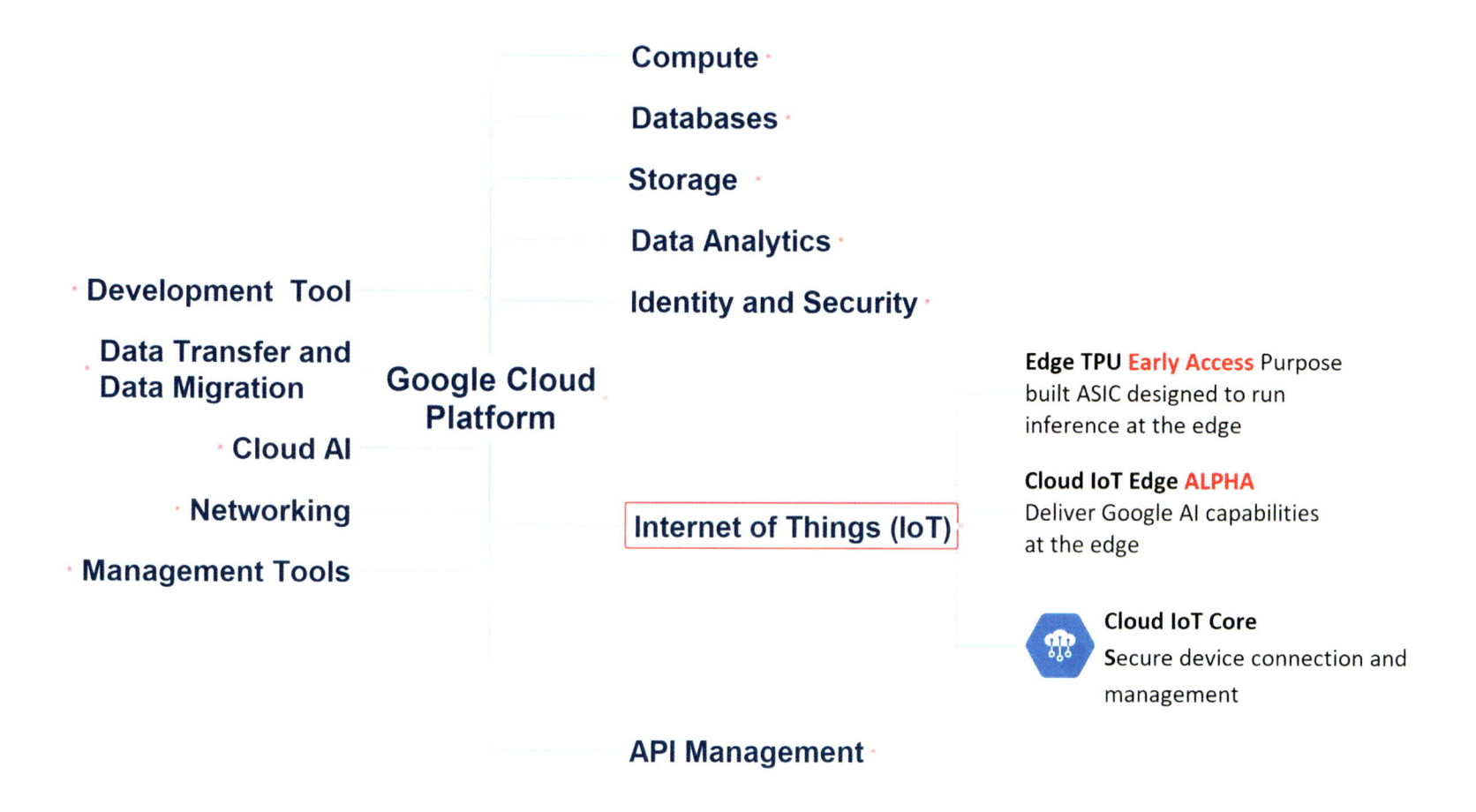

- Compute
- Databases
- Storage
- Data Analytics
- Identity and Security
- Internet of Things (IoT)
- API Management

Edge TPU Early Access Purpose built ASIC designed to run inference at the edge

Cloud IoT Edge ALPHA Deliver Google AI capabilities at the edge

Cloud IoT Core Secure device connection and management

Figure 81: Google Cloud Platform IoT

Google Cloud IoT is scalable, fully-managed cloud services and consists of a comprehensive set of capabilities for edge/on-premises computing with machine learning capabilities for all your IoT needs. It is a collection of tools to connect, process, store, and analyse data both at the edge and in the cloud.

Cloud IoT Core
The Google Cloud IoT Core is a fully managed service to easily and securely connect, manage, and ingest data from **millions of globally dispersed devices**, and with an integrated toolsets provides a complete solution for collecting IoT data stream in real time for advanced analytics, processing, analyzing, visualizing, combining with machine learning help to improve operational efficiency, anticipate problems, and build rich models that better describe and optimize your business. Cloud IoT Core enables ML connecting through the IoT Edge to deploy machine learning models on gateways and edge devices. This deployed model can tap into significantly powerful Edge TPU™ to run the trained **ML models at the edge** with unprecedented speed for real-time responses. The Cloud IoT Core supports the standard **MQTT** and **HTTP** protocols so that you can use your existing devices **with minimal firmware changes**.
Cloud IoT Core, using Cloud Pub/Sub underneath and <u>runs on Google's serverless infrastructure</u>, which scales automatically in response to real-time changes and adheres to stringent industry-standard security protocols that protect your business data.

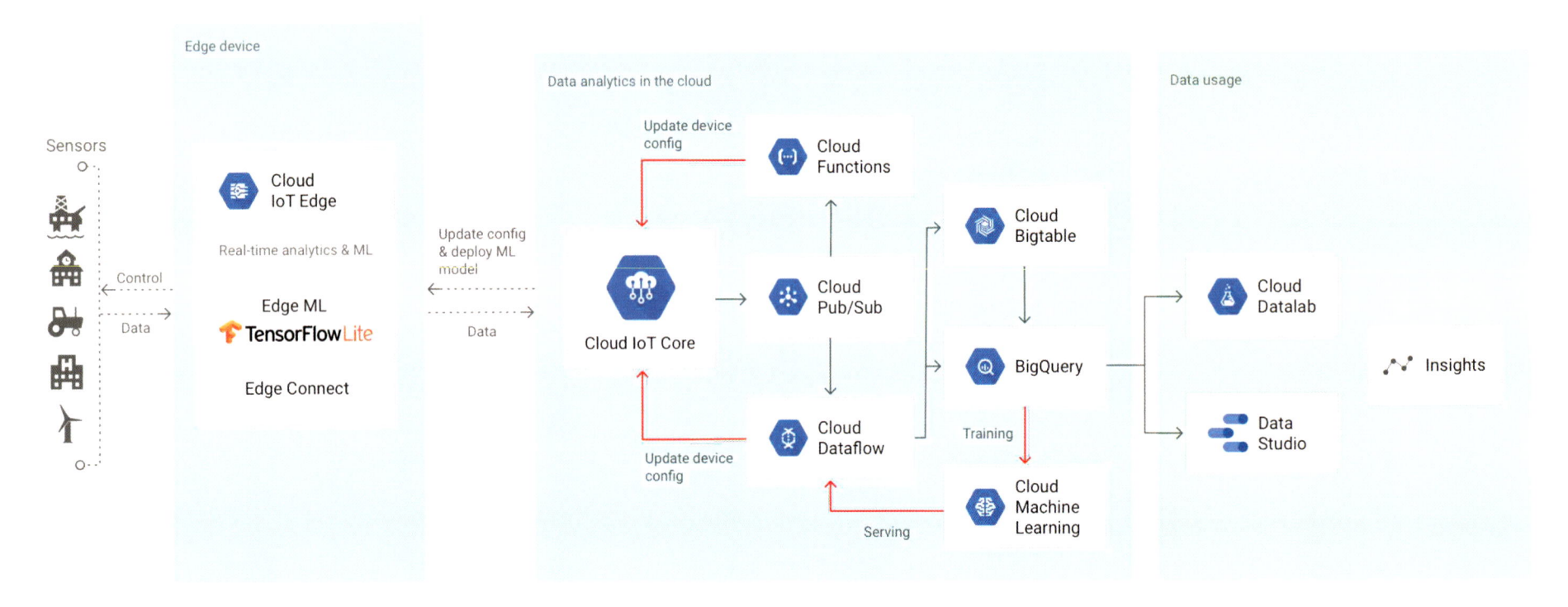

Figure 82: Cloud IoT Core

©2018 Google LLC, used with permission. Google and the Google logo are registered trademarks of Google LLC

Cloud IoT Edge
The Cloud IoT Edge extends Google Cloud's powerful data processing and machine learning to **billions of edge devices**, such as robotic arms, wind turbines, and oil rigs, so they can act on the data from their sensors in real time and make **real-time predictions** (predict outcomes locally) for **mission-critical IoT applications**. Cloud IoT Edge can run on Linux-based operating systems. Cloud IoT Edge is composed of two runtime components, **Edge Connect** and **Edge ML**, and also takes advantage of Google's purpose-built hardware accelerator ASIC chip, Edge TPU™.

Edge Connect securely connect edge devices to the cloud, enabling software and firmware updates, and manage the exchange of data with Cloud IoT Core.

Edge ML, built on a TensorFlow Lite runtime, run ML inferences of pre-trained TensorFlow Lite models locally and uses CPUs and hardware accelerators like Edge TPUs and GPUs to run on-device machine learning models. It also provides faster predictions for critical IoT applications than general-purpose IoT gateways — all while **ensuring data privacy and confidentiality**. This enables the next wave of machine learning applications and uses cases.

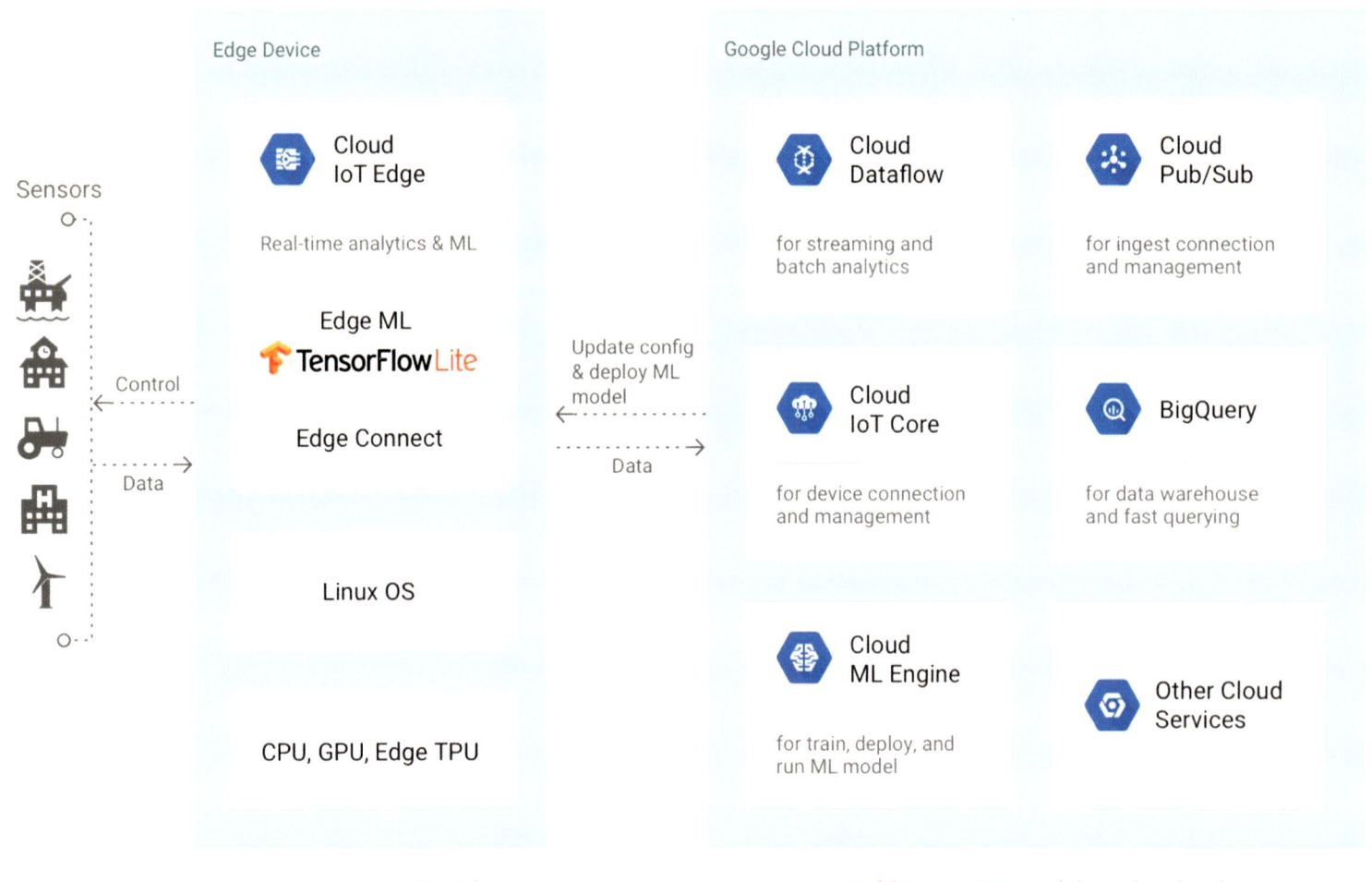

Figure 83: Cloud IoT Edge

Edge TPU

The Edge TPU is Google's purpose-built AI chip designed to run TensorFlow Lite ML models at the edge enabling through the deployment of high-quality ML inference at the edge complements Cloud TPU and Google Cloud services to provide an end-to-end, **cloud-to-edge**, augmented hardware and software infrastructure for facilitating the deployment of customers' AI-based solutions. Edge TPU offers high performance per watt with a small footprint, enabling a broad set of use cases such as predictive maintenance, anomaly detection, machine vision, robotics, voice recognition, and many more. It can be used in manufacturing, healthcare, retail, smart spaces, transportation, etc.. This hardware accelerator complements Cloud TPU, which is used for training models in the cloud. Edge TPU. It augments Google's Cloud TPU and Cloud IoT to provide an end-to-end (cloud-to-edge, hardware + software) infrastructure to facilitate the deployment of customers' AI-based solutions.

Further Reading:

- https://cloud.google.com/solutions/iot/
- https://cloud.google.com/iot-core/
- https://cloud.google.com/iot-edge/
- https://cloud.google.com/edge-tpu/

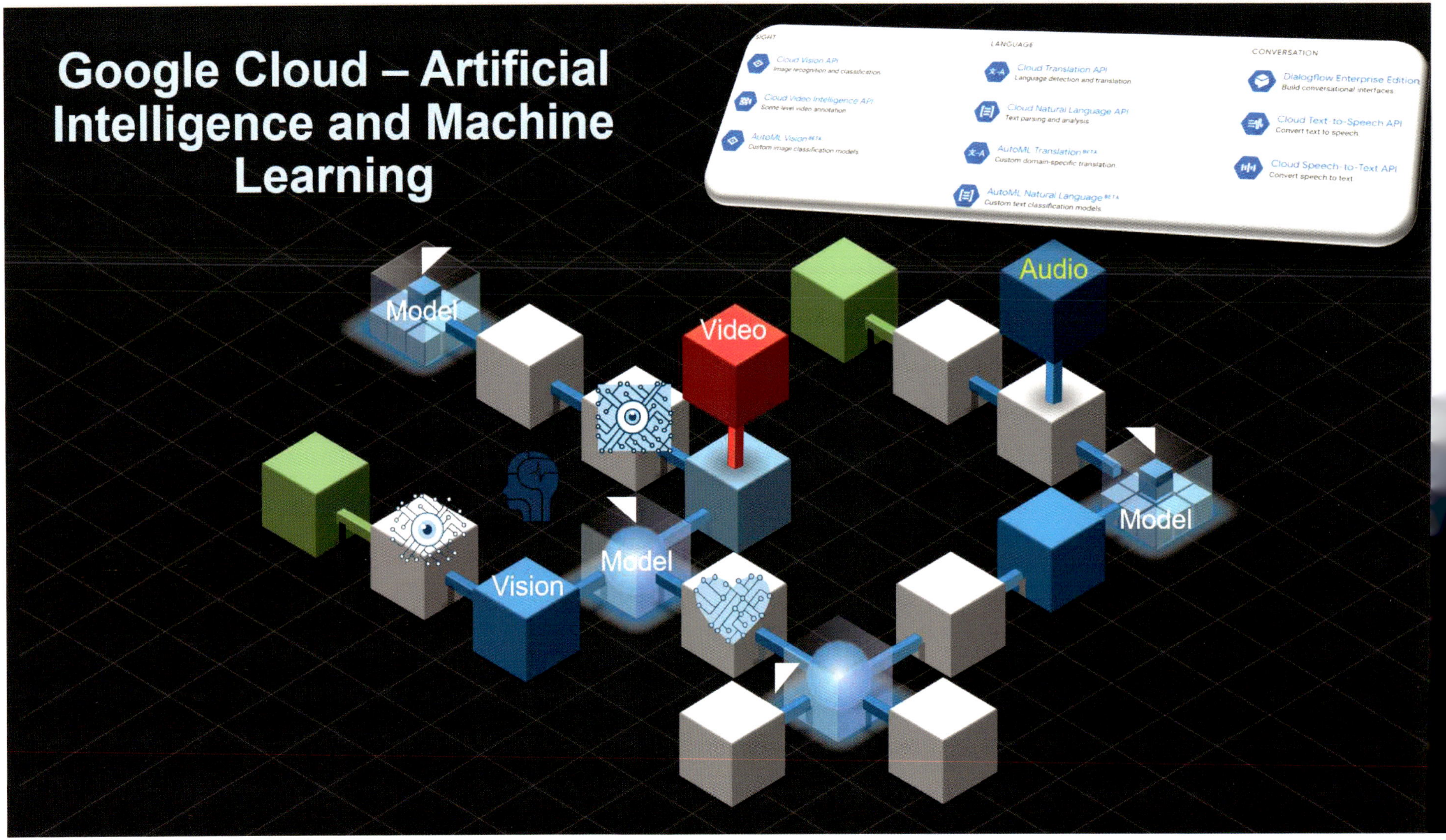
Google Cloud – Artificial Intelligence and Machine Learning
SIGHT
Cloud Vision API
Image recognition and classification
Cloud Video Intelligence API
Scene-level video annotation
AutoML Vision BETA
Custom image classification models
LANGUAGE
Cloud Translation API
Language detection and translation
Cloud Natural Language API
Text parsing and analysis
AutoML Translation BETA
Custom domain-specific translation
AutoML Natural Language BETA
Custom text classification models
CONVERSATION
Dialogflow Enterprise Edition
Build conversational interfaces
Cloud Text-to-Speech API
Convert text to speech
Cloud Speech-to-Text API
Convert speech to text
Model
Video
Audio
Model
Vision
Model

Cloud AI

Figure 84: Cloud AI Tools

Cloud AI, in my opinion, is one of the vital strength that Google Cloud Platform offers and has been building for some time to make AI real for the industry and crossing the chasm of data and analytics maturity of any organisation. Cloud AI is a crucial differentiator of the Google Cloud Platform. With its three critical pillars of AI :
- AI Building Blocks,
- AI Platform, and
- AI Solutions

Google is aiming at providing modern machine learning services, with its pre-trained models and service to generate your tailored models.

Cloud AI Tools allow you to take steps forwards to AI First Philosophy. Cloud AI's neural-net-based ML service has better training performance and increased accuracy compared to other deep learning systems. Major Google applications use Cloud machine learning, including Photos (image search), Translate, Inbox (Smart Reply), and the Google app (voice search).

There are two types of AI Building Blocks those enable you to introduce Cognitive and humanlike inherent capabilities of sight, language, and conversation abilities to your applications: **APIs for pre-trained models** and **AutoML for custom**

Google Cloud Certified Professional Cloud Architect, Second Edition

models. These building blocks can be used individually or in combination.

Figure 85: Cloud AI building blocks

APIs allow to utilise pre-trained models for everyday use cases along with your proven datasets without worrying about training models and access the latest fully trained models as Google makes breakthroughs in AI research.

On the other hand, Cloud AutoML uses Google's state-of-the-art transfer learning and neural architecture search technology to build domain-specific models and increase accuracy for a variety of use cases.

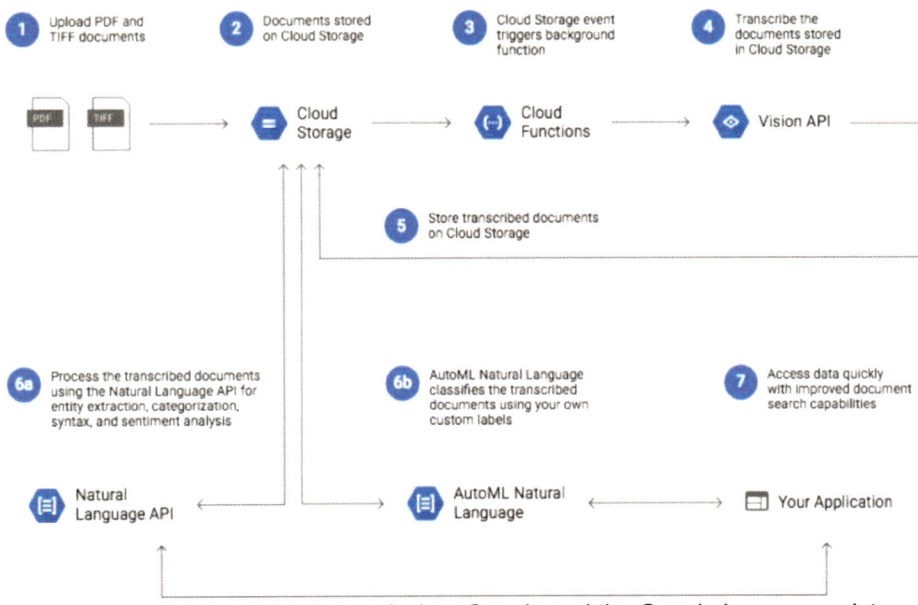

Figure 86: Example usage of Cloud ML and NLP APIs

Google Cloud Natural Language reveals the structure and meaning of text both through powerful pretrained machine learning models available through REST endpoints and through custom models that are easy to build with AutoML Natural Language^{BETA}. One can easily integrate the API into custom apps which would run on App Engine, GKE, Compute Engine, and mobile platforms such as Android and iOS. Cloud Natural Language could easily be integrated with the Vision OCR capabilities, or the Cloud Speech-to-Text features to create compelling apps or services those then could also be accessed from other GCP services including the Cloud Dataflow, Cloud Dataproc, or Cloud Datalab.

Cloud Natural Language can extract information about people, places, events, and much more mentioned in text documents, news articles, or blog posts, and at the same time able to understand the sentiment about products on social media or parse intent from customer conversations happening in a call centre or a messaging app. You can analyse text uploaded in your request or integrate with your document storage on Google Cloud Storage.

©2018 Google LLC, used with permission. Google and the Google logo are registered trademarks of Google LLC

An example of architecture that shows how to extract insights from and customer sentiments analysing phone calls data ingesting through Cloud Speech-to-Text and analytics derived from BigQuery.

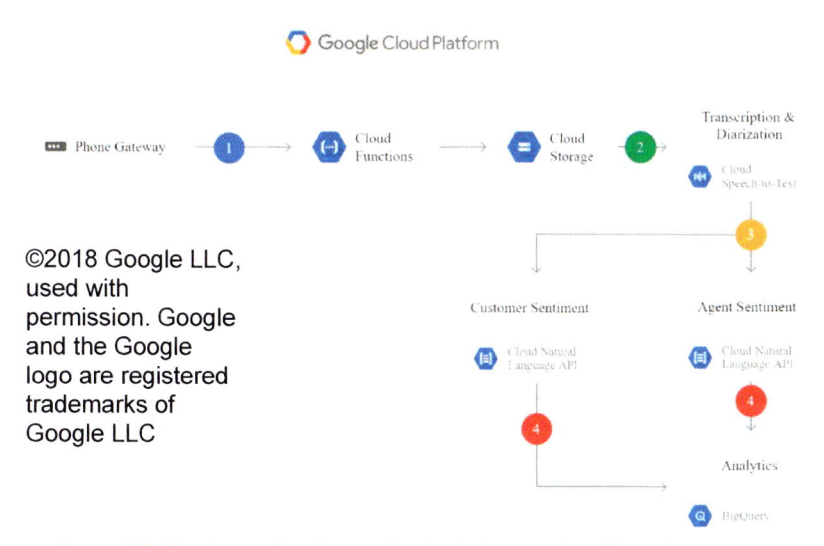

©2018 Google LLC, used with permission. Google and the Google logo are registered trademarks of Google LLC

Figure 87: Customer Sentiment Analysis Leveraging Cloud Natural Language API

TensorFlow is an open source library for machine learning, is designed to run on multiple computers to distribute training workloads. TensorFlow is Google's one of the earliest seed towards its AI Vision. Google made the TensorFlow as an open source release. TensorFlow contains a python code library to allows users to express mathematical operations within our ML models as a graph of data flows. **These flows represent how data moves between operations**. The API also **accelerates computation intensive neural networking and machine learning algorithms on multiple CPU and GPU components**.

©2018 Google LLC, used with permission. Google and the Google logo are registered trademarks of Google LLC

The following diagram illustrates the architecture for running a distributed configuration of TensorFlow on Compute Engine and using Cloud ML Engine with Cloud Datalab to execute predictions with your trained model.

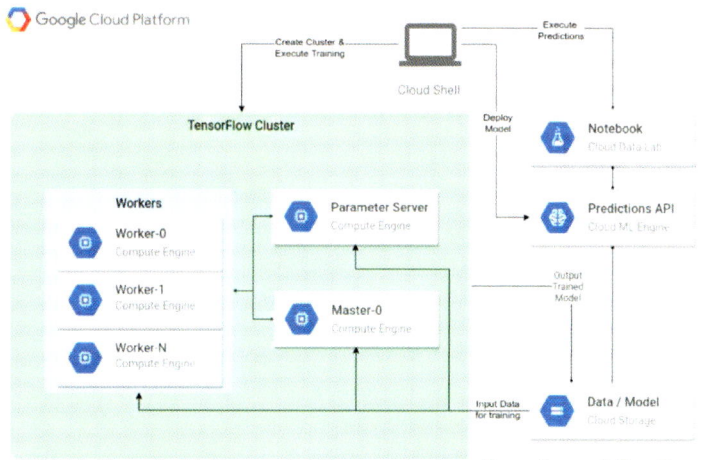

Figure 88: Running a distributed training job on Cloud ML Engine

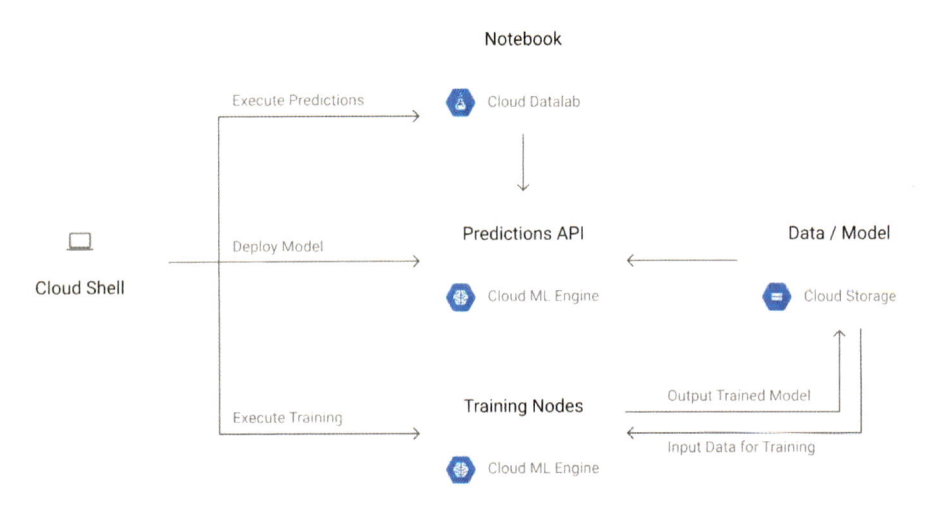

The following diagram describes an example of architecture that runs a distributed training job on Cloud ML Engine and uses the Cloud Datalab to execute predictions with your trained model.

Natural conversational interfaces
Dialogflow is an end-to-end, build-once deploy-everywhere development suite for creating conversational interfaces for websites, mobile applications, popular messaging platforms, and IoT devices. Dialogflow is used to build interfaces such as chatbots and conversational IVR those allow natural and rich interactions between your users and your business.
Below is one of my favourite usage example from Gary Stafford, Integrating Search Capabilities with Actions for Google Assistant, using GKE and Elasticsearch.

Below is a great example that illustrates how to stitch together Dialogflow, Google ML, CloudFunction and Kubernetes to build a fantastic search enabled intelligent interface.

©2018 Google LLC, used with permission. Google and the Google logo are registered trademarks of Google LLC

Google machine learning enables Natural language understanding through a user's intent and extracts prebuilt entities such as time, date, and numbers. Dialogflow comes with an integrated code editor to natively build serverless applications linked to your conversational interface through Cloud Functions for Firebase.

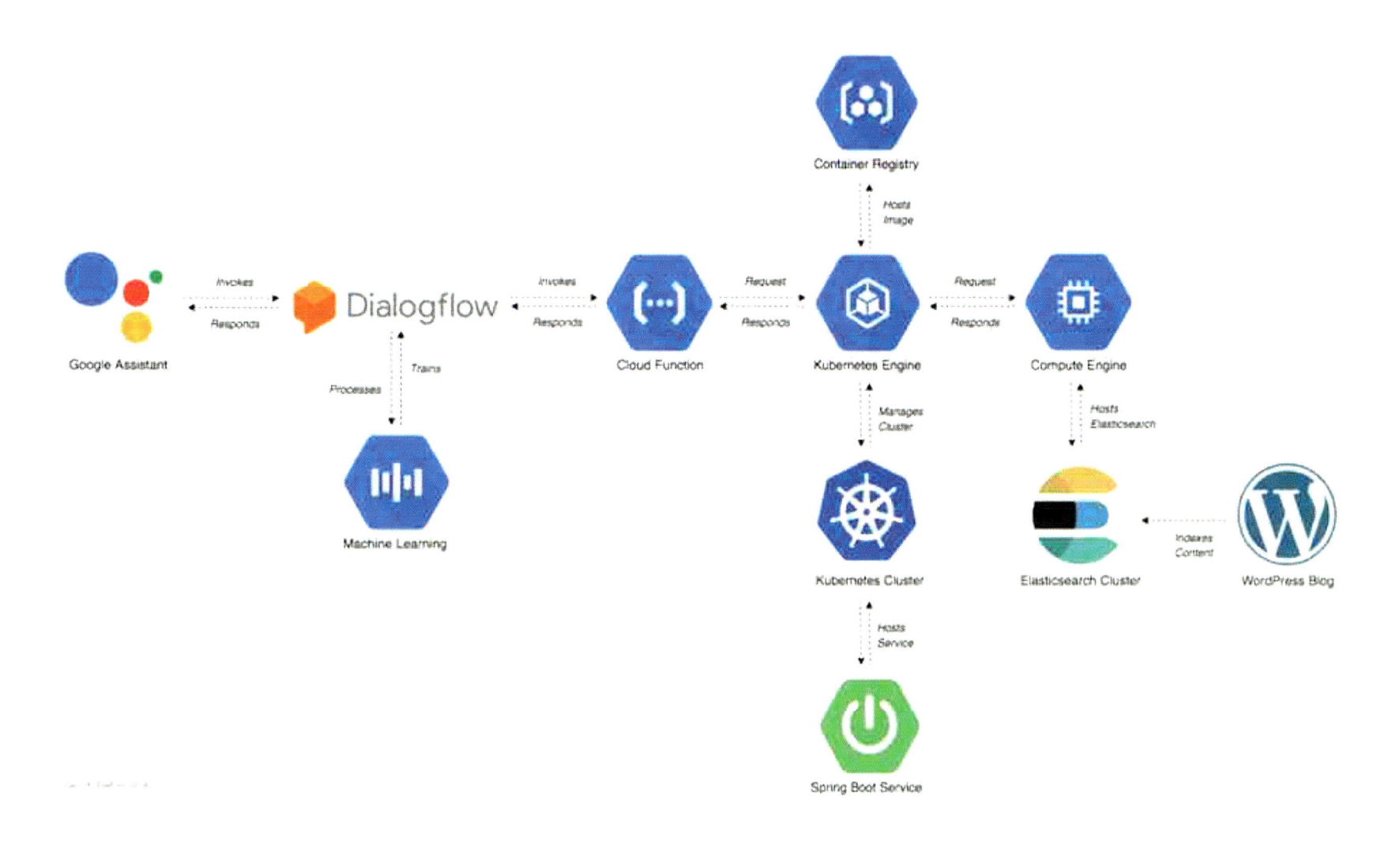

Figure 89: The high-level architecture of a search engine-enhanced Action for Google Assistant

Source: https://programmaticponderings.com/2018/09/24/integrating-search-capabilities-with-actions-for-google-assistant-using-gke-and-elasticsearch-part-2/
© Used with kind permission from Gary Stafford

Google Cloud Certified Professional Cloud Architect, Second Edition

You may also explore the **Dialogflow Knowledge Connectors** [Beta] introduces a mechanism allowing you to add bulk data, FAQs and knowledge-base articles from your enterprise to your agent. Knowledge Connectors use some of the same technologies used by Google Search and the Google Assistant to extract the right answers from the data corpus provided. Dialogflow could help you in enabling a great Enterprise Knowledge Graph.

Another brilliant example, building a chatbot that's capable of extracting texts from a picture (optionally translating it to different languages) and sending back the result to the user via SMS (or a phone call). Such an application could be used to extract other useful information from a given image or even a video stream and sends SMS notifications to the user or a group of users.

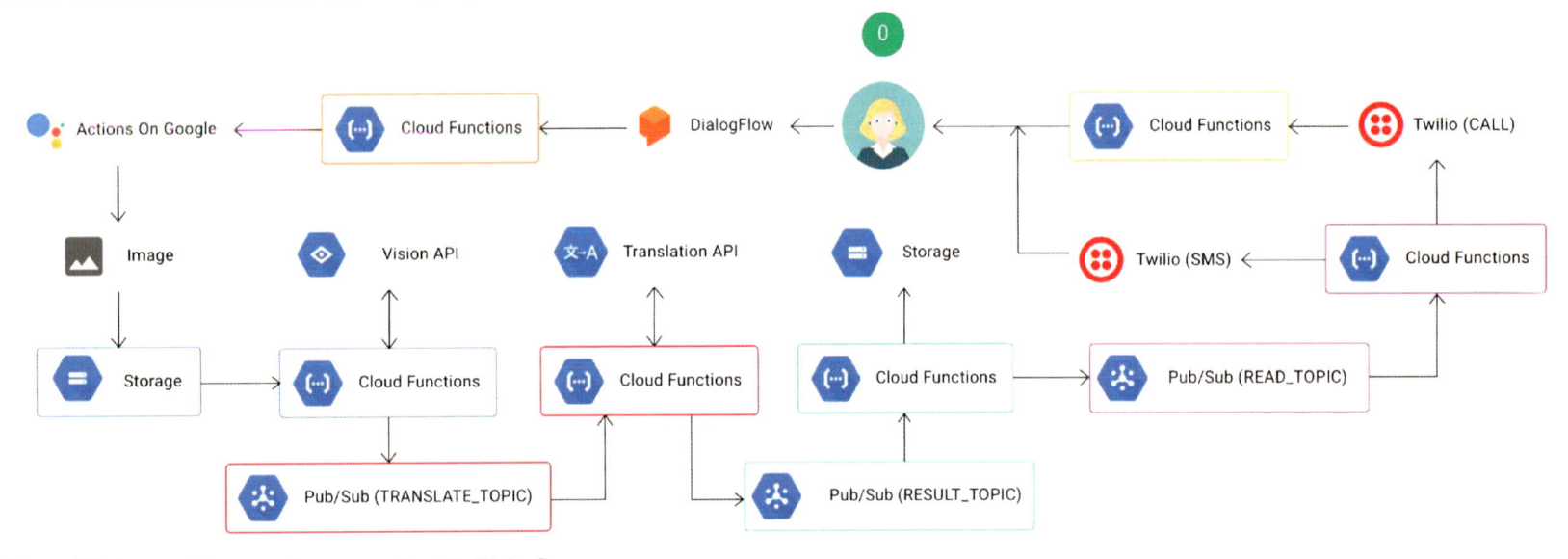

Figure 90: A complete serverless example with Dialogflow

Source: https://medium.com/google-developer-experts/building-your-next-serverless-application-the-complete-guide-98e48f85bd3c
Copyright: Used with Kind permission from Wassim Chegham

Machine learning and data
Machine learning has become a critical component of the analysis phase of the data lifecycle. It can be used to augment processed results, suggest data-collection optimisations, and predict outcomes in data sets. Consider the following use cases.
- **Product recommendations**: You can build a model that recommends products based on previous purchases and site navigation.
- **Prediction**: Use machine learning to predict the performance of complex systems, such as financial markets.
- **Automated assistants**: Build automated assistants that understand and answer questions asked by users.
- **Sentiment analysis**: Determine the underlying sentiment of user comments on product reviews and news stories.

Google Cloud ML Engine
Google Cloud Machine Learning (MLE) Engine is a **managed service** allowing developers and data scientists to **train** their ML models **at scale**, to host your trained model in the cloud, and to use your model to make predictions about new data build and bring superior machine learning models to production. Cloud ML Engine Cloud Machine Learning Engine brings the power and flexibility of TensorFlow to the cloud.
The diagram below highlights the stages in an ML workflow where the blue-filled boxes indicate where Cloud ML Engine provides managed services and APIs:
As the diagram suggests, you can use the Cloud ML Engine to accomplish the following stages in the ML workflow:
1. Train an ML model on your data:
    a. Train model
    b. Evaluate model accuracy
    c. Tune hyperparameters
2. Deploy your trained model and Send prediction requests to your model:
    a. Online prediction
    b. Batch prediction
3. Monitor the predictions on an ongoing basis
4. Manage your models and model versions.

Figure 92: Model building and tuning leveraging Tensorflow

What is Machine Learning?

Machine learning (ML) is a subfield of artificial intelligence (AI). The goal of ML is to make computers learn from the data that you give them. Instead of writing code that describes the action the computer should take, your code provides an algorithm that adapts based on examples of intended behavior. The resulting program, consisting of the algorithm and associated learned parameters, is called a trained model.

Figure 91: ML Workflow

©2018 Google LLC, used with permission. Google and the Google logo are registered trademarks of Google LLC

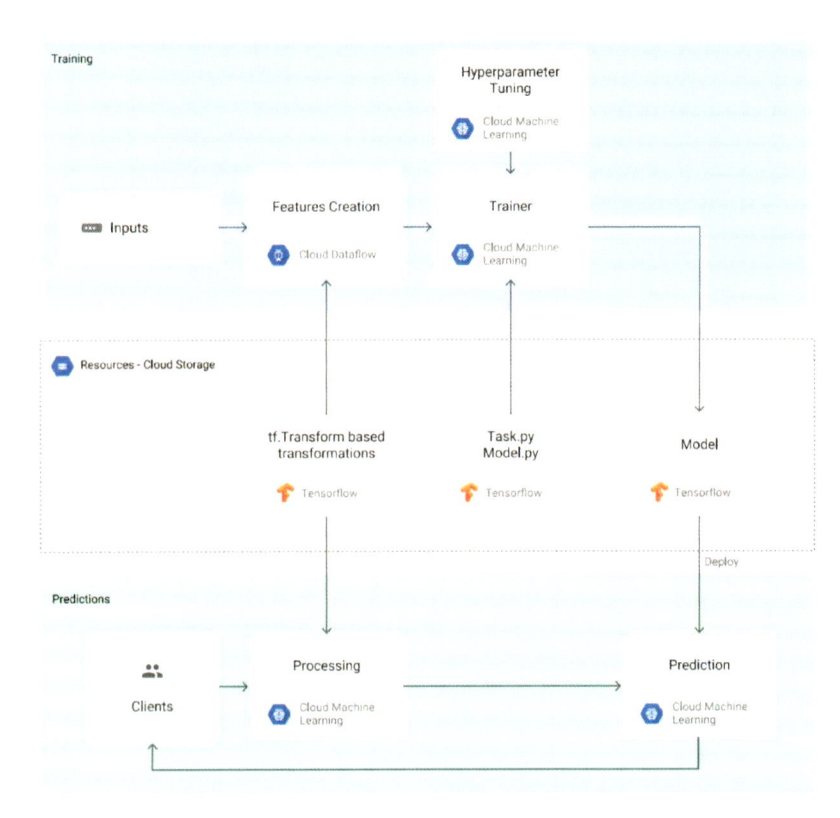

You create models using the TensorFlow framework, an open source framework for machine intelligence, and then use Cloud Machine Learning to manage to preprocess training and prediction.

Cloud ML Engine benefits over TensorFlow:
- It runs ML tasks in a serverless environment
- Facilitates hyperparameter tuning
- Hosts models as a RESTful API accessible from heterogeneous clients (not only Python)

Cloud Machine Learning is integrated with Cloud Dataflow for data pre-processing, which can access data stored in both Cloud Storage and BigQuery. It also works with Cloud Load Balancing to serve online predictions at scale.

You can develop and test TensorFlow models completely in GCP using Cloud Datalab and Jupyter notebooks, and then use Cloud Machine Learning for large-scale training and prediction workloads.

The following diagram illustrates the approach to leveraging TensorFlow instead of the Cloud ML Engine.

Portable Models
Use the open source TensorFlow SDK, or other supported ML frameworks (in beta) to train models locally on sample data sets and use the Google Cloud Platform for training at scale.

©2018 Google LLC, used with permission. Google and the Google logo are registered trademarks of Google LLC

The workflow of Cloud Machine Learning consists of the following phases:

- **Preprocessing**: Cloud Machine Learning converts features from input datasets into a supported format, and might also normalise and transform the data to enable more efficient learning. During preprocessing, the training, evaluation, and test data is stored in Cloud Storage. This also makes the data accessible to Cloud Dataflow during this phase for any additional required preprocessing.
- **Graph building**: Cloud Machine Learning converts the supplied TensorFlow model into a Cloud Machine Learning model with operations for training, evaluation, and prediction.
- **Training**: Cloud Machine Learning continuously iterates and evaluates the model according to submitted parameters.

- **Prediction**: Cloud Machine Learning uses the model to perform computations. Predictions can be computed in either batches or on-demand, as an online prediction service. Batch predictions are designed to be run against large datasets asynchronously, using services such as Cloud Dataflow to orchestrate the analysis. On-demand predictions are often used with custom apps running on App Engine, GKE, or Compute Engine.

Cloud ML Engine trained models can be downloaded for local execution or mobile integration. You can also import scikit-learn, XGBoost, Keras, and TensorFlow models that have been trained anywhere for **fully-managed, real-time prediction hosting** — no Docker container required.

Training and Online Prediction leverages multiple frameworks to train and serve classification, regression, clustering, and dimensionality reduction models.
- scikit-learn for the breadth and simplicity of classical machine learning
- XGBoost for the ease and accuracy of extreme gradient boosting
- Keras for easy and fast prototyping of deep learning
- TensorFlow for the cutting edge power of deep learning

You can also import models that have been trained anywhere.

Further Reading:

https://cloud.google.com/solutions/running-distributed-tensorflow-on-compute-engine
https://cloud.google.com/ml-engine/
https://cloud.google.com/solutions/data-lifecycle-cloud-platform
https://cloud.google.com/data-science/

How Google Cloud enhance your AI and ML Journey

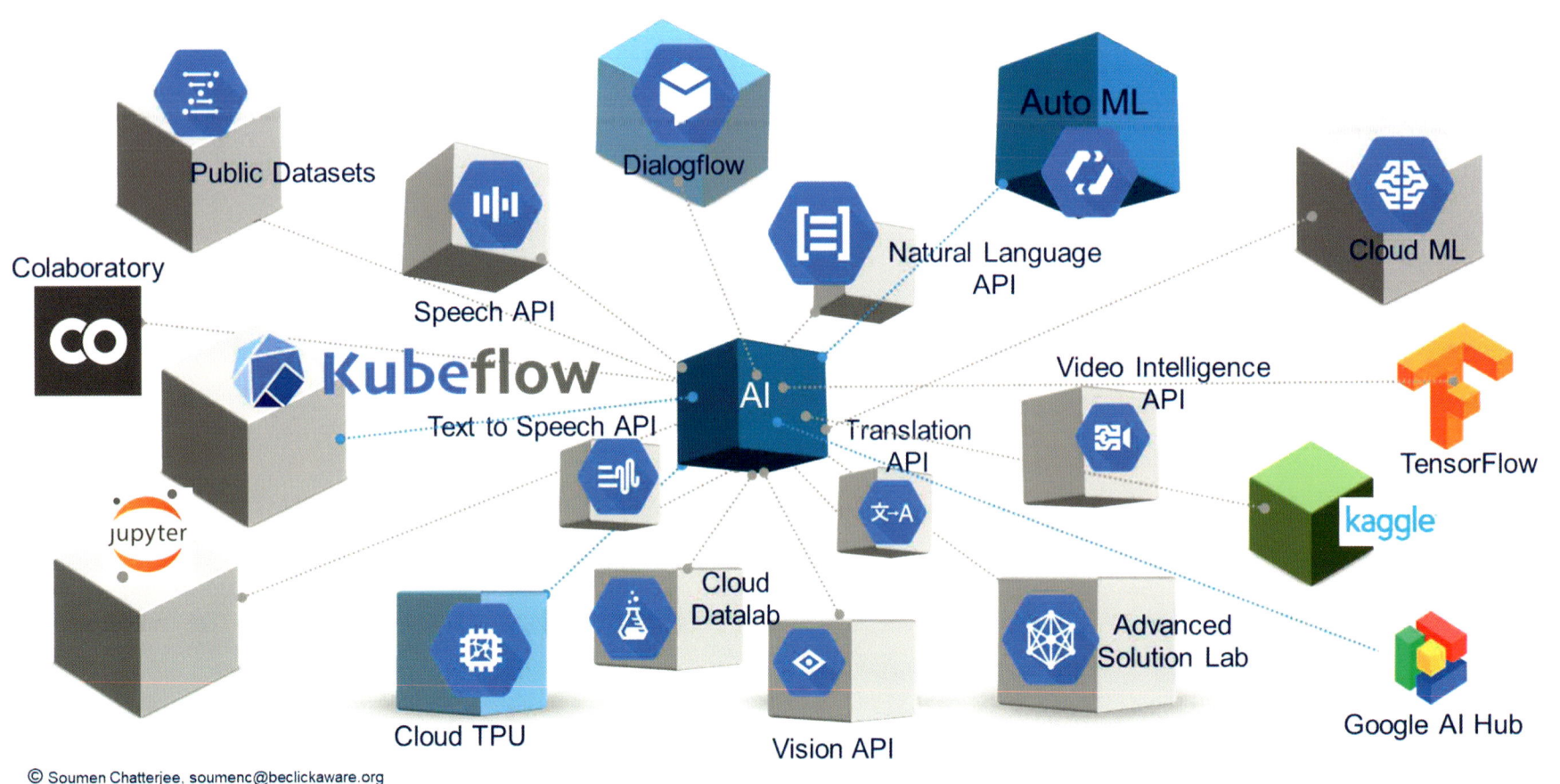

Tools for data scientists

- Public Datasets
- Colaboratory
- Dialogflow
- Auto ML
- Speech API
- Natural Language API
- Cloud ML
- Kubeflow
- AI
- Video Intelligence API
- Text to Speech API
- Translation API
- TensorFlow
- Jupyter
- kaggle
- Cloud TPU
- Cloud Datalab
- Vision API
- Advanced Solution Lab
- Google AI Hub

© Soumen Chatterjee, soumenc@beclickaware.org

Google Cloud Certified Professional Cloud Architect, Second Edition

AI First: Democratize AI

Google's vision as an "**AI First**" organisation, is embedded into its core DNA, reinforced by its large-scale investments in AI portfolio over the years and quarters and reflected on its continued focus on contextual information, machine learning, and developing intelligent technology infused with ML and Contextual information to improve customer experience. Google is leading the way with its impressive AI portfolios in the industry. AI now infuses almost all of Google's actions and products – its search engine, Pixel Phone, Google Assistant, Gmail, YouTube recommendations, data-centre cooling systems, G Suite product sets.

It is widely hyped up across the planet about AI and Machine Learning adoption and capabilities within organisations and 'An I First' is more of a buzz than actual action. Adoption of AI and ML would require a robust Data Native DNA within your Data-Centric organisation (DIVIDE approach within A Data-Centric Organization – How GCP enabling the CxO Vision) This is where Google is aiming at to capture and real differentiator of their Cloud Platform.

However, outside Google and the tech product sectors in general, the adoption of machine learning has not happened much. It is learned from various sources that only about 10,000 people estimated to be working in deep learning around the world, whereas the population of data scientists is in the range of 2 million. Google Cloud and its platform strategy is, therefore, aiming at making Artificial Intelligence is more accessible to every organisation bypassing the people, process and massive compute / storage infrastructure through its remarkably powerful Google Cloud Platform propositions those are setting Google Cloud apart from the fierce competition are Cloud AI, Auto ML and ML APIs (ML services, pre-trained models, and custom-generated solutions for tailored models), Serverless Platform, recent rolling out of the cloud tensor processing units (GPU, TPU). Google recent introduction of Kubeflow Pipelines - a workbench to compose, deploy and manage end-to-end ML workflows in Kubernetes and announcement of AI Hub - a central location for data scientists in enterprises to find various machine learning content, both public and private, such as data pipelines and notebooks to facilitate collaboration, reuse and deployment have reinforced their commitments to '**Democratize AI**', making it affordable and accessible for more significant benefits.

Further Read:

https://ai.google/
https://www.blog.google/products/google-cloud/cloud-automl-making-ai-accessible-every-business/
https://cloud.google.com/solutions/ai/

Grouping Google Cloud Platform resources

Grouping of resources is a great way to manage – whether it is to isolate tiered architecture (Development WebServers, Databases, Test environment etc.), management of traffic in or outflow, adhere to compliance to compliance demands through resource classification, monitor specific resources, or see those resources by billing account. GCP provides multiple ways to annotate your resources, to make them easier to track: security marks, labels and network tags.

Table 14: Labels, Tags and Security Marks

Grouping Mechanism	Description	GCP Resources
Labels	Labels are key/value pairs. Some of the key usages of labels are: • Identify the resources used by individual teams or cost centres • **Distinguish deployment environments** (production: web server, production: database, dev:web server) • Identify owners, state labels. • Use for cost allocation and billing breakdowns. • Monitor resource groups via Stackdriver, which can use labels accessible in the resource metadata.	• BigQuery • Cloud Bigtable • Cloud Dataflow • Cloud Dataproc • Cloud Deployment Manager • Cloud Functions • Cloud Key Management Service • Cloud Pub/Sub • Cloud Spanner • Cloud SQL • Cloud Storage • Compute Engine • Google Kubernetes Engine • Networking • Resource Manager

Security Marks	Main use cases for security marks:
	• Classifying and organising assets and findings independent of resource-level labelling mechanisms, including multi-parented groupings
	• Enabling tracking of violation severity and priority
	• Integrating with workflow systems for assignment and resolution of incidents
	• Enabling differentiated policy enforcement on resources, projects or groups of projects
		• Organisation
		• Project
		• App Engine
		   o Application
		   o Service
		• Compute Engine
		   o Address
		   o Disk
		   o Firewalls
		   o GlobalAddress
		   o InstanceGroup
		   o Network
		   o Route
		   o SslCertificate
		   o Subnetwork
		   o TargetVPNGateway
		   o VPNTunnel
		• Cloud Datastore
		   o Kind
		• Cloud Storage

	• Enhancing security focused insights into your resources, e.g., clarifying which publicly accessible buckets are within policy and which are not	o Image o Bucket o Instance
Network Tagging	Network tags apply to instances and are the means for controlling network traffic to and from a VM instance. On GCP networks, tags identify which VM instances are subject to firewall rules and network routes. You can use the cards as source and destination values in firewall rules. For routes, tags are used to identify to which instances a certain route applies. Using tags, you can create additional isolation between subnetworks by selectively allowing only certain instances to communicate.	• Compute Engine virtual machine (VM) instances. • Firewall rules and routes applicable to specific VM instances. Network tags could be added to VM instances or instance templates but cannot tag other GCP resources. Network tags could be assigned to new instances at creation time, or edit the set of assigned tags at any time later. **Network tags can be edited without stopping an instance**.

Further Reading:

https://cloud.google.com/blog/products/gcp/labelling-and-grouping-your-google-cloud-platform-resources
https://cloud.google.com/resource-manager/docs/creating-managing-labels
https://cloud.google.com/bigquery/docs/adding-using-labels
https://cloud.google.com/security-command-center/docs/how-to-asset-inventory#using_security_marks
https://cloud.google.com/vpc/docs/add-remove-network-tags

Filtering by Service account vs Network tag

If you need strict control over how firewall rules are applied to VMs, target service accounts and source service accounts are used instead of target tags and source tags:
- A network tag is **an arbitrary attribute**. One or more network tags can be associated with an instance by any IAM member who has permission to edit it. IAM members with the Compute Engine Instance Admin role to a project have this permission. IAM members who can edit an instance can change its network tags, which could change the set of applicable firewall rules for that instance.
- **A service account represents an identity associated with an instance**. Only one service account can be associated with an instance. You control access to the service account by controlling the grant of the Service Account User role for other IAM members. For an IAM member to start an instance using a service account, that member must have the Service Account User role to at least that service account as well as appropriate permissions to create instances (for example, having the Compute Engine Instance Admin role to the project).

You cannot mix and match service accounts and network tags in any firewall rule, and you cannot use target service accounts and target tags together in any firewall rule (ingress or egress).

Further Reading:
- https://cloud.google.com/vpc/docs/firewalls#service-accounts-vs-tags

- https://cloud.google.com/blog/products/gcp/three-ways-to-configure-robust-firewall-rules?hl=fa

Putting the puzzle together – A high-level Network Tagging Example

When you want to create a firewall rule restricting access to sensitive user billing information in a data store running on a set of VMs in your VPC. The traditional approach here is to attach tags to VMs and create a firewall rule that allows access to specific tags, e.g., the creation of a firewall rule that allows all VMs with the billing-frontend tag to access to all VMs with the tag billing-data. **The drawback of this approach is that any developer with Compute InstanceAdmin role for the project can now attach billing-frontend as a tag to their VM, and thus unintentionally gain access to sensitive data**.

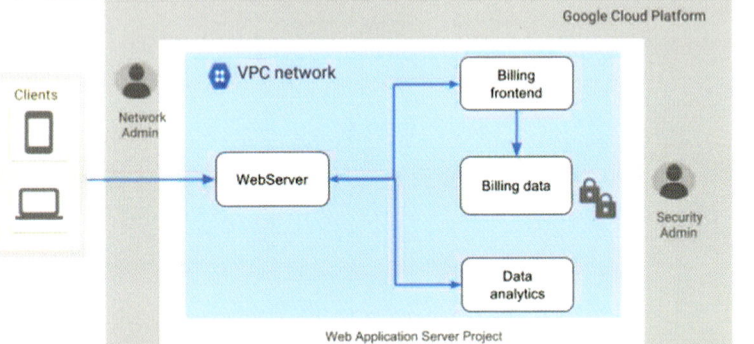

Figure 93: Firewall Rules leveraging Service Accounts

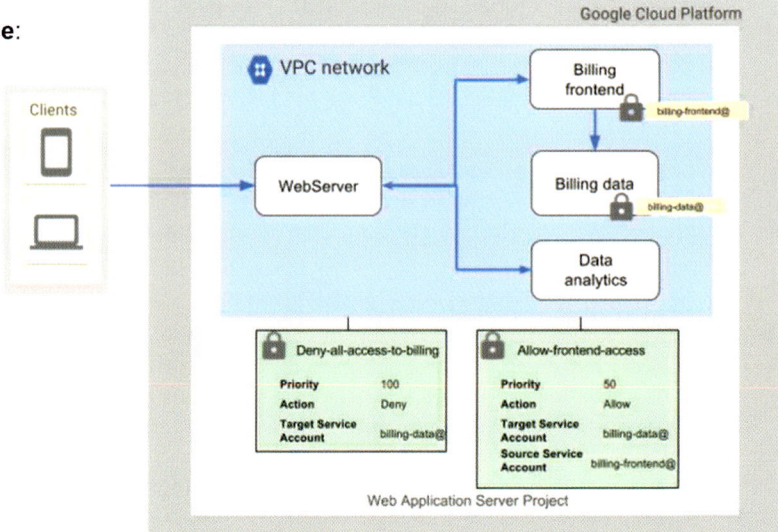

Using service accounts, instead of using tags, developers could be blocked from enabling a

firewall rule on their instances unless they have access to the appropriate centrally managed service accounts. We could create a firewall rule allowing access to the **billing-data@** service account only **if the originating source service account of the traffic is billing-frontend@**.

Adapted from source:

https://cloud.google.com/blog/products/gcp/three-ways-to-configure-robust-firewall-rules?hl=fa

Figure 94: Network Tagging

©2018 Google LLC, used with permission. Google and the Google logo are registered trademarks of Google LLC

©2018 Google LLC, used with permission. Google and the Google logo are registered trademarks of Google LLC

Google Cloud Platform – Built to Scale

Building applications those can scale seamlessly as demand flows up or down, and at the same time, be resilient and fault-tolerant enough to withstand the interim unavailability of one or more computing resources are crucial these days to run any 24/7/365 consumer-centric businesses. A highly-available, or resilient, the solution is one that continues to give you seamless experience despite expected or unexpected failures of any link in the chain of the eco-system. Google Cloud Platform ensures you a planet-scale infrastructure that remains uninterrupted at any moment in time.

Google Cloud Platform enables you with built-in components that allow you to develop scalable and resilient architecture leveraging:

- Load balancers to monitor servers and distribute traffic to servers that can best handle the requests
- Hosting virtual machines in multiple regions
- Configuring a robust storage solution

Table 15: GCP Built-in components to enable scale and resiliency

Architecture Requirement	Google Cloud Platform Service
Load balancing	HTTP load balancing
Server hosting	Compute Engine, Regions and Zones
Server Management	Instance templates, Managed instance groups, Autoscaler
Data Storage	Cloud SQL, Cloud Storage

Table 16: GCP Disaster Recovery Components Building Blocks

Networking and data transfer

- Cloud Load Balancing
  - Cross-region
  - Single Anycast IP
  - Health checks
  - Cloud CDN integration
  - Autoscaling integration

- Cloud Interconnect
  - Cloud VPN (IPsec VPN)
  - Direct peering

- Cloud DNS
  - Programmatic DNS management
  - Access control
  - Anycast to serve zones

Management and monitoring

- Cloud Status Dashboard
  - Status of GCP services

- Stackdriver
  - Uptime monitoring
  - Alerts
  - Logging
  - Error reporting

- Cloud Deployment Manager
  - Repeatable and consistent deployment process
  - Parallel deployment
  - Templates
  - Infrastructure as code

Compute and storage

- Compute Engine
  - Scalable compute resources
  - Predefined and custom machine types
  - Fast boot times
  - Snapshots
  - Instance templates
  - Managed instance groups
  - Persistent disks
  - Live migration

- Cloud Storage
  - Highly durable object store
  - Geo-redundant storage
  - Storage classes
  - Object lifecycle management
  - Data transfer from other sources
  - Encryption at rest by default

- GKE
  - Managed environment for deploying and scaling containerized applications
  - Persistent volumes
  - Node auto-repair
  - Liveness and readiness probes
  - Multi-zone and regional clusters
  - Command-line tool for managing cross-regional clusters

Figure 95: Designing DR - Building Blocks

The following diagram shows how these GCP components could be put together to build a scalable, resilient application:

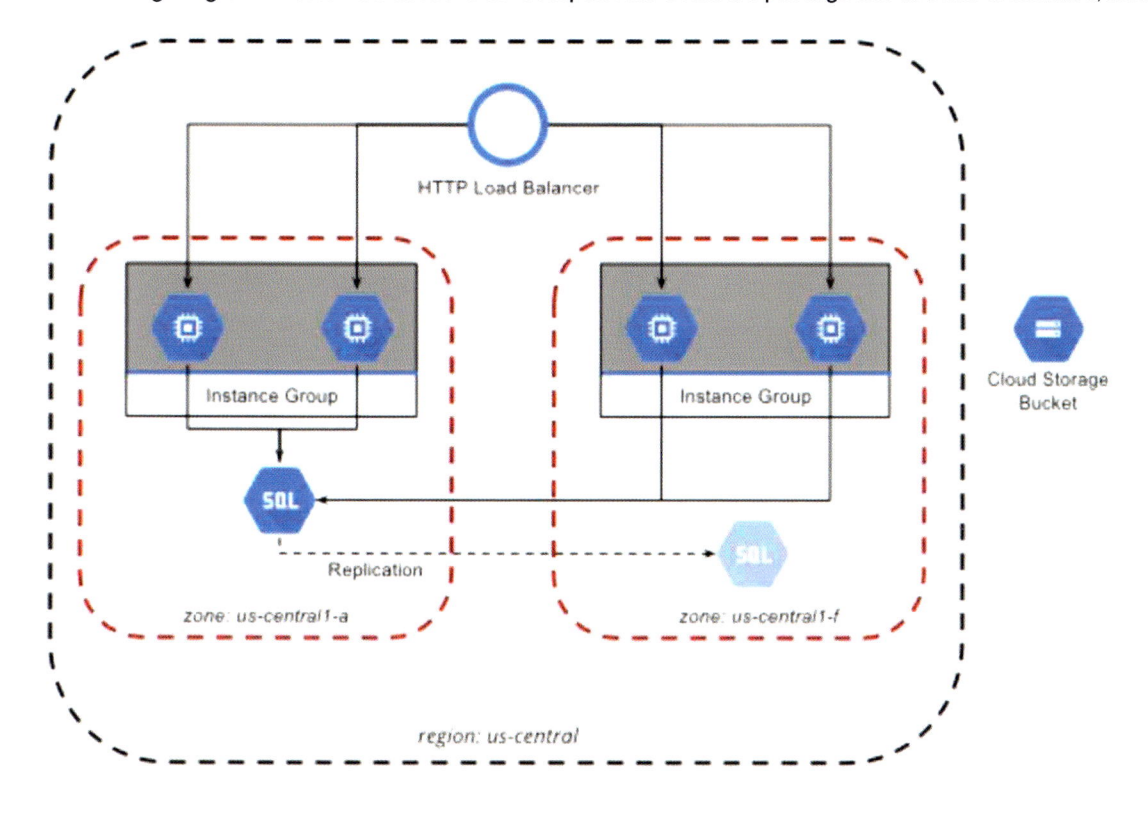

Figure 96: Building Scalable and Resilient Web Applications on Google Cloud Platform

Leveraging above way, we achieve Infrastructure as Service (IAAS) scalability mode.

©2018 Google LLC, used with permission. Google and the Google logo are registered trademarks of Google LLC

Disaster Recovery and Business Continuity

A disaster recovery plans must be developed to ensure a Business Continuity in the event of a failure and specify details on how you can avoid losing data during a disaster and also ensuring the application is up running.

Application Recovery – DR Scenario
A High Available (HA) pattern requires a well-architected HA application deployment in your production environment.
DR building blocks:
- Compute Engine
- Cloud Load Balancing
- Cloud SQL

The following diagram illustrates a High Available Production Deployment architecture:

Figure 97: An HA Deployment of Applications

Cold DR Scenario
In this scenario, in the event of a zonal failure, the regional instance group launches a replacement instance in a different zone in the same region. A new persistent disk is created from the latest snapshot and attached to the new instance. The following diagram illustrates this state:
The following diagram illustrates a Cold DR Production Deployment architecture that leverages a persistent disk-based snapshot:

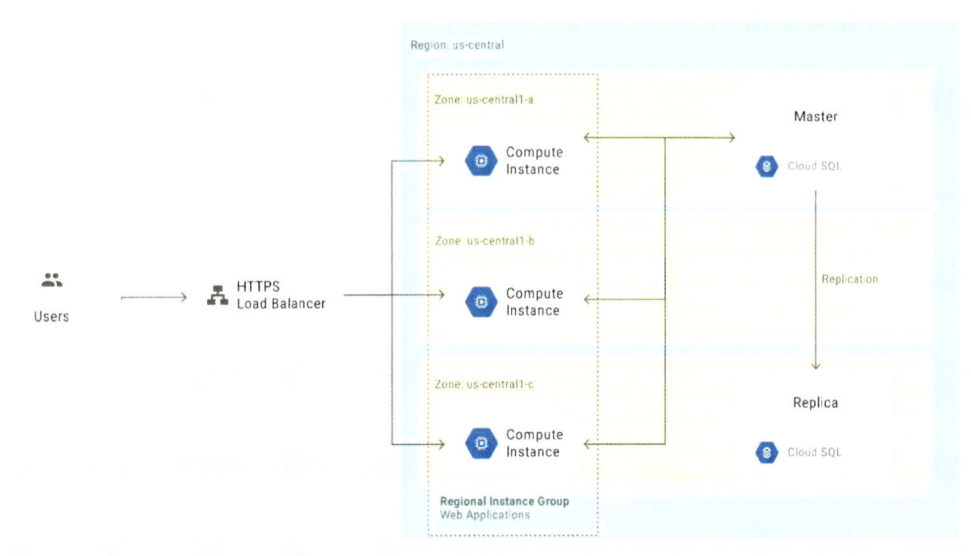

©2018 Google LLC, used with permission. Google and the Google logo are registered trademarks of Google LLC

Google Cloud Certified Professional Cloud Architect, Second Edition

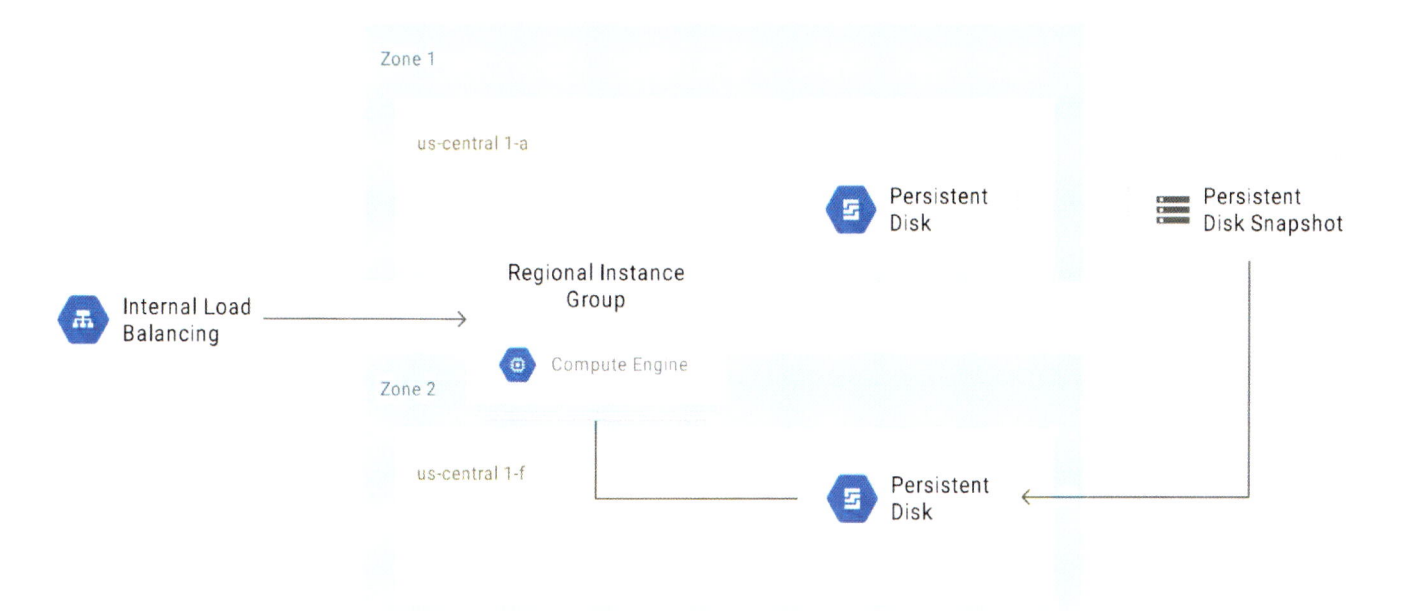

Figure 98: Cold DR - Deployment of Applications

©2018 Google LLC, used with permission. Google and the Google logo are registered trademarks of Google LLC

Data Recovery – DR Scenario

The following diagram illustrates an example of architecture that addresses a DR plan that reacts automatically to failure without requiring manual recovery, where the persistent disk snapshot has been used to restore the persistent disk in a different zone

DR building blocks used:
- Compute Engine
- Managed instance groups
- Cloud Load Balancing (internal load balancing)

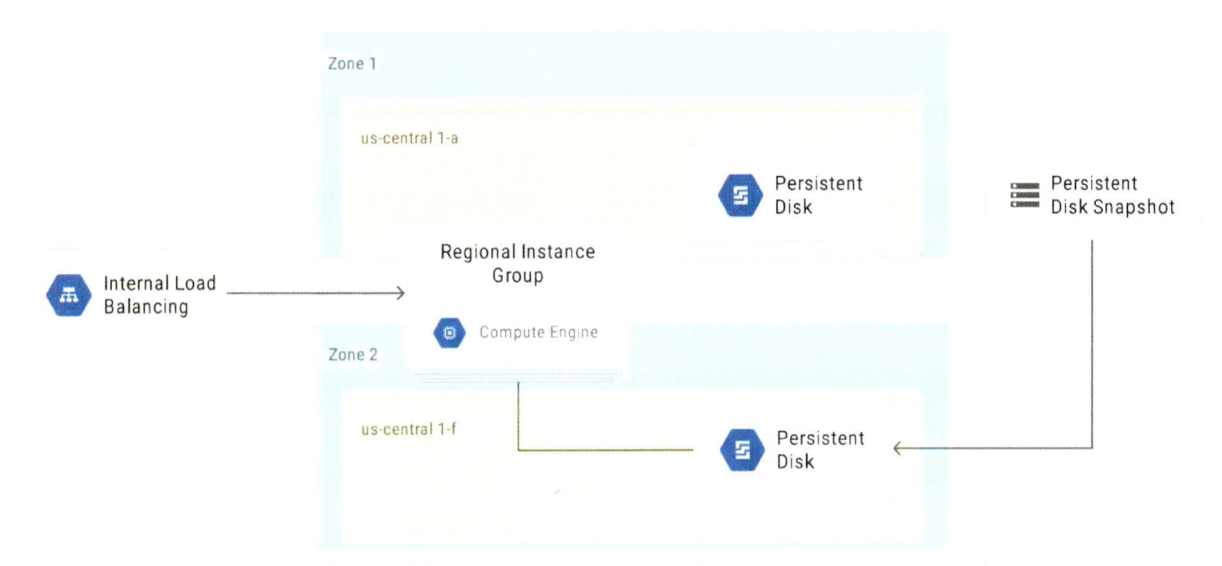

Figure 99: HA Data Recovery leveraging Persistent Disks

©2018 Google LLC, used with permission. Google and the Google logo are registered trademarks of Google LLC

The following diagram provides guidance about which transfer method to use, depending on how much data you need to transfer to GCP

Table 17: DR Data Transfer Mechanisms in GCP

Amount of Data

```
                                    gsutil
                                    Tervela
              Google                Bitspeed
              Transfer              Aspera                              Zadara
              Service               Komprise                Google Transfer Appliance (Beta)
                                    Signiant
                                    ...

100 TB -----------------------------------------------------------------------------------
                                                            Google Transfer Appliance (Beta)
                                                                   Iron Mountain
                                                              Prime Focus Technologies
 20 TB -----------------------------------------------------------------------------------
                                                                   Iron Mountain
                                                              Prime Focus Technologies

           In GCS | Other   | In a colo  | On-prem with      | On-prem with
                    Cloud                  good connectivity   low bandwidth
```

©2018 Google LLC, used with permission. Google and the Google logo are registered trademarks of Google LLC

There are many other ways that Google Cloud Platform enables Scalability and Resiliency. One of the best ways to achieve scalable architecture is through a

Serverless Architecture which is inherently a **Platform as a service**.
There are a few another indirect way to manage traffic and scale such as **Managed Instance Autoscaling** and ensuring the platform is built with infrastructure and components that can scale appropriately testing through

Distributed Load Testing Using Kubernetes.

GCP – Built to scale

Building resilient and scalable architectures with Google Cloud Platform

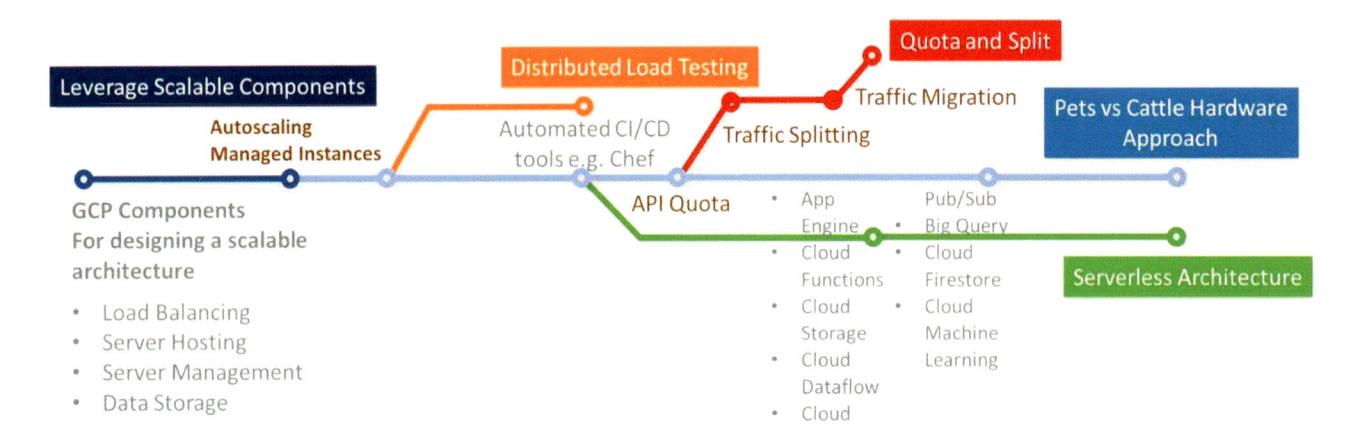

Leverage Scalable Components
- Autoscaling Managed Instances

GCP Components For designing a scalable architecture
- Load Balancing
- Server Hosting
- Server Management
- Data Storage

Automated CI/CD tools e.g. Chef

Distributed Load Testing

API Quota

- App Engine
- Cloud Functions
- Cloud Storage
- Cloud Dataflow
- Cloud

Quota and Split
Traffic Migration
Traffic Splitting

- Pub/Sub
- Big Query
- Cloud Firestore
- Cloud Machine Learning

Pets vs Cattle Hardware Approach

Serverless Architecture

Further Reading:
- https://cloud.google.com/solutions/scalable-and-resilient-apps
- https://cloud.google.com/tasks/docs/manage-cloud-task-scaling
- https://cloud.google.com/appengine/articles/scalability
- https://cloud.google.com/solutions/dr-scenarios-for-applications
- https://cloud.google.com/solutions/dr-scenarios-building-blocks

Serverless Architecture

Serverless computing is a cloud computing model that abstracts server management and low-level infrastructure decisions away from developers. Google introduced Serverless computing almost a decade ago through its App Engine. GCP enables you to build and deploy functions or applications using a fully managed end-to-end serverless platform.

Figure 100: A comprehensive serverless ecosystem

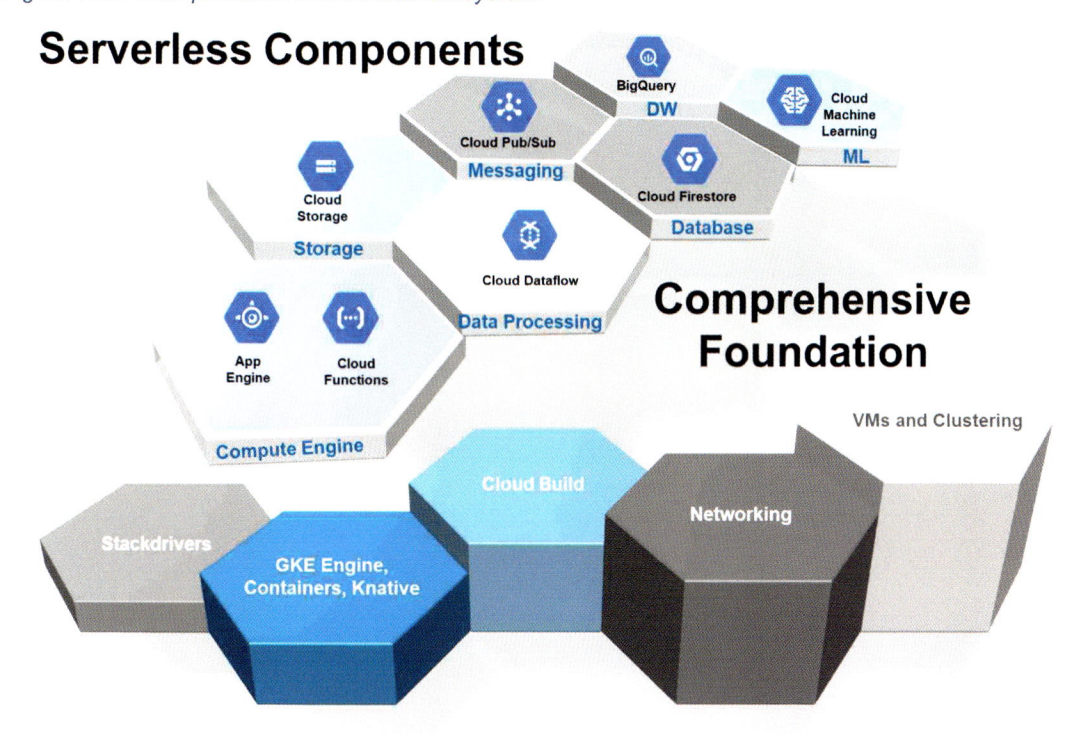

Google Serverless Architecture enables us to write and to deploy code without the hassle of managing the underlying infrastructure. This way, it enhances developer productivity by helping focus on building great business applications and under the hood, it introduces **Zero server management, no upfront provisioning, auto-scaling to meet traffic demands**, and paying only for the resources used.

Knative is Google's open source commitments to **build a serverless ecosystem with an open-source** set of components from the same technology that enables the GKE serverless add-on.

Knative provides powerful abstraction and flexible workflow for building, testing, or **deploying container images or non-container artefacts on a Kubernetes cluster**. By integrating Knative into your platform, you would benefit from both the portability aspects and containers and the automation and efficiency of delivering serverless computing on on-premises or in any other cloud.

Google Cloud Certified Professional Cloud Architect, Second Edition

Function as a service (FAAS) – Cloud Function

Cloud Functions allows you to build and deploy services at the level of a single function, not at the level of entire applications, containers, or VMs. With Cloud Functions, you can construct applications from bite-sized business logic billed to the nearest 100 milliseconds, only while your code is running. Serve users from zero to planet-scale, all without managing any infrastructure.

Cloud Functions Use Cases areas:

Serverless application backends
- Integration with third-party services and APIs
- Serverless mobile backends
- Serverless IoT backends

Real-time data processing systems
- Real-time file processing
- Real-time stream processing
- Event-driven ETL

Intelligent applications
- Virtual assistants and conversational experiences
- Video and image analysis
- Sentiment Analysis

Cloud Functions can access most major Google Cloud Platform services via language-specific API client libraries and REST APIs, including the following:

©2018 Google LLC, used with permission. Google and the Google logo are registered trademarks of Google LLC

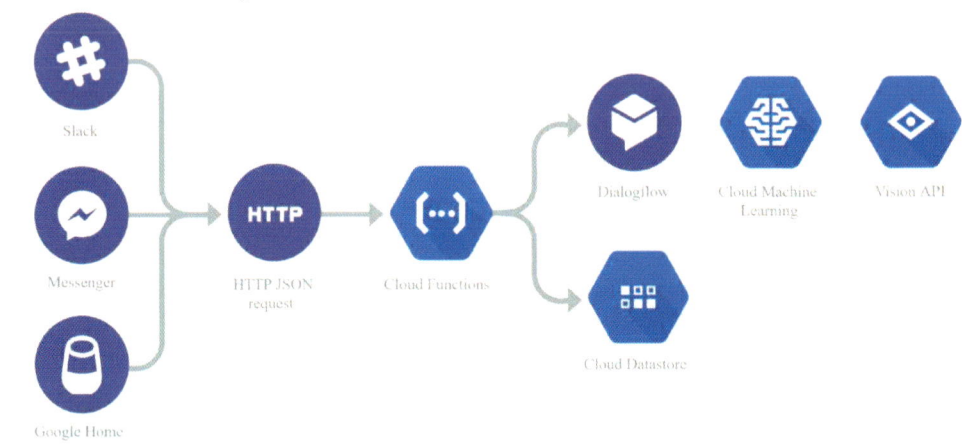

Figure 101: Cloud Functions integrates with other Google Cloud Platform Components

- Cloud BigQuery
- Cloud Bigtable
- Cloud Data Loss Prevention
- Cloud Datastore
- Cloud DNS
- Cloud Firestore
- Cloud Machine Learning Engine
- Cloud Natural Language API

- Cloud Pub/Sub
- Cloud Resource Manager
- Cloud Spanner
- Cloud Speech-to-Text API
- Cloud SQL
- Cloud Storage
- Cloud Translation API
- Cloud Vision API

- Cloud Video Intelligence API
- Firebase (DB, Storage, Analytics, Auth)
- Google Stackdriver Debugger
- Google Stackdriver Error Reporting
- Google Stackdriver Logging
- Google Stackdriver Monitoring
- Google Stackdriver Trace
- Google Compute Engine

Supported event providers

- HTTP—invoke functions directly via HTTP requests
- Cloud Storage
- Cloud Pub/Sub
- Firebase (DB, Storage, Analytics, Auth)
- Stackdriver Logging

Figure 102: Cloud Functions and Video Intelligence

©2018 Google LLC, used with permission. Google and the Google logo are registered trademarks of Google LLC

An example use of Cloud Functions, integrated with Video Intelligence.
Example architecture of a serverless machine learning (ML) model to enrich support tickets with metadata before they reach a support agent.

Further Reading:
https://cloud.google.com/blog/products/gcp/bringing-the-best-of-serverless-to-you

You could find some of the limits of Google Cloud Functions here:
https://cloud.google.com/functions/quotas
https://cloud.google.com/solutions/architecture-of-a-serverless-ml-model

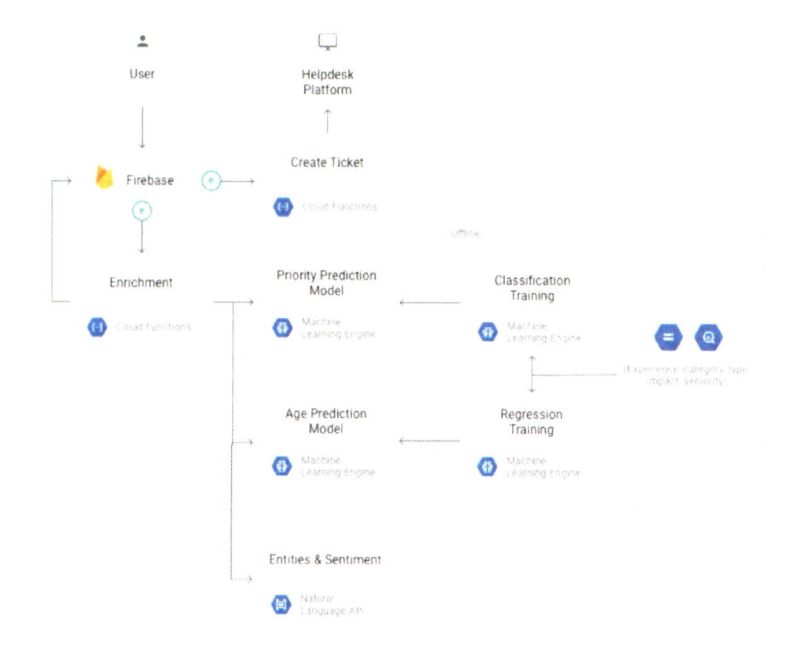

Figure 103: Serverless ML Example

©2018 Google LLC, used with permission. Google and the Google logo are registered trademarks of Google LLC

Regulatory Compliance and Standards

CLOUD COMPUTING COMPLIANCE CONTROLS CATALOG (C5)

DATA PRIVACY — Personal Data, Privacy, Confidentiality, Integrity, Accessibility

DATA SOVEREIGNTY — converted and stored in binary digital form is subject to the laws of the country in which it is located.

FCA FG 16/5 — Material outsourcing and Cloud Strategy for Financial Organizations under FCA in UK.

EU-US PRIVACY SHIELD

ISO 27001, 27017, 27018 → SOC 1,2,3 → GDPR → NIST 800-53 → PCI DSS → HIPAA

Standards, Regulatory Compliance & Certifications

Cloud Platform is a shared responsibility model for the implementation of security and controls. As a CxO organisation, this is the fundamental principle, we all must understand. Ideally, the cloud provider owns and operates the platform and its components whereas we are mostly responsible for the application or solution we build. It is the data that makes things complicated – Storage of data, Accessing the data, Data Transport Layer, Data Archival Layer and all the contact points where data touches as part of the journey. Data Lineage is a way to understand the lifecycle of the data, how it changes each state and value (a State Machine pattern really). Data Security in general in GCP is already discussed in here

Identity and Security.
Regulatory compliance mandates are adhering to defined controls applicable to specific industry, whereas some other standards are applied to the way security, data protection, data move or cloud computing platform designed.
There are also compliance standards mandated by certain industry-specific regulators regarding the adoption of cloud within your business to safeguard customers and consumers, and more importantly the ethical business.

Table 18: Regulatory Compliance in Finance - GCP Adherence

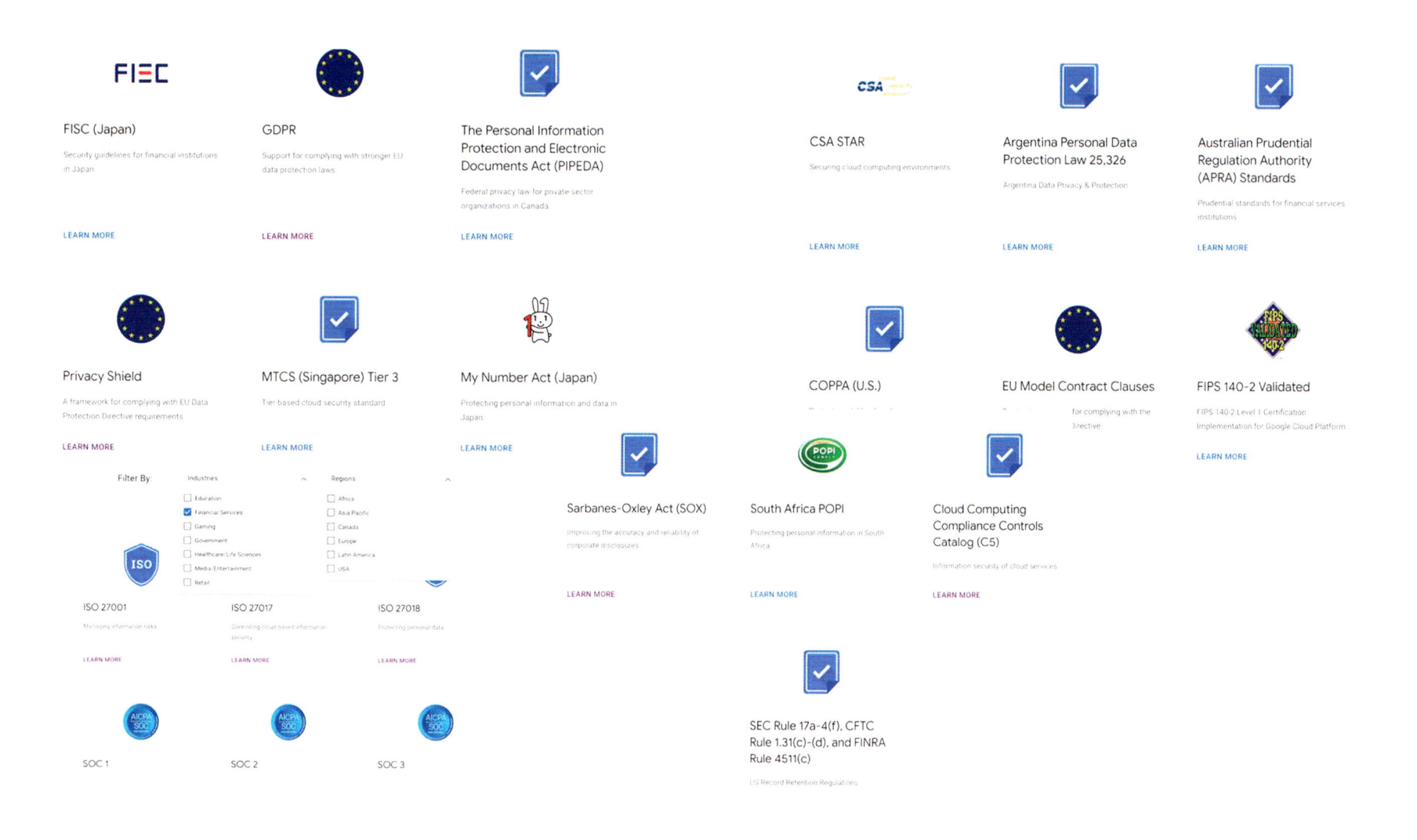

FISC (Japan)
Security guidelines for financial institutions in Japan.

LEARN MORE

GDPR
Support for complying with stronger EU data protection laws.

LEARN MORE

The Personal Information Protection and Electronic Documents Act (PIPEDA)
Federal privacy law for private sector organizations in Canada.

LEARN MORE

CSA STAR
Securing cloud computing environments

LEARN MORE

Argentina Personal Data Protection Law 25,326
Argentina Data Privacy & Protection

LEARN MORE

Australian Prudential Regulation Authority (APRA) Standards
Prudential standards for financial services institutions

LEARN MORE

Privacy Shield
A framework for complying with EU Data Protection Directive requirements

LEARN MORE

MTCS (Singapore) Tier 3
Tier based cloud security standard.

LEARN MORE

My Number Act (Japan)
Protecting personal information and data in Japan.

LEARN MORE

COPPA (U.S.)

EU Model Contract Clauses
for complying with the Directive.

FIPS 140-2 Validated
FIPS 140-2 Level 1 Certification Implementation for Google Cloud Platform

LEARN MORE

ISO 27001
Managing information risks

LEARN MORE

ISO 27017
Controlling cloud-based information security

LEARN MORE

ISO 27018
Protecting personal data

LEARN MORE

Sarbanes-Oxley Act (SOX)
Improving the accuracy and reliability of corporate disclosures.

LEARN MORE

South Africa POPI
Protecting personal information in South Africa

LEARN MORE

Cloud Computing Compliance Controls Catalog (C5)
Information security of cloud services

LEARN MORE

SOC 1

SOC 2

SOC 3

SEC Rule 17a-4(f), CFTC Rule 1.31(c)-(d), and FINRA Rule 4511(c)
US Record Retention Regulations

©2018 Google LLC, used with permission. Google and the Google logo are registered trademarks of Google LLC

Table 19: Google Cloud Components and Compliance Standards

Cloud adoption and especially 'cloud first' policy for most of the organisations, is a service provided by either cloud providers or outsourcing organisations (known as 'material outsourcing' construct) such as UK's Financial Conduct Authority's FCA FG 16/5 guidance would require a spectrum of other considerations:

- Global Strategy and accepting the risk by senior executives (Ensuring that senior leaders understand the consequences of using these kinds of technologies in case consumer data leakage or any financial data leak happens)
- Clear Data Owners and Responsibility of Data Producers and Maintenance of the same
- Following various International standards
- Monitoring the outsource and service provider's access to data and audit
- Data security
- Adherence to the Data Protection Act, Data Harbouring, Data Sovernity
- Managing secure access to a business premise
- Strict Change management procedure
- Data Recovery and Business
- Clear Exit plan (From one Cloud Providers to the other or Cloud to On-Premise).

Google Cloud Platform regularly undergo independent verification of security, privacy, and compliance controls, achieving certifications against global standards to earn your trust.

As a Google Cloud Platform adopter, your org should adopt a strict governance and security controls in place along with the GCP components applicable to your architecture as shown in the above table, Error! Reference source not found.

Further Reading

https://cloud.google.com/security/compliance/#/

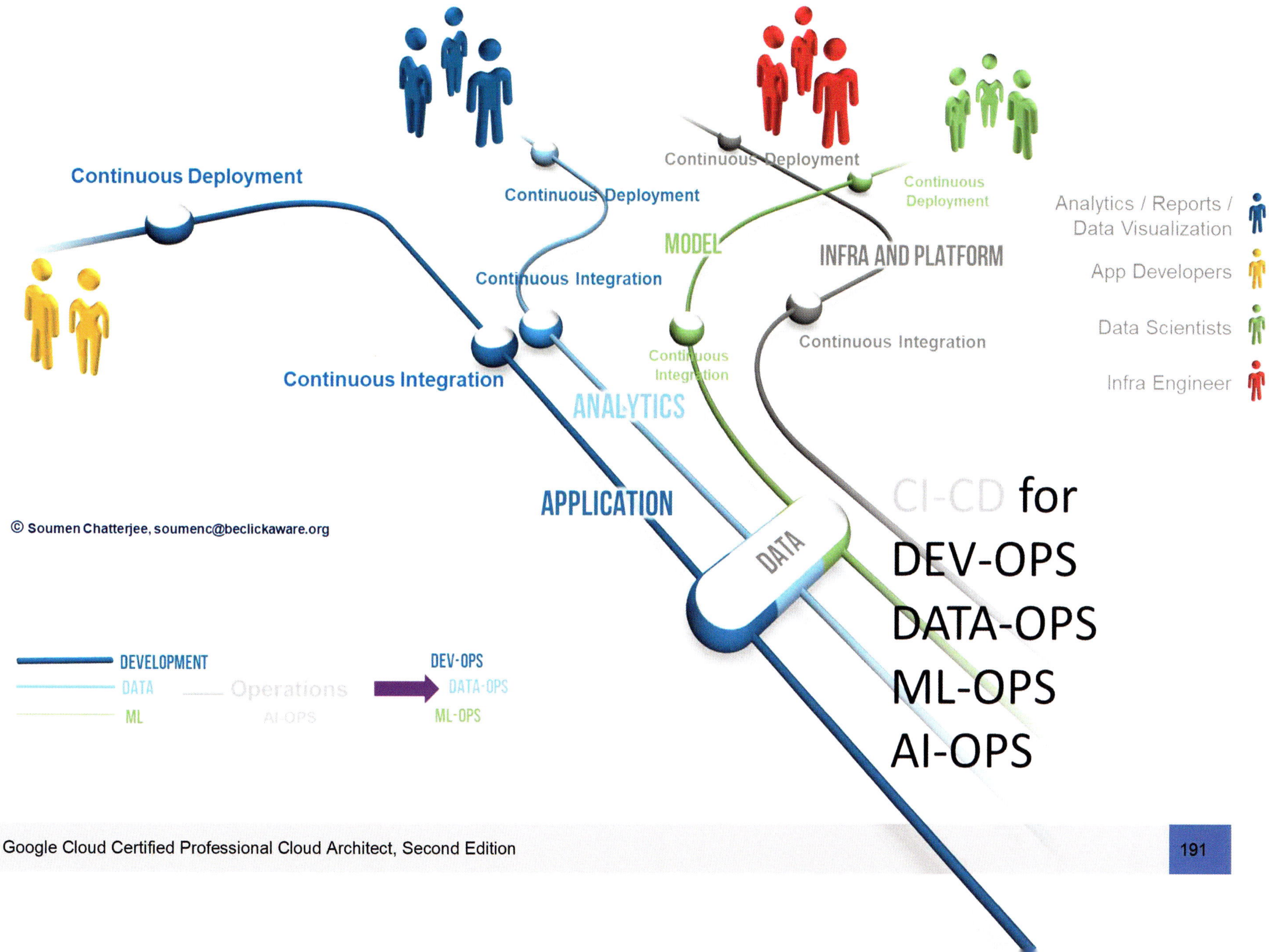
Continuous Deployment
Continuous Integration
Continuous Deployment
Continuous Integration
Continuous Deployment
Continuous Deployment
MODEL
INFRA AND PLATFORM
Continuous Integration
Continuous Integration
ANALYTICS
APPLICATION
DATA
Analytics / Reports / Data Visualization
App Developers
Data Scientists
Infra Engineer
CI-CD for
DEV-OPS
DATA-OPS
ML-OPS
AI-OPS
DEVELOPMENT
DATA
ML
Operations
AI-OPS
DEV-OPS
DATA-OPS
ML-OPS

Google Cloud NO-Ops: Catalyst Data to Wisdom to Enterprise Innovation Continuum

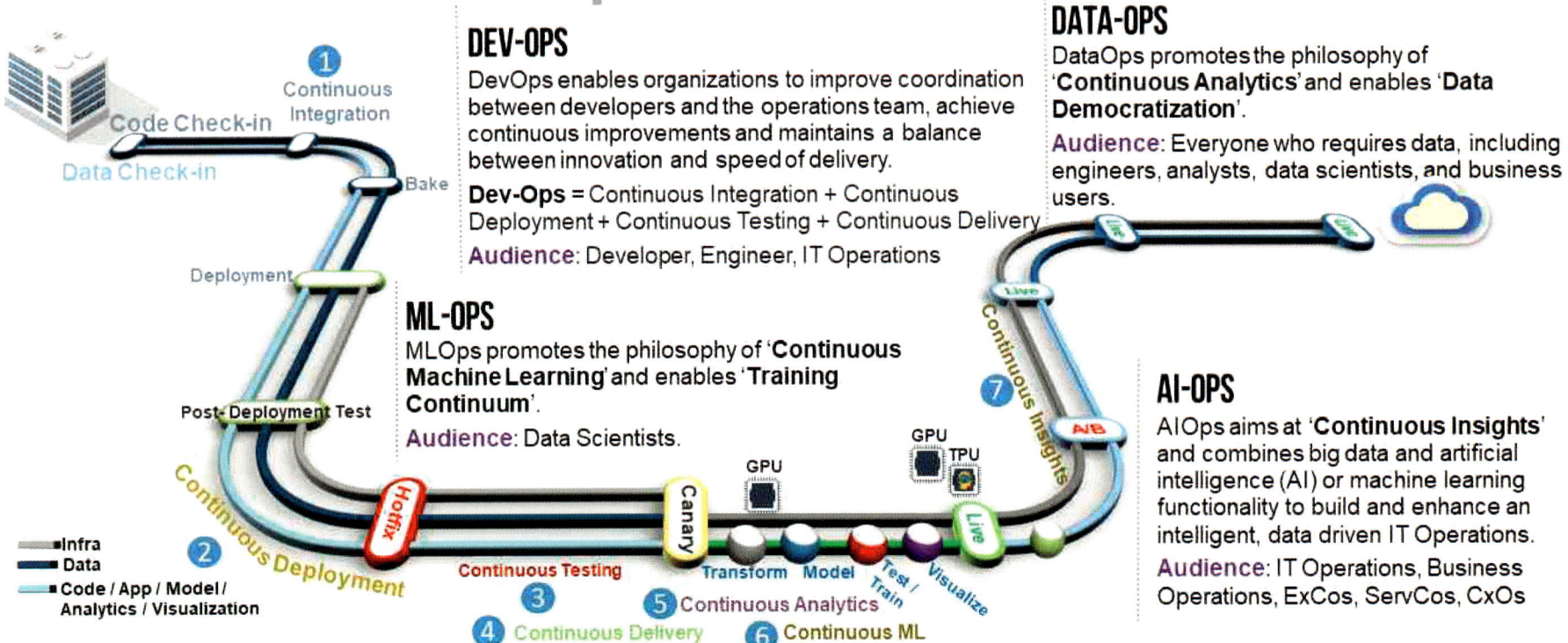

DEV-OPS
DevOps enables organizations to improve coordination between developers and the operations team, achieve continuous improvements and maintains a balance between innovation and speed of delivery.

Dev-Ops = Continuous Integration + Continuous Deployment + Continuous Testing + Continuous Delivery

Audience: Developer, Engineer, IT Operations

ML-OPS
MLOps promotes the philosophy of '**Continuous Machine Learning**' and enables '**Training Continuum**'.

Audience: Data Scientists.

DATA-OPS
DataOps promotes the philosophy of '**Continuous Analytics**' and enables '**Data Democratization**'.

Audience: Everyone who requires data, including engineers, analysts, data scientists, and business users.

AI-OPS
AIOps aims at '**Continuous Insights**' and combines big data and artificial intelligence (AI) or machine learning functionality to build and enhance an intelligent, data driven IT Operations.

Audience: IT Operations, Business Operations, ExCos, ServCos, CxOs

Pipeline stages: Code Check-in / Data Check-in → ① Continuous Integration → Bake → Deployment → Post-Deployment Test → ② Continuous Deployment → Hotfix → ③ Continuous Testing → Canary → ④ Continuous Delivery → Transform → Model (GPU) → ⑤ Continuous Analytics → Test/Train (GPU/TPU) → ⑥ Continuous ML → Visualize → Live → A/B → ⑦ Continuous Insights → Live

Legend:
- Infra
- Data
- Code / App / Model / Analytics / Visualization

© Soumen Chatterjee, soumenc@beclickaware.org

Google Cloud – Cloud Native Operations (DevOps CI/CD, Data Ops, AIOps and No Ops)

Google Cloud Immutable VM Infrastructure and Compute eco-systems, Container Cluster Management through Kubernetes Engine, Managed App Platform through App Engine and Serverless execution environment through Cloud Functions automatically let you reliably builds, tests, and updates, and production rollout. Google Cloud Platform also supports Dev-Ops releases, Data-Ops, Canary Release, and A/B testing.

CI/CD Pipeline using GKE and Spinnaker

With GKE and Spinnaker, it allows creating a robust continuous delivery flow that helps to ensure your software is shipped as quickly as it is developed and validated. The below diagram shows how to create a continuous delivery pipeline using Google Kubernetes Engine, Cloud Source Repositories, Cloud Build, and Spinnaker. Another way to build a continuous delivery pipeline using Ansible, Spinnaker and Google Compute Engine as described in the following diagram. This architecture uses baking and deploying immutable images as an example.

Spinnaker is an open source tool for orchestrating continuous delivery pipelines that deploy software to cloud resources. It is typically used for deployments based on Debian packages, but with Packer templates, you can configure Spinnaker to support your provisioner of choice.

©2018 Google LLC, used with permission. Google and the Google logo are registered trademarks of Google LLC

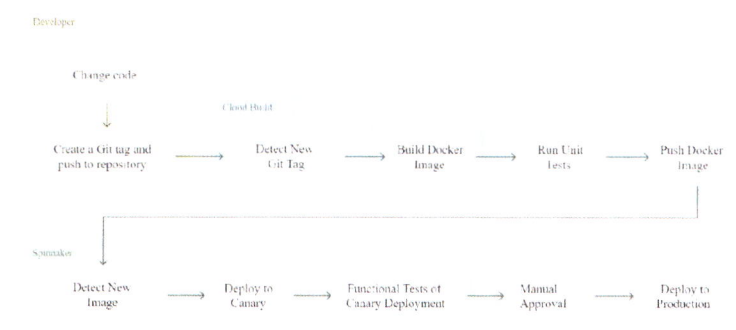

Figure 105: Continuous Delivery Pipelines with Spinnaker and Google Kubernetes

Figure 104: App Delivery pipeline with Google Cloud Components

CI/CD pipeline using GKE clusters

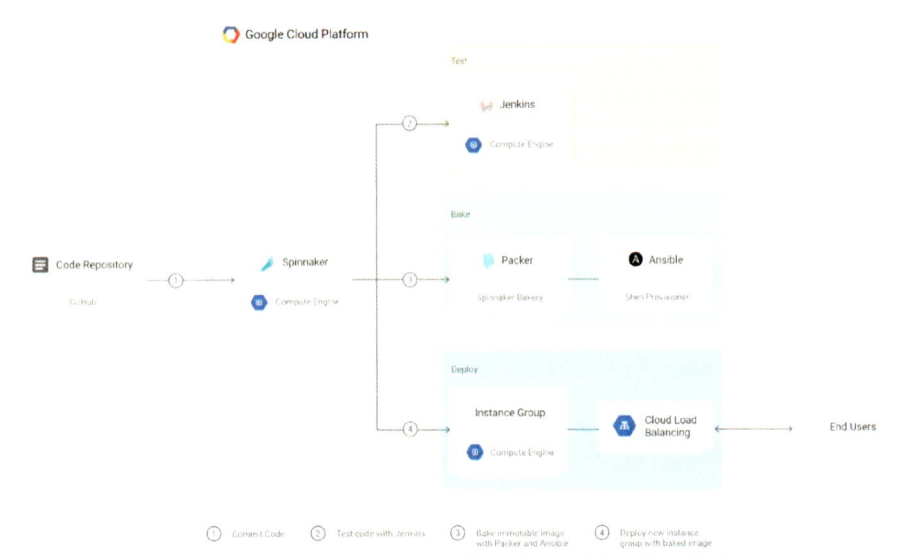

Figure 106: Building a continuous delivery pipeline using Ansible, Spinnaker and Google Compute Engine

The CI/CD pipeline uses two separate GKE clusters, one for testing and one for production. At the beginning of the pipeline, developers commit changes to the example codebase. This action triggers the pipeline to create a release and to deploy it to the development cluster. A release manager can then promote the release so that it's deployed into the production cluster. The following diagram illustrates this process.

Figure 107: CI/CD pipeline using two separate GKE clusters

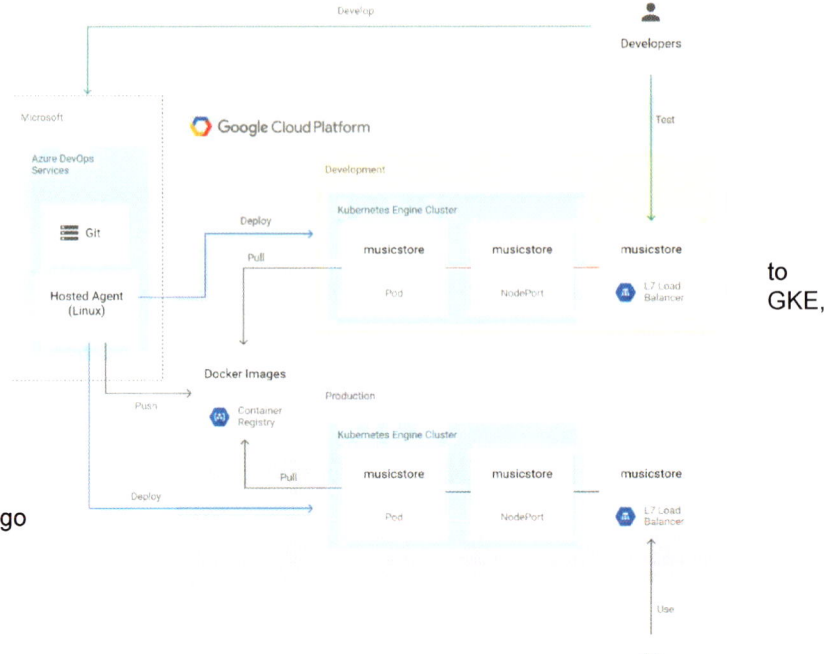

©2018 Google LLC, used with permission. Google and the Google logo are registered trademarks of Google LLC

Spinnaker is an open source, the continuous delivery system led by Netflix and Google manage the deployment of apps on different computing platforms, including App Engine, Compute Engine, AWS, and Azure. Using Spinnaker, you can implement advanced deployment methods, including canary deployments.

to GKE,

©2018 Google LLC, used with permission. Google and the Google logo are registered trademarks of Google LLC

Google Cloud Certified Professional Cloud Architect, Second Edition

Set up a continuous delivery pipeline using Jenkins and GKE

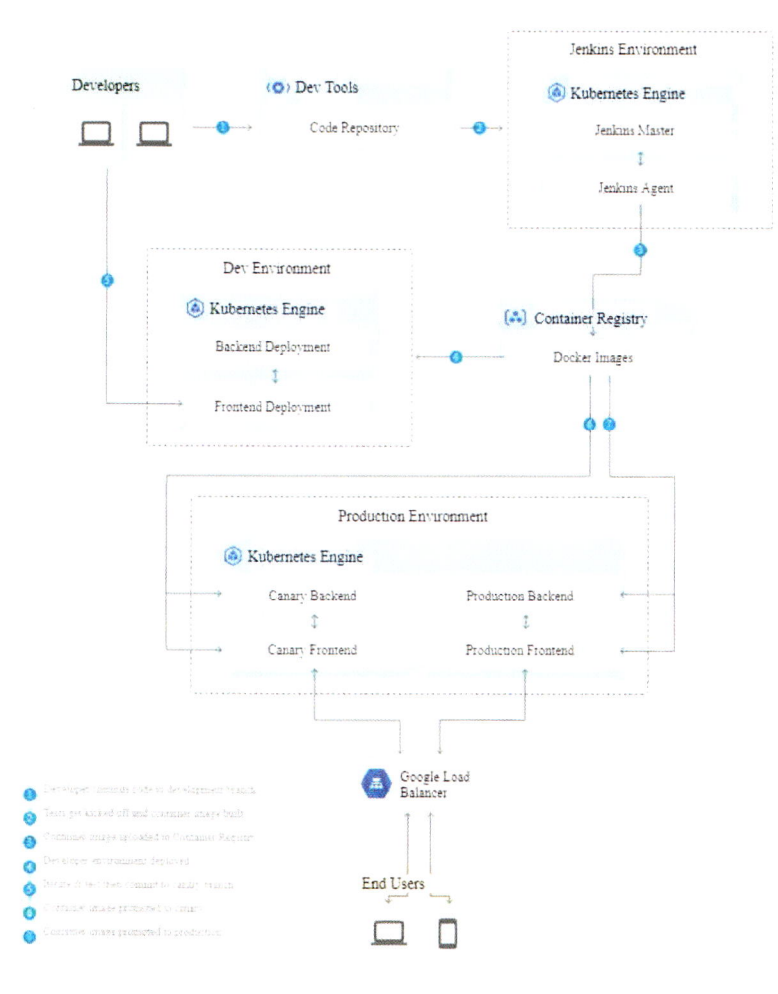

Figure 108: A continuous delivery pipeline using Jenkins and GKE

©2018 Google LLC, used with permission. Google and the Google logo are registered trademarks of Google LLC

Jenkins helps in setting up a CI/CD process which primarily involves the following stages:
- Checkout Code
- Run Unit Tests
- Dockerize App
- Push dockerized app to Container Registry
- Deploy the dockerized app on GKE

Further Reading

- https://cloud.google.com/solutions/creating-cicd-pipeline-vsts-kubernetes-engine
- https://cloud.google.com/solutions/ansible-with-spinnaker-tutorial
- https://cloud.google.com/solutions/spinnaker-on-compute-engine

Automating Canary Analysis on Google Kubernetes Engine with Spinnaker
A canary release is a technique to reduce the risk from deploying a new version of software or application (referred as the canary) into production and deployed to a small subset of users alongside the stable running version. In this approach, Traffic is split between these two versions such that a portion of incoming requests is diverted to the canary as well as the existing production version. As part of the analysis, the behaviour is accurately compared between the old and new versions of your app. The differences are analysed, and a range of different metrics are compared and get continued with deployment, where the canary behaves well or better than the baseline.

In a canary deployment, in a combination of Spinnaker, an automated canary analysis on an app is deployed on GKE and monitored by Stackdriver.

A/B Testing in the Google Cloud Platform

A/B testing, also known as split testing, is a randomized experiment with two variants of the same application, a widely used technique of testing additional features, usually UX in nature, in your application for various reasons like usability, popularity, noticeability, etc, and how those factors influence the bottom line - the one that gives a better conversion rate, wins.

A/B testing is also known as bucket tests or split-run testing or hypothesis testing. A/B testing sometimes could use more than two versions, and in that case, it becomes a multivariate testing or multinomial testing.

You could use Google App Engine to configure traffic splitting and also to develop various versions of the App to perform A/B testing where traffic migration smoothly switches request routing, gradually moving traffic from the versions currently receiving traffic to one or more versions that you specify. Please make a note that caching issues can exist for an App Engine application, especially when deploying a new version. Traffic splitting often makes subtle caching problems more apparent.

Microservices are widely used to build multiple versions of the App and promote the culture of automated A/B testing.

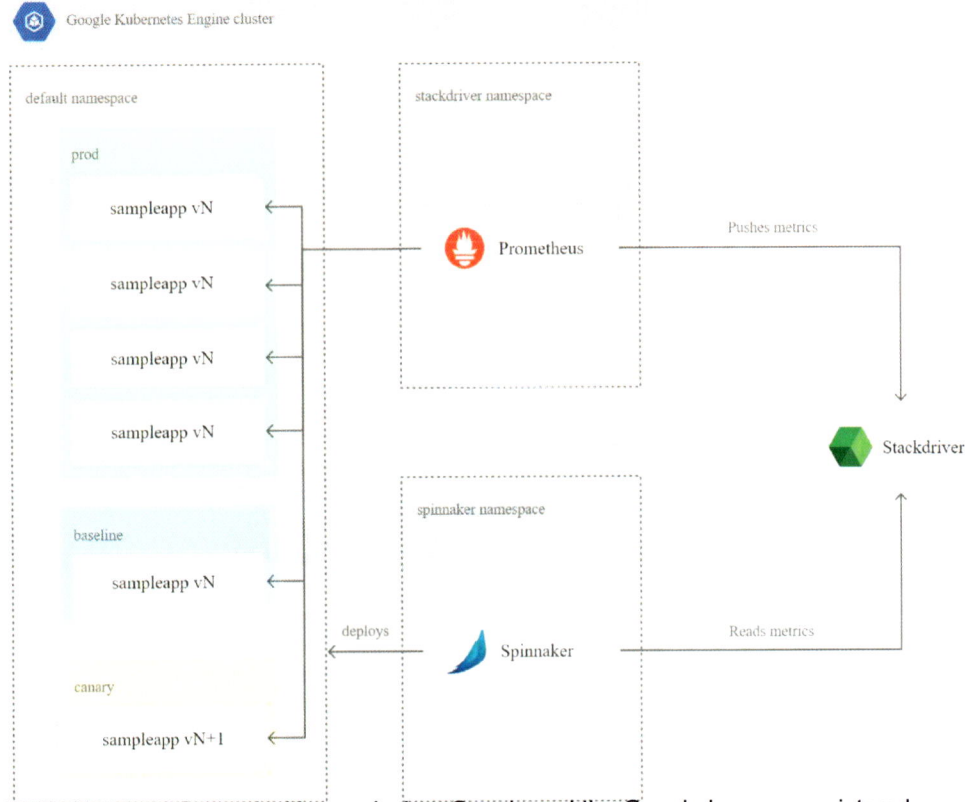

©2018 Google LLC, used with permission. Google and the Google logo are registered trademarks of Google LLC

Figure 109: Canary Testing on Google Kubernetes Engine with Spinnaker

applications and resources.

Distributed Load Testing Using Kubernetes

Google Cloud Platform is an excellent environment for distributed load testing using containers, leveraging through Google Kubernetes Engine (GKE), which is powered by the open source container-cluster manager Kubernetes. GKE provides the ability to quickly provision container infrastructure and tools to manage deployed

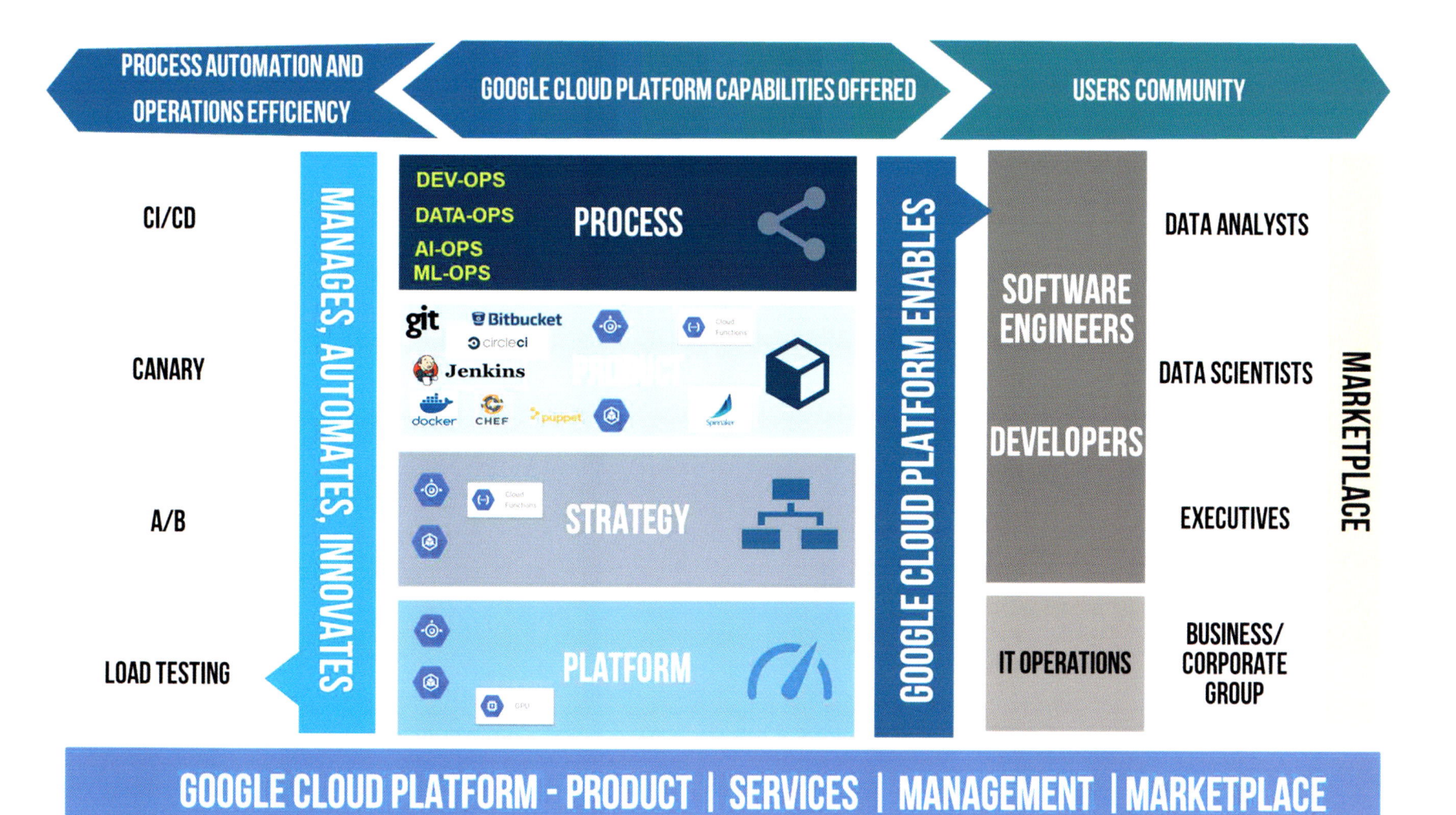

Google Cloud Certified Professional Cloud Architect, Second Edition

Further Reading

- https://cloud.google.com/solutions/continuous-delivery-jenkins-kubernetes-engine
- https://cloud.google.com/solutions/distributed-load-testing-using-kubernetes
- https://cloud.google.com/solutions/automated-canary-analysis-kubernetes-engine-spinnaker
- https://cloud.google.com/solutions/distributed-load-testing-using-kubernetes

Kubeflow: Simplifying machine learning on open hybrid clouds

The Kubeflow is an open-source initiative that enables using machine learning (ML) tools stacks like TensorFlow, PyTorch, Scikit Learn, XGBoost, Caffe, and others, all on Kubernetes. The Kubeflow framework ties infrastructure and machine learning solutions together, and simplifies moving models, and its associated dependencies from a developer's machine to a cloud cluster. The Kubeflow promotes the open hybrid cloud so that it can run both on-premises or in the cloud.

Kubeflow: Cloud-native machine learning with Kubernetes

The Kubeflow is the machine learning toolkit for Kubernetes, aiming to provide a simplified platform to develop, deploy, and manage composable, portable, and scalable machine learning on Kubernetes, and get running with your ML Workflow.

The **Kubeflow Pipelines** platform consists of:

- A user interface (UI) for managing and tracking experiments, jobs, and runs.
- An engine for scheduling multi-step ML workflows.
- An SDK for defining and manipulating pipelines and components.
- Notebooks for interacting with the system using the SDK.
- The following are the goals of Kubeflow Pipelines:
- End-to-end orchestration: enabling and simplifying the orchestration of machine learning pipelines.
- Easy experimentation: making it easy for you to try numerous ideas and techniques and manage your various trials/experiments.
- Easy re-use: enabling you to re-use components and pipelines to create end-to-end solutions without having to rebuild each time quickly.

Cisco and Google Cloud have been a great advocate of the open hybrid cloud and jointly building an open hybrid cloud architecture to maximise the investments across cloud and on-premises environments. Continuing this commitment, Cisco recently announced their release of the Unified Computing System (UCS) and HyperFlex platforms that leverage Kubeflow and provide a production-grade on-premise infrastructure to run AI/ML jobs

Further Reading

- https://www.kubeflow.org/docs/components/
- https://vwo.com/ab-testing/
- https://cloud.google.com/appengine/docs/standard/python/splitting-traffic
- https://cloud.google.com/appengine/docs/admin-api/migrating-splitting-traffic
- http://go.google-mkto.com/Bl0abT1CA000P2EP0TXCE82
- https://cloud.google.com/blog/products/gcp/simplifying-machine-learning-on-open-hybrid-clouds-with-kubeflow

Google Cloud Pricing Innovation

Introduces pay-as-you-go pricing to the, with industry leading innovations per-second billing

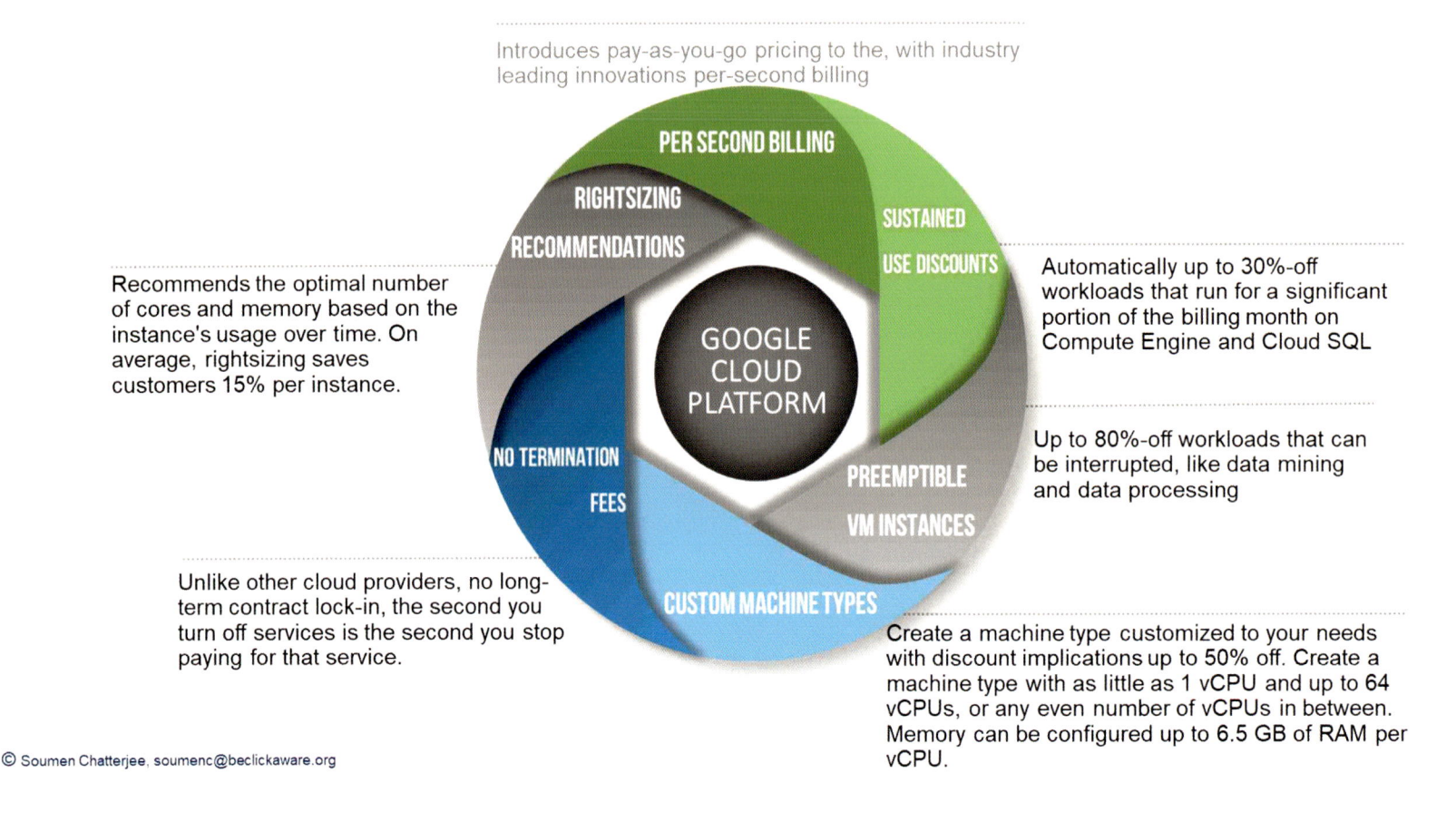

- **PER SECOND BILLING**
- **RIGHTSIZING RECOMMENDATIONS** — Recommends the optimal number of cores and memory based on the instance's usage over time. On average, rightsizing saves customers 15% per instance.
- **SUSTAINED USE DISCOUNTS** — Automatically up to 30%-off workloads that run for a significant portion of the billing month on Compute Engine and Cloud SQL
- **NO TERMINATION FEES** — Unlike other cloud providers, no long-term contract lock-in, the second you turn off services is the second you stop paying for that service.
- **PREEMPTIBLE VM INSTANCES** — Up to 80%-off workloads that can be interrupted, like data mining and data processing
- **CUSTOM MACHINE TYPES** — Create a machine type customized to your needs with discount implications up to 50% off. Create a machine type with as little as 1 vCPU and up to 64 vCPUs, or any even number of vCPUs in between. Memory can be configured up to 6.5 GB of RAM per vCPU.

© Soumen Chatterjee, soumenc@beclickaware.org

Google Cloud Certified Professional Cloud Architect, Second Edition

Google Cloud Pricing and Billing

Google Cloud Platform does not require any upfront costs or make commitments to get lower prices. Google Cloud Platform is significantly cheaper while used correctly. Google Cloud Pricing calculator is an easy way to calculate the cost of various Google Cloud components. One can easily configure billing on the Google Cloud Platform (GCP) in a variety of ways to meet different needs.

The diagram below represents an example GCP resource hierarchy within an organisation:

Figure 110: GCP Pricing Calculator Tool

©2018 Google LLC, used with permission. Google and the Google logo are registered trademarks of Google LLC

Figure 111: GCP Resource Hierarchy

The GCP resource hierarchy includes an Organisation node and folders. It allows you to map your organisation onto GCP and provides logical group together access management policies (Cloud Identity and Access Management) and Organisation policies. Both Cloud IAM and Organisation policies are inherited through the hierarchy.

Google Cloud Certified Professional Cloud Architect, Second Edition

The top of the hierarchy starts with an Organisation that comprises of folders group projects, as well as other folders. Projects contain resources. Resources can be further categorised using labels to enforce granular permissions at different levels to control the spend within GCP. Billing accounts are linked to and pay for projects. All lower level resources are parented by projects, which are the middle layer in the hierarchy of resources. You can use projects to represent logical projects, teams, environments, or other collections that map to a business function or structure. Any given resource can only exist in one project.

GCP resources are the fundamental components that make up all GCP services, such as Compute Engine virtual machines (VMs), Cloud Pub/Sub topics, Cloud Storage buckets, and so on. For billing and access control purposes, resources exist at the lowest level of a hierarchy that also includes projects and an organisation.

Labels help you categorise your Google Cloud Platform resources (such as Compute Engine instances). A label is a key-value pair. You can attach a label to each resource, then filter the resources based on their labels. Information about labels is forwarded to the billing system so that you can break down your billing charges by the label.

Figure 112: Google Cloud Billing Dashboards

©2018 Google LLC, used with permission. Google and the Google logo are registered trademarks of Google LLC

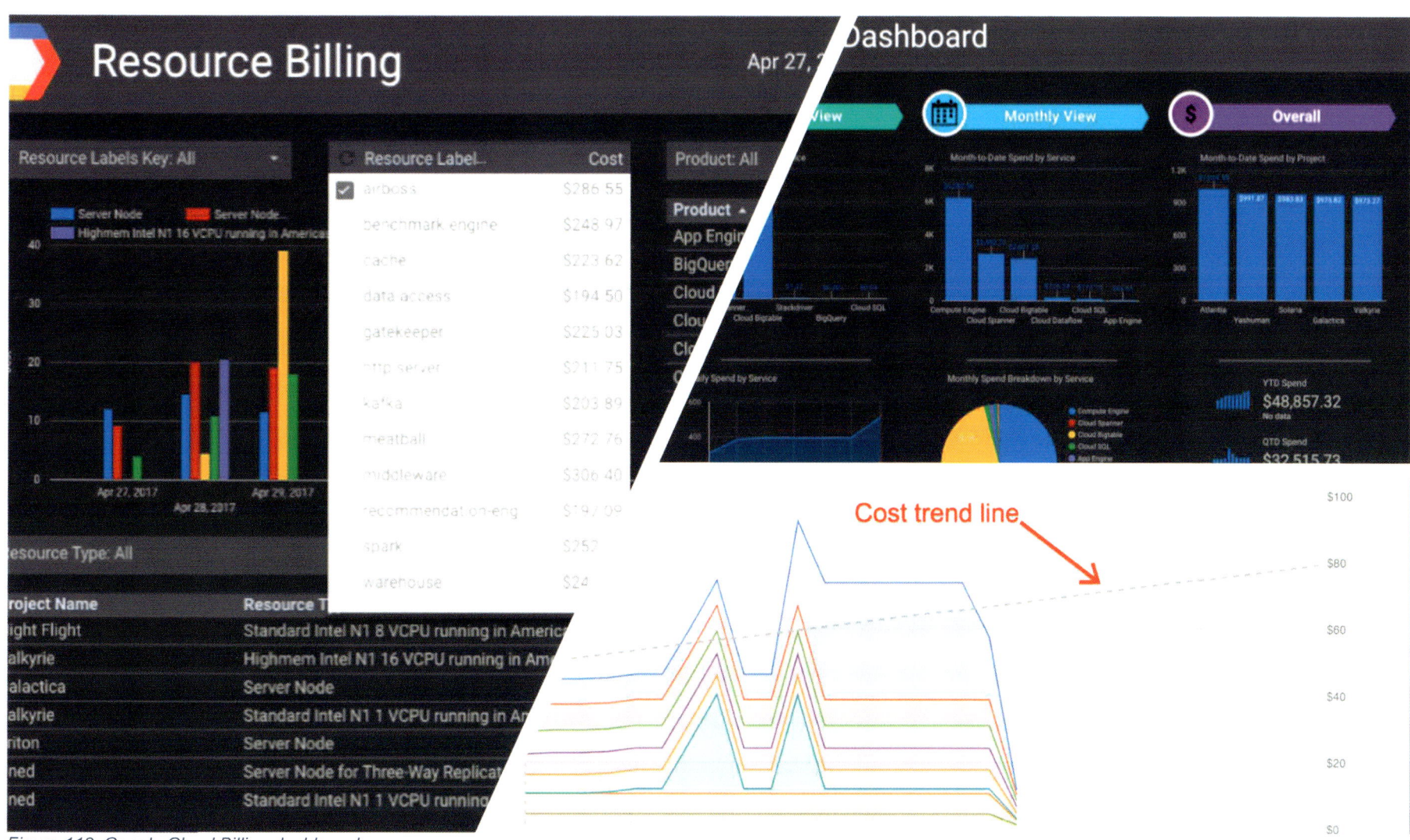

Figure 113: Google Cloud Billing dashboards

©2018 Google LLC, used with permission. Google and the Google logo are registered trademarks of Google LLC

Google Cloud Certified Professional Cloud Architect, Second Edition

203

Google recently announced the availability of a new cost forecast feature for Google Cloud Billing. This feature makes it easier to see at a glance how your costs are trending and how much you are projected to spend. You can now forecast your end-of-month costs for whatever bucket of spending is essential to you, from your entire billing account down to a single SKU in a single project.

Google Cloud Platform Sustained Discount

Google offers sustained use discounts which are automatic discounts that you get for running specific Compute Engine resources a significant portion of the billing month. Sustained use discounts apply to the following resources:
- The vCPUs and memory for predefined machine types
- The vCPUs and memory for custom machine types
- The vCPUs and memory for sole-tenant nodes
- The 10% premium cost for sole-tenant nodes, even if committed use discounts cover the vCPUs and memory in those nodes
- GPU devices

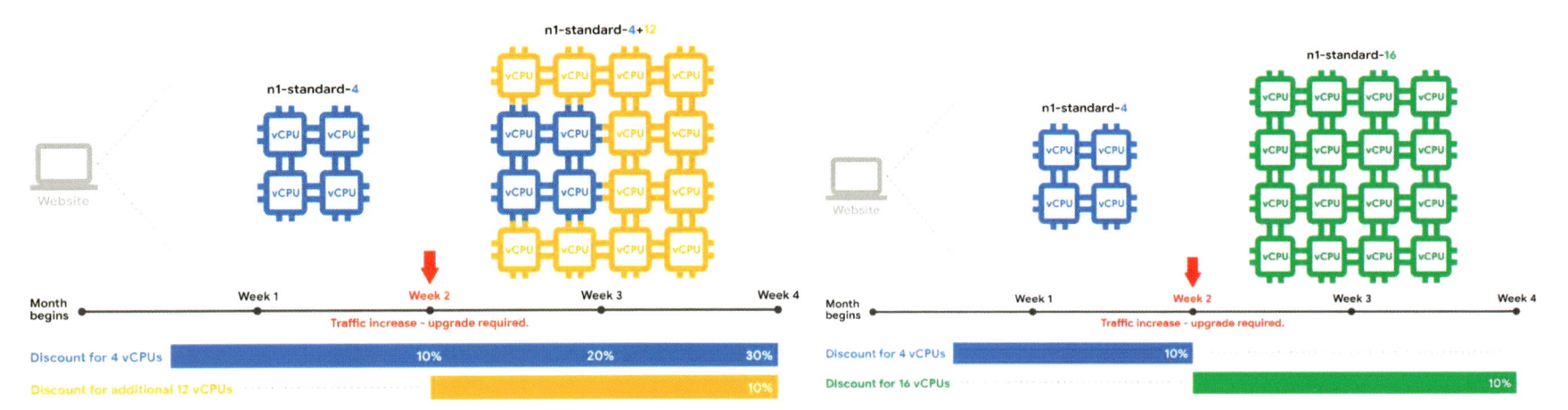

*Figure 114: Scenario A where Cost is The total monthly cost of the combined resources is **$284.3335035***

Figure 115: Scenario B – Sustained Discount where total monthly cost is $312.075.

©2018 Google LLC, used with permission. Google and the Google logo are registered trademarks of Google LLC

Calculation example detailed here in https://cloud.google.com/compute/docs/sustained-use-discounts

Compute Engine offers the ability to purchase committed use contracts in return for deeply discounted prices for VM usage. These discounts are known as committed use discounts.

If your workload is stable and predictable, you can purchase a specific amount of vCPUs and memory for a discount off of regular prices in return for committing to a usage term of 1 year or 3 years. The discount is up to 57% for most machine types or custom machine types. The discount is up to 70% for memory-optimised machine types.

Upon purchase, you will be billed a monthly fee for the term you selected, whether or not you use the services.

For further details, please refer: https://cloud.google.com/compute/docs/instances/signing-up-committed-use-discounts

Further Read:

- https://cloud.google.com/billing/docs/concepts
- https://cloud.google.com/pricing/
- https://cloud.google.com/pricing/price-leader

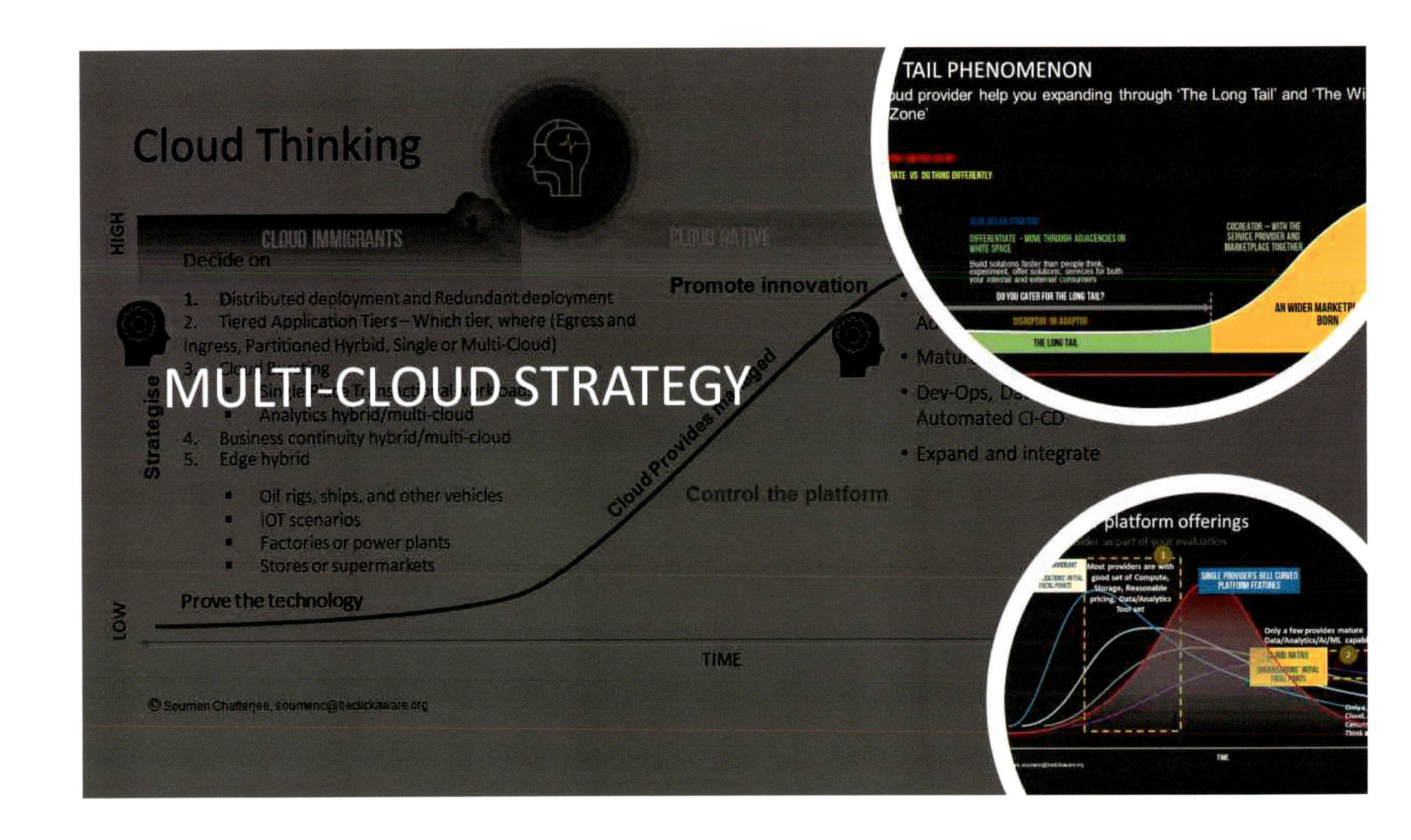

MULTI-CLOUD STRATEGY

Cloud Thinking

CLOUD IMMIGRANTS | **CLOUD NATIVE**

Decide on
1. Distributed deployment and Redundant deployment
2. Tiered Application Tiers – Which tier, where (Egress and Ingress, Partitioned Hyrbid, Single or Multi-Cloud)
3. Cloud Bursting
   - Single-use Transactional hybrid
   - Analytics hybrid/multi-cloud
4. Business continuity hybrid/multi-cloud
5. Edge hybrid

- Oil rigs, ships, and other vehicles
- IOT scenarios
- Factories or power plants
- Stores or supermarkets

Strategise / Prove the technology / Promote innovation / Control the platform

HIGH / LOW / TIME

Cloud Provides managed

© Soumen Chatterjee, soumenc@theclickaware.org

TAIL PHENOMENON

Cloud provider help you expanding through 'The Long Tail' and 'The Wi... Zone'

INNOVATE VS DO THING DIFFERENTLY

OUR SOLAR STRATEGY
DIFFERENTIATE – MOVE THROUGH ADJACENCIES OR WHITE SPACE

COCREATOR – WITH THE SERVICE PROVIDER AND MARKETPLACE TOGETHER

Build solutions faster than people think, experiment, offer solutions, services for both your internal and external consumers

DO YOU CATER FOR THE LONG TAIL?

DISRUPTOR OR ADAPTOR

THE LONG TAIL | AN WIDER MARKETPLACE BORN

platform offerings

...der as part of your evaluation

Most providers are with good set of Compute, Storage, Reasonable pricing, Data/Analytics Tool set

SINGLE PROVIDER'S BELL CURVED PLATFORM FEATURES

Only a few provides mature Data/Analytics/AI/ML capabil...

CLOUD NATIVE ORGANISATIONS' INITIAL FOCAL POINTS

Google Cloud Certified Professional Cloud Architect, Second Edition

Cloud Native, Cloud Neutral and Multi-Cloud Strategy

We come across to cloud-related topics now and then these days in forums, articles, analysts column. Almost all sizes organisations have already embraced cloud computing into their mainstream IT portfolio or in the process of moving in, budgeted as part of the core business strategies and recognised a significant enabler in the journey to their digital transformations. Cloud providers are every day strengthening their eco-system to unlock, manage and mine massive scale datasets at scale and serving millions and billions of users and handling millions and billions of events real-time from your **data production systems.** Cloud platforms can offer you an intelligent **data consumer platform** for your enterprise business leaders as well as all other user personas enabling advanced analytics, machine learning, and artificial intelligence at an affordable price point. One of the critical point we have to remember all the time that without being a **Data Native** or **Data Migrant**, your digital journey would remain incomplete and without adopting a cloud path, your digital transformation journey would remain as a distant dream. Chris Anderson, in his best selling and revolutionary book '**The Long Tail: How Endless Choice is Creating Unlimited Demand**' has rightly analysed the behavioural economy signal and beautifully explained to us how in digital master industries are reimagining their services to align to the behavioural economy and cloud providers, are also not an exception. Being '**Cloud Native**' means adopting a cloud provider and build your platforms on that preferred cloud providers. Your loyalty towards a selected provider is the most common scenario across the industry.

The 'Long Tail' phenomenon has inspired almost every leader, and those market-leading cloud providers are no exception. All the providers are in fierce competition to offer us architecturally creative Cloud Platform Solution, and turning from a mass market back into a niche adopters and tailoring their offering accordingly. Due to the 'Long Tail' service revolution, all the cloud providers are innovating their pricing strategy and coming up with not only a better pricing strategy but also enhancing their tools, components and platform is getting better every day. It would be unwise for 'Data Immigrants' getting locked into a specific cloud provider until the point you understand the offerings, impact on your technology, pricing, cost and satisfying your enterprise requirements.

Cloud Native signifies that your organisation embraces cloud platforms as your DNA and in every services and solution that were offered. There is a spectrum of things associated than just leveraging underlying cloud infrastructure, to become a native cloud enterprise. This is a significant journey and can't happen overnight unless you start on the cloud as a start-up and set off your journey. Cloud Native organisation not necessarily be tied with one provider but usually with more than one providers.

The term Multi-Cloud describes setups that combine at least two public cloud providers which might also involve some private computing environments.

THE LONG TAIL PHENOMENON

Does your cloud provider help you expanding through 'The Long Tail' and 'The Wider Marketplace Zone'

Business model usefulness and targeted behavioural fitness

BUSINESS CHALLENGE AND RED OCEAN
DO YOU DIFFERENTIATE VS DO THING DIFFERENTLY

SERVICE PROVIDER

THE HEAD

BLUE OCEAN STRATEGY
DIFFERENTIATE - MOVE THROUGH ADJACENCIES OR WHITE SPACE

Build solutions faster than people think, experiment, offer solutions, services for both your internal and external consumers

DO YOU CATER FOR THE LONG TAIL?

DISRUPTOR OR ADAPTOR

THE LONG TAIL

COCREATOR – WITH THE SERVICE PROVIDER AND MARKETPLACE TOGETHER

Google AI Hub. Limitless possibilities.

AN WIDER MARKETPLACE IS BORN

Services / Solutions / Products

© Soumen Chatterjee, soumenc@beclickaware.org

Cloud Thinking

HIGH → **LOW** (vertical axis)
TIME (horizontal axis)

Strategise

CLOUD IMMIGRANTS
Decide on
1. **D**istributed deployment and Redundant deployment
2. Tiered Application Tiers – Which tier, where (Egress and Ingress, Partitioned Hyrbid, Single or Multi-Cloud)
3. Cloud Bursting
   - Single Place Transactional workloads
   - Analytics hybrid/multi-cloud
4. Business continuity hybrid/multi-cloud
5. Edge hybrid

- Oil rigs, ships, and other vehicles
- IOT scenarios
- Factories or power plants
- Stores or supermarkets

Prove the technology

CLOUD NATIVE
Promote innovation

Cloud Provides managed

Control the platform

CLOUD FIRST
- Think Cloud – Stable Cloud Strategy and Cloud Adoption Framework
- Matured Single or Multiple Cloud Adoption
- Dev-Ops, Data-Ops, ML-OPS, AI-OPS, Automated CI-CD
- Expand and integrate

© Soumen Chatterjee, soumenc@beclickaware.org

Cloud provider platform offerings
Areas you must consider as part of your evaluation

CLOUD IMMIGRANT ORGANISATIONS' INITIAL FOCAL POINTS

Most providers are with good set of Compute, Storage, Reasonable pricing, Data/Analytics Tool set

SINGLE PROVIDER'S BELL CURVED PLATFORM FEATURES

Only a few provides mature Data/Analytics/AI/ML capability

CLOUD NATIVE ORGANISATIONS' INITIAL FOCAL POINTS

CLOUD FIRST MUST THINK ABOUT THESE AREAS

Only a few enables you Open Cloud, Muli-Cloud, AI / ML, Take you on a fast track Data Centricity and Price Leaderships
Think about feature 1, 2 and 3

TIME

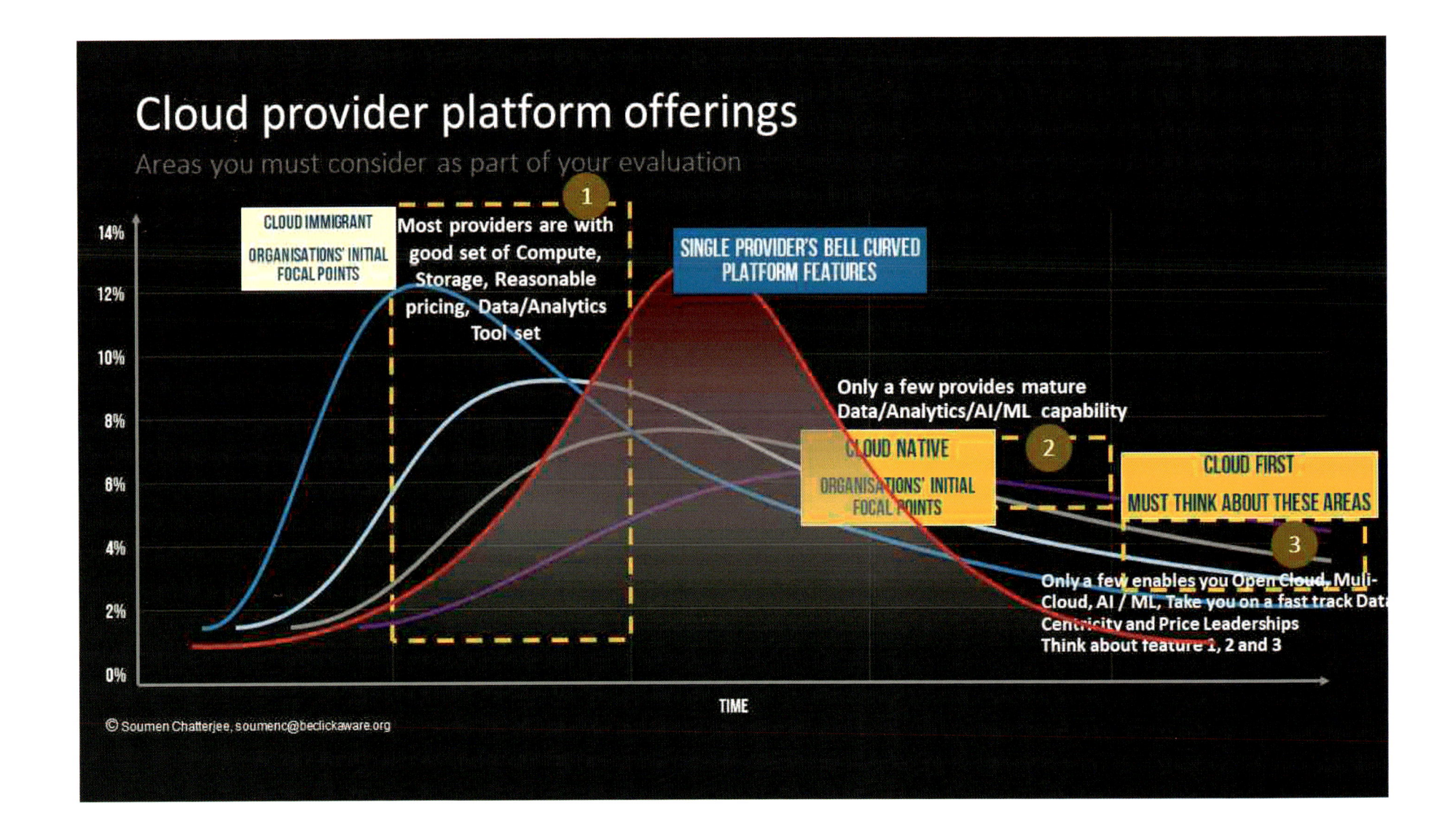

© Soumen Chatterjee, soumenc@beclickaware.org

Google Cloud Certified Professional Cloud Architect, Second Edition

CLOUD NATIVE, HYBRID AND MULTI CLOUD WORKLOADS

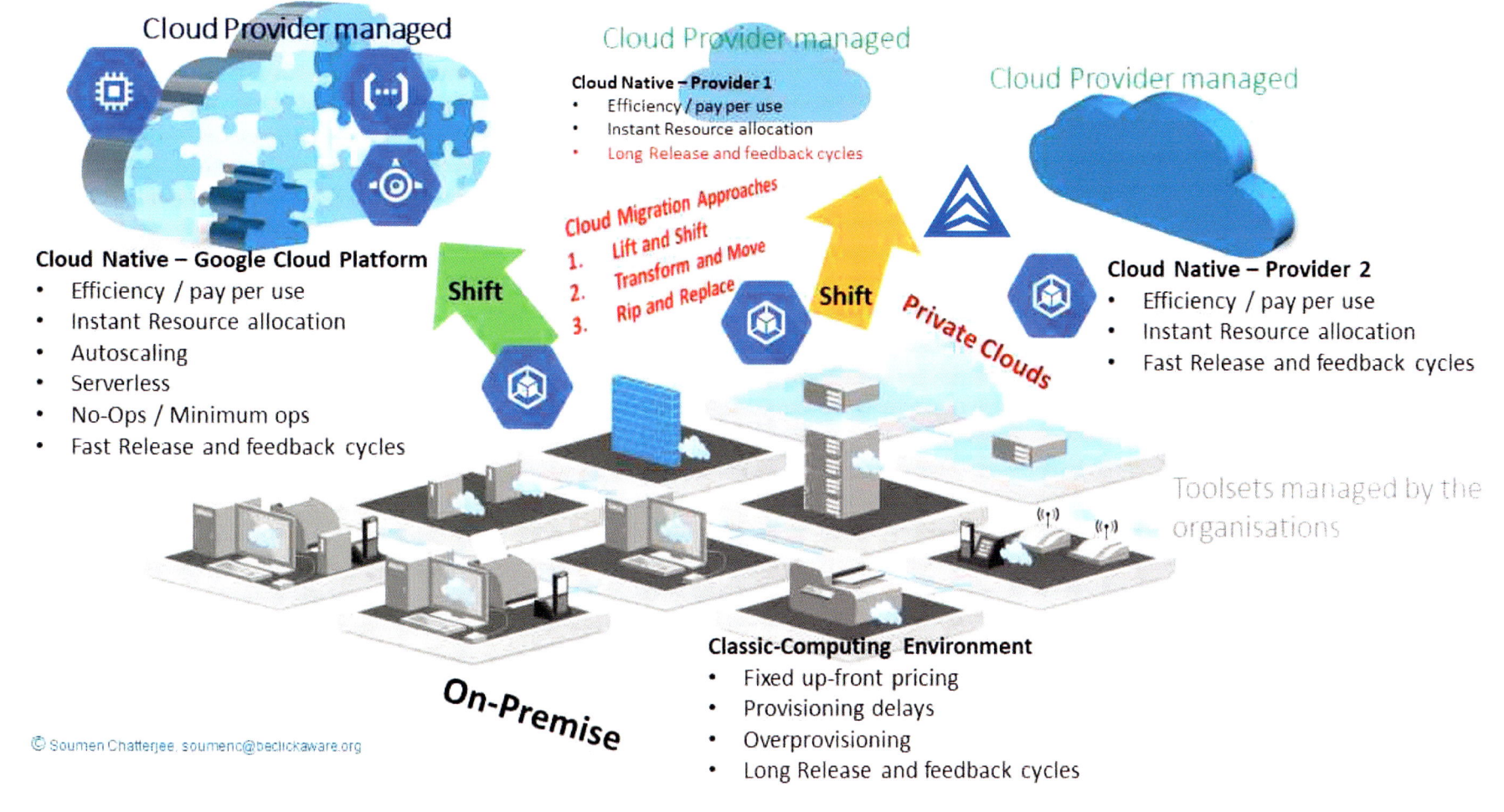

Cloud Provider managed

Cloud Provider managed

Cloud Native – Provider 1
- Efficiency / pay per use
- Instant Resource allocation
- Long Release and feedback cycles

Cloud Provider managed

Cloud Migration Approaches
1. Lift and Shift
2. Transform and Move
3. Rip and Replace

Cloud Native – Google Cloud Platform
- Efficiency / pay per use
- Instant Resource allocation
- Autoscaling
- Serverless
- No-Ops / Minimum ops
- Fast Release and feedback cycles

Shift

Shift

Private Clouds

Cloud Native – Provider 2
- Efficiency / pay per use
- Instant Resource allocation
- Fast Release and feedback cycles

Toolsets managed by the organisations

On-Premise

Classic-Computing Environment
- Fixed up-front pricing
- Provisioning delays
- Overprovisioning
- Long Release and feedback cycles

© Soumen Chatterjee, soumenc@beclickaware.org

Google Cloud Certified Professional Cloud Architect, Second Edition

Moving to Multi-clouds

Once you decide to move to could, it would involve three key areas: infrastructure, workloads and applications to move to the cloud. When we migrate a workload to the cloud, it is essential to consider the different components of your infrastructure including service availability, scaling and management activities. We have already discussed **Cloud Platform Storage** and **Compute Engine** in detail. We have shown a rich set of data and analytical tools within Google Cloud in the **Cloud Databases** section. The methodology and destination of data depend on the type of load (Transactional vs Analytical vs Operational vs Complex Event Processing vs Unstructured vs Media) and differs from the methodology for moving databases.

Embrace Google Cloud

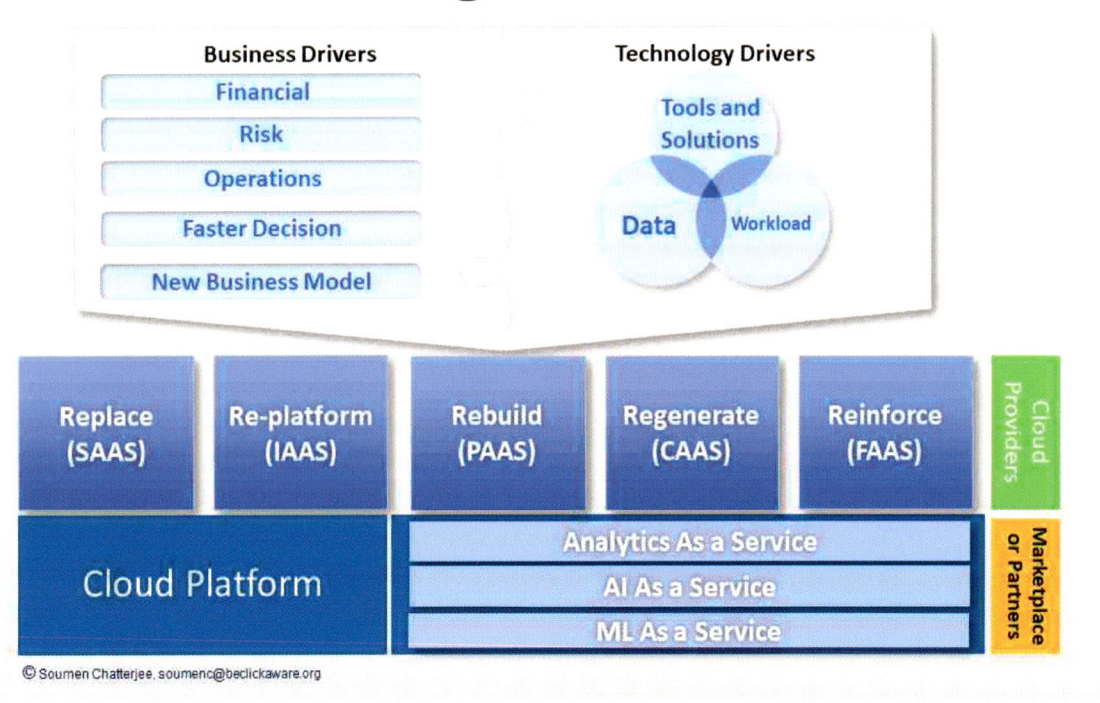

Business Drivers
- Financial
- Risk
- Operations
- Faster Decision
- New Business Model

Technology Drivers
- Tools and Solutions
- Data
- Workload

| Replace (SAAS) | Re-platform (IAAS) | Rebuild (PAAS) | Regenerate (CAAS) | Reinforce (FAAS) | Cloud Providers |

Cloud Platform | Analytics As a Service / AI As a Service / ML As a Service | Marketplace or Partners

© Soumen Chatterjee, soumenc@beclickaware.org

The cost of the move is one critical driver and decides the destination, and you could get significant advantage considering various pricing options, sustained use discounts (SUD) and committed discounts on Google Compute Engine virtual machines (VMs), and costs can be significantly lower than managing hardware or virtual machines on on-premise.

The decision about which workloads to run on which computing environments has a profound impact on the effectiveness of a hybrid and multi-cloud strategy. Putting the wrong workload on the cloud can complicate your deployment while providing little benefit. Putting an appropriate workload in the right place not only helps the workload but helps you learn about the benefits of each environment.

Cloud migration of data requires a data pipeline comprising workflows that connect data, processing, and services across clouds, giving you a unified data environment.
Google Cloud provides a rich set of workflows:
    a. Cloud Composer
    b. Google Cloud ML Engine
    c.

d. Kubeflow: Simplifying machine learning on open hybrid clouds
e. Kubeflow: Cloud-native machine learning with Kubernetes
f.

g. Serverless Architecture

Figure 116: What moves to cloud

Table 20: Moving on-premise infrastructure to GCP

On-Premise / Private Cloud Service Type	Data Center	Google Cloud Platform
Compute	Physical hardware, virtualized hardware (VMWare ESXi, Hyper-V, KVM, XEN)	Google Compute Engine
Storage	SAN, NAS, DAS	Persistent disk, Google Cloud Storage
Network	MPLS, VPN, hardware load balancing, DNS	Google Cloud VPN, Google Cloud Interconnect, Compute Engine load balancing, Google Domains, Google Cloud DNS
Security	Firewalls, NACLs, route tables, encryption, IDS, SSL	Compute Engine firewalls, encryption, IDS, SSL
Identity	Active Directory, LDAP	IAM, GCDS, LDAP
Management	Configuration services, CI/CD tools	Deployment Manager, configuration services, continuous integration/continuous delivery (CI/CD)

Open Source / Cloud Neutral Product	Compatible GCP product
Apache HBase	Cloud Bigtable
Apache Beam	Cloud Dataflow
Apache Hadoop	Cloud Dataproc
MySQL, PostgreSQL	Cloud SQL
Redis	Cloud Memorystore
Network File System (NFS)	Cloud Filestore
JMS, Kafka	Cloud Pub/Sub

Table 21: Moving Cloud Neutral Technologies to GCP

Moving applications follow a separate approach which could involve moving tools as shown in the above table or rebuild leveraging **Google App Engine (GAE)**, **API Management**, and **Function as a service (FAAS) – Cloud Function**

Cloud Migration Topology
Connecting private computing environments to Google Cloud Platform securely and reliably delivers successful hybrid or multi-cloud deployment, and a great detail level of design consideration is required to meet the unique requirements of your enterprise workloads and suit the architecture patterns that you intend to apply.

One of the widely used patterns is the '**Mirrored**' topology to primary set up a range of environments in a hybrid fashion, and this design could be tailored in various ways with a combination of separate VPCs with the CI/CD VPC, bastion hosts and squid proxy depending on use-cases.

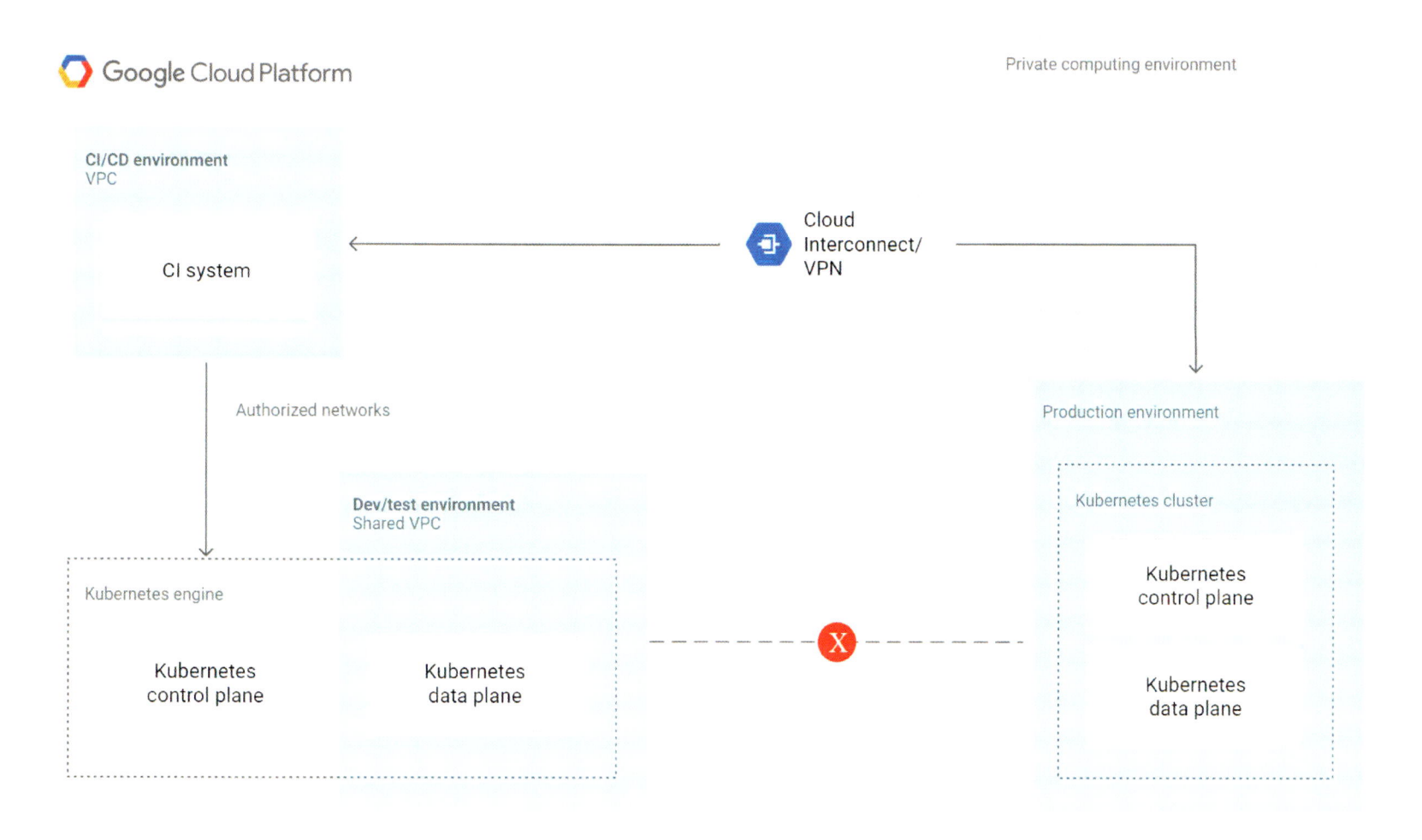

Figure 117: Cloud Migration – One example variety of Mirror Topology

Another successful pattern is '**Meshed**' topology that establishes a flat network spanning across multiple computing environments.

©2018 Google LLC, used with permission. Google and the Google logo are registered trademarks of Google LLC

Figure 118: Cloud Migration – One example a variety of Mesh Topology

©2018 Google LLC, used with permission. Google and the Google logo are registered trademarks of Google LLC

This 'Meshed' topology could be improvised with the introduction of an additional deep packet inspection or other advanced firewalling mechanisms exploiting the capabilities of GCP firewall rules.

Another widely popular topology is the '**Gated egress**' to expose selected APIs from the private computing environment to workloads that are deployed in GCP without exposing them to the public internet.

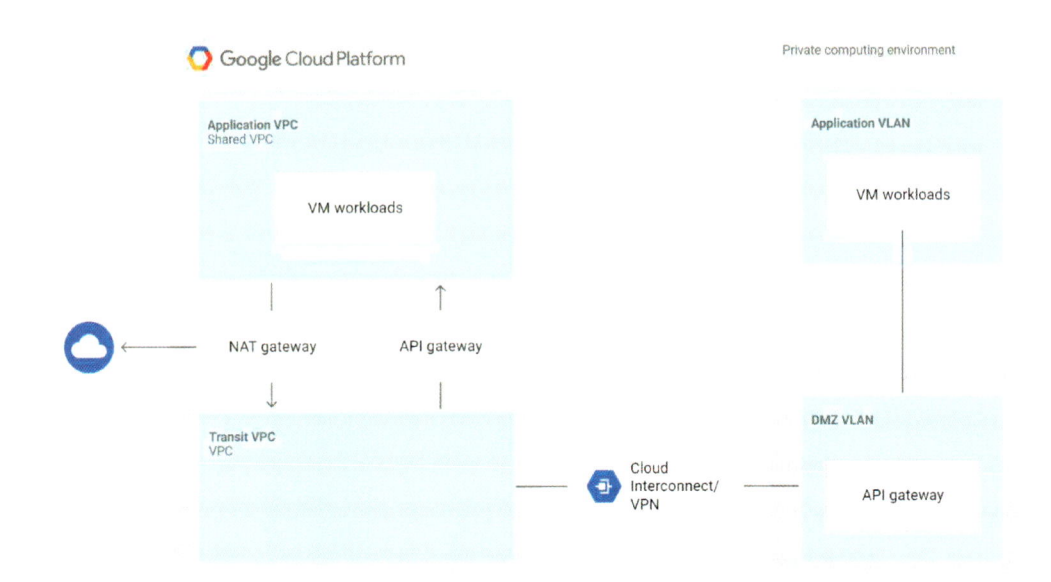

The '**Gated ingress**' topology exposes selected APIs of workloads running in GCP to the private computing environment without exposing them to the public internet.

Figure 119: Cloud Migration - Gated Egress and Ingress Topology

©2018 Google LLC, used with permission. Google and the Google logo are registered trademarks of Google LLC

Further Reading

- https://cloud.google.com/solutions/best-practices-migrating-vm-to-compute-engine
- https://cloud.google.com/solutions/hybrid-and-multi-cloud-architecture-patterns#tiered_hybrid
- https://cloud.google.com/solutions/hybrid-and-multi-cloud-patterns-and-practices
- https://cloud.google.com/solutions/hybrid-and-multi-cloud-architecture-patterns#tiered_hybrid
- https://cloud.google.com/solutions/hybrid-and-multi-cloud-architecture-patterns#cloud_bursting
- https://cloud.google.com/solutions/hybrid-and-multi-cloud-network-topologies
- https://cloud.google.com/solutions/migration/hadoop/hadoop-gcp-migration-overview

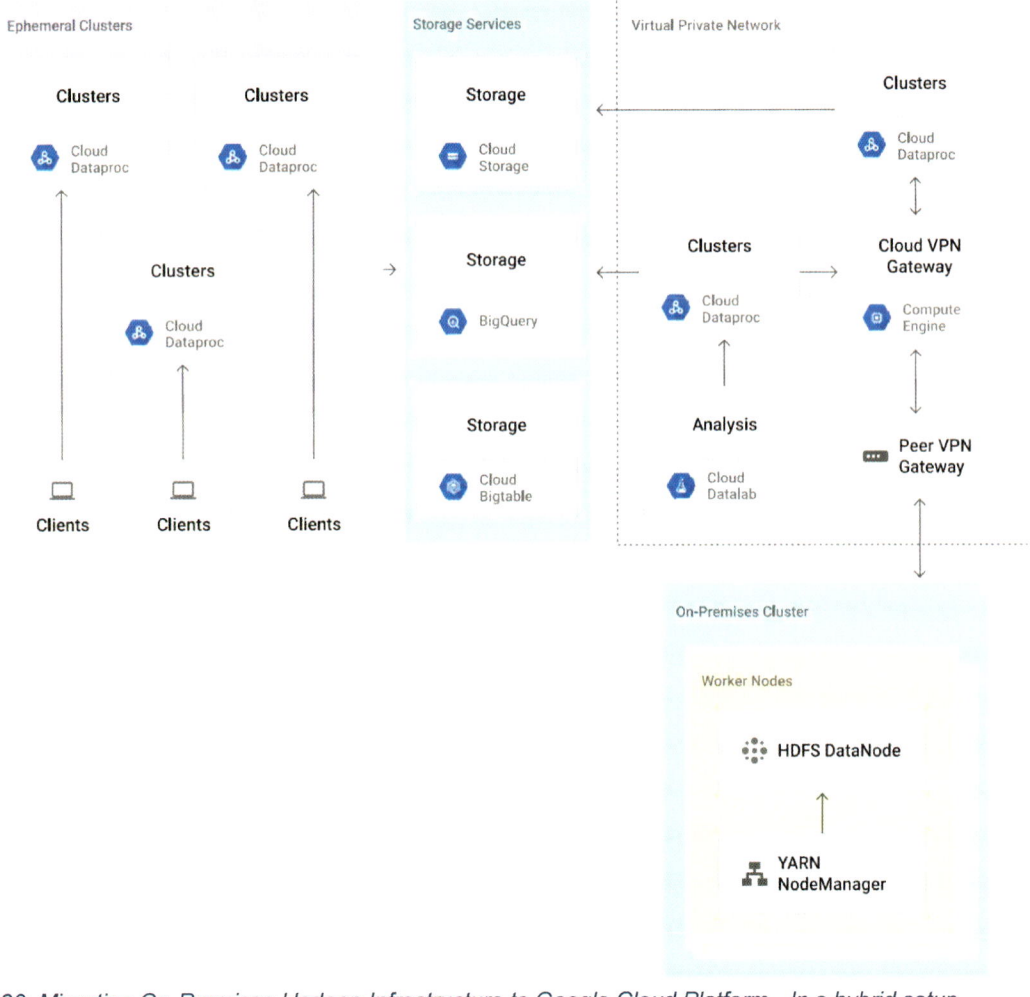

Figure 120: Migrating On-Premises Hadoop Infrastructure to Google Cloud Platform - In a hybrid setup

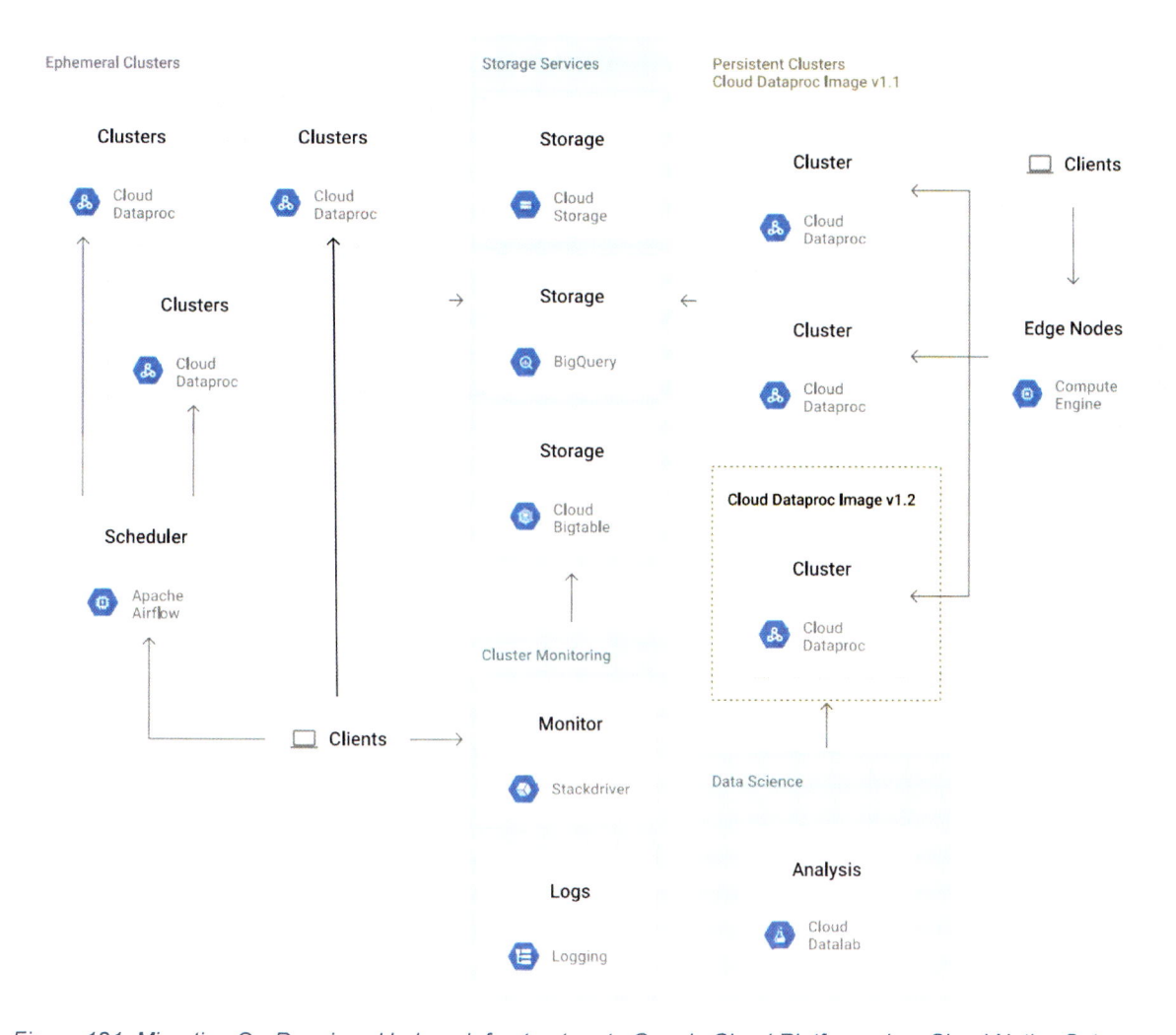

Figure 121: Migrating On-Premises Hadoop Infrastructure to Google Cloud Platform - In a Cloud Native Setup

©2018 Google LLC, used with permission. Google and the Google logo are registered trademarks of Google LLC

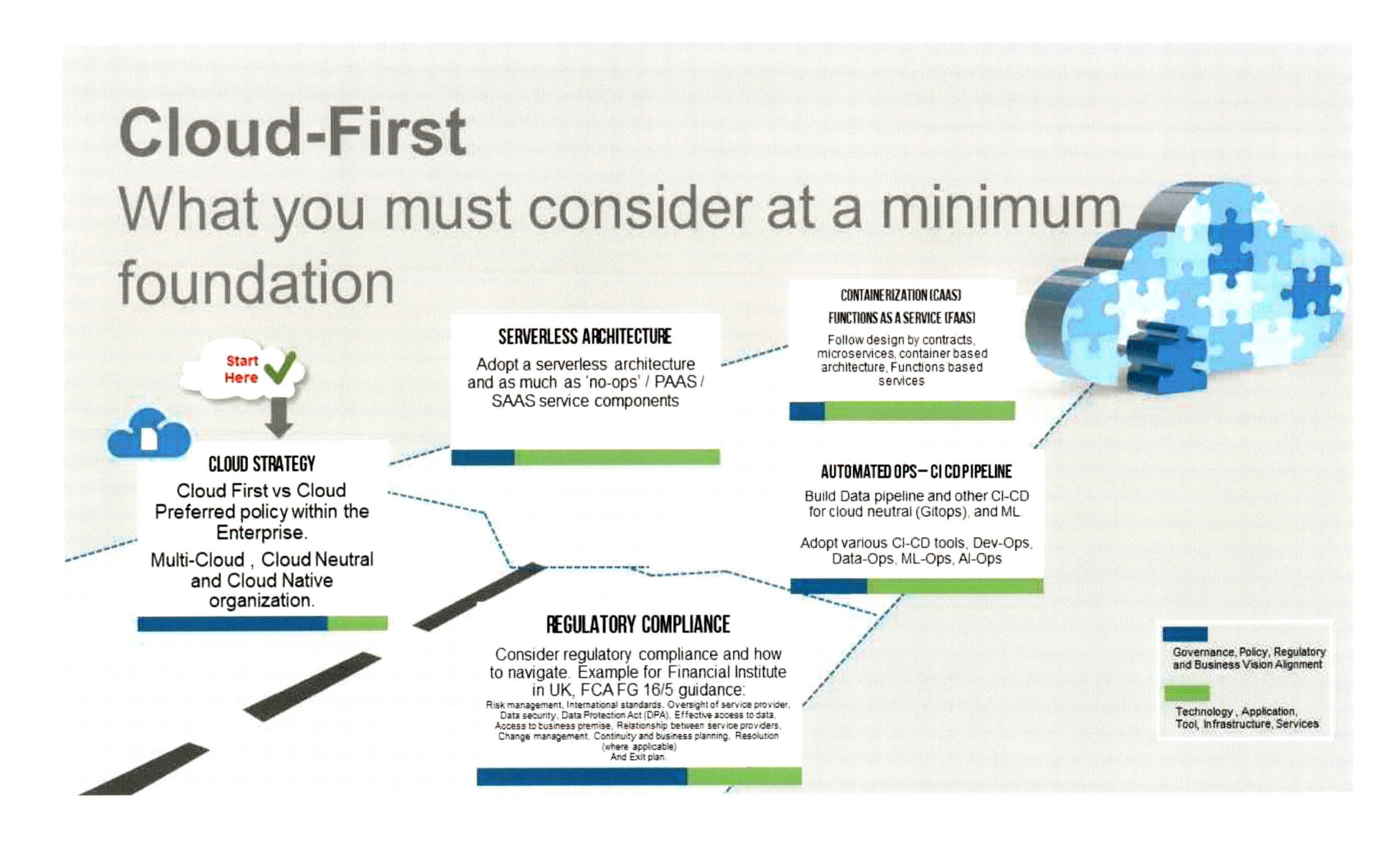

Cloud-First
What you must consider at a minimum
foundation

Start Here ✓

CLOUD STRATEGY
Cloud First vs Cloud Preferred policy within the Enterprise.
Multi-Cloud, Cloud Neutral and Cloud Native organization.

SERVERLESS ARCHITECTURE
Adopt a serverless architecture and as much as 'no-ops' / PAAS / SAAS service components

CONTAINERIZATION (CAAS)
FUNCTIONS AS A SERVICE (FAAS)
Follow design by contracts, microservices, container based architecture, Functions based services

AUTOMATED OPS – CI CD PIPELINE
Build Data pipeline and other CI-CD for cloud neutral (Gitops), and ML.
Adopt various CI-CD tools, Dev-Ops, Data-Ops, ML-Ops, AI-Ops

REGULATORY COMPLIANCE
Consider regulatory compliance and how to navigate. Example for Financial Institute in UK, FCA FG 16/5 guidance:
Risk management, International standards. Oversight of service provider, Data security, Data Protection Act (DPA), Effective access to data, Access to business premise, Relationship between service providers, Change management, Continuity and business planning, Resolution (where applicable) And Exit plan.

Governance, Policy, Regulatory and Business Vision Alignment

Technology, Application, Tool, Infrastructure, Services

Google Cloud Certified Professional Cloud Architect, Second Edition

Cloud First vs Cloud Enabled

A common way to begin your cloud journey leveraging the public cloud is starting with a '**Cloud First**' policy, assess and initiate deployment of new workloads to the public cloud. You could follow **Moving to Multi-cloud** approach and allow a private computing infrastructure or internal cloud environment if a restrictive data or highly restrictive data scenario or tools/application limitations or any other regulatory compliance or organisational reasons.

The cloud-first strategy introduces a series of benefits, and you can deploy new workloads in a clean and cloud-native fashion while avoiding (or at least minimising) the hassles of migrating existing workloads.

On the downside, using a cloud-first strategy might introduce some opportunity loss factors generating insights and discovering interesting patterns leveraging existing workloads. New workloads might constitute only a fraction of your overall IT workload, and also introduces risks increasing the overall complexity of your IT environment. This approach might offer cost-savings and on the outset simplifies the overall enterprise architecture, however, might not be the best architecture for various use-cases. We should use Cloud First with significant care and not with a blanket approach and must take into accounts each candidate application and associated workloads.

Cloud-enabled Data Native organisations are much more successful with a hybrid and multi-cloud approach in reality.

Google Next 19 – Key Announcements

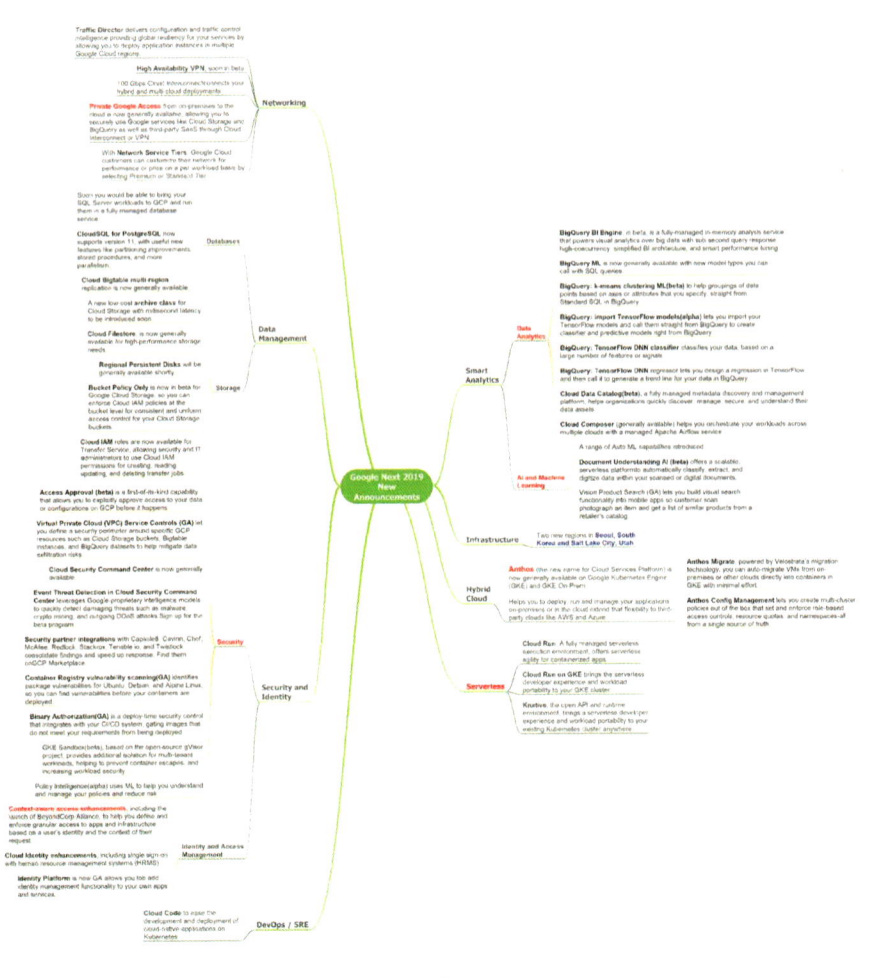

Figure 122: Google Next 19 Announcement Summary

Google Cloud Certified Professional Cloud Architect, Second Edition

Further reading in details: 122+ announcements from Google Cloud Next '19 (https://cloud.google.com/blog/topics/inside-google-cloud/100-plus-announcements-from-google-cloud-next19)

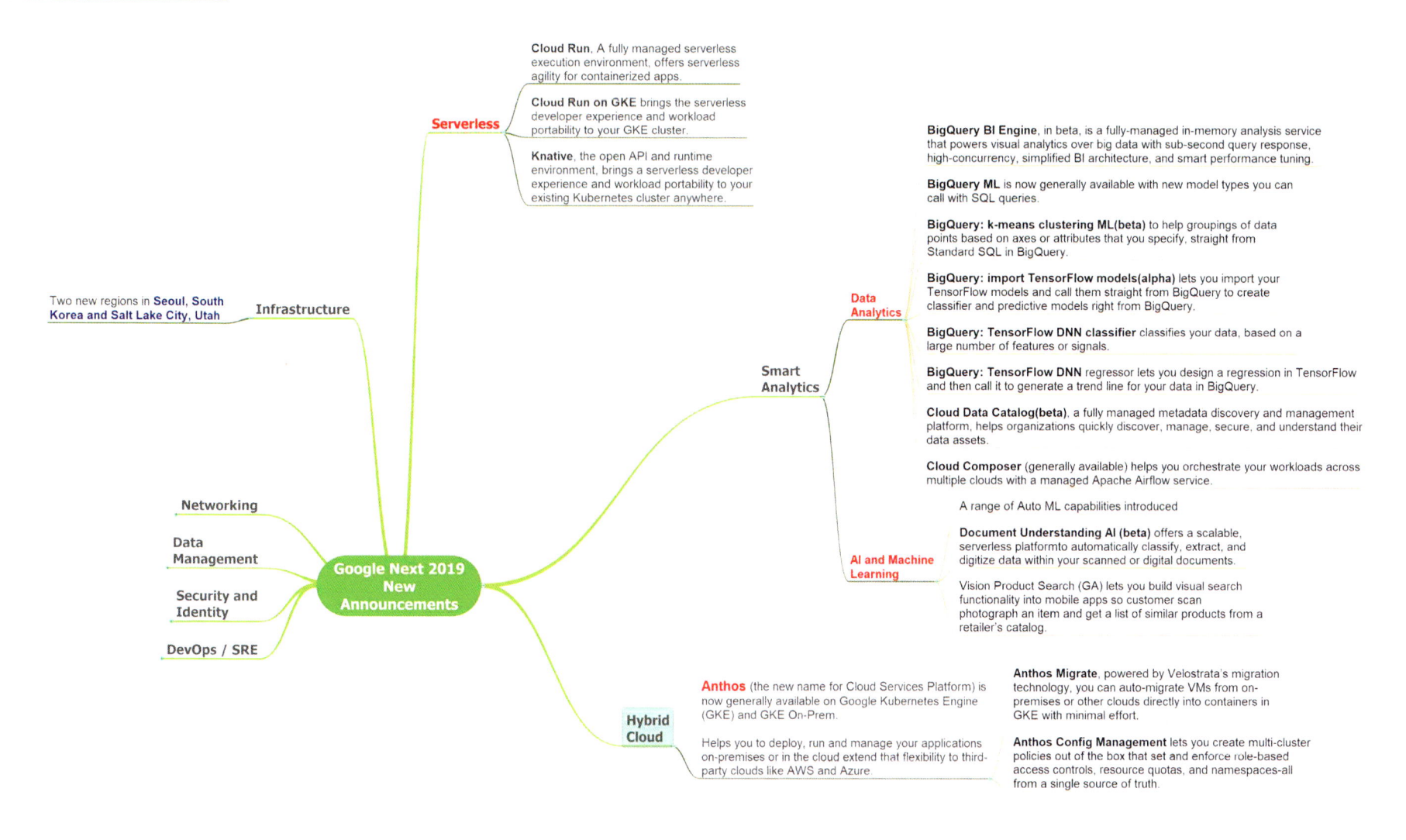

Google Next 2019 New Announcements

Infrastructure
- Two new regions in **Seoul, South Korea** and **Salt Lake City, Utah**

Networking

Data Management

Security and Identity

DevOps / SRE

Serverless
- **Cloud Run**, A fully managed serverless execution environment, offers serverless agility for containerized apps.
- **Cloud Run on GKE** brings the serverless developer experience and workload portability to your GKE cluster.
- **Knative**, the open API and runtime environment, brings a serverless developer experience and workload portability to your existing Kubernetes cluster anywhere.

Smart Analytics

Data Analytics
- **BigQuery BI Engine**, in beta, is a fully-managed in-memory analysis service that powers visual analytics over big data with sub-second query response, high-concurrency, simplified BI architecture, and smart performance tuning.
- **BigQuery ML** is now generally available with new model types you can call with SQL queries.
- **BigQuery: k-means clustering ML(beta)** to help groupings of data points based on axes or attributes that you specify, straight from Standard SQL in BigQuery.
- **BigQuery: import TensorFlow models(alpha)** lets you import your TensorFlow models and call them straight from BigQuery to create classifier and predictive models right from BigQuery.
- **BigQuery: TensorFlow DNN classifier** classifies your data, based on a large number of features or signals.
- **BigQuery: TensorFlow DNN** regressor lets you design a regression in TensorFlow and then call it to generate a trend line for your data in BigQuery.
- **Cloud Data Catalog(beta)**, a fully managed metadata discovery and management platform, helps organizations quickly discover, manage, secure, and understand their data assets.
- **Cloud Composer** (generally available) helps you orchestrate your workloads across multiple clouds with a managed Apache Airflow service.

AI and Machine Learning
- A range of Auto ML capabilities introduced
- **Document Understanding AI (beta)** offers a scalable, serverless platformto automatically classify, extract, and digitize data within your scanned or digital documents.
- **Vision Product Search (GA)** lets you build visual search functionality into mobile apps so customer scan photograph an item and get a list of similar products from a retailer's catalog.

Hybrid Cloud
- **Anthos** (the new name for Cloud Services Platform) is now generally available on Google Kubernetes Engine (GKE) and GKE On-Prem.
- Helps you to deploy, run and manage your applications on-premises or in the cloud extend that flexibility to third-party clouds like AWS and Azure.
- **Anthos Migrate**, powered by Velostrata's migration technology, you can auto-migrate VMs from on-premises or other clouds directly into containers in GKE with minimal effort.
- **Anthos Config Management** lets you create multi-cluster policies out of the box that set and enforce role-based access controls, resource quotas, and namespaces-all from a single source of truth.

Google Cloud Certified Professional Cloud Architect, Second Edition

Google Next 2019 New Announcements

Security and Identity

Security

- **Access Approval (beta)** is a first-of-its-kind capability that allows you to explicitly approve access to your data or configurations on GCP before it happens.
- **Virtual Private Cloud (VPC) Service Controls (GA)** let you define a security perimeter around specific GCP resources such as Cloud Storage buckets, Bigtable instances, and BigQuery datasets to help mitigate data exfiltration risks.
- **Cloud Security Command Center** is now generally available.
- **Event Threat Detection in Cloud Security Command Center** leverages Google-proprietary intelligence models to quickly detect damaging threats such as malware, crypto mining, and outgoing DDoS attacks. Sign up for the beta program.
- **Security partner integrations** with Capsule8, Cavirin, Chef, McAfee, Redlock, Stackrox, Tenable.io, and Twistlock consolidate findings and speed up response. Find them on GCP Marketplace.
- **Container Registry vulnerability scanning(GA)** identifies package vulnerabilities for Ubuntu, Debian, and Alpine Linux, so you can find vulnerabilities before your containers are deployed.
- **Binary Authorization(GA)** is a deploy-time security control that integrates with your CI/CD system, gating images that do not meet your requirements from being deployed.
- **GKE Sandbox(beta)**, based on the open-source gVisor project, provides additional isolation for multi-tenant workloads, helping to prevent container escapes, and increasing workload security.
- **Policy Intelligence(alpha)** uses ML to help you understand and manage your policies and reduce risk.

Identity and Access Management

- **Context-aware access enhancements**, including the launch of BeyondCorp Alliance, to help you define and enforce granular access to apps and infrastructure based on a user's identity and the context of their request.
- **Cloud Identity enhancements**, including single sign-on with human resource management systems (HRMS).
- **Identity Platform** is now GA allows you tob add identity management functionality to your own apps and services.

Data Management

Databases

- Soon you would be able to bring your SQL Server workloads to GCP and run them in a fully managed database service.
- **CloudSQL for PostgreSQL** now supports version 11, with useful new features like partitioning improvements, stored procedures, and more parallelism.
- **Cloud Bigtable multi-region** replication is now generally available.

Storage

- A new low-cost **archive class** for Cloud Storage with millisecond latency to be introduced soon.
- **Cloud Filestore**, is now generally available for high-performance storage needs.
- **Regional Persistent Disks** will be generally available shortly.
- **Bucket Policy Only** is now in beta for Google Cloud Storage, so you can enforce Cloud IAM policies at the bucket level for consistent and uniform access control for your Cloud Storage buckets.
- **Cloud IAM** roles are now available for Transfer Service, allowing security and IT administrators to use Cloud IAM permissions for creating, reading, updating, and deleting transfer jobs.

DevOps / SRE

- **Cloud Code** to ease the development and deployment of cloud-native applications on Kubernetes

Networking

- **Traffic Director** delivers configuration and traffic control intelligence providing global resiliency for your services by allowing you to deploy application instances in multiple Google Cloud regions.
- **High Availability VPN**, soon in beta
- 100 Gbps Cloud Interconnect connects your hybrid and multi-cloud deployments.
- **Private Google Access** from on-premises to the cloud is now generally available, allowing you to securely use Google services like Cloud Storage and BigQuery as well as third-party SaaS through Cloud Interconnect or VPN.
- With **Network Service Tiers**, Google Cloud customers can customize their network for performance or price on a per-workload basis by selecting Premium or Standard Tier.

Serverless

Infrastructure

Hybrid Cloud

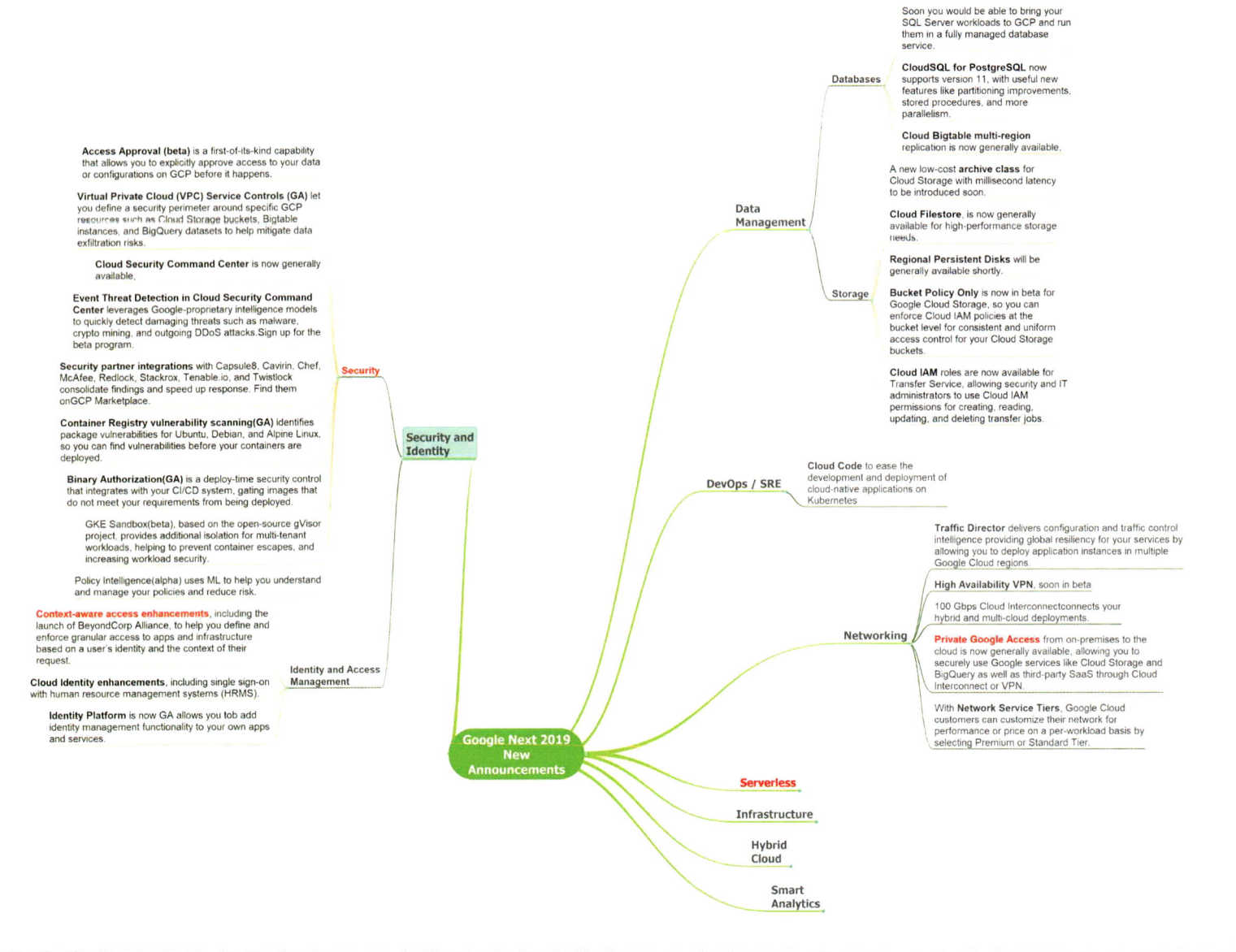

Smart Analytics

Certification Exam: Sample Case Studies

Case Studies are detailed here: https://cloud.google.com/certification/guides/professional-cloud-architect/

All these case studies are similar to those which you would encounter in real-life Google Cloud projects. Your first success formula is to understand all the highlighted areas that I developed from those three sample case studies Google would expect you all to understand and grasp the concepts behind them. All the necessary concepts and areas you have read so far in the book would make you ready to stand out.

Best wishes! Please send me your feedback about the book, and in case you appear for the exam, email me your experience directly to me
soumenc@beclickaware.org

Mountkirk Games Case Study

TerramEarth Case Study

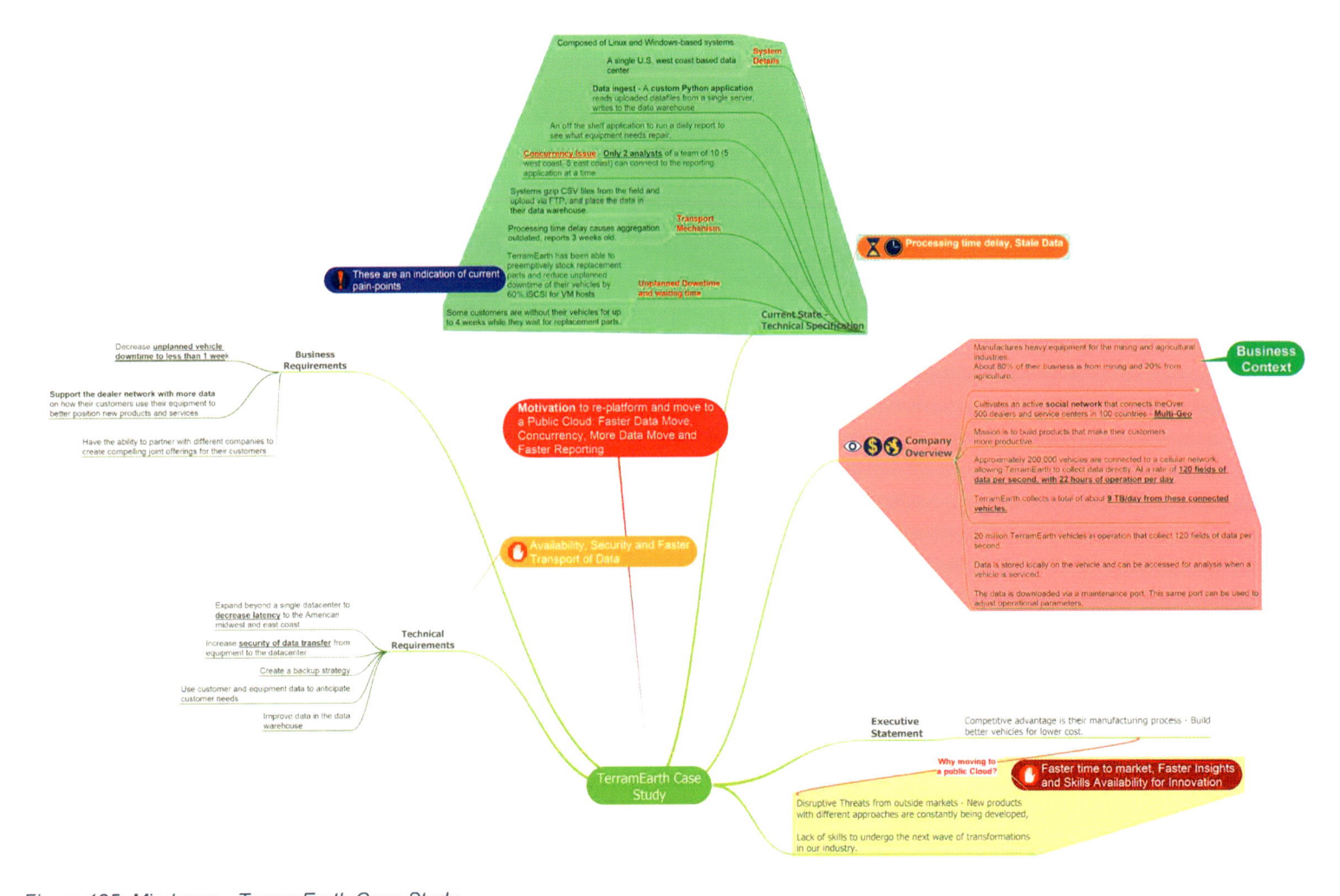

Figure 125: Mind map - TerramEarth Case Study

Certification Exam: Sample Case Studies

Case Studies are detailed here: https://cloud.google.com/certification/guides/professional-cloud-architect/

All these case studies are similar to those which you would encounter in real-life Google Cloud projects. Your first success formula is to understand all the highlighted areas that I developed from those three sample case studies Google would expect you all to understand and grasp the concepts behind them. All the necessary concepts and areas you have read so far in the book would make you ready to stand out.

Best wishes! Please send me your feedback about the book, and in case you appear for the exam, email me your experience directly to me
soumenc@beclickaware.org

Mountkirk Games Case Study

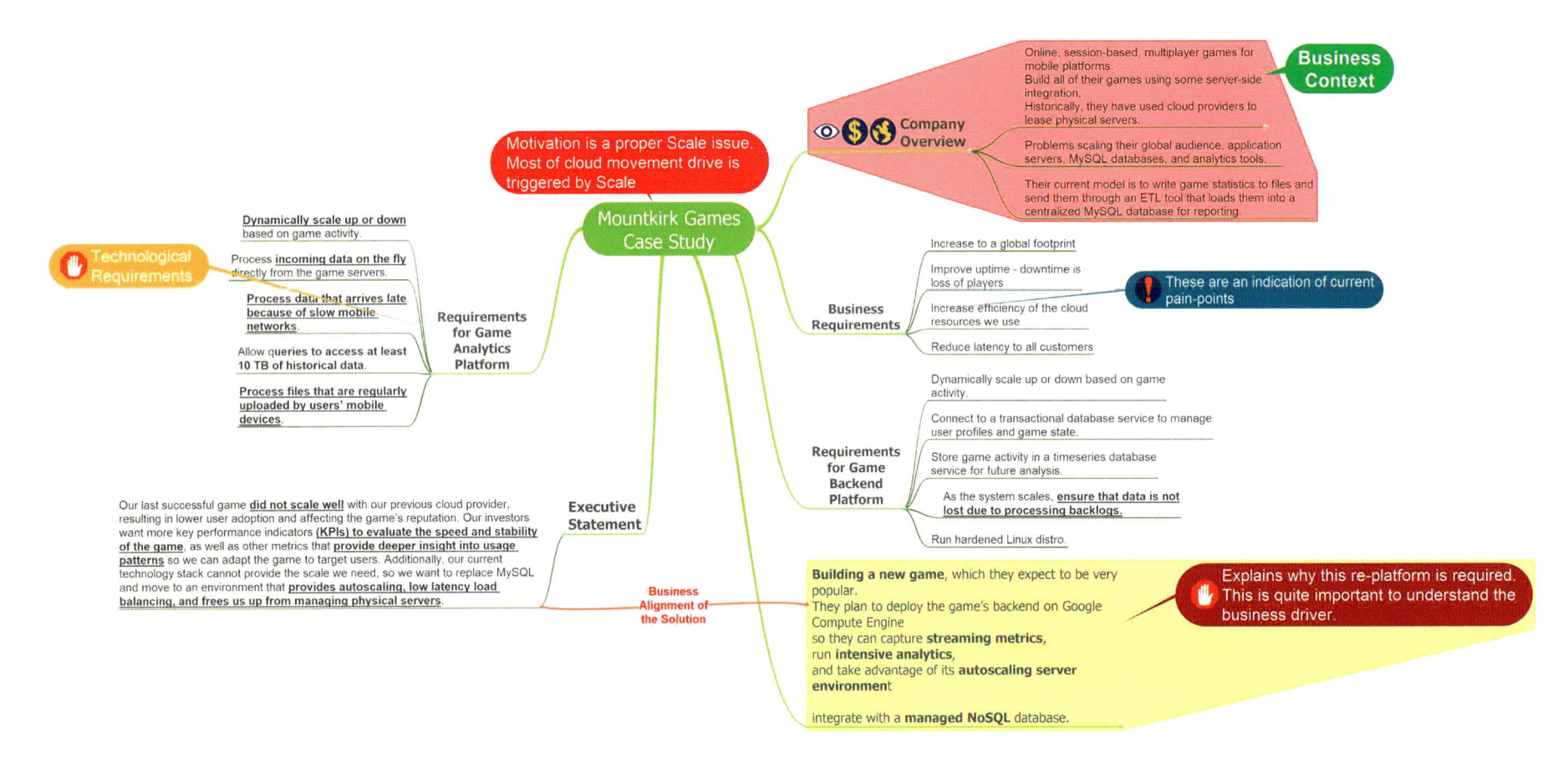

Figure 123: Mindmap - Mountkirk Games Case Study

Dress4Win Case Study

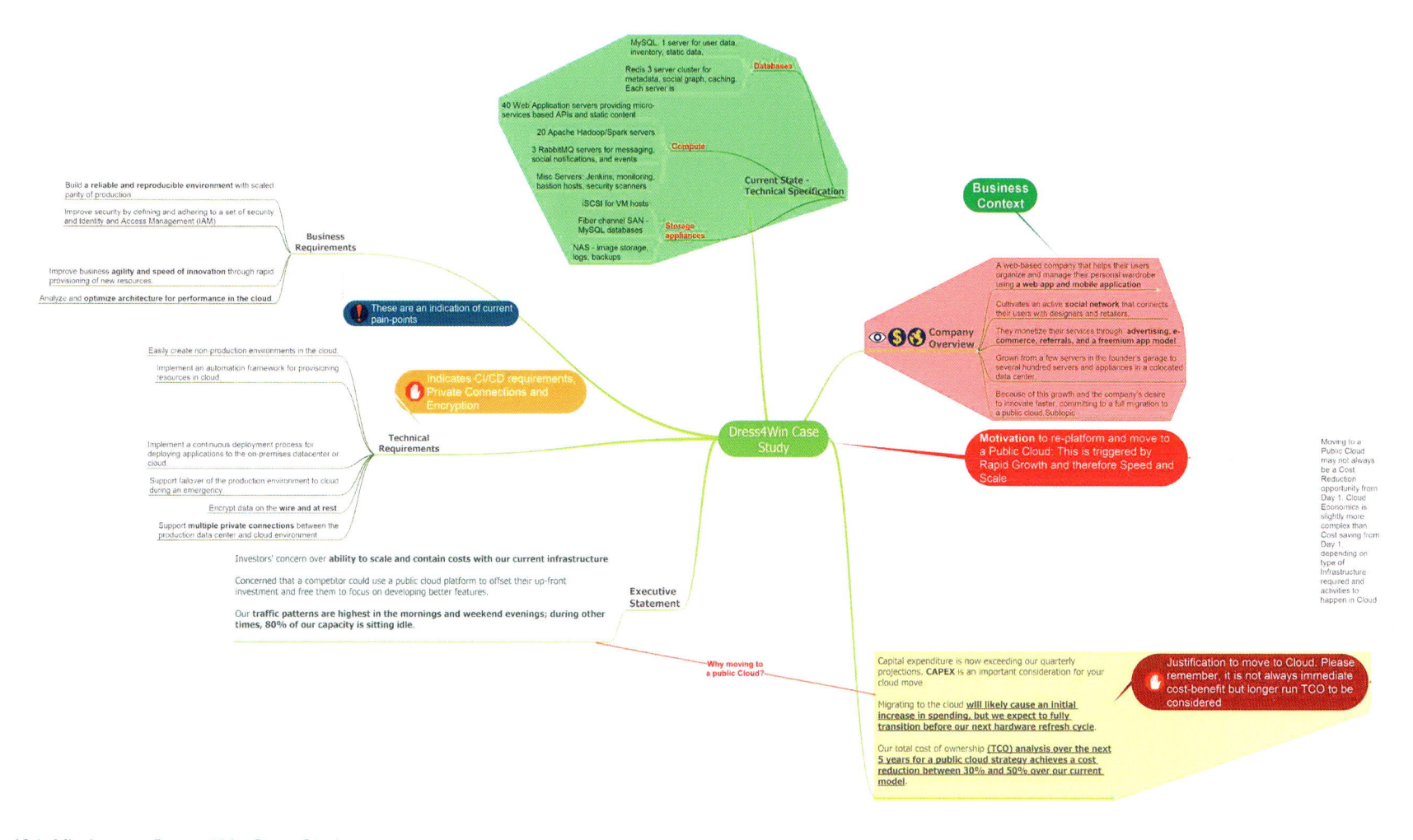

Figure 124: Mind map - Dress4Win Case Study

TerramEarth Case Study

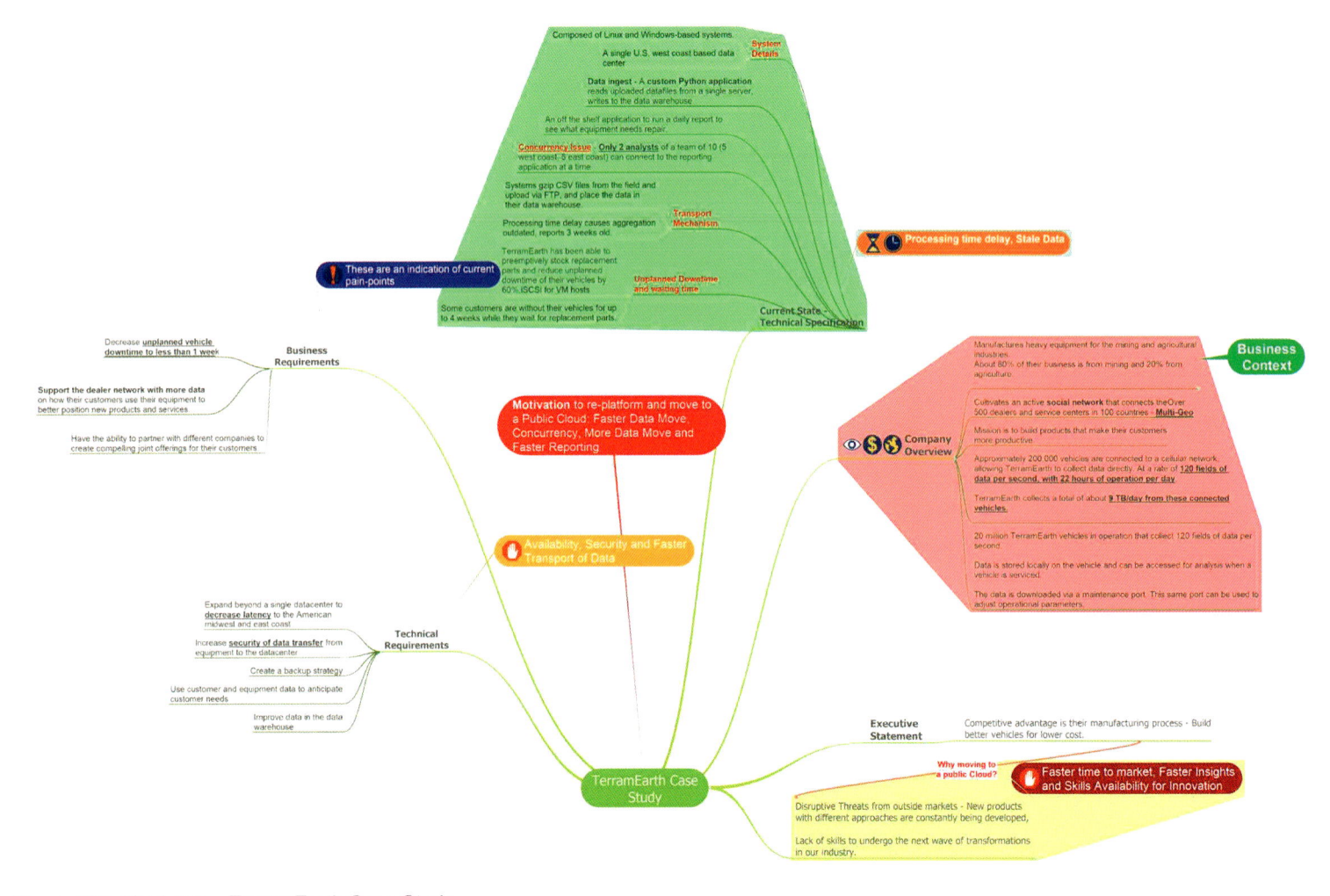

Figure 125: Mind map - TerramEarth Case Study

Test your exam readiness

There would be 100 sample questions available for you to help you in your exam preparation. Please check here after 31st May 2019:

In case, this QR code does not work, please visit www.beclickaware.com and you would find the URL to download the sample questions and answers pdf.

Alternatively email to: chatterjee.soumen@gmail.com

Google Cloud Platform diagramming & documentation

Generate Technical Documentation, and Complete Diagrams is one of the other aspects for a successful Cloud Native or Cloud Immigrant organisation. The Cloudockit with their recent tools help you to visualise your GCP Projects, generate a complete detailed documentation moreover, ensure that your GCP environment is compliant.

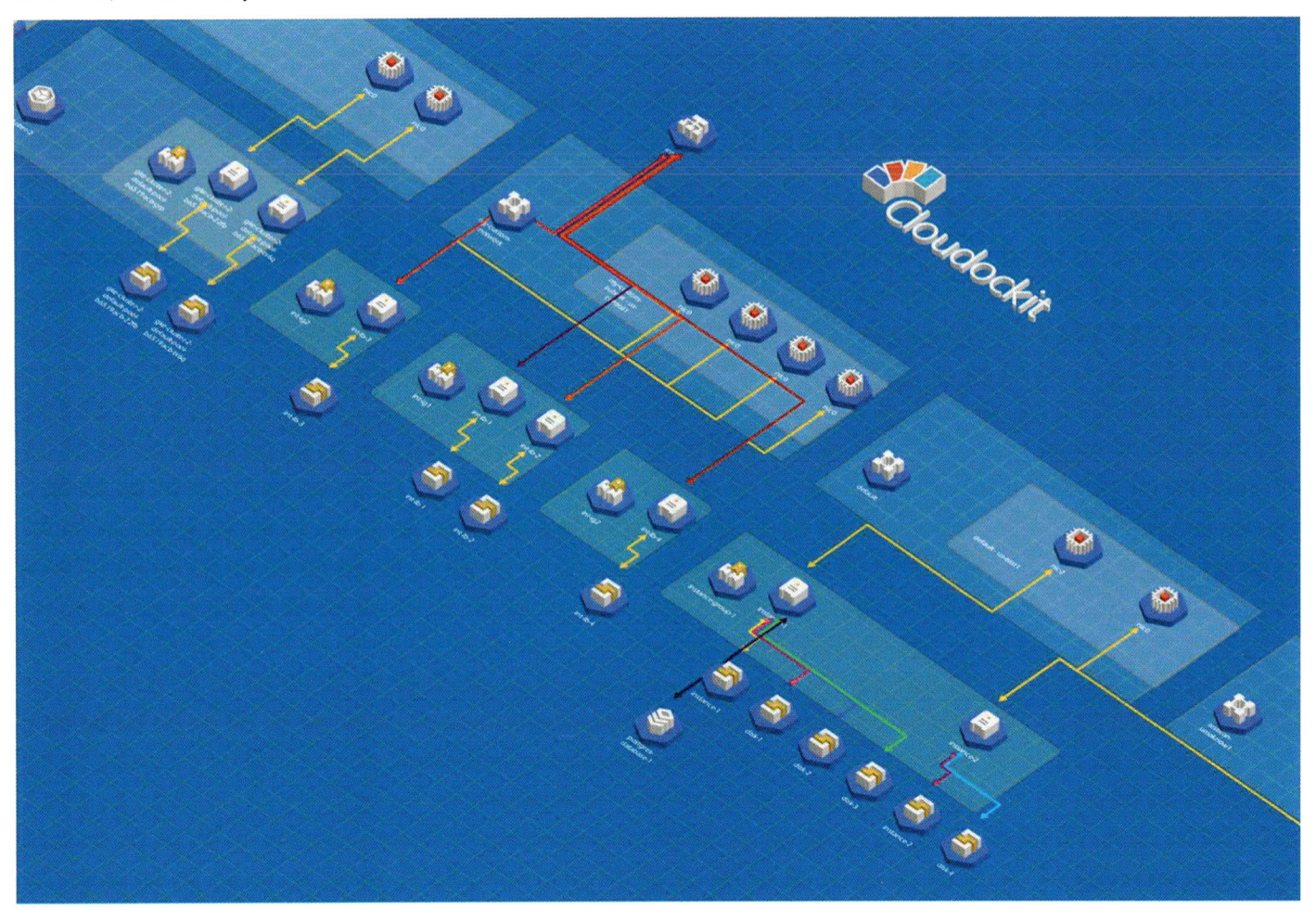

© 2019 Cloudockit

Cloudockit does a massive job for you! It will automatically scan your Google Cloud Projects and detect the dependencies between all the components. Here is an example of Diagram automatically generated by Cloudockit:

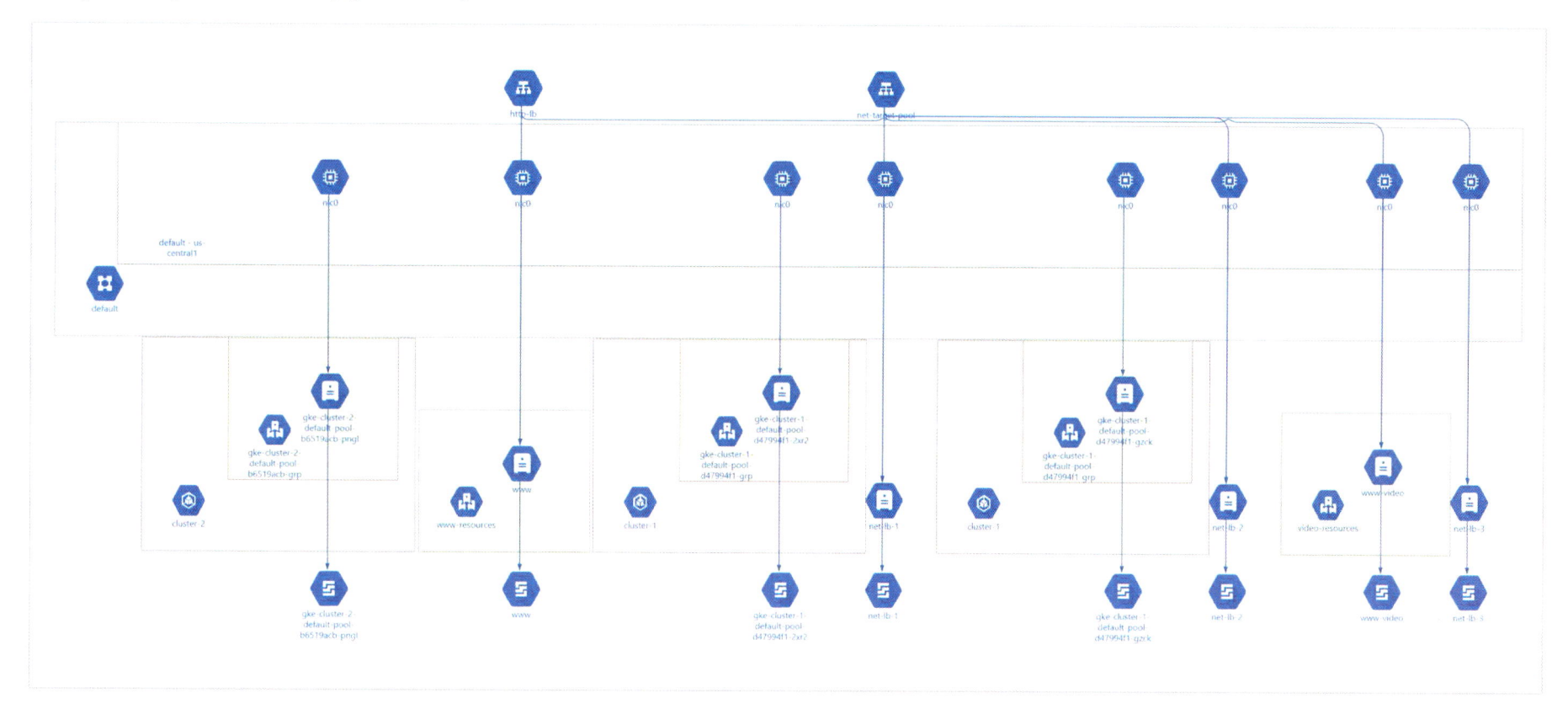

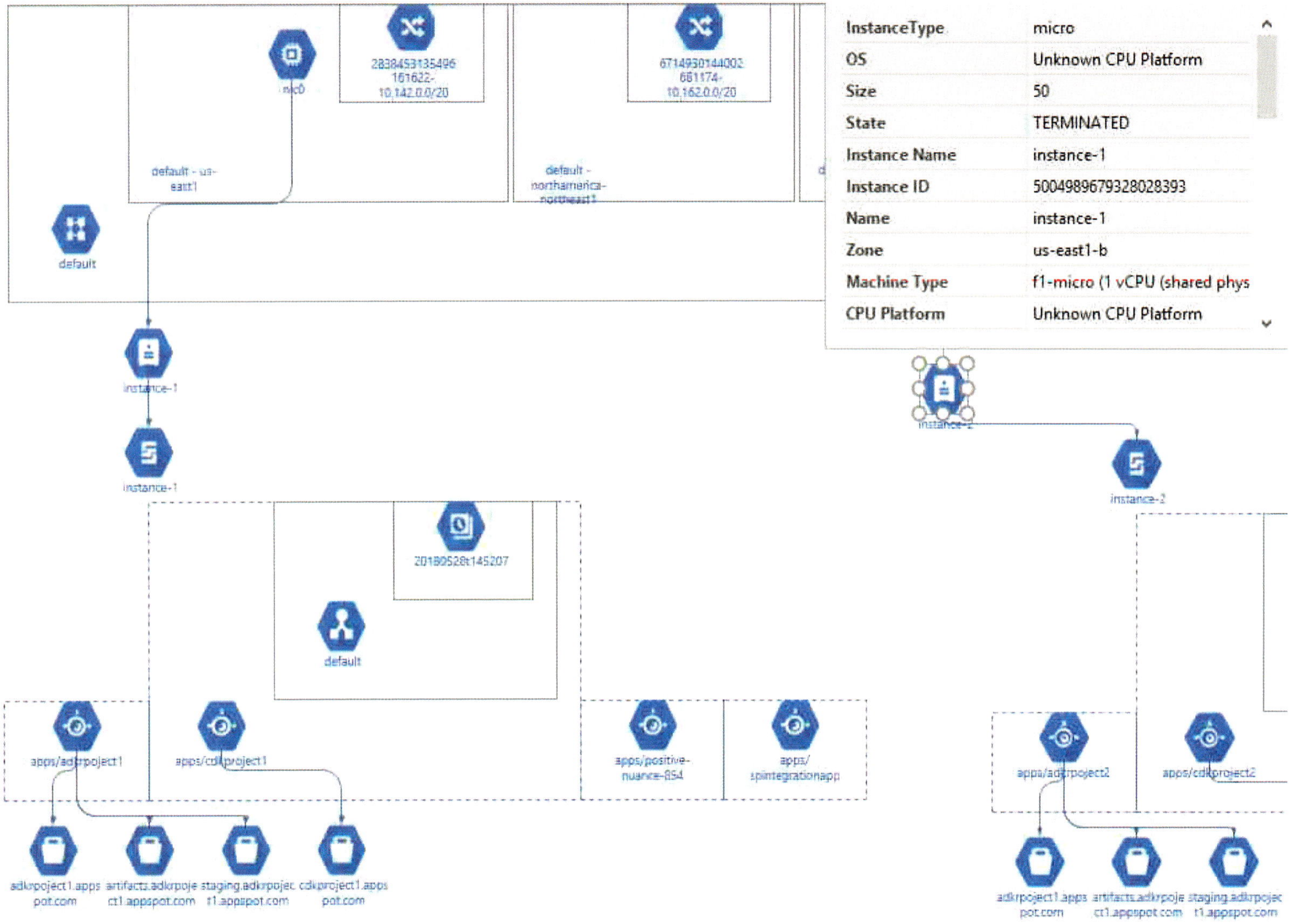
InstanceType micro
OS Unknown CPU Platform
Size 50
State TERMINATED
Instance Name instance-1
Instance ID 5004989679328028393
Name instance-1
Zone us-east1-b
Machine Type f1-micro (1 vCPU (shared phys
CPU Platform Unknown CPU Platform
nic0
2838453135496 161622- 10.142.0.0/20
6714930144002 681174- 10.162.0.0/20
default - us-east1
default - northamerica-northeast1
default
instance-1
instance-1
instance-2
instance-2
20180528t145207
default
apps/adkrpoject1
apps/cdkproject1
apps/positive-nuance-854
apps/ spintegrationapp
apps/adkrpoject2
apps/cdkproject2
adkrpoject1.appspot.com
artifacts.adkrpoject1.appspot.com
staging.adkrpoject1.appspot.com
cdkproject1.appspot.com
adkrpoject1.appspot.com
artifacts.adkrpoject1.appspot.com
staging.adkrpoject1.appspot.com

KUBERNETES ENGINE

CLUSTER-2

Cluster description

Cluster Name	cluster-2
Description	
Master zone	us-central1-a
Master version	1.9.7-gke.3
Endpoint	104.198.18.248
Cluster size	3
Total cores	3 vCPUs
Total memory	1.8 GB
Client certificate	Enabled
Kubernetes alpha features	Disabled
Created time	2018-08-03 09:35:56.00
Status	RUNNING
Node zones	us-central1-a
Network	default
Subnet	default
VPC-native (alias IP)	Disabled
Container address range	10.12.0.0/14
Service address range	10.15.240.0/20
Stackdriver Logging	Enabled
Stackdriver Monitoring	Enabled
Logging service	logging.googleapis.com
Monitoring service	monitoring.googleapis.com
Private cluster	Disabled
Master authorized networks	Disabled
Network policy	Disabled
Legacy authorization	Disabled
Maintenance window	None
Expired time	

Add-ons

Kubernetes dashboard	Enabled
HTTP load balancing	Enabled

NodePool

DEFAULT POOL

Node Pool Description

CLOUD FUNCTIONS

FUNCTION-1

Function

Name	function-1
Version ID	1
Last deployed	2018-07-20 12:59:20
Memory allocated	128 MB
Timeout	60s
Executed function	helloGCs
Service Account	cdkproject1@appspot.gserviceaccount.com
Runtime	nodejs6
Status	ACTIVE

BACKGROUND FUNCTION - TRIGGER - CLOUD STORAGE BUCKET

Event Type	google.storage.object.finalize
Resource	projects/_/buckets/cdkproject1.appspot.com
Service	storage.googleapis.com

FUNCTION-2

Function

Name	function-2
Version ID	1
Last deployed	2018-08-03 13:37:07
Memory allocated	256 MB
Timeout	60s
Executed function	helloWorld
Service Account	cdkproject1@appspot.gserviceaccount.com
Runtime	nodejs6
Status	ACTIVE

VPC NETWORK

MY-CUSTOM-NETWORK

Network description

Name	my-custom-network
ID	4708358712233722350
Description	
Subnet creation mode	Custom subnets
Dynamic routing mode	REGIONAL
IPv4 range	None
Gateway IPv4	None
Created	jeudi, août 2, 2018, 13:27:29.34

Subnetworks

MY-CUSTOM-SUBNET

Name	my-custom-subnet
ID	3234514270562451940
Description	None
Region	us-central1
IP address range	10.128.0.0/20
Gateway	10.128.0.1
Private Ip Google access	Off
Flow logs	Off

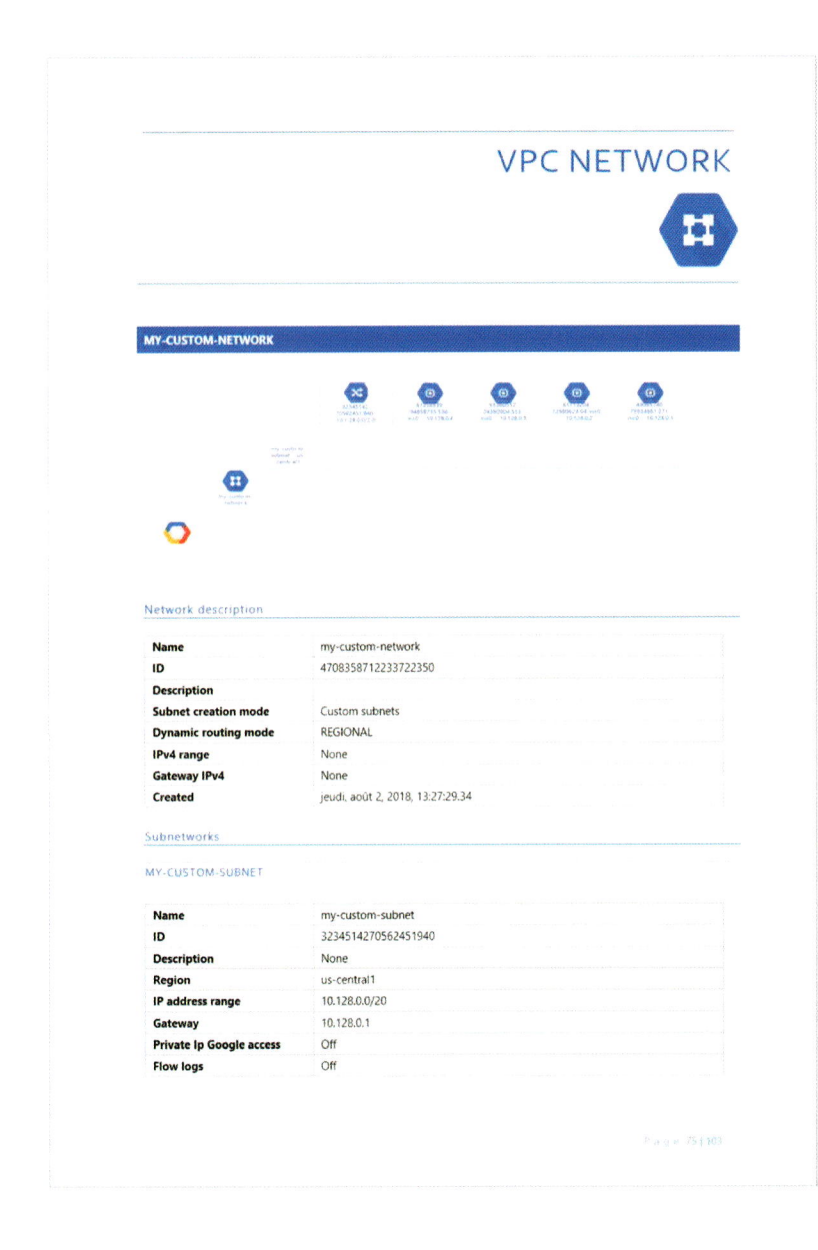

APP ENGINE

APPS/ANNIE-PROJECT-210619

Properties

ID	annie-project-210619
Name	apps/annie-project-210619
Location ID	northamerica-northeast1
Serving Status	SERVING
Default HostName	annie-project-210619.appspot.com
Auth Domain	gmail.com
Code Bucket	staging.annie-project-210619.appspot.com
Default Bucket	annie-project-210619.appspot.com
GCR Domain	us.gcr.io

Services

Note: If you are interested in Cloudockit Tool, please get in touch directly with Cloudockit Team here at https://www.cloudockit.com

Reference:

https://www.cloudockit.com/google-cloud-platform-automated-document-diagrams-generation/

Google Cloud Product and Services Glossary

Last Checked: May 15, 2019
Source: https://cloud.google.com/terms/services

©Google LLC All rights reserved. Google Cloud and Google Cloud Platform is a trademark of Google LLC

1. **Google App Engine:** Google App Engine enables you to build and host applications on the same systems that power Google applications. App Engine offers fast development and deployment; simple administration, with no need to worry about hardware, patches or backups; and effortless scalability.
2. **Google BigQuery Service:** Google BigQuery Service is a fully managed data analysis service that enables businesses to analyze Big Data. It features highly scalable data storage that accommodates up to hundreds of terabytes, the ability to perform ad hoc queries on multi-terabyte datasets, and the ability to share data insights via the web.
3. **Google Cloud Bigtable:** Google Cloud Bigtable is a fast, fully managed, highly-scalable NoSQL database service. It is designed for the collection and retention of data from 1TB to hundreds of PB.
4. **Google Cloud Build:** Google Cloud Build is a service that executes your builds on Google Cloud Platform infrastructure. Google Cloud Build can import source code from Google Cloud Storage, Cloud Source Repositories, GitHub, or Bitbucket; execute a build to your specifications; and produce artifacts such as Docker containers or Java archives.
5. **Google Cloud Dataflow:** Google Cloud Dataflow is a fully managed service for strongly consistent, parallel data-processing pipelines. It provides an SDK for Java with composable primitives for building data-processing pipelines for batch or continuous processing. This service manages the life cycle of Google Compute Engine resources of the processing pipeline(s). It also provides a monitoring user interface for understanding pipeline health.
6. **Google Cloud Datalab:** Google Cloud Datalab is an interactive tool for exploration, transformation, analysis and visualization of your data on Google Cloud Platform. It runs in your cloud project and enables you to write code to use other Big Data and storage services using a rich set of Google-authored and third party libraries.
7. **Google Cloud Dataproc:** Google Cloud Dataproc is a fast, easy to use, managed Spark and Hadoop service for distributed data processing. It provides management, integration, and development tools for unlocking the power of rich open source data processing tools. With Cloud Dataproc, you can create Spark/Hadoop clusters sized for your workloads precisely when you need them.
8. **Google Cloud Datastore:** Google Cloud Datastore is a fully managed, schemaless, non-relational datastore. It provides a rich set of query capabilities, supports atomic transactions, and automatically scales up and down in response to load. It can scale to support an application with 1,000 users or 10 million users with no code changes.
9. **Google Cloud Endpoints:** Google Cloud Endpoints is a tool that helps you to develop, deploy, secure and monitor your APIs running on Google Cloud Platform.
10. **Cloud Firestore:** Cloud Firestore is a NoSQL document database for storing, syncing, and querying data for mobile and web apps. Its client libraries provide live synchronization and offline support, while its security features and integrations with Firebase and Google Cloud Platform accelerate building serverless apps.
11. **Google Cloud Functions:** Google Cloud Functions is a lightweight, event-based, asynchronous compute solution that allows you to create small, single-purpose functions that respond to cloud events without the need to manage a server or a runtime environment.
12. **Cloud Healthcare:** Cloud Healthcare is a fully managed service to send, receive, store, query, transform, and analyze healthcare and life sciences data and enable advanced insights and operational workflows using highly scalable and compliance-focused infrastructure.

13. **Google Cloud IoT Core:** Google Cloud IoT Core is a fully managed service that allows you to easily and securely connect, manage, and ingest data from internet connected devices. It permits utilization of other Google Cloud services for collecting, processing, analyzing, and visualizing IoT data in real time.
14. **Cloud Talent Solution:** Cloud Talent Solution offers access to Google's machine learning, enabling company career sites, job boards, ATS, staffing agencies, and other recruitment technology platforms to improve the talent acquisition experience.
15. **Google Cloud Hardware Security Module:** Google Cloud Hardware Security Module is a cloud- hosted key management service that lets you protect encryption keys and perform cryptographic operations within a managed HSM service. You can generate, use, rotate, and destroy various symmetric and asymmetric keys.
16. **Google Cloud Key Management Service:** Cloud KMS is a cloud-hosted key management service that lets you manage cryptographic keys for your cloud services the same way you do on premises. You can generate, use, rotate, and destroy AES256, RSA 2048, RSA 3072, RSA 4096, EC P256, and EC P384 cryptographic keys.
17. **Google Cloud Machine Learning Engine:** Cloud Machine Learning Engine is a managed service that enables you to easily build machine learning models with the powerful TensorFlow framework. It provides scalable training and prediction services that work on large scale datasets.
18. **Google Cloud Memorystore:** Cloud Memorystore provides a fully managed in-memory data store service to build application caches or provide sub-millisecond data access. Cloud Memorystore is a scalable and highly available Redis service fully managed by Google.
19. **Google Cloud Pub/Sub:** Google Cloud Pub/Sub is designed to provide reliable, many-to-many, asynchronous messaging between applications. Publisher applications can send messages to a "topic" and other applications can subscribe to that topic to receive the messages. By decoupling senders and receivers, Google Cloud Pub/Sub allows developers to communicate between independently written applications.
20. **Google Cloud Spanner:** Cloud Spanner is a fully managed, mission-critical relational database service. It is designed to provide a scalable online transaction processing (OLTP) database with high availability and strong consistency at global scale.
21. **Google Cloud SQL:** Google Cloud SQL is a web service that allows you to create, configure, and use relational databases that live in Google's cloud. It is a fully-managed service that maintains, manages, and administers your databases, allowing you to focus on your applications and services.
22. **Google Cloud Storage:** Google Cloud Storage is a RESTful service for storing and accessing your data on Google's infrastructure. The service combines the performance and scalability of Google's cloud with advanced security and sharing capabilities.
23. **Google Cloud Test Lab:** Google Cloud Test Lab enables you to test mobile applications using physical and virtual devices in the cloud. It runs instrumentation tests and script-less robotic tests on a matrix of device configurations, and reports detailed results to help improve the quality of your mobile app.
24. **Google Cloud Translation (and Google Cloud Translation v2 or any subsequent general availability version/release)** is a RESTful API that automatically translates text from one language to another language (e.g. French to English). You can use the API to programmatically translate text in your webpages or apps.
25. **Google Compute Engine:** Google Compute Engine offers scalable and flexible virtual machine computing capabilities in the cloud, with options to utilize certain CPUs, GPUs, or Cloud TPUs. You can use Google Compute Engine to solve large-scale processing and analytic problems on Google's computing, storage, and networking infrastructure.
26. **Google Container Registry:** Google Container Registry is a private Docker image storage system on Google Cloud Platform. The registry can be accessed through an HTTPS endpoint, so you can pull images from your machine, whether it's a Google Compute Engine instance or your own hardware.
27. **Google Data Loss Prevention:** The Google Data Loss Prevention helps you understand and manage sensitive data. It provides fast, scalable classification and optional redaction for sensitive data elements like credit card numbers, names, social security numbers, passport numbers, US and selected international driver's license numbers, phone numbers, and more.
28. **Google Kubernetes Engine:** Google Kubernetes Engine, powered by the open source container scheduler Kubernetes, enables you to run containers on Google Cloud Platform. Kubernetes Engine takes care of provisioning and maintaining the underlying virtual machine cluster, scaling your application, and operational logistics such as logging, monitoring, and cluster health management.

29. **Google Stackdriver:** Google Stackdriver is an integrated monitoring, logging, and diagnostics hosted solution that helps you gain insight into applications that run on Google Cloud Platform and other public cloud platforms. Stackdriver helps you keep your cloud-powered applications fast and available. Stackdriver includes Monitoring, Logging, Error Reporting, Debugger, Profiler, and Trace components.
30. **Cloud Data Fusion:** Cloud Data Fusion is a fully managed, cloud native, enterprise data integration service for quickly building and managing data pipelines. Cloud Data Fusion provides a graphical interface to help increase time efficiency and reduce complexity and allows business users, developers, and data scientists to easily and reliably build scalable data integration solutions to cleanse, prepare, blend, transfer, and transform data without having to wrestle with infrastructure.
31. **Cloud Filestore:** Cloud Filestore is a scalable and highly available shared file service fully managed by Google. Cloud Filestore provides persistent storage ideal for shared workloads. It is best suited for enterprise applications requiring persistent, durable, shared storage which is accessed by NFS or requires a POSIX compliant file system.
32. **Identity Platform:** Identity Platform provides you with functionality and tools to manage your users' identities and access to your applications. Identity Platform supports authentication and management of users with a variety of methods, including email & password, phone number, and popular federated identity providers like Google and Facebook.
33. **Google Cloud Platform Machine Learning Services Group**:
    a. **Cloud AutoML** is a machine learning product suite that enables developers with limited machine learning expertise to provide their data sets and obtain access to quality trained models produced by Google's transfer learning and Neural Architecture Search (Google's technology for finding, generating, evaluating, and training numerous neural architectures to automatically select a solution for the customer's application)
        i. **AutoML Tables** enables your entire team of data scientists, analysts, and developers to automatically build and deploy state-of-the-art machine learning models on structured data at increased speed and scale.
        ii. **Cloud AutoML Video** is a simple and flexible machine learning service that lets businesses and developers easily train custom and scalable video models for their own domain or use cases.
        iii. **Cloud AutoML Vision** is a simple and flexible machine learning service that lets businesses and developers with limited machine learning expertise train custom and scalable vision models for their own use cases.
        iv. **Cloud AutoML Natural Language** enables customers to categorize input text into their own custom defined labels (supervised classification). Users can customize models to their own domain or use case.
        v. **Cloud AutoML Translation** is a simple and scalable translation solution that allows businesses and developers with limited machine learning expertise to customize the Google Neural Machine Translation (GNMT) model for their own domain or use-case.
        vi. **Recommendations AI** enables you to build an end-to-end personalized recommendation system based on state-of-the-art deep learning ML models, without a need for expertise in ML or recommendation system architecture.
34. **Cloud Text-to-Speech** synthesizes human-like speech based on input text in a variety of voices and languages.
35. **Dialogflow Enterprise Edition** is a development suite for voice and text conversational apps including chatbots. Dialogflow is cross-platform and can connect to your own apps (on the web, Android, iOS, and IoT) or existing platforms (e.g., Actions on Google, Facebook Messenger, Slack). Dialogflow Enterprise Edition is the paid enterprise tier of Dialogflow provided under the Google Cloud Platform Terms of Service. The free tier of Dialogflow (Dialogflow Standard Edition) is not offered via the Google Cloud Platform Terms of Service and is provided under the Dialogflow Standard Edition Terms of Service.
36. **Google Cloud Data Labeling** is a service that helps developers obtain high quality data to train and evaluate their machine learning models. It supports labeling for image, video, text, and audio as well as management of all of your labeled data in one place.
37. **Google Cloud Natural Language** provides powerful natural language understanding as an easy to use API. This API enables application developers to answer the following questions: 1) What are the entities referred to in the block of text?; 2) What is the sentiment (positive or negative) for this block of text?; 3) What is the language of this

block of text?; and 4) What is the syntax for this block of text (including parts of speech and dependency trees)? Users can call this API by passing in a block of text or by referring to a document in Google Cloud Storage.
38. **Google Cloud Speech-to-Text** allows developers to convert audio to text by applying powerful neural network models in an easy to use API.
39. **Google Cloud Video Intelligence** makes videos searchable, and discoverable, by extracting metadata with an easy to use REST API. It quickly annotates videos stored in Google Cloud Storage, and helps you identify key noun entities of your video and when they occur within the video.
40. **Google Cloud Vision** enables developers to understand the content of an image by encapsulating powerful machine learning models in an easy to use API. It quickly classifies images into thousands of categories (e.g., "sailboat", "lion", "Eiffel Tower"), detects individual objects and faces within images, and finds and reads printed words contained within images. You can build metadata on your image catalog, moderate offensive content, or enable new marketing scenarios through image sentiment analysis. You can also analyze images uploaded in the request and integrate with your image storage on Google Cloud Storage.
41. Google Cloud Platform Networking Products:
    a. **Cloud Armor:** Google Cloud Armor offers a policy framework and rules language for customizing access to internet-facing applications and deploying defenses against denial of service attacks.
    b. **Cloud NAT (Network Address Translation):** Cloud NAT enables instances in a private network to communicate with the internet.
    c. **Google Cloud CDN:** Google Cloud CDN uses Google's globally distributed edge points of presence to cache HTTP(S) load balanced content close to your users.
    d. **Google Cloud DNS:** Google Cloud DNS is a high performance, resilient, global, fully managed DNS service that provides a RESTful API to publish and manage DNS records for your applications and services.
    e. **Google Cloud Interconnect:** Cloud Interconnect offers enterprise-grade connections to Google Cloud Platform using Google Services for Dedicated Interconnect, Partner Interconnect and Cloud VPN. This solution allows you to directly connect your on-premises network to your Virtual Private Cloud.
    f. **Google Cloud Load Balancer (GCLB):** Google Cloud Load Balancing provides scaling, high availability, and traffic management for your internet-facing and private applications.
    g. **Google Cloud Router:** Google Cloud Router enables dynamic Border Gateway Protocol (BGP) route updates between your VPC network and your non-Google network.
    h. **Network Service Tiers:** Network Service Tiers enable you to select different quality networks (tiers) for outbound traffic to the internet: the Standard Tier primarily utilizes third party transit providers while the Premium Tier leverages Google's private backbone and peering surface for egress.
    i. **Traffic Director:** Traffic Director is Google Cloud Platform's traffic management service for open service meshes.
    j. **Virtual Private Cloud:** Virtual Private Cloud provides a private network topology with IP allocation, routing, and network firewall policies to create a secure environment for your deployments.
    k. **VPC Service Controls:** VPC Service Controls provide administrators the ability to configure security perimeters around resources of API based cloud services (such as Cloud Storage, BigQuery, Bigtable) and limit access to authorized VPC networks, thereby mitigating data exfiltration risks.
    l. **VPN:** VPN allows you to connect your existing network to your Google Compute Engine network via an IPsec connection or connect two different Google managed VPN gateways.
42. Other Google Cloud Platform Services:
    a. **Access Approval** allows customers to approve eligible manual, targeted accesses by Google administrators to their data or workloads before those accesses happen.
    b. **Access Context** Manager allows Google Cloud organization administrators to define fine-grained, attribute based access control for projects, apps and resources.

c. **Access Transparency** captures near real-time logs of manual, targeted accesses by Google administrators, and serves them to customers via their Stackdriver Logging account.
d. **BigQuery Data Transfer Service** automates data movement from SaaS applications to BigQuery on a scheduled, managed basis. With the BigQuery Data Transfer Service, you can transfer data to BigQuery from SaaS applications including Google Ads, Campaign Manager, Google Ad Manager, and YouTube.
e. **Cloud Asset Inventory** is an inventory of cloud assets with history. It enables users to export cloud resource metadata at a given timestamp or cloud resource metadata history within a time window.
f. **Cloud Composer** is a managed workflow orchestration service that can be used to author, schedule, and monitor pipelines that span across clouds and on-premises data centers. Cloud Composer allows you to use Apache Airflow without the hassle of creating and managing complex Airflow infrastructure.
g. **Cloud Run** lets you run stateless HTTP containers on a fully managed environment.
h. **Cloud Scheduler** is a fully managed enterprise-grade cron job scheduler. It allows you to schedule virtually any job, including batch, big data jobs, cloud infrastructure operations, and more. You can automate everything, including retries in case of failure to reduce manual toil and intervention. Cloud Scheduler even acts as a single pane of glass, allowing you to manage all your automation tasks from one place.
i. **Cloud SDK:** Google Cloud SDK is a set of tools to manage resources and applications hosted on Google Cloud Platform. It includes the gcloud, gsutil, and bq command line tools. The gcloud command-line tool provides the primary command-line interface to Google Cloud Platform.
j. **Cloud Security Command Center** helps security teams gather data, identify threats, and act on them before they result in business damage or loss. It offers deep insight into application and data risk so that you can quickly mitigate threats to your cloud resources and evaluate overall health.
k. **Cloud Source Repositories:** Cloud Source Repositories provides Git version control to support collaborative development of any application or service, including those that run on App Engine and Compute Engine.
l. **Cloud Storage Transfer Service** enables you to import large amounts of online data into Google Cloud Storage, quickly and cost-effectively. With Storage Transfer Service, you can transfer data from Amazon Simple Storage Service (Amazon S3) and other HTTP/HTTPS locations as well as transfer data between Google Cloud Storage buckets.
m. **Cloud Tasks** is a fully managed service that allows you to manage the execution, dispatch, and delivery of a large number of distributed tasks. Using Cloud Tasks, you can perform work asynchronously outside of a user or service-to-service request. Cloud Tasks provides all the benefits of a distributed task queue such as task offloading wherein heavyweight, background and long running processes can be dispatched to a task queue, loose coupling between microservices allowing them to scale independently, and enhanced system reliability as tasks are persisted in storage and retried automatically, making your infrastructure resilient to intermittent failures.
n. **Event Threat Detection** helps detect threats in log data. Threat findings are written to Security Command Center and optionally to Stackdriver Logging.
o. **Google Cloud Console App** is a native mobile app that enables customers to manage key Google Cloud services. It provides monitoring, alerting, and the ability to take actions on resources.
p. **Google Cloud Deployment Manager** is a hosted configuration tool which allows developers and administrators to provision and manage their infrastructure on Google Cloud Platform. It uses a declarative model which allows users to define or change the resources necessary to run their applications and will then provision and manage those resources.
q. **Google Cloud Identity-Aware Proxy** is a tool that helps control access, based on a user's identity and group membership, to applications running on Google Cloud Platform.
r. **Cloud Identity & Access Management (Cloud IAM)** provides administrators the ability to manage cloud resources centrally by controlling who can take what action on specific resources.

- s. **Google Cloud Resource Manager** API allows you to programmatically manage Google Cloud Platform container resources (such as Organizations and Projects), that allow you to group and hierarchically organize other Google Cloud Platform resources. This hierarchical organization lets you easily manage common aspects of your resources such as access control and configuration settings.
- t. **Google Cloud Security Scanner** is a web application security scanner that enables developers to easily check for a subset of common web application vulnerabilities in websites built on App Engine and Compute Engine.
- u. **Google Cloud Shell** is a tool that provides command-line access to cloud resources directly from your browser. You can use Cloud Shell to run experiments, execute Cloud SDK commands, manage projects and resources, and do lightweight software development via the built-in web editor.
- v. **Google Genomics** provides an API to store, process, explore and share DNA sequence reads, reference-based alignments, and variant calls, using Google's cloud infrastructure.
- w. **Google Persistent Disk** is durable and high performance block storage for Google Cloud Platform. Persistent Disk provides SSD and HDD storage that can be attached to instances running in either Google Compute Engine or Google Kubernetes Engine.
- x. **Google Service Control** is a Google Cloud Platform infrastructure service that provides control plane functionality to managed services, such as logging, monitoring, and status checks.
- y. **Google Service Management** is a Google Cloud Platform infrastructure service that manages APIs and services, including GCP services and APIs and services created using Google Cloud Endpoints.
- z. **Phishing Protection** helps detect phishing attacks targeting end users and provides the ability to submit URLs to Google Safe Browsing.
- aa. **reCAPTCHA Enterprise** helps detect fraudulent activity on websites.
- bb. **Service Consumer Management** provides utilities to help service producers manage their relationships with their services' consumers, including the ability to create and manage tenancy units.
- cc. **Transfer Appliance** is a solution that uses hardware appliances and software to transfer large amounts of data quickly and cost-effectively into Google Cloud Platform.
- dd. **Web Risk API** is a Google Cloud service that lets client applications check URLs against Google's constantly updated lists of unsafe web resources.

43. Firebase and associated services:
    a. **Firebase Authentication**: Firebase Authentication provides a service as part of the Firebase platform to authenticate and manage users in your applications. It supports authentication using email & password, phone number and popular federated identity providers like Google and Facebook.
    b. **Firebase Test Lab**: Firebase Test Lab lets you test your mobile app using your test code or automatically on a wide variety of devices and device configurations hosted in a Google data centre, with test results made available in the Firebase console.
    c. **Google Cloud Functions for Firebase**: Cloud Functions for Firebase lets you write code that responds to events and invokes functionality exposed by other Firebase features, once you deploy JavaScript code in a hosted, private, and scalable Node.js environment that requires no maintenance.
    d. **Google Cloud Storage for Firebase**: Cloud Storage for Firebase adds customizable Google security (via Firebase Security Rules for Cloud Storage) to file uploads and downloads for your Firebase apps, as well as robust uploads and downloads regardless of network quality through the Firebase SDK. Cloud Storage for Firebase is backed by Google Cloud Storage, a service for storing and accessing your data on Google's infrastructure.
44. **Cloud Identity Services**: Cloud Identity Services are the services and editions as described at http://cloud.google.com/terms/identity/user-features.html

References

https://cloud.google.com/blog/products/gcp/every-gcp-blog-post-2018 A Must Read
https://cloud.google.com/forrester-wave-leader/ Report could be obtained by filling the form in the linked page.
https://cloud.google.com/forrester-public-cloud-platform-native-security-wave/ Report could be obtained by filling the form in the linked page
https://cloud.google.com/ml-engine/docs/tensorflow/regions
https://peering.google.com/#/infrastructure
https://cloud.google.com/about/locations/?region=europe#regions-tab
https://www.blog.google/products/google-cloud/cloud-automl-making-ai-accessible-every-business/
https://www.zdnet.com/article/cloud-providers-ranking-2018-how-aws-microsoft-google-cloud-platform-ibm-cloud-oracle-alibaba-stack/
https://www.zdnet.com/article/google-launches-cloud-automl-an-effort-to-simplify-and-automate-the-grunt-work-behind-ai-and-machine/
https://cloud.google.com/solutions/pci-dss-compliance-in-gcp
https://cloud.google.com/solutions/data-analytics-partner-ecosystem
https://cloud.google.com/solutions/data-lifecycle-cloud-platform
https://cloud.google.com/icons/
https://cloud.google.com/storage/docs/access-logs
https://cloud.google.com/billing/docs/how-to/export-data-bigquery
https://cloud.google.com/blog/products/gcp/every-gcp-blog-post-2018
https://cloud.google.com/interconnect/docs/concepts/colocation-facilities
https://cloud.google.com/solutions/architecture-of-a-serverless-ml-model
https://cloud.google.com/blog/topics/inside-google-cloud/100-plus-announcements-from-google-cloud-next19

Copyright Declarations and Acknowledgements

©Google LLC All rights reserved. Google Cloud and Google Cloud Platform is a trademark of Google LLC
Google and the Google logo are registered trademarks of Google LLC, used with permission
All the Google Cloud Platform and Products described are produced and consulted from the content available from Google Cloud Platform https://cloud.google.com/
and Google Cloud Blog https://cloud.google.com/blog/ website.
Google Cloud Platform is a registered trademark of Google. Contents and images Used with kind permission of Google

Registered Logo:

Google Cloud

Google Cloud Platform

TensorFlow

Illustrations and Images are developed leveraging licensed tools / software / design agency such as ConceptDraw, Draw.io and PresentationLoad

Microsoft Office 365 Business Edition is also used to produce contents and illustrations.

All other images are acknowledged and used with kind permission from the creators/sources of the image owner/copyright owner appropriately next to the illustration

Special Mention

This book wouldn't have been possible without my great friend Sanj. He is not only my friend but also a real Dev-Ops Cloud Expert by trade. This book was conceptualised during our so many coffee sessions and discussions. He helped me all the time with his SME knowledge whenever I needed to find something. I am grateful to your help Sanjeev.

This is the time to also mention about Ketan who helped me with his OS and Dev-Ops expertise and Cloud SME knowledge. Ketan, I appreciate your guidance.

My other forthcoming titles this year Q2 and Q3 2019

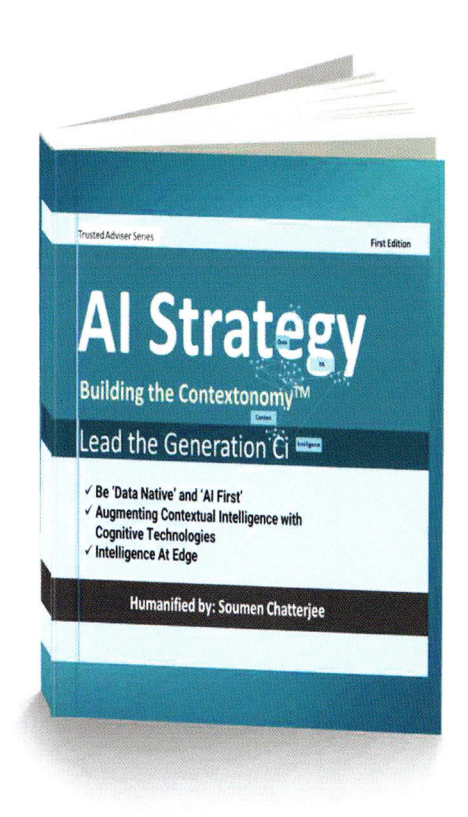

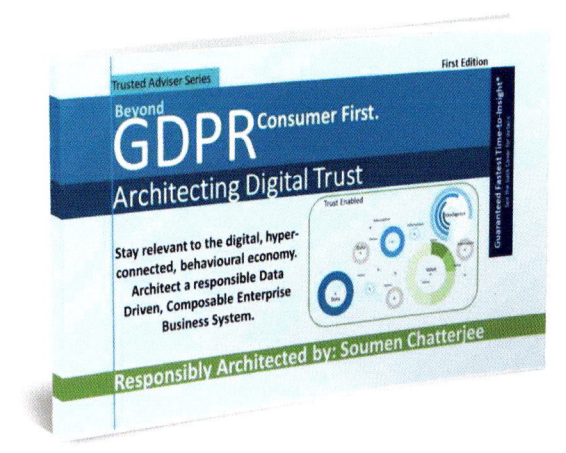

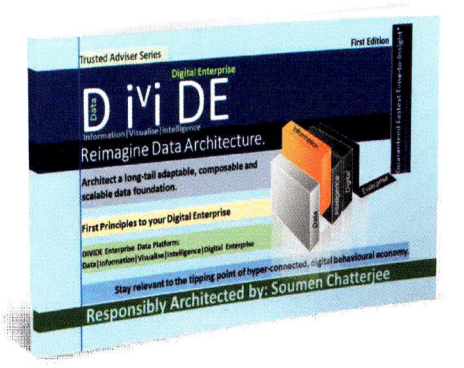

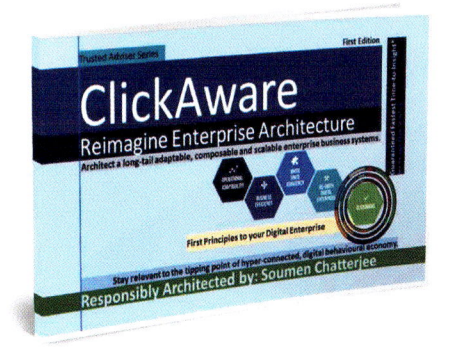

www.beclickaware.com

Index

3

3M · 30

A

a full lifecycle API management platform · 152
a key encryption key (KEK). · 143
a single anycast IP · 68
A/B testing · 192, 195
AccuWeather · 28
ACID transactions · 117
ACL · 105
Ad tech · 124
adtech · 115
Adtech workloads · 117
advertising technology · 117
AES-256 encryption · 107
AI Building Blocks · 161
AI First · 161
AI Platform · 161
AI Solutions · 161
AI-based solutions · 159
AI-first
    AI First · 26
always encrypted · 110
Amazon Simple Storage Service (Amazon S3) · 107
An App Engine · 91
analytical and operational workloads · 116
Analytical workloads · 117
Analytics events · 114
annotate · 172
anomaly detection · 128, 159
Ansible · 192
Ant Financials · 30
Anthos
    Cloud Service Platform · 52
anticipate problems · 156
Apache Airflow · 134
Apache Cassandra
    Cassandra · 117
Apache Hadoop · 130
Apache HBase · 117
Apache Kafka · 127, 128
Apache Spark · 128, 130
API management gateway · 152
Apigee · 152
App Engine · 101, 151, 162, 169
App Engine Flex instances · 70
App Engine flexible · 117
App Engine Limitations · 89
AppEngine · 128
Apple · 28
Application Scaling · 68
Archiving cold data · 101
Artificial Intelligence · 43
    AI · 26
At A Moment in Time' · 35
At Google-scale · 49
at rest · 110
at scale · 167
at the edge · 156
at-least-once delivery · 127
augmented hardware and software · 159
Auth · 151
Auth0 · 151
authentication API · 88
authorised view · 143
auto healing · 75
Automated assistants · 167
automatic scaling · 102
automatically encrypted · 102
AutoML for custom models · 162
auto-scaling · 183
Autoscaling · 75, 85
Avro · 101

B

Backend services · 76
batch · 112
Batch prediction · 167
batch process · 114
BATX · 30, 35
Bazaarvoice · 28
Beam-based SDK · 128
behavioural economy · 30, 206
Best Buy · 28
Big data · 52
Big Table
    Cloud BigTable · 109
BigQuery · 38, 72, 101, 107, 109, 110, 113, 125, 128
BigQuery GIS · 112
BigQuery ML · 110, 111
Bigtable · 116, 125
Billie · 28
billing · 174, 200
billing-frontend · 174
billions of edge devices · 157
BIOS upgrades · 82
Blobstore · 125
block storage · 102
BMW · 30
Border Gateway Protocol (BGP) · 74
Borg · 49, 111
Box · 27
bucket tests · 195

Build and operationalise · 110
Build' vs 'Run' vs 'Change · 43
<u>built on Jupyter</u> · 131
Built to Scale · 175
Business Continuity · 178
Business intelligence · 115
business models · 43

C

C# · 112
Caffe · 198
Caffeine · 49
Canary Release · 192
Cassandra · 109
CDO · 37
Chat and social · 103
Chief Digital Officer · 37
Chief Information Security Officer · 37
Chile's Health Care Sector · 27
CI/CD pipeline · 193
CIO · 37
classification · 169
ClickAware · 30
clickstream · 115
Clickstream · 128
ClickStream · 105
Cloud AI · 161
Cloud Armor · 70
Cloud AutoML
    AutoML · 28
Cloud Bigtable · 109, 117
    Bigtable · 117
Cloud Billing · 203
Cloud Build · 52, 148, 192
Cloud Composer · 134
Cloud Dataflow · 38, 112, 117, 127, 128, 130
Cloud Datalab · 131
Cloud Dataprep · 128

Cloud Dataproc · 38, 101, 128, 130
Cloud Datastore · 91, 102, 125
Cloud Deployment Manager · 148
Cloud enabled Data Native · 219
Cloud Endpoints · 151
Cloud Filestore · 102
Cloud Firestore · 102, 109
Cloud First · 219
Cloud Functions · 184
Cloud IAM · 138
Cloud IAM policy · 141
Cloud Identity and Access Management (Cloud IAM) · 144
Cloud Identity domain · 140
Cloud Identity Services · 239
Cloud IoT · 156
Cloud KMS · 138
Cloud Load Balancing · 68
Cloud Logging · 112
Cloud Machine Learning · 128, 168
Cloud Machine Learning Engine · 131
    MLE · 107
Cloud Memorystore
    Memorystore · 102
Cloud MemoryStore · 109
Cloud migration · 211
Cloud ML · 128
Cloud ML Engine · 111, 164
Cloud Native · 206
Cloud native Data Warehouse · 113
Cloud Natural Language · 101, 162
Cloud Neutral · 43
Cloud Pub/Sub · 72, 113, 117, 127, 128, 156
Cloud Pub/Subtopic · 102, 114
Cloud Resource Manager · 138
Cloud Router · 74
Cloud SDK · 151
    SDK · 148
Cloud Security Controls and Threat Management · 140
Cloud Security Scanner · 138

Cloud Services Platform · 52
Cloud Shell · 148
Cloud Source Repositories · 148, 192
Cloud Spanne · 125
Cloud Spanner · 109, 123
Cloud SQL · 109, 122, 125
Cloud SQL Proxy · 122
Cloud Storage · 101, 103, 109, 125
Cloud Storage bucket · 107
Cloud Storage bucket) · 107
Cloud Vision · 101
cloud-first · 44
CloudFunction · 164
cloud-native · 43, 102
Cloud-native · 130
Cloud-native machine learning · 198, 212
cloud-to-edge · 159
clustering · 169
Coca Cola · 28
cold path · 114
cold paths · 114
Coldline Storage · 100, 101
Colossus · 49, 111
columnar storage · 110
committed use discounts · 203
Complex Adaptive Systems (CAS) · 30
complex aggregations · 117
Complex Event Processing (CEP)
    CEP · 136
comprehensive API management platform · 152
compute (Borg) · 111
Compute Engine · 78, 85, 101, 117, 162, 169
Computing and hosting · 52
congestion control algorithm · 62
connected intelligence · 31
Console · 102
consumer-centric · 31
<u>container for your clusters and nodes</u> · 117
Container Registry · 148, 151
Content distribution · 101

context aware · 140
Context Economics · 31
Contextonomy · 6, 31
conversational experiences · 184
cost forecast · 203
Cost reduction · 114
Couchbase · 109
CPU · 163
CRM · 125
cross-site-scripting (XSS) · 140
CSV · 101
CTO · 37
Custom images · 81
Customer orders · 122
Customer-managed encryption keys (CMEK) · 143
Customer-supplied encryption keys (CSEK) · 143
CxO · 40

D

Daily quotas · 89
Daimler · 30
Data Analytics lifecycle · 126
Data backup · 101
Data Centric Organisation · 37
data consumer platform · 38, 206
Data DNA · 35
Data Economics · 28
data encryption key (DEK) · 143
Data Immigrants · 40
Data ingestion · 117
Data Locality · 111
Data Loss Prevention (DLP) API · 144
Data Migrant · 206
Data Native · 35, 40, 206
Data path · 74
data pipeline · 103
Data Pipeline · 104
Data processing · 105

data production platform · 38
  Data Production Platform · 38
data production systems · 38, 206
Data Studio · 110
Data Visualisation · 126
data warehouse · 38
Data warehouses · 109
database for mobile app development · 102
data-driven · 25
Dataflow · 112, 113, 128
data-ops · 18
Data-Ops · 192
datapipeline · 211
Dataproc · 117
DataStore · 109
DDoS attacks · 70
Dedicated Interconnect · 63
democratise AI
  Democratise AI · 26
deploying container · 183
Deployment tools · 148
Developer tools · 52
Device and operational metrics · 115
dev-ops · 18
Dev-Ops · 192
Dialogflow · 164
Digital Immigrants · 35
Digital Natives · 35
dimensionality reduction · 169
directed acyclic graphs (DAGs) · 134
disaster recovery · 101, 178
Disney · 30
Distributed Load · 181, 195
Dockerize App · 194
document database · 102, 117
Domino · 28
DR building blocks · 178
Dremel · 110, 111
Dremel query engine · 111
durable · 111, 116

Durable Reduced Availability (DRA) · 102
dynamic schemas · 122

E

eBay · 30
eCommerce · 125
Edge Connect · 157
Edge ML · 157
Edge TPU™ · 157
elastic data warehouse · 111
Elasticsearch · 164
embraces cloud platforms · 206
Encryption at rest · 138
ensuring data privacy and confidentiality · 157
enterprise data warehouse
  EDW · 110
enterprise mobility management (EMM) · 140
environmental medical or financial data · 107
ERP · 125
ETL · 112, 113
ETL data pipeline
  ETL · 135
ETL pipeline
  ETL · 113
Evaluate model accuracy · 167
Evernote · 28
Exactly-once Processing · 128
Extensible Service Proxy (ESP) · 151

F

faster predictions for critical IoT applications · 157
fault-tolerant · 175
FCA FG 16/5 · 189
Federated Query · 111
FIDO standards · 143
Financial data · 116

Financial services · 123
Financial transactions · 122
fine-grained · 140
Firebase · 151
Firebase Authentication · 239
Firebase Real-time Database · 102
Firebase Test Lab · 239
Firestore · 125
Firewall Rules · 71
Flash injection · 140
Forrester Research · 29
Forseti Audit · 138
Forseti findings and actions · 144
Forseti Security · 144
Foundation for AI · 111
Fraud detection · 128
Free quotas · 89
fully managed · 102
fully-managed cloud services · 156

G

G Suite domain · 140
GAE · 88
GAFAM · 30, 35
game · 115
garbage-collection · 117
Gartner · 29
Gated egress · 214
Gated ingress · 214
GE · 30
Generate GCP Technical Documentation · 228
Generation Ci' · 31
Genomics · 132
geographic · 107
GeoJSON · 112
Geospatial · 112
Geospatial datasets · 125
GKE · 52, 101, 117, 162, 169

GKE clusters · 70
GKE On-Prem · 52
global endpoints · 127
global network · 62
global resource · 57
Global Resources · 64
global service · 127
global supply chain · 124
Global supply chain · 125
globally dispersed devices · 156
globally-distributed · 123
Gmail · 49
Go · 112
Google account · 140
Google app (voice search). · 161
Google App Engine · 88, 136
Google Assistant, · 164
Google Cloud Adoption Framework · 43
Google Cloud APIs · 144
Google Cloud CDN · 72
Google Cloud Dataflow
    Dataflow · 107
Google Cloud DNS · 72
Google Cloud Functions for Firebase · 239
Google Cloud Interconnect · 62
Google Cloud Machine Learning (MLE) · 167
Google Cloud Natural Language · 162
Google Cloud Platform Machine Learning Services Group · 236
Google Cloud Platform Networking Products · 237
Google Cloud Storage · 49
Google Cloud Storage for Firebase · 239
Google Compute Engine · 102, 131, 136
Google Data Studio · 132
Google Data Studio 360 · 137
Google Docs · 49
Google File System (GFS) · 49
Google group · 140
Google Kubernetes Engine · 102, 134
Google Kubernetes Engine (GKE) · 151

Google managed service · 68
Google Sheets · 112, 113
Google Stackdriver · 149
GPU · 163
Graph building · 168
Graph data · 116
Graphs · 125
gRPC · 127
gsutil · 101, 102, 107
guidance about which transfer method · 180

H

Hadoop · 38, 101, 117
hardware accelerator · 159
hardware accelerators · 157
HBase · 109, 130
HDD · 102, 117
HDFS · 49
health checking · 76
healthcare · 159
Heavy Read / Write · 125
High Available (HA) · 178
high performance per watt · 159
High Throughput · 125
highly scalable
    Scale · 110
highly-available · 175
high-throughput · 117
Home Depot · 28
Horizontally scalable · 123
Host OS · 82
hot paths · 114
HSBC · 28
HTC · 28
HTTP · 156
Human Exchange (**HX**) · 30
human experience (HX) · 43
hybrid and multi-cloud · 219

Hybrid computing · 52
HyperFlex platforms · 198

I

IBM · 30
Identity and Access Management
    IAM · 138
Identity Aware Proxy (IAP) · 135
Identity is an Identity as a Service (IDaaS) · 140
Immutable · 192
immutable blobs · 117
immutable disk · 79
import models · 169
    Model Import · 169
in the cloud · 156
in transit · 110
Inbox (Smart Reply) · 161
information consumption platform
    Information Consumption Platform · 38
Infrastructure as Service (IAAS) · 177
infrastructure-as-a-service (IaaS) · 78
ingestion · 113
ingress or egress
    Firewall Rules · 173
in-memory databases · 111
Instance Groups Limitations · 75
Intelligent applications · 184
intelligent Autoscaling · 68
interactive analysis · 131
interactive dashboard · 113
interactive dashboards · 132
interactive data exploration · 131
Interactive Query · 125
IoT analytics · 128
IoT data · 116, 117
IoT data stream · 156
IoT devices · 115
IoT time series data · 117

IPython · 131
ISO 27001 · 78
ISO/IEC 27001 · 122

J

Java · 112
JavaScript · 131
JDBC · 113
Jenkins · 194
JSON · 101, 109, 128, 151
JSON API · 101, 102
Jupiter · 49, 111
Jupyter notebooks · 137

K

Kaggle · 27
Keras · 169
Kewpie · 27
key/value data · 125
key-value pair · 201
Knative · 183
Knowledge Connectors · 166
Kubeflow · 198
Kubernetes
    GKE · 164
Kubernetes Engine · 102, 136

L

label · 201
labels · 172
Lambda Architecture · 104
large-scale cluster management · 111
Lead · 45
lead effectively · 43

Learn · 45
learn continuously · 43
Lifecycle configurations · 102
Lifecycle Management · 101
Live migration · 82
live migrations · 26
Log integrity · 113
Logical Control path · 74
Logical Data Warehousing · 111
Looker · 110, 115
low latency · 101
Low latency · 116
Low Latency · 125
lower cost · 101

M

machine learning · 101, 130
Machine learning · 167
Machine Learning · 6
    ML · 26
Machine Learning Engine (MLE) · 28
    MLE · 26, 28
machine learning models on gateways and edge devices · 156
machine learning solutions · 110
machine vision · 159
machine-learning
    ML · 117
Magic Quadrant · 29
MainAd · 28
managed columnar storage · 110
managed MySQL · 109
managed Network Attached Storage (NAS) · 102
managed NoSQL · 116
managed serverless application · 88
managed service · 167
Managed Service · 25
manufacturing · 159

MapReduce · 49
MapReduce jobs · 101
Marine · 27
Marketing data · 116
massively scalable
    Planet-Scale · 116
Memcache · 88, 91
Meshed topology · 213
mess for less · 43
microservices · 19
Microservices · 91, 195
MicroStrategy · 110
minimal firmware changes · 156
Mirrored' topology · 212
mission-critical IoT applications · 157
mix and match service accounts · 173
mixed content (HTTP in HTTPS) · 140
ML models at the edge · 156
ML pipeline
    pipeline · 128
Mobile games · 103
Model Monetisation · 28
Monetisation · 28
Monitoring · 125
MQTT · 156
multi-cloud · 25
Multi-cloud · 134
Multi-Cloud · 206
multi-reader capability · 102
multi-regional location · 101
Multi-Regional Storage · 100, 101
Multi-Regional Storage bucket · 107
multi-row transactions · 117
multivariate testing · 195
MySQ · 113
MySQL · 113, 122

N

N+2 redundancy · 63
NATU · 30, 35
Natural conversational interfaces · 164
Nearline Storage · 100, 101
Nearline Storage bucket · 107
Netflix · 193
Network endpoint · 75
Network Peering · 71
network tags · 172, 173
Networking · 52
networks · 57
no downtime · 102
no more eventual consistency · 102
NO SQL
    NoSQL · 125
Node.js · 112
non-structured · 125
NoSQL · 102, 109
NoSQL databases
    NoSQL · 109
NoSQL datastores · 88

O

OAuth · 101
Object Lifecycle Management · 102
object storage · 111
Ocado · 27
OLAP · 117, 125
OLTP · 117, 122
on-demand backups · 122
Online prediction · 167
OpenAPI · 152
operational efficiency · 156
opportunity loss factors · 219
Ops tooling · 52

Organization policies · 200
outflow · 172

P

Partner Interconnect · 63
performant infrastructure · 111
Persistent Disk · 102
persistent disk snapshot · 180
personal and sensitive data · 128
Personalisation · 125
petabyte-scale · 116
Philips · 28
phishing-resistant two-factor authentication (2FA) · 143
Photos (image search) · 161
PHP · 112
pipeline · 134
planet-scale · 40, 78, 184
Platform as a service · 181
    PAAS Scalability · 181
point-in-time recovery · 122
Point-of-Sale · 128
PostgreSQL · 113, 122
pre-built report templates · 132
predict outcomes locally · 157
Prediction · 167, 169
predictive maintenance · 159
preemptible VM · 84
Preprocessing · 168
pre-trained models · 161
private IP · 122
Product recommendations · 167
Programmatic Interaction · 112
projects · 201
Provisioning · 81
pseudonymizing · 128
Public images · 81
PubSub · 128
purpose-built AI chip · 159

PySpark · 135
Python · 112, 131, 134
PyTorch · 198

Q

QlikView · 115
queue-based workload · 75

R

randomized experiment · 195
ransaction histories · 116
rapid scaling · 90
Real-time app data · 117
Real-time data processing systems · 184
Real-time Message processing · 126
real-time predictions · 157
recommendations · 125
redact sensitive data · 144
Regional instance · 75
Regional Resources · 64
Regional Storage · 100
Regional Storage bucket · 103
regions · 57
regression · 169
regulatory compliance · 219
Relational · 125
Relational databases · 109
Reserved query · 114
resilient · 175
resource hierarchy · 141, 200
resources · 201
RESPONSE · 27
REST · 127, 149, 162, 184
REST API · 112
RESTful API · 168
retail · 159

Retail · 124
Right Action · 35
robotics · 159
Rolls Royce · 27
Ruby · 112
Running · 81

S

Safety limits · 89
Samsung · 30
scalable · 111
scale · 175
Scale · 45
scale efficiently · 43
scikit · 131
Scikit Learn · 198
scikit-learn · 169
SDLC (Software Development Lifecycle).
    SDLC · 148
Secure · 45
secure your environment comprehensively · 43
security marks · 172
segmentation analysis · 128
Semi-structured · 125
sensors · 117
Sentiment analysis · 167
Sentiment Analysis · 184
sequential filenames · 103
serverless · 38, 102, 110, 128
Serverless · 183
Serverless application backends · 184
serverless computing
    serverless · 127
Serverless computing · 52
serverless eco-system with an open-source
    Serverless Open Source · 183
server-side load balancing · 68
Service account · 140

Service Account · 173
service accounts · 173
Service Control · 151
Service Management · 151
Service mesh · 52
sharding · 127
Shielded VM · 85
smart spaces · 159
Snapchat · 28
SOC 1 · 78
SOC 2 · 78
SOC 3 · 78
software-defined networking (SDN) · 61
source service accounts · 173
Spark · 38, 101, 117
sparsely populated table · 116
Speech-to-Text · 162
Speech-to-Text and analytics · 163
Spending limits · 89
Spinnaker · 192
split testing · 195
Spotify · 28
SSAE-16 · 78
SSD · 102, 117
SSL termination · 70
SSTable format · 116
Stackdriver · 72, 114, 122
Stackdriver Debugger · 149
Stackdriver Error Reporting · 149
Stackdriver Logging · 150
Stackdriver Monitoring · 149
Stackdriver Profiler · 150
Stackdriver Trace · 149
Staging · 81
Stopping · 81
Storage · 52
storage (Colossus) · 111
storage transfer · 101
Storage Transfer Service · 107
Storing data · 101

Google Cloud Certified Professional Cloud Architect, Second Edition

Storing ETL data · 101
Strategic · 45
stream analytics · 126
Stream ingestion · 126
Stream processing · 117
streaming input · 114
streams · 112
<u>strongly consistent</u> · 123
structured data · 111
sub-10ms latency · 116
sub-millisecond data access · 102
<u>Subnets</u> · 71
sustained use discounts · 203

T

Tableau · 110, 115
Tactical · 45
tags · 173
Target · 28
task orchestrator · 113
Task Queues · 91
TCP BBR · 62
telemetry · 115
TensorFlow · 111, 131, 163, 167, 169, 198
TensorFlow Lite ML models · 159
TensorFlow models · 168
Terminated · 81
The Long Tail · 206
Third Wave · 43
Time to Live (TTL) · 102
Time-series data · 116
time-series schemas · 117
<u>timestamp-based filenames</u> · 103
Titan Security Keys · 143
TLS · 103

Traffic split · 194
Train model · 167
trained anywhere · 169
Training · 168
training models in the cloud · 159
transactional consistency · 123
transactional databases · 111
Transfer Appliance · 107
transferred to Google Cloud Storage · 107
Transformational · 45
Translate · 161
transportation · 159
Trifacta · 128
Tune hyperparameters · 167
two different versions of APIs · 152

U

Unified Computing System (UCS) · 198
unified data environment · 134, 211
<u>uptime checks</u> · 149
User analysis · 115
User credentials · 122
User-generated events (UGEs) · 136

V

vendor-lock-in · 134
Video and image analysis · 184
Video Intelligence · 185
Virtual assistants · 184
virtual machines · 26
virtual machines (VMs) · 55
Virtual Network · 61
Virtual Private Cloud (VPC) · 70

Vulnerability Scanning · 140

W

Walmart · 30
Websites, blogs, and content · 125
Wide Column · 125
workflow orchestration service · 134
workflows · 211
workloads · 211, 219

X

XGBoost · 169, 198
XML API · 101, 102

Y

YouTube · 49

Z

Zero Moments of Truth · 6
zero server management · 88
Zero server management, · 183
zero-configuration · 88
zonal failures · 116
Zonal instance · 75
zonal resources · 57
Zonal Resources · 64
zones · 57

About the author

Soumen is a data adviser and helps business staying relevant to the consumer first digital revolution. In the last two decades, Soumen contributed to many global leading organisations' data-driven business change and digital journey.

Soumen is a Google Certified Professional Cloud Architect.

Soumen sees **Contextonomy**™ is the next big thing that would change the way we work today and reimagine the business dimensions, society and the service industry.

Soumen dreams taking AI in the society to redefine Human Experience (HX) and lead the **'Generation Ci'** Data Natives where intelligence is infused with the Context, and AI.

Soumen loves music and history.

Soumen could be reached out to chatterjee.soumen@gmail.com

Stay Connected

www.beclickaware.com

Any forthcoming revised version, you would be entitled to have a free contents digitally.
Please register your interest and be in touch: chatterjee.soumen@gmail.com or soumenc@beclickaware.com with your Order No.

As my supporter and supporting my vision and dream, you are entitled to get **a special appreciation discount for my future publications**. Please drop a note with your details.

This book is printed in United Kindom
Printed by Dolman Scott Ltd
www.dolmanscott.co.uk